The Changing World in Plays and Theatre

The Changing World in Plays and Theatre

BY ANITA BLOCK

DA CAPO PRESS · NEW YORK · 1971

A Da Capo Press Reprint Edition

This Da Capo Press edition of *The Changing World in Plays and Theatre* is an unabridged republication of the first edition published in Boston in 1939. It is reprinted by special arrangement with the estate of the author.

Library of Congress Catalog Card Number 73-77721
ISBN 0-306-71359-4

Published by Da Capo Press, Inc.
A Subsidiary of Plenum Publishing Corporation
227 West 17th Street, New York, New York 10011

Manufactured in the United States of America

The Changing World in Plays and Theatre

THE Changing World IN Plays AND Theatre

BY ANITA BLOCK

BOSTON
LITTLE, BROWN AND COMPANY
1939

FIRST EDITION

Published March 1939

PRINTED IN THE UNITED STATES OF AMERICA

To my husband

S. JOHN BLOCK

whose knowledge and love of the theatre
and whose invaluable criticism
are all reflected in this book

Acknowledgments

The author is grateful to the following playwrights, publishers and others for permission to quote from plays written and published by them:

To Charles Scribner's Sons, New York, for permission to quote a passage from Henrik Ibsen's *A Doll's House.*

To William Heinemann, Ltd., London, for permission to quote a passage from Gerhart Hauptmann's *The Weavers.*

To George Bernard Shaw for permission to quote passages from *On the Rocks.*

To Little, Brown and Company for permission to quote passages from *My Life in Art* by Constantin Stanislavsky.

Passages from Anton Chekhov's *The Cherry Orchard* and *The Three Sisters.* By courtesy of Mr. Morris Gest.

To Sidgwick and Jackson, Ltd., London, for permission to quote a selection from Stanley Houghton's *Hindle Wakes.*

Selections from *The Constant Wife* by W. Somerset Maugham, copyright, 1927, and from *For Services Rendered* by W. Somerset Maugham, copyright, 1932, 1933, reprinted by permission of Doubleday, Doran & Company, Inc.

To The Theatre Guild, Inc., New York, for permission to quote a few sentences from W. Somerset Maugham's unpublished translation of Luigi Chiarelli's *The Mask and the Face.*

To Edouard Bourdet, Arthur Hornblow, Jr., and Coward-McCann, Inc., New York, for permission to quote passages from Hornblow's translation of *The Captive.*

To Samuel French, New York, for permission to quote excerpts from Robert Nichols' and Maurice Browne's *Wings Over Europe* (Copyright, 1927, 1929, by Robert Nichols and Maurice Browne. Copyright, 1935 [Acting Edition] by Samuel

French. All rights reserved.); Virgil Geddes' *The Earth Between* (Copyright, 1928, by Virgil Geddes. Copyright, 1930 by Samuel French. All rights reserved.); George Sklar's and Albert Maltz' *Peace on Earth* (Copyright, 1933 by George Sklar and Albert Maltz. Copyright, 1934, by Samuel French. All rights reserved.).

Selections from the plays of Eugene O'Neill and Clifford Odets. Reprinted by courtesy of Random House, Inc., New York City.

To Ernst Toller for permission to quote passages from *Masses and Man* and *The Machine-Wreckers.*

To Liveright Publishing Corporation, New York, for permission to quote from Ernst Toller's *Hinkemann.*

To Elmer Rice and to Samuel French, New York, for permission to quote selections from *The Adding Machine.*

To John Howard Lawson and to Thomas Seltzer, Inc., New York, for permission to quote passages from *Processional.*

To Longmans, Green & Co., New York, for permission to quote passages from Maxwell Anderson's and Harold Hickerson's *Gods of the Lightning.*

To Anderson House for permission to reprint passages from Maxwell Anderson's *Winterset* and *The Masque of Kings.*

To Paul Green and Robert M. McBride & Company, New York, for permission to quote passages from *In Abraham's Bosom.*

To John Wexley and Maxim Lieber, New York, for permission to quote portions of *They Shall Not Die.*

To Covici-Friede, Inc., New York, for permission to quote passages from Paul Peters' and George Sklar's *Stevedore.*

Passages from *What Price Glory?* from *Three American Plays,* copyright, 1926, by Maxwell Anderson and Laurence Stallings. By permission of Harcourt, Brace and Company, Inc.

To Coward-McCann, Inc., New York, for permission to quote passages from Hans Chlumberg's *Miracle at Verdun.*

ACKNOWLEDGMENTS

Passages from John Haynes Holmes' *If This Be Treason.* By permission of The Macmillan Company, publishers.

To Houghton, Mifflin Company, Boston, for permission to quote from *Six Soviet Plays,* edited by Eugene Lyons.

To International Publishers Co., New York, for permission to quote from Sergei M. Tretyakov's *Roar China* and Nikolai Pogodin's *Aristocrats.*

To The Theatre Guild, Inc., New York, for permission to quote passages from Vladimir Kirchon's and André Uspenski's *Red Rust.*

Contents

The Changing World
in Plays and Theatre

Chapter 1 Introductory

Love of the theatre, like every other kind of love, may be merely an unthinking emotional response, or it may be a rich emotional experience enhanced by fully aroused critical, analytical and discriminatory faculties. Thus those who "love" the theatre may be roughly divided into two main classes: those who express their "love" for the theatre by the desire to "go to a show," and those who, in the fine phrase alas no longer current, desire to "go to the play." The number of the former is legion; the number of the latter pitifully small. Indeed the one unshakable conviction to which my long and varied experience as a dramatic critic, a play reader and a lecturer on the drama has brought me is that those who "love" the theatre most, care least about the play. Nor is there here the slightest contradiction. Because the great theatre-going public which so "loves" the theatre may be described as suffering from excessive "*theatre-consciousness*" and at the same time as almost totally deficient in "*play-consciousness.*"

To define these terms further: *Theatre-consciousness* is the condition of being entranced by the glamour and by the often spurious trappings of the theatre — such as clever acting, smart dialogue, dazzling costumes and effective scenery — into a drugged indifference to the values of the play content. *Play-consciousness* is the condition of being critically alive, in the theatre, to the play as literature, judging the values of its content as one judges those of a novel, or a biography, or any other literary art-form. Once a theatre-goer has developed play-consciousness he can never be deceived in the theatre again. Once he goes to the theatre with his play-criticizing faculties trained and alert he not only sees right through the theatrical trappings into the play itself, but he also learns to desire and to demand in the theatre plays which would satisfy him as literature, if read quietly between the covers of a book, far away from the theatre's too often meretricious, albeit enchanting glamour.

The chief purpose of this book, then, is to develop *play-consciousness* among theatregoers. Because *theatre-consciousness* alone, like patriotism, is not enough. Mere theatre-consciousness not only stultifies the theatregoer and is one of the most pernicious influences under which the art of the theatre suffers, but it also actually prevents the broadest success of which the theatre is capable. Merely theatre-conscious audiences can and do easily make a hit of theatrical claptrap like *Grand Hotel.* But it takes play-conscious audiences to carry beautiful and meaningful plays like *Wings Over Europe* or *The Moon in the Yellow River* to success. And since play-conscious audiences are still distressingly small, the large, unthinking, uncritical theatre-conscious audiences have the power to doom to failure plays which, because of their content, transcend ephemeral theatre and are worthy to live on as dramatic literature.

Thus the first step in the development of play-consciousness is to establish critical standards and values according to which we can judge plays as either important or unimportant. That this judgment of plays must, in the last analysis, be made *outside* the theatre, is amply demonstrated by the fact that in recent years constantly increasing numbers of plays which first sought their audiences in the theatre, later sought and still seek further audiences as printed plays. In other words, a permanent life is sought for the *play,* after its ephemeral existence as *theatre* is over. It is then and then alone, when it is presented as literature, that the values of the play can be judged. Read *The Wingless Victory* removed from the aura of a popular "star" and see what a verbose, tortured, confused, unsound parable-melodrama remains! But read *Candida* and you require nor actors nor stage to vitalize its content. It acts itself for you as you sit in your armchair, holding the printed play in your hands. Morell and Marchbanks, Candida and Prossy, are warm and real and alive. You need no stars to interpret them as you chuckle or grow tender over the lines and situations and delightedly admire the profound revelation of character and of the fundamental relation between the sexes the play so limpidly presents. Just so, we need never see a production of Ibsen's *Ghosts* or *Hedda Gabler* to realize that these are great plays. True, to watch an outstanding actress play Hedda or Mrs. Alving is an unforgettable experience in the theatre, but this experience has nothing to do with one's judgment of Ibsen's plays.

Therefore the prime essential both for the theatregoer and for the theatre is to end as speedily as possible the confused identification between the play and the theatre. The play must be regarded as an independent art-form which stands or falls on its own intrinsic merits. It is shocking to listen to groups of educated and informed persons invariably discussing plays in terms of their productions. What, one rather sardonically muses, would have been the fate of *Winterset* had it been judged solely on its merits as a play, rather than as the dramatic emanation of that famous setting of the bridge, undoubtedly one of the most effectively executed stage designs in the current theatre, but surely entirely extraneous to the values of the play as such! Or the fate of *Dead End* if judged on its written words, instead of on the sure-fire "show" values of real water, dripping boys and the tooting of boats sounding all through the theatre during the intermissions! Not that a fine production is not of great importance to any play. It is; but what theatregoers and students of drama and the theatre must learn is that, while a good production, in transforming the written play into what we call "theatre," may and usually does add certain theatrical values, neither good directing, nor good acting, nor good scenery can ever add a hair's weight of value to the play itself. A fine production may enhance the play's values as theatre, but it can never supply any values which would entitle the play to live on as dramatic literature, to live an honorable life of its own, after its short career as theatre is over. How, for example, would it affect our judgment of Ibsen's *Rosmersholm* today, to be informed in a footnote that when it was produced the waters of the millrace were heard to rush wildly all through the intermissions?

So, just as the proverbial traveler does not see the woods for the trees, the theatregoing public does not see the plays for the theatre. And the effect on the theatre of audiences deficient in what I have called *play-consciousness* is a vicious one. Because only play-conscious audiences, deeply critical of play values, deeply concerned with the content of the plays offered to them, can inspire and sustain a *vital* theatre. For an active, successful theatre is not necessarily a vital theatre, any more than a hit is necessarily a vital play. What, then, is our definition of a *vital* theatre? To say that a vital theatre is one which depicts or reflects life is not enough. Because a theatre, in order to be vital, must deal with what is *essential to life,* with such matters as are important to our very existence. But matters which are essential to life are not a constant and unvariable quantity. They change in kind and in degree of importance according to the age in which we live. Plays vital to the Greeks dealt with the unescapable laws of the vengeful Gods to which little humans, even in their awfulest agony, were less than worms. When we of today witness a production, even a rarely fine one, of *Oedipus Rex,* a play most vital to the Greeks, this great tragedy of Sophocles does not tear at our hearts. We are vaguely moved by a sense of far-off unhappy things, we turn a little sick at the barbarous cruelty and torture, but Oedipus, King of Thebes, is not really vital to us. We are much more deeply moved by O'Neill's Emperor Jones, the least of America's black folk who dwell in our midst, and whose terrors, inherited and immediate, we understand, or by Lavinia Mannon, defeated and doomed by our unescapable modern gods: the laws of heredity and environment, in his great neo-Greek tragedy of New England, *Mourning Becomes Electra.*

Thus a vital theatre must deal with matters that are *essential to life in any given epoch.* That is the implication of the epithet "dated," today more and more frequently hurled at the great iconoclasts and revolutionaries among dramatists, such as Ibsen and even Shaw. Yes, the fight that Nora made to function as a human being instead of as some man's doll is no longer vital to women who vote, who adjust homes and husbands to outside "jobs" and to whom the state gives leave of absence from their work to bear babies. What bond is there between these freed women of today and Nora? Indeed, we may even ask, is there still a real bond between the women of today and the remorseful and tortured Mrs. Alving? Today no mother, however indirectly responsible she may feel herself, is fearfully called upon to give her son the release of death rather than let him decay physically and mentally through the ravages of syphilis. This dread disease is still a scourge, but medical science can and does cure it. Do these changes in play values then imply that Ibsen's plays are no longer great? By no means. They merely signify that Ibsen's plays no longer offer us vital theatre. They no longer deal with subjects essential to life today. But because they were great works of art, vital to their own day, which transcended the passing theatre, they have achieved immortality for the true lover of the drama.

A vital theatre, then, in any epoch, calls for plays which furnish commentary, interpretation, illumination and criticism of that epoch. When a theatre fails to do this it may represent a charming ornament, it may afford a pleasant diversion for the seekers of pleasure or of escape, it may exhibit literary, histrionic and other technical talents, but it is not a vital theatre. A perfect example of a theatre which has hardly any appreciable relation to the basic realities of life is the French theatre. It is like a little island around which for generations the surging seas of French thought and action have swirled unnoticed. On this little island of the theatre, men and women, still apparently regarding the triangle as eternal, continue to fret over artificially induced complications of the erotic life. True, Steve Passeur and the younger set of play artisans treat the erotically complicated more rawly and pitilessly than did (and still does) the kid-gloved Henry Bernstein. Or, they revise the classics and present theatrically brand-new versions of *The Birds* by Aristophanes or Shakespeare's *Coriolanus*. They love the theatre, these French, but they care very little about plays. They demonstrate perfectly that excessive theatre-consciousness and deficient play-consciousness produce an unimportant theatre. The French theatre is unimportant for the people of France and for the rest of the world because it does not deal essentially with matters vital to human life today. The theatre of Soviet Russia, on the other hand, because it today presents plays which, with all their shortcomings, constantly place before audiences matters of vital concern to them, realizes more nearly than any other the highest function of the theatre, which is to integrate audiences with the age in which they live.

It is because of this integration which exists, or should exist, between playwrights and audiences and the age in which they live that this book will confine itself to a discussion of *modern and contemporary drama.* The terms *modern* and *contemporary* are in no sense synonymous. There is a distinct line of cleavage between them, caused by the World War with its vast consequences of upheaval, individual as well as social, which divides the modern period and our own contemporary period into two distinct epochs. The profound differences between these epochs will be discussed in the next chapter. But it should be clear to us at once that it is our own age, the age in which our own life is lived, which, if we are normal, healthy human beings, should interest us more than anything else in the world. Our age is flesh of our flesh and spirit of our spirit and try, as some neurotics may, to escape from it, they never really can. Indeed the richness of our own lives, creative and receptive, depends on how closely we identify ourselves with the struggles and problems, individual and social, as well as with the hopes and ideals of the age in which we live. We understand our own age as we understand ourselves, with our own life-blood beating in our temples and in our veins. We may fondly think we understand other ages, but we can never be inside the skin of an ancient Greek, an Elizabethan, a beau or lady of the Restoration, a Girondist, or a German of Goethe's Weimar. We can never walk their streets or drink in the sights and sounds and smells that were life to them. However close we may think we get, our knowledge of the past will always remain remote and second-hand. But our knowledge of our own time is immediate and first hand. Here we may hope, if we fully merge ourselves with it, perhaps to clarify a little for our fellow travelers the struggles and confusions of our own age, to impart to them perhaps a little of our own convictions and faith. We of today *can* get inside the skin of a desperately courageous Spanish Loyalist, of an abdicating Edward VIII, with his inner psychological conflicts, and we can understand, even though we abhor, an Italian Fascist or a German Nazi, because these are all inseparable segments of our own age. For better or for worse, we are inextricably bound up with them.

Something of all this must animate the playwright who is to have any validity for his own age. He must concern himself with matters essential to the life of his time and he must regard it as the highest function of the theatre to present to audiences plays which endeavor to clarify and illumine some aspect of import and meaning to our common life. This purpose is the criterion according to which playwrights have been judged as qualified, to a greater or a lesser degree, for inclusion in this book. I do not know whether or not some of the playwrights whose work is to be discussed in these pages will "live" — if, for example, the future will place the plays of Ernst Toller or Clifford Odets on the shelves beside those of Wedekind or Galsworthy. Nor does this matter. What matters is that these and other contemporary playwrights are important to us who are living today, both as theatre and as dramatic literature, and that they are endeavoring to perform the same sort of service for us that the great modern dramatists tried to perform for their contemporaries, namely, to write for the theatre, plays which shall have some relation to and significance for people's lives as they must, in their own given time, be lived.

Outstanding modern dramatists are therefore included in this book for two reasons. First, because the subjects about which Ibsen, Hauptmann, Schnitzler and others wrote are still so close to us, psychologically and socially, as to be a part of our immediate heritage and therefore both understandable and valuable to us. In the case of Shaw, the great social problems the plays present, such as, for example, the problems of poverty and war, not only are still with us, but exist in forms even more acute and menacing. The only change is that the younger playwrights deal with these questions, as we shall see later in these pages, in a very different style and approach from that used by the great Irishman in his then single-handed attempt to utilize the theatre to awaken a smug and indifferent world to a sense of social responsibility. The second reason for the inclusion of the important moderns in these pages is that they form the foundations of our own contemporary drama, the roots out of which the drama of our own time has grown. Different as our current plays are, in style and technique, nevertheless O'Neill, Toller, Maugham, Bourdet, Bruckner, Wexley and other contemporaries are the direct descendants of Ibsen, Hauptmann, Wedekind and the rest. Our playwrights of today, in spite of the gulf of the World War which separates them from the moderns, are, nevertheless, their logical successors, their intellectual inheritors. Tremendously changed as our contemporaries are in tempo, in psychological and social knowledge and in philosophical outlook, they did not, any more than did the immortal Topsy, "just grow." Therefore, if we are to have any real understanding of our contemporary drama, if we are to have any sound convictions about and any clearly conceived hopes and aspirations for our theatre of today, we must understand the powerful drama of the moderns which still brushes our own theatre with its great wings.

One of the most prevalent fallacies, growing out of our overdeveloped theatre-consciousness and our underdeveloped play-consciousness, is that plays with content and meaning for their audiences, such as concern us in this book, must necessarily be solemn, if not actually tragic — in any case overheavy doses to swallow in the theatre. Nothing could be further from the truth. Plays with content illuminating to audiences run, as we shall see, the entire gamut, from tragedy to lightest satiric comedy. W. Somerset Maugham's *The Constant Wife* and Chiarelli's *The Mask and the Face* both deal frankly and uncompromisingly with an important subject, namely the passing of the "double standard" of sexual morality in relation to marital fidelity, the former in an Anglo-Saxon country, the latter in a Latin country. But audiences witnessing these plays are almost continuously in a state of delighted laughter induced, on the one hand, by the brilliant satiric wit of Maugham and, on the other, by the satirically farcical situations created by Chiarelli. Yet this does not prevent these playwrights from tellingly making their points in dealing with a subject of vital interest to audiences who have to meet the problems of changing sexual standards in their own lives. By the same sign was Sidney Howard's *The Silver Cord,* ostensibly a light comedy, an illuminating contribution to the contemporary American theatre. Here, profiting by Freudian interpretation, Howard portrayed for delighted and comprehending audiences the type of mother who destroys the future happiness of her men-children, her sons, by keeping them bound to her in a really abnormal emotional involvement. Nor need the dread "social" play be other than absorbing theatre, as *Stevedore, Peace on Earth, Waiting for Lefty,* and *Awake and Sing* amply testify. These held their audiences spellbound and would have had far longer runs were theatregoers play-conscious and did they go to the theatre avid for the play instead of blindly seeking a "show" or what they are pleased to call "entertainment."

By this time the reader may have begun to wonder if there is a place for this so-called "entertainment" in the play-conscious theatre. But what is this thing called "entertainment"? What is the meaning of the term? What does the person mean who looks at one truculently and announces: "I go to the theatre for entertainment"? To this, I and those who think like me might parry: "Well, we also go to the theatre for entertainment. Surely we don't go to be bored! But our idea of being entertained is being interested in something which possesses inherent value and not being merely amused." People are entertained by symphony concerts, they are not amused by them. People are entertained, not amused, by art exhibitions. To ask nothing of an art but that it amuse you, is to degrade that art, and those who seek nothing in the theatre but amusement, which they wrongly call entertainment, are constantly degrading the art of the theatre. Art makes demands on the spectator, on the listener. It asks that he respond to the ideas set forth by the creative artist and it is this shared effort which stimulates and inspires both the creative artist and the public as well as the art which is their common possession. But amusement asks nothing of anybody. It deceives the jaded and the, for the most part, unconsciously life-weary by seeming to afford them surcease. And to such pitiful and ignoble purposes of "entertainment" is the great art of the theatre very largely dedicated. What better evidence of this can we have than that in America in 1937 the Pulitzer Prize was awarded to an incredibly trifling and deliberately contrived piece of theatre amusement called *You Can't Take It With You!* Surely no stronger argument than this is needed to prove not only that theatregoers in general fail to evaluate the play and its supreme importance to the theatre, but also that among the allegedly critical elect there is no comprehension of the significance the play has for our theatre. Nor does this mean for a moment that the theatre should be devoid of light entertainment. A well-balanced theatre must and should have its lusty farces, its gentler comedies, its gay musical shows and satiric topical revues. But always the glory of the theatre is the play shedding light on dark places, fraught with meaning for its own time.

There is of course one other indispensable feature of the well-balanced theatre—the inclusion of the classics. For despite the fact that they never really lose their quality of remoteness for us and that we cannot identify ourselves directly with the inner and outer conflicts they portray, yet the classics hold significant values for us. First, whether we consciously realize it or not, witnessing performances of the classics give us that sense of historic continuity, not only of the theatre but of life itself, which is always a stabilizing experience, emotionally and intellectually. Secondly, we are so closely identified with the race's psychic past that we do recognize in a Hamlet or in a Richard II the seemingly eternal symbol of man's tragically devastating inner conflicts and in an Ophelia the seemingly eternal symbol of the destructive force of erotic frustration. Finally the classics afford us an ever-fresh impact with art that has achieved immortality, with plays important enough to have survived as literature and living enough to inspire each new generation to renew them as theatre, as ever-living Nature is freshly renewed for us each spring.

Here, in these pages, however, we shall be concerned chiefly with the plays of our own time and more specifically with such plays as, in accordance with the point of view toward the play and toward the theatre set down in this introductory chapter, may be said to be integrated with life today. Because our thesis is that the importance and value of the theatre in any given epoch depend on the awakened and active interest of playwrights and of theatregoers in all that vitally concerns themselves and their own age, individually and socially. This integration, as we shall see in later chapters, may express itself in the most variegated ways. It may express itself through an O'Neill, completely absorbed in the inner psychological conflicts today harassing the individual. It may express itself through a John Wexley or a John Howard Lawson, completely absorbed in the great social and economic conflict harassing the entire world. It may even express itself *negatively* through a Maxwell Anderson's baffled efforts to find integration. But whatever the form, it is only out of significant material, such as these playwrights have fashioned into plays, that there can grow a living theatre of meaning and import for its own age.

Before we proceed to our study of Contemporary Drama, however, we must pause to consider its relations to the great period of Modern Drama which preceded it.

Chapter 2 Modern Foundations of Contemporary Drama

Before we can have any clear understanding of contemporary drama and discover its integral relation to our own time, we must rid ourselves of the all too prevalent confusion of regarding the terms *modern* and *contemporary* as interchangeable. For example, we constantly hear Ibsen and Toller, Schnitzler and O'Neill indiscriminately referred to as *modern* dramatists. Indubitably Ibsen and Schnitzler *are* modern dramatists, but Toller and O'Neill are just as indubitably *contemporary* dramatists and the difference between them must be measured by a gauge far deeper and more significant than that of mere chronology. The difference between modern and contemporary, placing, as it does, some of the world's most important playwrights in one category or the other, is, as we shall see, a matter, not of time, but of world events of the first magnitude. For close as we still are to the year 1914, we who are living today already know with a positive, historical conviction that probably so long as our world lasts, that year will stand as one of the most fateful in history. For the World War precipitated the end of the modern world and the beginning of the contemporary world which we faced breathlessly and bewilderedly in 1918.

The World War tore the modern world convulsively out of what had seemed its destined course. The guiding star of that modern, prewar period had been faith in orderly and peaceful progress as man's forward way of life. As a result, all the engrossing vital psychological and sociological questions presented in their plays by the modern playwrights were offered by them for consideration and solution to their own world, assumedly ruled by scientific knowledge, reason, and civilized human behavior. To this world the Great War came as a destroying shock, and when the first four years of upheaval had passed, the modern world was no more. In its place, astride the ruins, was a violently and completely changed world, changed not only politically and economically, nationally and internationally, but in all its basic concepts of life and behavior — sexual, psychological, social. This new postwar world, then, with its Communism, Fascism, Nazism, Aryanism, New Dealism, civil wars, "imperial" conquests and depressions, constitutes our own contemporary world. Incredible even to ourselves who are living in it, this period seems to bear no real relation to the modern period which preceded it. The line of cleavage between prewar modern and postwar contemporary is almost complete.

It is because of this violent passage, then, from one kind of world to another that the usual element of transition, the time element between two historical epochs, is so almost completely lacking as a bond between the prewar and our postwar period. Counted as a matter of years, the time lapse between modern and contemporary playwrights is so small that, under the normal conditions of transition, the former should almost imperceptibly merge into the latter. Indeed, chronologically, in the instance of several playwrights, the two periods actually do overlap. We know very well that Schnitzler wrote after the year 1918, as did Galsworthy, and that Gerhart Hauptmann is still physically alive in Germany today. As for the mentally and spiritually indestructible Shaw, not only did he write three of his finest and most evocative plays after 1918 — *Heartbreak House* (1919); *Back to Methuselah* (1921); *Saint Joan* (1923) — but he is fulminatingly among us still. His is a unique position because the titanic subjects he dealt with in his plays, as a pioneer, such as the economic injustice of capitalism and its attendant horrors of poverty and war, are with us still. Indeed they are not only with us but actually more violently and threateningly so than in the days when Shaw first took such subjects as the only ones he regarded worthy of attention in the theatre and shook them right in the faces of hostile audiences. And not satisfied with that, he further implemented his plays with his sharply illuminating, inimitable prefaces, written to shock into social consciousness an ever-growing audience of fascinated, if often frightened, readers.

Yet — and this is the startling anomaly in the relation between the wise, prescient, brave moderns and ourselves — those pioneers no longer "belong." Due to the deep chasm between our essential time and their essential time, in spite of the still compelling immediacy of much of their subject matter and the extreme recency of their flowering, the great moderns often have about them, for us, something of the aroma of the archaic. Hauptmann and Schnitzler, Galsworthy and Chekhov and the rest, their vital work scarcely finished, are already "classics." So close to us in time that they are chronologically still with us, they no longer seem *of* us. Their prewar reality is not our postwar reality; their measured prewar rhythm has none of the frenzy of our postwar rhythm; their legitimate fears nothing of our neo-atavistic terrors. Our very vocabulary, although often little more than a superficial jargon, completes this sense of the already archaic in these moderns so near and yet so strangely far from us. An illustration of this is Schnitzler's play *The Vast Domain* (*Das weite Land*). This is his symbolic title, designating the human soul, and the play is a characteristically sound and deeply felt psychological study, but it will mean little to the contemporary reader who expects to hear psychological difficulties discussed in the Freudian terms popularized by an O'Neill or even by a Sidney Howard. An age which sees the individual's personal psychological problems mercilessly exposed in terms of complexes, repressions, neuroses, under the powerful searchlight of the new psychology, will find little that seems revealing or important in the gentle, pitying understanding in which Schnitzler envelops the tragic blunders and frustrations of the human soul.

In the same way Hauptmann's epoch-making play, *The Weavers* (1892), the first deliberately written *social* drama, provocative of fierce hostility and even riots, with its realistic picture of a group of exploited and starving Silesian weavers daring a spontaneous and unorganized rebellion in the 1840's against the conditions of their labor, is today, when it is produced at all, presented as an "art" production, as a sacred classic. Why? Are there no longer any starving workers in the world, ready to rebel? The answer, of course, is that there are today more such rebellious workers than Hauptmann ever dreamed of. But in these postwar times, workers' protest-action has taken the form, not of sporadic and unpremeditated rebellion, but of stupendously prepared organization, of actual revolution and of civil war. Thus a postwar social drama like Ernst Toller's *Masses and Man* (1919) scarcely bears any recognizable resemblance to *The Weavers*. Toller's play was written in a cell in a German military prison during the first year of the German revolution. On the title page we read: To THE WORKERS; and above this dedication are these lines:—

World-Revolution:
Mother of New
Power and Rhythm,
Mother of New
Peoples and Patterns.
Red Flames the Century in Blood of Expiation:
The Earth Nails Itself
To the Cross

Contrast with this Hauptmann's dedication of *The Weavers:* To MY FATHER; and under it these lines:—

You, dear father, know what feelings lead me to dedicate this work to you and I am not called upon to analyse them here. Your stories of my grandfather, who in his young days sat at the loom, a poor weaver like those here depicted, contained the germ of my drama. Whether it possesses the vigor of life or is rotten to the core, it is the best "so poor a man as Hamlet is" can offer.

Yours,

GERHART.

While Hauptmann in his *The Weavers* asked an uncomprehending and indignant society, "Do you realize that starved workers may revolt?", Toller, in the light of revolution actually experienced and accepted by him as inevitable, asks in *Masses and Man,* not "Must we have revolution?" but "Is it still possible to have revolution without mass-murder, without bloodshed?"

Manifestly, therefore, we cannot use the terms *modern* and *contemporary* interchangeably. Nor does it matter whether the particular writer in question concerns himself with social matters or with those personal problems which involve only the individual. Both social and individual questions have suffered the same sea-change in the short but rough passage from the shore of yesterday to that of today. Let no reader, however, hastily deduce that the great moderns are not important to us. They are, since it is just because we are so sharply separated from their world that the great moderns constitute almost our only bridge back to it. This is especially true of the great modern dramatists because they stand out as men of the highest courage, as intrepid pioneers whose plays were vital to the development of thought and behavior in their own age. To them we owe our most vivid and informing picture of what constituted the essential character of those three decades or so which preceded the World War. No feminist treatise, not even John Stuart Mill's deservedly famous classic, *The Subjection of Women,* ever portrayed for us the male-dominated slave-woman of those unregenerate days as fearlessly and unforgettably as did Ibsen's *A Doll's House*. No treatise on the crying need in the 90's for the most elementary sex education of the young ever aroused a world of benighted Mr. and Mrs. Grundys as did Wedekind's children's tragedy *The Awakening of Spring*. No Socialist treatise on the cynical lust for profits engendered by capitalism ever exposed some of its quite amoral beneficiaries more bitingly than did Shaw's *Mrs. Warren's Profession*.

The great modern dramatists left us a rich heritage and exerted a powerful influence from which no thinking playwright of today can escape or would wish to escape. If today we can no longer respond with high emotional tension to the great modern plays themselves, we can and do thrill to the magnificent courage of those modern playwrights who dared introduce into the theatre vital subjects that were taboo to the accepted standards of morals and manners of their time. Into a society ridden by ignorance and hypocrisy, not only on sexual but on social and economic questions, they deliberately hurled truths and discussions of truths which their smug frightened world, shamed and resentful, could meet only with sham moral horror, with abuse heaped on the offending playwrights.

But so deeply integrated were these dramatists with their own time, so passionately concerned were they with the matters they regarded as of vital moment to their fellow men, that the theatre, as such, was for them infinitely less important than the truths they felt must be uttered in it. In this fact lies the crux of the matter for playwrights, indeed the crux of all art: namely, that the artist must care infinitely more for what he has to say than for the medium through which he says it. Nor does this attitude imply for an instant, as some would have us believe, that such an artist must inevitably care less for his art. What it does imply is that he cares *more* for life and for truth and that for him the highest function of art is to serve life by revealing some aspect of truth which the artist feels the supreme need of expressing. "I write for the theatre because I regard it as the best means to reach people," said Ibsen, and the young Hauptmann uttered words to the same effect. Thus to these and to all playwrights taking this view of their art, the theatre is always the *means* and never the end. Naturally, a creative artist selecting the theatre as his means of expression makes that choice because he deems this medium best suited to his own individual talents. Obviously it would be quite absurd for anyone, however noble his ulterior purpose, to set out to be a playwright if he had no love for the theatre and the play and if he did not instinctively see his own creative work in terms of both. But once he is convinced that the theatre is his medium, then, if his first interest is in the service of life and of truth, the theatre will represent for him, as it did for its great genius, Ibsen, the means with which he hopes "to reach people."

The great modern dramatists, then, wrote about vital subjects deliberately calculated to shock their benighted and timorous fellow beings into an awareness of the realities of life which the prewar world could not bring itself to face. What some of these tabooed subjects were which our great modern playwrights felt compelled to drag out in the open we shall see shortly. But most important for us will be to discover how far they took us on that road of liberating revelation, along which our contemporary playwrights have been traveling so much faster and so much more furiously. For each new age must bring forth new Saint Georges to slay new dragons. Our brash and uninhibited postwar period still has its own taboos to wrestle with. If leading newspapers can now dare to print the word "syphilis" without violent shock to their readers, the word "homosexuality" must still appear concealed in the euphemistic cloak of "abnormal sex relation." And audiences, who now watch without inner or outer protest the physical ravages of syphilis in Ibsen's once reviled and anathematized *Ghosts,* still wriggle with embarrassed distaste at the startling impact of Lesbianism in *The Children's Hour*. In my extensive lecturing before the most variegated audiences I have never been asked if I consider the subject of *Ghosts* a fit one for the theatre, but whenever I discuss *The Children's Hour* I know that a query as to the fitness of *its* subject for "our stage" is coming with swift inevitability.

We can have no thorough comprehension of the part our contemporary dramatists are playing in lifting the taboos of our time, unless we know the extent of the foundations laid by the modern dramatists before the World War changed the entire fabric of thought and conduct. Even a World War could not destroy those foundations. True, the superstructure of contemporary drama seems out of plumb and out of harmony with them. But the foundations are there, admirably strong and firm, exhaling inspiration, evoking the kind of courage and social devotion that a changed world demands.

The mighty forerunner of our great modern dramatists was Henrik Ibsen. And Ibsen it is who becomes our first telling example of the playwright who, while he excelled as a writer *for the theatre,* as a master of stage technique, has achieved his immortality and lives for us today only rarely as a person of the theatre and almost entirely as a writer of imperishable dramatic literature. If in the theatre of today, in comparison with the tense, clipped, nervous, almost monosyllabic dialogue we accept as "natural," reflecting as it does the elliptical speech of our own radio timetabled and generally speeded-up age, Ibsen's meticulously evolved, carefully analytical lines seem to amble and creak and fill us overwrought contemporary theatregoers with impatience, these luminous lines do not creak when encountered in the theatre-of-the-armchair. Instead they excite the reader who, freed from the demands of the time schedule, can enjoy the inimitable development of a typical Ibsen scene without losing a single indispensable line.

But the reader or student who is eager for knowledge of Ibsen will never get such knowledge from the mutilated versions that make of an Ibsen play popularly acceptable "theatre" today. Let no one who saw the recent Alla Nazimova production of *Ghosts* fancy that he was listening to Ibsen's drama. What he witnessed was an abbreviated version that lacked whole pages of dialogue absolutely necessary to any true understanding of the motivation of the behavior of the characters. These passages deleted, the irreducible residue of the original play was then "pepped-up" for Broadway and road consumption by grotesquely transforming any satiric note into a laugh-provoking "comedy" element, thus distorting the mood of the play as well as some of its most subtle and important values. What remained was a theatrical vehicle in which it was hoped that a star actress could in the late 1930's successfully act Mrs. Alving. This Nazimova did superbly, but in a defective tabloid version. Even more flagrant was Thornton Wilder's version of *A Doll's House*. This production actually changed the lines of the play's ending and of Ibsen's explicit stage directions, so as to create the impression that Nora has left her husband forever instead of giving that intended by Ibsen: that she is leaving him only until they shall both have developed into human beings capable of making a true marriage of their hitherto mutually degrading relation. Ibsen's constructive purpose in writing this revolutionary play was thus lost and the merely theatre-conscious audiences who had not read their Ibsen received a false concept of the play's true values. Certainly it is not because of such abortive "revivals" of Ibsen that the great modern dramatist lives. Ibsen lives because the play-conscious reader, following the play's limpidly clear dialogue, in which every character is either driven to strip himself of his lying pretenses or to rise to unexpected heights as the result of new growth and insight, would not wish to lose a line. One of my students, a young man from the West, had never seen or read an Ibsen play. After reading *Ghosts* and *A Doll's House* he said: "And here I've been spending all my spare time and money on Broadway shows. What I want now is to know some more Ibsen!" Thus is play-consciousness born.

Ibsen's real contribution, then, is not that he developed dramaturgy to a higher point of perfection than had previously been attained; it is not even that his special technique exerted a serviceable influence on the entire art of playwriting. This technical advance gives him undoubted value for students of the evolution of dramatic technique, although any study of Ibsen's method of playwriting is today largely academic. For us the significance of Ibsen is his pioneering in the field of human thought and behavior, is his recognition of the vital truth that the evolving individual must struggle to free himself in every age from what he realizes has become obnoxious and outworn among the established social usages and institutions still accepted by an unthinking, complacent and timid majority. Into whatever such established social institutions Ibsen's searching eyes peered, whether these involved marriage, the family, business or politics, he saw there struggling individuals, men and women, strangled emotionally and spiritually by codes of conduct that were vicious and venal and clearly anti-social.

Above all, Ibsen saw the women of his time and recognized in them its essential victims, because he understood that it was their status as a submerged sex that was responsible not only for the wrongs committed against them, but for the wrongs they were committing themselves. He saw clearly that so long as women continued to function solely as sex creatures, to live through men as mere appendages, so long would both sexes suffer the penalty of this destroying inequality. And Ibsen realized even more. He realized that the women of his time had begun to experience the birth-pangs of their emergence, however confused and inarticulate they still were. This conviction of Ibsen went far deeper than the demand for woman suffrage, which had begun in earnest some years before he uttered his clarion call in *A Doll's House* in 1879. Ibsen's concept of the needs of women and therefore of society as a whole can best be described by a term invented only recently—*feminism,* which includes not only political and legal equality for women but the much more fundamental economic equality, as well as the abolition of all the unwritten codes of sex discrimination such as the "double standard of morality," both within and without marriage, which from the beginnings of organized society had warped and degraded woman.

So, in a series of great plays he created an extraordinary galaxy of women who revealed woman's unhappy and untenable position in the modern world. The "doll" Nora rudely awakened to a sense of personal dignity and human responsibility; the too late enlightened and tragically remorseful Mrs. Alving; the buoyant Rebecca West, too free-thinking and free-living for the traditions of her time; the gentle but firm Ellida, insisting that not the claims of the husband but freedom of erotic choice is woman's only law; and finally the neurotic Hedda, so frustrated by false bourgeois standards of conduct that she becomes a cruel, destroying monster driven to the ultimate negation of self-destruction—all these superbly drawn women testify to Ibsen's profound understanding of some of the basic defects in the social structure and the social behavior of his own time. Also—and this is far more admirable and important—they further evidence his determination to use his great dramatic gifts to reveal to audiences the kind of people they themselves really were, by showing them the kind of society they were willing to tolerate. If it was of the highest importance for the nascent Noras in those audiences to drink fresh courage from the wells of resolution with which Ibsen had supplied his Nora, then it was quite as important for the still unregenerate males there to watch, with uneasy astonishment, what happened to Nora's husband, Helmer.

To Ibsen, then, belongs the distinction of being the first to regard as a *dramatic* subject, as a subject *for the theatre,* a woman in revolt against the accepted social code of her time. Ibsen had no doubt that absorbing theatre could be created by showing such a woman in the actual process of evolution. So *A Doll's House* was written, and countless persons in the actual theatre and in the theatre-of-the-armchair have raptly watched Nora emerge from her chrysalis. In the beginning quite unconscious of the fact that her entire marriage is a sham and an indignity, when subjected to a series of mental and moral shocks, Nora changes under our very eyes from a doll-wife into an adult woman, who not only realizes the tragic truth of her position, but in whom the strength has been born to reject a wifehood that degrades her and a motherhood in which she functions as an ignorant and irresponsible bungler. But like all true pioneers Ibsen is never negative. Let us turn for illustration to the famous ending of *A Doll's House.* Nora has announced to her husband her decision to leave him, her home and her children, because she is convinced that only in this way can she think through the new truths and convictions that have come to her.

"You talk like a child," cries her husband. "You don't understand the society in which you live!" "No, I do not," replies Nora, very simply, "but now I shall try to learn. I must make up my mind which is right — society or I."

Is it to be wondered at that the society that listened to such "subversive" intentions, especially on the part of a mere woman, clutched the arms of its theatre seats in consternation and alarm and assailed Ibsen as a "destroyer of the home" and "an enemy of society"? Finally, realizing that Nora is determined to go, Helmer, now in genuine anguish, asks her:—

Nora, can I never be more than a stranger to you?

NORA

(*Taking her bag.*) Oh, Torvald, then the miracle of miracles would have to happen!

HELMER

What is the miracle of miracles?

NORA

Both of us would have to change so that—Oh, Torvald, I no longer believe in miracles.

HELMER

But *I* will believe! Tell me! We must so change that—?

NORA

That communion between us shall be a marriage. Good-bye. (*She goes out.*)

HELMER

(*Sinks into a chair with his face in his hands.*) Nora! Nora! Nora! (*He looks around and rises.*) Empty! She is gone. (*A hope springs up in him.*) Ah! The miracle of miracles—?!

(*From below is heard the reverberation of a heavy door closing.*)

The curtain falls.

And the reverberation of that door closing, as someone well said, was heard around the world.

Thus does Ibsen "the destroyer of the home" end his play on a ringing note of hope and promise. The miracle *will* happen. A new order of men and women, equal and freely questioning the validity of society's accepted institutions, will build real marriages and real homes. But that Ibsen was a master-builder and not an enemy of society, the "compact majority" of his own day, as Ibsen tersely called them, who feared and hated him as intensely as he hated and despised them, could of course never believe. So, hurt and stung by the attacks *A*

Doll's House brought down on him, Ibsen struck back at the "compact majority" in his next play. If they proclaimed Nora an immoral monster who violated her marriage vow and shamefully deserted husband and children, he would show them a woman who allowed herself to be persuaded that the marriage bond is inviolable and who remained with her husband in the home when her highest sense of responsibility as well as her deepest sense of outrage convinced her, like Nora, that her one, clear duty was to go.

The play which Ibsen wrote to confound his hostile critics was *Ghosts* (1881), undoubtedly his most powerful work and a great play. But it was more than that. *Ghosts* was also the most daring, the most revolutionary play that had, up to that time, been written for the theatre. Because, not content with writing a scathing indictment of the hypocrisy that animated public asseveration of the sacredness of the marriage bond, Ibsen, in his new play, expressed that indictment in terms of a subject so taboo that for anyone then to regard it as fit for the ears of audiences in the theatre seemed unthinkable. This taboo subject was venereal disease, at that time scarcely even whispered about in private. Yet Ibsen dared to present on the stage, as his crowning argument against those who had called him a destroyer of marriage and morality, a living picture of the tragic ravages of syphilis, inherited within the bonds of holy matrimony.

A young woman discovers soon after her marriage that her husband is not only a low profligate but also diseased. Rebelling against such a marriage, but especially against bearing the possible child of such a marriage, she decides to leave husband and home and goes to tell her pastor of her decision. Her pastor, Pastor Manders, today still the classic example of the clerical upholder of conventional morality at all costs, tells her she cannot violate her marriage vow and commands her to go back to her husband. The young woman in question, being Mrs. Alving of *Ghosts* and not Nora of *A Doll's House,* obeys. She returns to her husband and in due course of time she bears a son. But the father continues his debauched life, and when the boy approaches adolescence, in spite of the fact that her entire emotional life is centered in this only child Mrs. Alving sends him away from her to Paris — less to develop his talent for painting than to remove him from his father's contaminating influence. There he reaches young manhood before his father's death finally permits Mrs. Alving to bring her longed-for son, Oswald, home again. But to her horror the mother soon discovers, in the tensely dramatic closing scene of Act I, that Oswald has not only inherited his father's profligacy, but, what is more tragic, as is revealed in the moving scene between mother and son in Act II, that he is already suffering from paresis, the result of the tainted blood inherited from his diseased father, and that it is only a matter of time before his mind will collapse entirely. How that final mental collapse inexorably comes, and how the tortured mother finds the strength to keep her word to her son that she herself will release him from the lingering decay of a life she never should have given him, is told in a closing scene overwhelming in its tragedy and powerful in its implications.

But did the "compact majority" rise to Ibsen's play and recognize in the tragedy of Mrs. Alving and her son a warning to the Pharisaical society which had hypocritically condemned Nora? Decidedly not; and there exist few more revealing commentaries, both on the treatment accorded to pioneers and on the radical changes in concepts of social morality effected between one age and the next, than are to be found in the London press comments following a private performance of *Ghosts* in 1891. "Amazing feats of vituperation" they are called by William Archer, who with Bernard Shaw was the fearless Ibsen champion of those early days. Archer collected those comments in an article later quoted by Shaw, and I have selected the most pungent of them to reprint here.

Ibsen's positively abominable play entitled *Ghosts*. . . . An open drain; a loathsome sore unbandaged; a dirty act done publicly; a lazar-house with all its doors and windows open . . . offensive cynicism. . . . Ibsen's melancholy and malodorous world. . . . Gross, almost putrid indecorum. . . . Literary carrion . . . crapulous stuff.

—*Daily Telegraph* (leading article).

Morbid, unhealthy, unwholesome and disgusting story . . . a piece to bring the stage into disrepute and dishonour with every right-thinking man and woman.

—*Lloyd's.*

Lugubrious diagnosis of sordid impropriety. . . . Maunderings of nookshotten Norwegians. . . . It is no more of a play than an average Gaiety burlesque.

—*Black and White.*

Noisome corruption.

—*Stage.*

And the following are some of the choicest descriptions of Ibsen himself:

A crazy fanatic . . . not only consistently dirty, but deplorably dull.

—*Truth.*

A gloomy sort of ghoul, bent on groping for horrors by night and blinking like a stupid, old owl when the warm sunlight of the best of life dances into his wrinkled eyes.

—*Gentlewoman.*

And now finally some descriptions of those who had the insight and the courage to attend the performances of *Ghosts* and to hail Ibsen as a great social iconoclast and a great dramatist: —

> Lovers of prurience and dabblers in impropriety who are eager to gratify their illicit tastes under the pretence of art.
>
> — *Evening Standard.*

> The sexless. . . . The unwomanly woman, the unsexed females. . . . Educated and muck-ferreting dogs. . . . Effeminate men and male women. . . . They all know . . . that they are doing not only a nasty but an illegal thing. . . . Outside a silly clique, there is not the slightest interest in the Scandinavian humbug or all his works.
>
> — *Truth.*

And what was Ibsen's answer to this obscene onslaught? A new play, this time an exposé of worse than hypocrisy among a group of these "pillars of society" in their political life, namely their deliberate conspiracy of silence on a condition in their city actively dangerous to the public health, because to admit this menace would mean to deprive themselves of a rich source of personal income. This play he named with bitter irony *An Enemy of the People,* because with none of his characters is Ibsen so deeply identified as with that of the social-minded and truth-telling Dr. Stockmann, who, in return for behaving with what he properly regards as ordinary social decency, finds himself reviled and ostracized and deprived of his livelihood. But just as such treatment led Dr. Stockmann to declare that he had "only begun to fight," so it also impelled his creator, Ibsen, to continue undaunted his battle against the destroying shams of bourgeois society as he saw them.

The savagery with which this society hit back at Ibsen is the clearest evidence that they sensed instinctively that here was the first mighty blast of a new order hostile to themselves and to the social codes which protected them. If enough Noras and

Mrs. Alvings and Rebecca Wests knocked basically false and destructive concepts of marriage and sex and social morality out of the minds of the Helmers and the Pastor Manders and the Rosmers; if enough Heddas shuddered and got themselves jobs and developed the courage of their normal sexual instincts; if enough Dr. Stockmanns were sufficiently fearless to expose their discoveries of political and social corruption, and enough Gregers Werles were made to understand that "ideals" of conduct can come only out of the deepest inner convictions of the individual; and if, finally, enough Solnesses would joyously walk hand in hand with the younger generation instead of being terrified of its keener courage and more breath-taking goals — then what would happen to that society's intrenched and satisfied beneficiaries?

Henrik Ibsen, intrepid founder of modern drama, belongs to that noble brotherhood beloved for the enemies they make. It is they who remain of import for the age that follows them because they express the advance thought and new social concepts still violently unacceptable to the majority of their own age. Therefore to have any understanding of the values of our contemporary drama it is as essential to be familiar with the plays of Ibsen as it is for those interested in contemporary painting to know the work of the great modern, Cézanne. A real experience awaiting the reader of Ibsen is the discovery of how deeply involved we still are today with his indignations, indeed with his entire ideology of the responsibility of the individual to himself and to society. And finally the contemporary reader will discover in Ibsen's drama that perfect balance between the play and the theatre, which, as this book predicates, is the theatre's only valid reason for existence. In order that theatre audiences might be more powerfully held, he evolved a stage technique which he hoped would make the theatre more of a living reality than it had been before. This, were Ibsen writing today, he would describe as a technique whereby the "identification" between the persons in the audience and the characters on the stage is made more complete. In short, Ibsen was not writing "closet-drama"; he was writing plays to be produced on a stage, in a theatre, before an audience. He wanted those plays to be successes in the theatre, but in order to achieve such success he wrote no word that did not satisfy him as being intrinsically essential to his play as a work of art, nor did he ever omit a word essential to his play as the expression of his convictions. Ibsen scorned what I have termed merely *theatre-conscious* audiences; it was for *play-conscious* audiences that he wrote with his heart's blood.

It was in 1892, the year in which Ibsen wrote *The Master Builder,* his fourth play from the last, that a young German wrote his fourth play. The young German was Gerhart Hauptmann, and his play was *The Weavers.* Unescapable, for any serious-minded young playwright of the time, had been the influence of Ibsen, prodigiously admired by the progressive element in Germany. *A Doll's House* had enjoyed enormous popularity there since 1880, and after some private performances, the first in 1886, *Ghosts* had the honor of being the initial play to be presented by the famous *Freie Bühne* (Free Stage) in Berlin in 1889. In the same year Hauptmann, himself a member of the Free Stage Society, had his own first play produced there. This was *Before Dawn,* an outspoken portrayal of degeneracy among the peasants and the more affluent farmers, who had nothing but alcohol and sexual excesses to relieve the monotony of their lives. As might have been expected, such truthtelling aroused the canting hushers-up and a storm broke over play and playwright. Clearly, then, here was a younger man thoroughly impregnated with Ibsen's concept of the function of the theatre and determined to carry forward the kind of drama with which his precursor had shocked the world.

I use the phrase *carry forward* advisedly, because Hauptmann's contribution to modern drama lies in the fact that it was he who carried the social play forward into its next phase.

For Hauptmann had grown to manhood during the years when Socialism, with its disturbing new analysis of society, had been outlawed in Germany. In the light of this new social philosophy, the progressive thinker no longer viewed the individual in the terms in which Ibsen had depicted him, but saw him always *conditioned* by the social group, the economic class to which he belonged — submerged in the group, in the class, with which all the interests most vital to his life were identified and of which he was an inseverable part. And so Hauptmann and the others imbued with these new social and economic beliefs were convinced that individuals behave as they do because they belong to the working class, because they belong to the poverty-stricken masses, or because they belong to those forgotten men, the unregenerate peasants. Therefore, since they believed that membership in a clearly defined social group is chiefly responsible for making individuals what they are, these writers were further convinced that a new kind of literature and drama must be created, not in the old terms of highly individualized heroes and heroines, but in new terms of social groups and classes. This, Emile Zola was doing in France in his novels; and it was Gerhart Hauptmann who was the first dramatist with the vision and the courage to discard the individual as hero and present instead a social group as hero.

Thus he made *the workers the hero* in *The Weavers.* While this play is socialistic and revolutionary in tone, Hauptmann nevertheless did not take as his subject the workers of his own day, whose public socialist avowals were then under the ban, but reverted to the Silesian weavers of the 1840's, letting them express the new spirit of working-class revolt vicariously and by unmistakable implication. It was still a far cry from even this unprecedented social play to the unequivocal immediacy of a *Waiting for Lefty.*

In Hauptmann's opening description in the first act of *The Weavers* are inherent his approach to and treatment of his subject: —

> A large whitewashed room on the ground floor of Dreissiger's house at Peterswaldau, where the weavers deliver their finished fabric and the cloth is stored. . . . To the right a glass door through which weavers, male and female and children, are passing in and out. Against the right wall stands a long bench on which a number of weavers have already spread out their cloth. In the order of arrival each presents his piece to be examined by Pfeifer, Dreissiger's manager, who stands with a magnifying glass behind a large table on which the fabric to be inspected is laid. When Pfeifer has satisfied himself, the weaver lays the cloth on the scale and an office apprentice tests its weight. . . . Pfeifer calls out the payment due in each case to the cashier, who is seated at a small table.
>
> It is a sultry day toward the end of May. The clock is on the stroke of twelve. Most of the waiting people have the air of standing before the bar of justice, in torturing expectation of a decision that means life or death to them. They are marked, too, by the anxious timidity characteristic of the receiver of charity who has suffered many humiliations and, conscious that he is barely tolerated, has acquired the habit of self-effacement. Add to this an expression on every face that tells of constant, fruitless brooding. There is a general resemblance among the men. . . . The majority are flat-chested, short-winded, sallow and ill-looking creatures of the loom, their knees bent with much sitting. At a first glance the women show fewer typical traits. They look overdriven, worried, reckless, whereas the men still make some show of a pitiful self-respect; and their clothes are ragged, while the men's are patched and mended. Some of the young girls are not without a certain charm, consisting in a wax-like pallor, a slender figure and large, projecting melancholy eyes.

Whenever I read this description there flashes before my eyes Van Gogh's tragic picture of the "Potato Eaters." That is how these Silesian weavers must have looked, a subject extraordinary enough for a painting, but what a subject for a play! This drab picture of mass-misery, of poverty, of semi-starvation, of cowering abjectness before the masters of their bread, with all its implications of uncontrolled greed and social injustice! Add this, then, to the story of a spontaneous revolt of these lowly workers, suddenly singing revolutionary songs and finding unsuspected wells of courage to protest, to demand, aye even to take — and it is not difficult to understand that the play's production led to riots and the riots led to its being forbidden for a time by censorship.

If Ibsen, then, was the founder of social drama in its more general aspects, Hauptmann was the founder of social drama in its specific aspect of bringing into the theatre the workers *as such,* as the chief protagonists, *en masse,* of the conflict between labor and capital. Thus *The Weavers* will live as the prototype of plays deliberately written to bring the cause of the workers before the attention of audiences in the theatre. But ask those who know their Nora and their Hedda, their Ekdal and their Solness, to name *individual* characters in *The Weavers* and they are likely to answer: "There was a splendid old man — what was his name? And a fiery young woman — now what was she called?" That is all they will remember of individuals, but unforgettable to them are the weavers, the *workers,* bound together by common interests, common sufferings and common hopes. In the creation of this vital, new type of play, then, lies Hauptmann's contribution. However pitiful is the political conformance of his old age in Germany today, Hauptmann will live as the pioneer who carried Ibsen's philosophy of individual responsibility forward to its logical next step of *social responsibility.*

This preoccupation with the tragedy of the disinherited Hauptmann expresses in a different fashion in the poetic dream-play *Hannele,* his most perfect artistic creation. Tender and heartbreaking, *Hannele* combines factors which we accept in our social plays of today quite as a matter of course, but which represented a rare perceptiveness in the social thinking of Hauptmann's day—for he merges the psychological factor with the social as constituting the true basis of human behavior. Without discussing how far psychological factors are themselves the results of social conditioning, we know that there are complicated processes involved in our conduct as human beings which must be described as psychological and which are clearly distinguishable from the social. That Hedda Gabler marries Tesman without love, because as a female parasite untrained to earn her own living she is compelled to adopt marriage as a profession, is a *social* factor. That Tesman is physically repulsive to her and that the fact of her pregnancy is unendurable to her are *sexual* and *psychological* factors. And it is the introduction of the latter factors into the social play *Hannele* that, together with its poetic quality, give it its moving attributes.

Poverty-stricken little fourteen-year-old Hannele, distraught because the death of her beloved mother has left her at the mercy of a drunken and debauched stepfather, tries to drown herself. She is saved by her schoolmaster, Gottwald, with his gentle, Christlike face, who carries her to the poorhouse. There, surrounded by the gaping faces of derelicts like herself, her emaciated little body shivering, she shrieks with terror of her stepfather, but closes her lips in silence when they ask her what he has done to her. The doctor orders her put to bed and the Deaconess, Sister Martha, torn with pity for this neglected child who begs to die, herself takes care of her. There follow then the scenes of Hannele's delirious phantasy, which for profound psychological insight and tragic pathos, expressed in lines of inspired beauty and simplicity, have seldom been equaled. In the troubled confusion of her adolescent emotions, her worshiped

Saviour Jesus and her adored schoolmaster Gottwald become merged as the bridegroom of her unconscious dreams; her beloved mother appears to bring her the flower called "heaven's key" and angels come to tell her that the bread and milk the earth denied her are awaiting her in their Eternal City. So Hannele knows that she will die and shyly she asks Sister Martha: "Must I lie in my coffin in rags, torn and tattered?" But at once the village tailor enters to dress her as a bride with veil and wreath and he places a pair of glass slippers on her incredibly tiny feet. Soon a funeral march is heard and the entire village comes to pay its respects to her. Her beloved schoolmaster Gottwald weeps and Hannele hears him say that he mourns because his two violets have faded — the dead eyes of his dear Hannele. And the village children stand reverently at her bed, overcome by her splendor, and ask "Princess" Hannele to forgive them for always having called her "Rag-princess." Finally there appears the Stranger, clad in the shabby overcoat and with the gentle features of the schoolmaster. To the accompaniment of harp-strains, with an angel choir to escort her, the Stranger, in lines of rich lyric beauty, describes to Hannele, shuddering in ecstasy, the ineffable glories to which he is even now taking her. . . . Then we are once more in the dingy poorhouse and Hannele is lying in bed, a poor, sick child. The doctor is bending over her. "Dead?" anxiously asks Sister Martha. And sorrowfully the doctor replies: "Dead."

In thus regarding the social problem, especially its appalling manifestation of poverty, as not only suitable but also as morally prescribed subject matter for the theatre — a veritable *noblesse oblige* for the socially awakened playwright — Hauptmann expressed his own deep integration with his time. For it was during these years of his early manhood that the struggle of the masses for a place in the sun was beginning to be generally recognized as a significant issue. If it was considered a dangerous impropriety to expose publicly the subjects with which Ibsen dealt, it was considered infinitely more dangerous and far more reprehensible to exhibit, as Hauptmann did again and again, the ravages of poverty. And even if the forms and inevitably the substance also of our postwar social plays seem today to have little resemblance to the dramas of Hauptmann, are not the forgotten Americans of *Tobacco Road* Hauptmann's degenerate German peasants reincarnate? And are not the savagely exploited textile workers whose struggle is set forth in *Let Freedom Ring* blood brothers and sisters to Hauptmann's Silesian weavers? If our age is still emotionally and intellectually involved with many of the questions propounded by Ibsen, how much more deeply is it involved with the problems of poverty and exploitation first brought into the modern theatre by Gerhart Hauptmann.

If one German playwright, then, carried forward the social challenges of Ibsen, it was another German playwright who advanced to its logical next step Ibsen's pioneer challenge in the field of sex. This was Frank Wedekind; and one can find no more convincing argument for the unfailing logic that animates the evolution of human thought, however tortuously illogical it may seem at certain junctures of human history, than that the year 1892, which gave to the world Ibsen's *The Master Builder,* should also give it Hauptmann's *The Weavers* and then further startle it with Wedekind's quite incredibly bold challenge *The Awakening of Spring.* Like Hauptmann, Wedekind regarded Ibsen as the great master and indeed for a number of years he went about in Germany giving public readings of Ibsen's plays. Above all he shared Ibsen's loathing of the accepted hypocritical conventional morality which hid sexual ignorance, sexual excesses and sexual suffering, indeed the elementary facts of sex, behind a smoke-screen of "purity" and "decency." What Wedekind unfortunately lacked, however, was Ibsen's or even Hauptmann's capacity for consistent orderly thinking and writing. His was an unstable personality, and so his hate of sexual hypocrisy expressed itself through his own undisciplined and often violent reactions, in a series of savage and sometimes confused plays. These, with the exception of his masterly and moving *The Awakening of Spring* and his frank if repellent *Earth-Spirit,* will find little sympathetic understanding on the part of the reader or theatregoer of today who, fed on Freudian revelations, can scarcely believe that there was ever anything secret about sex and that its manifestations, normal or even abnormal, should lead to the violence of feeling expressed by Wedekind.

But *The Awakening of Spring* is another story. This "children's tragedy," as Wedekind himself calls it, will cause the reader's well of sympathy to overflow. And it will do more: it will also arouse intense admiration for the man who had the courage to write with such frankness on a subject then so completely taboo as the troubled awakening of children and adolescents to the consciousness and emotions of sex and their urgent need for the fullest instruction in sexual matters. It was now Wedekind's turn to be treated as pariah for his pains — he was even imprisoned on a trumped-up charge of *lèse majesté. The Awakening of Spring,* however, became an enormous success and the play itself will live as the great link between *Ghosts,* that first effort directed toward the lifting of sexual taboos, and those more numerous contemporary plays which brought into the theatre of our own time sexual subjects that, even in this age of unparalleled sex enlightenment and liberalism, still are attacked as taboo.

In *The Awakening of Spring* we meet a group of school boys and girls, between the ages of fourteen and seventeen. They range from the mediocre to the exceptional, and Wedekind dares to tell the then unwelcome truth about them: that in those adolescent years boys and girls alike are preoccupied with the overpowering facts of sex and with the disturbing consciousness of their own sexual impulses and emotions. Wedekind then shows, through successive scenes that are at once frank and heartbreaking, the tragedy that comes to these children because their parents and teachers, themselves still under the indoctrinated curse of regarding sex as a shameful thing, are powerless to guide them through the days of their urgent young need. Because her mother simply cannot bring herself to respond to the earnest imploring of her sexually awakened fourteen-year-old daughter to tell her the facts of sex, the uncomprehending but tremulously responsive Wendla is not prepared to resist the sudden sexual advances of the schoolboy Melchior, to whom she is strongly attracted. And how can Melchior, fine and lofty in spirit, the most serious and brilliant student in his class, commit such a reprehensible act? Because, as Wedekind vividly demonstrates, this splendid boy, together with his schoolfellows, is left to welter in a morass of sexual muck by an adult world which withholds clarifying truth and constructive information. For the same reason Melchior's best friend, the gentle Moritz, whose parents are making financial sacrifices for his education, after an unequal struggle between the havoc caused by sex disturbances and his need for single-minded cramming to keep his scholastic place, in desperation blows his brains out. And when there is found among the effects of poor Moritz a paper written by Melchior in which he tried to explain the facts of sex, as he understood them, for his shy friend who could not bring himself to learn about such things orally, Melchior's so-called teachers, blastingly portrayed by Wedekind, vote to expel him as a moral delinquent and he is committed to the uplift of a House of Correction. In the meantime bewildered little Wendla is subjected by her horrified mother to the mercies of a midwife to whose septic ministrations the lovely, innocent child succumbs. But these three are not the only victims.

Through the other young characters of his play, every phase of adolescent sexual perplexity and aberration caused by ignorance is portrayed by Wedekind, with understanding, courage and artistry.

By the turn of the century the grave import and rare quality of this "children's tragedy" had attained recognition, and soon the young Reinhardt gave it a characteristically fine production in Berlin which enjoyed close to four hundred performances, an unheard-of achievement in the European theatre. The printed play, too, was widely read and translated, again demonstrating that the value of drama significant in itself always transcends that of mere theatre. Thus in America, during those prewar years, a progressive minority, pitifully small in number, who were interested in modern European drama, had read *The Awakening of Spring;* but it was not until 1917, when the war had already loosened the world from its old moorings, actual and conceptual, that an attempt was made to give the play an American production. To theatregoers of today, accepting as a matter of course O'Neill's great plays on sexual themes, as well as lesser works, the fact that an ordinary, public production of *The Awakening of Spring* was unthinkable in New York in 1917 will sound incredible. Today it seems fantastic that in order to prevent interference by the police, a highly elaborate machinery for a performance was evolved by a private group whose sole interest in presenting the play was its educational value in the field of sexual enlightenment. Thus *The Awakening of Spring* was presented under the auspices of *The Medical Review of Reviews,* a progressive medical magazine which further organized as sponsors a "committee" of representative citizens prominent in various branches of education and finally a formidable array of "co-workers" selected from widely varied activities and interests. And last but not least the sale of tickets was by subscription only, so that every holder of a ticket became a subscriber to the enterprise. Thus swathed and protected against the onslaughts of American "morality," one of the great dramatic masterpieces received its first production in English on this side of the Atlantic. And even then the Commissioner of Licenses refused a theatre for the play, on the ground that its performance would be "contrary to public welfare," and not until a court injunction against his stopping the performance was obtained, did the delayed matinee curtain rise at half-past three o'clock.

How urgently needed here was the play's liberating influence may be judged from the press reviews, as well as from an incident, unforgettable to me as one of the production's ardent "co-workers," that occurred during the performance. In the course of the play there arose from her seat another "co-worker," a woman, well-known not only as an author's representative and theatrical producer, but also as a leader in one of America's major political parties. Outraged she proceeded up the aisle, proclaiming in loud tones: "I've had enough! I didn't know I'd been asked to sponsor a *dirty show!*" Nor did the play reviewers, by courtesy called critics, with one or two notable exceptions, acquit themselves any more worthily than had their London confrères twenty-five years before on the production of Ibsen's *Ghosts.* In one New York newspaper appeared the headline "All Childhood Shamed," with the play described as "this nasty and prurient product of Kultur." Elsewhere the play was referred to, in the flippant smartness already then the curse of American drama criticism, as a "spring offensive"; and the reader was told that the drama is "of no great interest or consequence, which saves us the trouble of telling why one girl was ruined, one boy committed suicide and another was arrested." But the highest point of American theatre "criticism" in 1917 was reached by the gentleman who informed his reading public that in one scene of *The Awakening of Spring* a mother in literal terms explains to her young daughter the "facts of nature" and that "in a later episode the children take advantage of their newly-gained information."

Against such vicious ignorance and abysmal stupidity on the part of newspaper reviewers even the gods still continue to cry out in vain; and it was through these channels of the press that the American theatre-going public received its first knowledge of Wedekind. Nor does the fact that both the translation and the production were admittedly unsatisfactory offer the slightest excuse for this reception in America of a play which by 1917 had in Europe won its place, not only as an important milestone in the historical development of drama, but also as an accepted classic. Such reactions of ignorance, hypocrisy and cowardice, typical of the American "compact majority," as in the case of Ibsen's *Ghosts* had the effect, however, of stones thrown into a dormant pool: they created a series of active, ever-widening circles of sympathetic readers, responsive to the play's liberating influence. When we regard the sex-enlightened youth of our own time, the date, 1892, which we read on Wendla's tombstone seems indeed of a bygone age. Yet those who today share Wedekind's faith in the high function of the play and of the theatre will place in a very special niche all its own *The Awakening of Spring.*

Finally, viewing the works of Wedekind as a whole, in their larger aspect, from the lesser known to the best known such as *Earth-Spirit* and *The Box of Pandora,* we find that his one underlying theme, however wild its divagations, reiterated over and over again with terrific emphasis, is the supreme importance to struggling mortals of physical sex. Wedekind refuses to draw the veil over this primal force, this great potential for happiness. In addition there runs through his plays, merging with this theme of sex, the social, or even the Socialist note, which we saw was ever the dominant note in the plays of Hauptmann. Wedekind, too, understood that not only was a new sexual orientation needed to make men free, but a "new deal," social and economic, as well. For example, Dr. Schön, the *diabolus ex machina* of *Earth-Spirit,* is as much enslaved by his lust for property and wealth as by his lust for the primitive Lulu. Both lusts are jointly responsible for his destruction. And in a lesser play, *Marquis von Keith,* Wedekind draws a striking portrait of a man so unbalanced by the lust for success and the unscrupulous acquisitiveness of his age that he becomes a dehumanized and amoral swindler. Thus, in spite of the violence and therefore often the confusion of his attacks, through which the coherence and clarity necessary to art are too often lost, Frank Wedekind, rationaliser of the tabooed subject of sex, takes his place among the important modern dramatists.

That extraordinary year, 1892, remains a focal point in the rich field of modern drama, for all that was most clearly visioned, most iconoclastic, most savagely repudiated and destined to be most significant for our contemporary age. In that year, not only was the aging Ibsen welcoming the younger generation in *The Master Builder,* Hauptmann proclaiming new social truths in *The Weavers* and Wedekind new sexual truths in *The Awakening of Spring,* but also there was heard for the first time in England the voice of a great modern dramatist. No more perfect evolutionary conjunction can be imagined than that the year 1892 should also have seen the production of a play called *Widowers' Houses,* the first play written by an Irishman named George Bernard Shaw. Like Hauptmann and Wedekind, a disciple of Ibsen, whose champion for the English-speaking world he became, Shaw now carried forward into new realms, in a manner and style distinctly his own, the type of drama established by Ibsen, the avowed purpose of which was to serve life.

For life, as he observed it about him, did not satisfy the

young Shaw at all. He could not reconcile himself to the prevalence of corroding poverty in a world of plenty; and so his searching, analytical mind soon led him to recognize in Socialism the solution of the many social problems he realized were inherent in the economic world order of capitalism. And from the day on which Shaw became convinced of the soundness of Marxian economics to the present, Socialism has remained the motive force of his life and thought. Always frankly active and outspoken as a Socialist propagandist in word and pen, his many writings in this field, notably his *Intelligent Woman's Guide to Socialism and Capitalism,* were never tempered by any concern as to how his political and economic unorthodoxy might affect his career as a playwright. Indeed, in all his most important plays, no matter what the subject, the underlying Socialist philosophy is discernible. Surely no one but a Socialist could have written the limpid economic analysis of slum landlordism, which was for that day the daring theme of his first play *Widowers' Houses.* Nor could anyone but a Socialist have written *Mrs. Warren's Profession, Man and Superman, Major Barbara, Heartbreak House* or *Saint Joan.* For Socialism to Shaw was not, as to many others, merely the red badge of youth. It was the guiding philosophy of a lifetime; and the splendid white-bearded man, now eighty-three, although he has seen his own modern world and his hopes for it collapse, nevertheless today looks across the wreckage of war and Fascism and still sees in the lodestar of his youth, Socialism, the one invincible hope of the world. To the prattlers of today who patronizingly refer to this eternally young pioneer in that favorite current epithet of intended demolition — "dated" — I recommend a reading, in the light of current events, of *all* the plays just referred to above; and in addition, for the sake of their souls, the Preface to *Plays: Pleasant and Unpleasant,* Volume II; the Preface to *Heart-*

break House; and *The Revolutionist's Handbook,* printed as an Appendix to *Man and Superman.*

But such a recommendation can of course be made only to the play-conscious. For the merely theatre-conscious, Shaw scarcely exists, since even the finest production of his plays gives the listener little more than a fragmentary glimmer of the brilliance and the profundity that are Shaw. In the theatre there is no lingering over lines, and "getting" the lines of almost any play becomes for the audience an exercise in catch-as-catch-can. Where the play-content is of no moment, losing some of it here and there does not seriously matter. But where the lines are packed with meaning as in Shaw and where, because of his feats of mental legerdemain, his logic is not always instantaneously apparent, the play is always ahead of the listener, especially of the thoughtful listener intent on missing nothing. It is the *play-conscious* theatregoer at a Shaw play who is distressed at losing lines, meaning, logic, and continuity and for whom the laughs and the ephemeral amusement induced by any Shavian drama are not enough. Thus the value of Shaw as *theatre* is very secondary to the value of Shaw as *drama.*

If this sounds like a depreciatory statement to make about the work of a playwright who wrote for the theatre, let us consider for a moment the case of Shakespeare. Obviously, if Shakespeare's immortality depended on the theatrical production of his plays, his name would never have been a household word for generations. The number of persons who have *read* Shakespeare's plays in comparison with the number who have seen them on the stage is legion. What does seeing *Hamlet* in the theatre really mean in comparison with reading it, not once, but many times? Or *Macbeth?* Or *Richard II?* What, for example, did those who rushed to see Maurice Evans play Richard II, without a careful reading of the play, know about one of the most psychologically illumined and most superbly written of Shakespeare's plays? I can tell you, as the result of questioning dozens of such theatregoers: Exactly nothing. As an experience in *playgoing,* their attendance at this production is without significance. They did not even have a real experience in the art of acting, because one's true enjoyment of an actor depends on one's appreciation of the actor's interpretation of the material supplied him by the dramatist, and of the material supplied to Maurice Evans by Shakespeare these audiences know nothing. Thus continued large audiences, when a much-heralded star plays Shakespeare, are devoid of any inspiriting meaning. Of play-consciousness, even though the play is Shakespeare, there is here a complete absence.

By the same sign, then, is the work of Shaw essentially for the play-reader. As vital for the happiness of the world today as when they were written, the works of Shaw offer a storehouse of mental treasure, stimulating, witty, provocative. With the exception of a few of the earlier plays, such as *Candida* and later *Saint Joan,* Shaw's discursive discussion-pieces certainly do not suit the temper and tempo of our own age as reflected in the theatre of today. All of us more or less neurotic, all victims of the destructive evils of a civilization so brilliantly defined by Freud as "a community neurosis," we are, for example, comforted in the theatre by our identification with the neurotic sufferers depicted by a Eugene O'Neill. Their vernacular is far closer to the groping needs of today's audiences than the sharp, intellectual exercises, however witty, of the Shavian puppets, so cleverly manipulated by their master ventriloquist. In the half-articulate idiom of the street, spoken by the ordinary folk who constitute the throbbing characters of a Clifford Odets, their counterparts in the audience hear their own inarticulate cries; in the taut monosyllables of frustration and longing, they hear their own eager and bursting hearts. There is little time in the theatre of today for Shaw. The audience comes in from passing a picket line and goes out to get news of a war. In between, in the theatre, there is no time to become mentally and spiritually adjusted to the vein and temper of a Bernard Shaw. But apparently there is plenty of time outside of the theatre, because those who can find it in this age to read novels like *Anthony Adverse* and *Gone with the Wind* cannot plead that it is lack of time that keeps them from seeking the stimulation of one of the most informed and provocative minds of our time.

It is into the mouth of his revolutionist, John Tanner, in *Man and Superman,* that Shaw puts the words: "I declare that according to my experience moral passion is the only real passion." It is this moral passion which Shaw so admired in Ibsen, that was the animating force of his own work. Let us see how this moral passion expresses itself in the play of his that is most directly the lineal descendant of the drama of Ibsen and of Wedekind, the play that ran foul of the British censor and later of the New York City police, namely *Mrs. Warren's Profession.* Disgusted at the cruel hypocrisy which branded the prostitute as an outcast, Shaw determined to express his Socialist conviction that if there was any immorality in prostitution, it was the immorality of the hypocrites who benefited from it financially and not of the underpaid women who were driven into "a life of shame" through poverty. Shaw's purpose was to show that this "profession" was deliberately utilized by the exploiters as a source of economic gain. Thus is the English aristocrat, Sir George Crofts, exposed as co-owner with Mrs. Warren of a chain of houses of prostitution. But Mrs. Warren herself is shown as having escaped from the lot of a starved working girl into the far better paid occupation of a prostitute and later "risen" to her position of wealth and security. And it is not at all cynically but with honest conviction that Mrs. Warren tells her daughter Vivie, in the famous scene closing Act II, that the girls in her houses are far better treated and better paid than women in other employments. Thus it was not the immorality of prostitution as such that aroused Shaw's moral passion, but the immorality of a system that bred prostitution, battened on it and then denounced its victims as moral outcasts. It was this same moral passion which later in *Major Barbara* impelled Shaw to proclaim that "poverty is the only crime." Clearly no British censor of the time, just before the turn of the century, would permit the public production in England of *Mrs. Warren's Profession.* A few years later, in 1905, an attempt was made to ban a New York production and the play was closed by the police as "offensive to decency." There is no doubt that the outraged protest that followed on the part of a vocal minority of New York's enlightened citizens influenced the court to acquit the defendants of the charge of "committing a public nuisance." The opinion of the learned justice should be read *in toto* to enjoy the full aroma of its rich Victorian flavor. I quote, with italics of my own, a few of the choicest sentiments:—

"That his [Shaw's] main idea is not the discussion of the social evil, so-called, seems to be demonstrated by the fact that not one of the characters of the play refutes the sophistical reasoning of the courtesan mother, with the statement which we *judicially know* that the prostitute is not ordinarily driven to her *choice* of calling by anything other than her motive *to satisfy the desires of her senses without work;* that the only social condition which would keep her from the life which she chooses would be one where man is not compelled to eat his bread in the sweat of his brow—where the delights of the senses are furnished without money and without price. Surely the playwright is not so superficial a scholar that he is ignorant that the ordinary prostitute is on the same plane with the common vagrant in this regard. In fact the statute classes her with the vagrant. . . ."

Nevertheless, in spite of all this abysmal ignorance and error betrayed by the "superficial" Shaw, the erudite judge is finally compelled to ask grudgingly the decisive legal question: "Is the suggestion of the play in its essence moral or immoral?" To which he incredibly answers: —

"In no scene of the play is Mrs. Warren's 'profession' presented *as a stage picture*. It is merely referred to, and that *in a most indirect way*. The prostitute does not flaunt herself upon the stage. The penalty which the mother pays in the loss of the child, for whom she exhibits some motherly love *at least,* is not one which would be likely to attract her sex to her mode of life. If virtue does not receive its usual reward in this play, vice, at least, is presented in an odious light and *its votaries are punished. . . .*"

Because of such pharisaical opinions, then, was Shaw's vitally important play, with its new social approach to the solution of an age-old problem, permitted to resume, unmolested, its run in New York City. And appearing at the same time in book form, an innovation for those days, *Mrs. Warren's Profession* with its coruscating Preface was widely discussed, spreading its influence far beyond that of a passing theatrical production. This influence was further increased by preachers fulminating against the "dangerous" teachings of this iconoclast. I remember one famous New York preacher, who sought to dispose of Shaw by hurling at him the epithet "unspeakable clown" and this offensive epithet of "clown" has clung to him through the years. Today we have a new insight into the inner meaning of the heartbreaking cry, "*Ridi, pagliaccio*" — a new comprehension of those highly sensitive, often seemingly unsensitive souls who laugh that they may not weep. We know now that wit and satire are often the defense mechanisms of those to whom life is intensely tragic. "When a comedy of mine is performed," says Shaw in one of his prefaces, "it is nothing to me that the spectators laugh — any fool can make an audience laugh. I want to see how many of them, laughing or grave, have tears in their eyes."

And now, at fourscore years and more, having lived to see the world for which he had hoped so much in his prime blunder blindly from one catastrophe into another, Shaw achieves the miracle of facing this new age of violently clashing ideologies with as keen an understanding and as fresh a hope as ever. To those who question Shaw's intellectual grasp of world problems today, I recommend one of his recent plays, *On the Rocks,* as keen and outspoken a dramatic document as ever he penned in his physical prime. In its Preface he not only reaffirms his belief in "the economics of Socialism," but also evidences, most delightfully, his clear understanding of the treatment he is receiving today in the "Western world suffering badly from Marxphobia": —

> When I say anything silly, or am reported as saying anything reactionary, it runs like wildfire through the Press of the whole world. When I say anything that could break the carefully inculcated popular faith in Capitalism, the silence is so profound as to be almost audible.

But a change in Shaw's approach to current social problems there naturally has been, just as there has been a change in the outlook of even the youngest Socialist who lived through the War and who now lives in the transformed postwar world. And it is this inevitable change of outlook, but *not* of social philosophy, which *On the Rocks* reveals. For although it continuously crackles with satiric wit and is extraordinarily lively, its grave theme is one which the prewar world did not even envisage — namely, a bankruptcy of capitalist democracy so complete as to render impossible any social transformation within its own framework. Here are the rocks on which the Western world has foundered, and for this impotence of political democracy Shaw blames timid and hopelessly divided

Labor quite as sharply as he blames the visionless, bungling, self-interested captains of the ship of state. In his play he shows them all to us, from the Liberal Prime Minister of a National Government to a Labor Alderman from the Isle of Cats — all seemingly quite incapable of getting their world off the rocks.

Thus we behold the British Prime Minister, a perfect Shavian character, tolerant, lovable, making endless speeches of outworn clichés, muddling along, working himself nearly to death and accomplishing exactly nothing until a lady doctor, a shrewd psychologist, tells him that he is suffering, not from overwork, but "from that very common English complaint, an underworked brain," and takes him off to her sanitarium, to use his mind before he loses it entirely. Preceding her appearance, however, in the Cabinet Room in Number 10 Downing Street, while crowds of the unemployed noisily demonstrate without, we are privileged to view a succession of animated scenes, which, for all their wit, are a merciless exposé of the political crisis which today seems to face a capitalist democracy. Inimitable is the scene of the Prime Minister's meeting with a Labor deputation from the Isle of Cats, each member of which is a vividly realized satiric character, from the heavy but energetic little Mayor and the wealthy young Viscount, unshaven and in a sweater, who fancies he is a Communist, to the clearheaded young Alderwoman, really of the working class, passionately determined to be continuously militantly class-conscious to her last oratorical phrase. There is also in the deputation the elderly Mr. Hipney, one of those sons of the "lower classes," rich in shrewd philosophy, whom Shaw so delights to draw. After the meeting is over and the rest take their leave, he remains behind, now really to "talk a bit" with the Prime Minister. For fifty years Mr. Hipney has been devoted to the cause of labor, during which time he has lived through twelve unemployment crises. He has never read "Dr." Marx, whom his father knew well, and the conversation that follows between Mr. Hipney and the Prime Minister, who has also never read Marx, on the part played by the "old doctor" in the world's present social crisis, is as illuminating as it is riotously entertaining.

After learning how to use his brain in the sanitarium, the Prime Minister returns to throw the country into an uproar by the program he now publicly proposes. It is a program calling for the nationalization of ground rents; the nationalization of banks; the nationalization of collieries; the nationalization of transport; the abolition of tariffs; collective farming; compulsory public service for all — among other equally drastic measures. And now Shaw, with devastating truthtelling lets us hear the reaction of various social groups to the Prime Minister's program of socialization as the way off the rocks. So long as some of the Cabinet members think they see in the program a means for serving their own special interests, they are for it, as is, for example, a Cingalese plutocrat, symbolizing both British colonial possessions and high finance, who delivers one of the most coruscating speeches of the play. But the Labor deputation, with symbolic blindness, seeing in the new social program nothing but "compulsory labor," "doing away with strikes" and depriving the workers of their "last scrap of liberty," reappear to fight it savagely. And now Shaw, in order to point the tragic truth of men's stupidity, resorts to his favorite method of mental legerdemain and offers, in the light of its inescapable and destructive antithesis, the social salvation they reject. For the mentally transformed Prime Minister has foreseen that his plan of progress would be blindly blocked on every hand and he is ready. So when the Conservative Leader now threatens to carry the issue to the voters, the Prime Minister presents his "ace of trumps": —

Well, here is my ace of trumps. The people of this country, and of all the European countries, and of America, are at present sick of being told that, thanks to democracy, they are the real government of the country. They know very well that they don't govern and can't govern and know nothing about Government except that it always supports profiteering, and doesn't really respect anything else, no matter what party flag it waves. They are sick of twaddle about liberty when they have no liberty. They are sick of idling and loafing about on doles when they are not drudging for wages too beggarly to pay the rents of anything better than overcrowded one-room tenements. They are sick of me and sick of you and sick of the whole lot of us. They want to see something done that will give them decent employment. They want to eat and drink the wheat and coffee that the profiteers are burning because they can't sell it at a profit. They want to hang people who burn good food when people are going hungry. They can't set matters right themselves; so they want rulers who will discipline them and make them do it instead of making them do the other thing. They are ready to go mad with enthusiasm for any man strong enough to make them do anything, even if it is only Jew baiting, provided it's something tyrannical, something coercive, something that we all pretend no Englishman would submit to, though we've known ever since we gave them the vote that they'd submit to anything.

And when one of those present says: "A dictator: eh? That's what you want," it is Mr. Hipney who minces no words in reply:—

Better one dictator standing up responsible before the world for the good and evil he does than a dirty little dictator in every street responsible for nobody, to turn you out of your house if you don't pay him for the right to exist on the earth, or to fire you out of your job if you stand up to him as a man and an equal. You can't frighten me with a word like dictator. Me and my like has been dictated to all our lives by swine that have nothing but a snout for money, and think the world is coming to an end if anybody but themselves is given the power to do anything.

Thus, if a nation has demonstrated its incompetence to improve its lot democratically and to eliminate its little dictators, how is it going to escape having its lot "improved" by one big dictator?

This, then, is the barbed challenge of *On the Rocks;* and one can picture Shaw — here, as ever, unmistakably the champion of Socialism — smiling wryly and a little hopelessly at being called a "Fascist" for his pains. . . .

Deserted by Capital and Labor alike, as he knew he would be, the Prime Minister is filled with deep relief that his futile "whitewashing" political career is over. And he knows, too, that he is precluded from ever becoming a revolutionary leader, both by his traditions and his temperament. But just as we heard the unemployed demonstrating on the streets as the curtain rose, so now do we again hear, from without, excited shouts and the breaking of windows. Through the window of the Cabinet Room the Prime Minister, with his wife and young secretary, watch with horror as the police club and break heads. Suddenly the sound of defiant singing is heard. It is the revolutionary song: "England, arise!" Hearing it, the young secretary, moved by an irresistible impulse, rushes out to join the singers. And as the Prime Minister says to his wife

> . . . What she felt just now other girls and boys may feel tomorrow. And suppose — ! . . . Suppose England really did arise!

the curtain falls.

To this social document in dramatic form, making continuous mental demands on the actors, as well as on the audience, the Federal Theatre gave a superb production. What a happy augury for Shaw's own social ideals that thinking, socially alert audiences, at theatre prices so low as to be accessible to practically all, should be able to enjoy as fine a production of a Shaw play as any Broadway has ever offered!

And, indeed, I can think of no more symbolic epitome of the career of this great social dramatist, unique in that his integration with his time has spanned two epochs, than the approximation to his lifelong ideals which the production of his plays by the American Federal Theatre affords. Organized as a Government relief measure, the Federal Theatre soon evolved into something infinitely more important. It became a genuine National Theatre, delighting millions of men, women and children who had been denied the cultural as well as the emotional and spiritual experience provided by the living theatre. Prophetically this happy production of his timely play seems to unite the great pioneer modern dramatist with that world of the future for whose coming he has fought so valiantly.

In Ibsen, Hauptmann, Wedekind and Shaw, then, are to be found the dramatists most profoundly integrated with the modern age, because they were the most acutely aware of the evils inherent in the social, sexual and economic standards of that age and the most clearly positive in their constructive exposition of those evils. But a discussion of these modern foundations would be inadequate without the inclusion of other dramatists of high rank and purpose. One of these is Shaw's compatriot, the Englishman, John Galsworthy. Lacking the robust mentality and the pioneering zeal of an Ibsen or a Shaw, Galsworthy nevertheless is, within the limits of his personality, organically inseparable from his age and time. This bond is clearly recognizable in the fact that it is always the underdog, the individual who has been "put upon" by the dominant elements in the social structure, who enlists Galsworthy's deep interest. Like Shaw, he understood that the basic "crime" of the society about which he wrote was poverty, breeding the pitifully innocent "criminals" whose tragedies he portrayed so eloquently. What a heartbreaking gallery of them: the helpless

Falder and the woman he loves in *Justice;* the equally helpless Jones and Mrs. Jones in *The Silver Box;* the derelicts in *The Pigeon* — to mention only a few, all testifying to the utter sham of the smug assumption that the Haves and the Have-nots are equal before the law! And, like Ibsen, Galsworthy understood that the ultimate victim of a bourgeois society is woman. If economic necessity drives poor John Falder into prison, it is his mate who is driven into prostitution and who then, as a prostitute, is, under the English law, denied the right to a divorce from a menacing husband. If Jones becomes a brutal drunkard because of continued unemployment, it is Mrs. Jones who, now compelled to support the three children she has borne him, becomes not only an underpaid charwoman, but the victim, physically and morally, of the drunken Jones.

It was, however, with subtle comprehension, that Galsworthy portrayed the woman of his own class who was the economic dependent of the "man of property," untrained to gain her livelihood except by sex alone. Where in the drama is there a more appealing figure than *The Fugitive?* Clare is the perfect Galsworthian Hedda Gabler — soft where Hedda is hard, gentle where Hedda is cruel, selfless where Hedda is selfish, passionate where Hedda is sensual. But like Hedda she is the helpless victim of the bourgeois tradition which makes her the sexual property of the man who "keeps" her, whether in or out of wedlock. A fugitive from the embraces of a husband who is repulsive to her, Clare is relentlessly pursued by all the social forces she finds arrayed against her: the laws his humiliation and lust of possession impel him to invoke; her hopeless inability to earn her own living; the ruin which the notoriety of association with her is bringing to the man who has befriended her; her final confrontation with the fact that the only profession open to her is the oldest and the ugliest in the world. But just as Hedda refused to accept life on the terms of sexual submission to a man into whose power she had fallen, so Clare also commits the ultimate act of the fugitive from life because she will not accept it on the terms of what she has always considered woman's supreme debasement: her dedication to the act of love without the urge of love. As contrasted as were their dramatic creators, these two women, nevertheless, together supply a complete picture of the degradation inherent in the economic dependence of women upon men. It is further interesting to note that while *Hedda Gabler* was written in 1890, *The Fugitive* was written in 1913. And how deeply responsive Galsworthy was to the needs of this type of woman may be judged from his much more richly documented portrait, Irene in *The Forsyte Saga.*

In yet another play did Galsworthy carry forward a dictum proclaimed by the embattled Ibsen, to the effect that the strongest man is he who is able to stand alone, come what may. This play is *The Mob,* with a theme that is freshly pertinent for our own age, when cynical imperialist conquests and the throttling of opposition opinion go hand in hand. The date of its first production in Manchester, England is significant — March, 1914. It is the Boer War, however, which Galsworthy uses as his example of shameful imperialist adventure against which every true patriot must raise his voice, even after his country is actually at war. This is what Stephen More, Member of Parliament, does, although his position is that of Under-Secretary of State and a place in the Cabinet is ahead of him. On the very night when the troops have been ordered to South Africa, More nevertheless makes his speech in Parliament asking his country, which he so deeply loves, "to avoid placing before the searchlight eyes of History the spectacle of yet one more piece of national cynicism." "In the name of Justice and Civilization we pursue this policy," concludes Stephen More, "but by Justice we shall hereafter be judged and by Civilization — condemned." How strangely prophetic sound these words, as if they were being uttered of events destined to happen a quarter-century later! Well, that speech is the beginning of the end for Stephen More. " 'Ware Mob!" — so his friend, the big newspaper editor, warns him at the start; and now with relentless logic we are shown how the mob tracks him down. And characteristically Galsworthy includes in this mob not only the ignorant, passion-ridden, war-inflamed people of the streets, but More's own class, his own people, even including his adored wife whose father is a General and whose three brothers are fighting at the front. So at the end the street mob, which he has with his speeches braved so often, crashes into his own house, now deserted by family and servants; and there, still defiantly telling the mob: "My country is not yours," he meets his death. But with that irony of which he is such a master, Galsworthy has yet one more scene to present. For what seemed the final curtain immediately rises again to disclose a statue in a sunlit London Square; on its pedestal we read: —

Erected
To the Memory
of
Stephen More
"Faithful to his Ideal"

Galsworthy, like Shaw, lived to write much in this contemporary age which followed the World War, but he was never of it. In his novels especially he tried to interpret the "lost" post-war generation, but he failed dismally. He caught many of the externals of this strange, new world, but he could not get inside the skins of those who were never really *his* contemporaries, because he was a modern to the core. Yet, a tender-minded playwright of meticulous skill, Galsworthy will move and delight the reader of today.

How extraordinarily strong was the influence of Ibsen in the decade before and after 1900 may be judged from the fact that it penetrated France, a country whose drama has never, with a few exceptions, concerned itself with the problems of life. Thus the appearance there of a Eugene Brieux is almost unique in the annals of French drama. For if elsewhere the theatre was being made an integral part of the life of the time, then, Brieux decided, he would use the theatre similarly in France. In the opening paragraph of his Preface to a volume of three translated plays of Brieux, Shaw writes: "There is no summit in the barren plain that stretches from Mount Molière to our own times until we reach Brieux" and I might add that, so far as significant French drama is concerned, the "barren plain" has continued almost uninterruptedly ever since.

Brieux is best known for his play *Damaged Goods,* which was directly fathered by Ibsen's *Ghosts* and which, like it and like *Mrs. Warren's Profession,* was censored both in France and in England. The subject of *Damaged Goods* is venereal disease, then called the "unmentionable diseases," but the problem is considered from a different angle from that of *Ghosts.* Indeed, it is just this unmentionableness that Brieux attacked as criminal—showing that to keep the subject taboo was knowingly to spread venereal disease. Especially, he condemned the law that places the oath of "professional secrecy" upon physicians, thus forbidding them to "betray" the diseased condition of morally unscrupulous patients to those in danger of being infected by them. In *Damaged Goods* we see a doctor thus prevented from securing a young patient's promise to postpone his marriage until he shall have been cured. The results of his marriage are the birth of a syphilitic child, the hideous shock of revelation to the innocent young wife, the possible infection of the child's wet-nurse—the chain of consequences is endless. Brieux used his fable as little more than a peg on which to hang, especially in Act III, the most outspoken and informing discussion on venereal disease ever conceived for the ears of the general public.

Indeed so "shameless" was this "perverted" playwright that he actually wanted this "unmentionable" subject discussed on a stage! Nor did his fellow countrymen, who delightedly accepted as a matter of course the ever-popular boulevardier type of "sex" play which, night after night, presenting extra-marital sex adventures as the most hilariously amusing thing on earth, grasp the grim irony of their anathematizing Brieux as "a soulless wretch without morality." When *Damaged Goods* was forbidden a production in Paris, Brieux himself read the play before an audience gathered in the famous Théâtre Antoine where others of his dramas, notably *Blanchette, The Three Daughters of M. Dupont* and *The Red Robe* had already been successfully produced. Thus there was started on its stormy career a play which stands as a milestone on the forward road so indomitably traveled by modern drama. In 1910 the volume containing translations of *Damaged Goods, The Three Daughters of M. Dupont,* and *Maternity,* with a brilliant Preface by Shaw, from the beginning the champion of Brieux as he had been of Ibsen, was published in America and, like the printed play of *Mrs. Warren's Profession,* caused widespread discussion. In that same year, too, Eugène Brieux was elected a member of the Académie Française, for despite the fact that Brieux, like Zola, was essentially a maverick and fundamentally alien in his artistic point of view to the genius of the French people, the stature of the man and his contribution to French dramatic literature could not be denied.

In 1913, a single performance of *Damaged Goods* in New York was planned by Richard Bennett and his "co-workers" under the auspices of *The Medical Review of Reviews,* which was a few years later also to sponsor a single performance of *The Awakening of Spring*. That this "notorious" play was to have an American production caused considerable advance excitement, and the performance itself was received with cheers and many curtain calls. The newspaper reviewers, however, with one or two exceptions, found it insufferably "dull." Still, in spite of this dictum from on high, the demand for a regular "run" was so persistent that the play opened as a Broadway production and a month after its opening a leading theatrical weekly reported that "certain scenes and lines are applauded to the echo at every performance." *Damaged Goods* had the extraordinary long run for that time of sixty-six performances on Broadway, after which it was presented in various American cities; and the influence of the publicity given to the play's subject matter cannot be overestimated. It is when we remember that only in recent years have our newspapers permitted the word "syphilis" to be printed in their columns that we feel the full measure of contempt for the shallow parrots to whom the mention of Brieux is the occasion for an attack of spurious artistic shudders.

Brieux consistently wrote for the kind of theatre which he regarded as vital to the needs of society—the theatre which would present problems calling for solution. Only a few of his plays remain permanently valuable. These are, in addition to *Damaged Goods: The Three Daughters of M. Dupont,* a scathing portrayal of the sufferings of women under the hypocritical moral code of the period, but especially under the system of loveless, financially "arranged" marriages; *The Red Robe,* an exposé of the corruption to be met with in obtaining advancement in the field of law administration, but especially of the criminal methods used to procure convictions, even of innocent persons, because what the State rewards is the largest possible number of convictions; and finally *Les Hannetons*—a quite untranslatable title, literally, *The May-Bugs*—by far the most artistic and liveliest of Brieux's plays, demonstrating, with sardonic humor, that for the man who rejects the "chains" of marriage there is no bondage quite so inescapable as that of "free" love. The play-reader will find these plays exciting and profitable and for the student of the drama they are indispensable.

Meanwhile in Austria, the Viennese, Arthur Schnitzler, to whom the life of prewar Vienna was flesh of his flesh and spirit of his spirit, was utilizing the theatre from a completely different angle. But nothing is further from the truth than the uncritical estimate of him, repeated *ad nauseam,* as the depicter in all its "nuances" (that is the favorite word) of the amatory life of Vienna's smart set. Indeed his outstanding plays, such as *Light o' Love, Living Hours, The Lonely Way, The Vast Domain,* and *Professor Bernhardi,* are as far removed in content and spirit from such an unjust characterization as would be *Romeo and Juliet* if described as a play dealing with the love-life of the smart set in Verona. Schnitzler was a physician, and his patients as well as everyone he encountered were to him revelations of the tortuous human soul agonizing underneath its surface layer of gaiety and struggling incessantly to attain its bit of happiness. Thus it is the *individual* that supremely interested this sensitive, wise doctor.

The human soul was to Schnitzler a "vast domain," which descriptive phrase he uses as the title of one of his most subtle tragic plays. He explored what was then so uncharted a land, presenting his discoveries often with melancholy and always without illusion, frankly yet tenderly, but above all seeking to find the basic motives which cause the individual to behave and suffer as he does. In other words, Schnitzler brought into modern drama the *psychological* play as Ibsen, Hauptmann and the others we have here discussed created the *social* play. Like Wedekind, Schnitzler believed that the single most compelling force in the life of the individual is that of sex, so dominating him that its ecstasy and happiness are but slight compared with its pain and disillusionment. But where Wedekind savagely attacks society for allowing sex to continue as a socially destructive force, Schnitzler is absorbed in the psychological effects on individuals of their usually tragic and rarely satisfying sex experiences. *Light o' Love* is the tragedy of a fine girl of the people caused by her relation with a young man of a higher social class. For to her this is not an "affair," but the deepest kind of love, which drives her also to seek death when her lover is killed in a duel involving a married woman of his own class. *Living Hours,* a one-act play, technically perfect, is a psychological study of the reactions to an invalid woman's suicide: that of her artist son for whose release she has killed herself, and that of the inconsolable friend who was her lover years ago. *The Lonely Way,* perhaps his most finely wrought and most poignant play, portrays with mellow understanding and pity the ultimate tragic isolation of the individual. Here the experience of every character reveals how, in all our griefs and frustrations, in the various deaths we die, including the last and final one, we are fearfully and unreachably alone. Not even the seeming complete union of sex, the seeming complete fusion of love, can save the individual, doomed by the inner laws of his own ego, from having to meet the struggles and the shocks of life in this ultimate isolation. Whoever does not know the Schnitzler of these plays is missing precious contact with the modern dramatist whose warm, tolerant understanding and insight were expressed in the most deeply felt and illuminating psychological plays before those of Eugene O'Neill.

Treated in a seemingly light vein, but expressing a fundamental philosophy, the one play of Schnitzler that incurred the ban of censorship, even in his own Vienna, was the famous *Hands Around* (*Reigen* — literally *The Round Dance*). This is a brilliant satiric commentary on that great leveler, the driving force of sex, which keeps all dancing to its tune, in a vicious circle, hand in hand. Schnitzler divides his play into "Ten Dialogues." There are also ten characters, five men and five women, who in each of the ten scenes pair in a new sexual combination. In Scene I the Street-girl and the Soldier have their dialogue until asterisks advise us that the great urge has had its way; in Scene II the Soldier repeats the pattern with the Chambermaid in an amusement park; in Scene III it is the Chambermaid and the Young Master for whom asterisks must be set down. Follow the remaining seven scenes of the Young Master with the Young Married Woman; the Young Married Woman with her Husband; the Husband with the Sweet Little Pick-up; the Sweet Little Pick-up with the Playwright; the Playwright with the Actress; the Actress with the Count, and finally the sex circle is completed with the Count and the Street-girl of Scene I. Each of these ten scenes is a psychological *tour de force.* A five-hundred-page novel could give us little more that is essential to the understanding of these men and women than do these incomparably written short scenes in which the characters completely reveal themselves, their social position, their philosophy of life, their culture, their breeding, or the lack of it, their egotism, their sensuality. To observe the difference in the Young Master's sexual approach to the Chambermaid and in his sexual approach to the Young Married Woman of his own class is in itself a social treatise, as is the Husband's treatment of his wife and of his Little Pick-up, or the Playwright's treatment of the latter and of the famous Actress who acts in one of his plays. But always at the psychological moment come the asterisks. At that point every social chasm is bridged by the all-compelling life-force. Nor does Schnitzler do anything so inartistic as to use the asterisks for scene endings. No, they come when they logically must and the dialogue, properly changed in key and mood, is resumed again.

It was in 1897 that Schnitzler wrote his frank *Hands Around,* but it was not until after the World War, in 1920, that it was first produced in Vienna. In America, highly artistic and inoffensive as the play must seem to all adult minds, certain New York societies, self-appointed watchdogs of "morality," succeeded, in 1923, in preventing even a private production for men only (!) in a New York theatre by a private club. And once more, as when Brieux read *Damaged Goods* to an audience in the Théâtre Antoine, was a banned play read aloud — this time *Reigen,* in a room of this club. Apparently this commentary on our sex-life struck a contemporary note highly disturbing in its implications. Three years later, in 1926, a crude production in a tiny theatre in Greenwich Village enjoyed a short run unmolested, "pursuing its pornographic course there," to quote a typical bit of newspaper *esprit.* And, incredible though it seems, as recently as 1930 the printed play of *Hands Around* was banned from public sale by a New York State court decision. This purblind decision held: —

It is very clear that the author of the book now before us for consideration was not thinking of the spiritual, but devoted the whole book to the animal instincts of the human race. His efforts were not a lesson in morality, nor an attempt to uplift the mind of the reader, but an attempt to depict, in a manner that might possibly be called clever, adulterous relations, vulgar and disgusting in the extreme. While some people may think this quite smart, a book of this kind, which has nothing to recommend it, and dealing wholly with such details, is properly held to be disgusting, indecent and obscene. . . . No better appraisal of its value is needed than that given by the introduction. The facts show that the whole book deals with the sensual. It has no other object or purpose.

True, that particular edition suffered from its meretricious introduction. But today, in New York City, at any rate, *Hands Around* may be freely purchased and may also be read in our public libraries.

Although he survived the end of the World War well over a decade, Schnitzler, like Galsworthy, was spiritually homeless in the postwar world. While he, like Freud, was a Vienna physician, deeply concerned with the strange workings of the human soul, Schnitzler's great work was finished long before the revolutionary effect on literature and art and thought generally of Freud's epochal findings in the field of psychology had made themselves felt. The Freudian interpretation that has now saturated not only the writing of O'Neill but all our more serious psychological playwriting, we of today naturally miss even in Schnitzler's plays. Shortly before his death Schnitzler attempted to utilize the new vein, notably in his psychological novelette *Fräulein Else,* which is little more than a hundred-and-thirty-five page monologue expressing the unspoken thoughts of a young girl as she lives through an intense emotional crisis which leads to her suicide. But Schnitzler is no James Joyce, no postwar neurotic steeped in Freudian psychology. He is the old keen, searching, humane, understanding Schnitzler, his Else resembling a prewar young lady of the Vienna *haut monde;* for Schnitzler can no more get into the psychological skin of postwar youth than could Galsworthy. As a perfect illustration of the chasm between prewar and postwar psychological revelation, read the famous unspoken monologue of Mrs. Bloom at the end of James Joyce's post-Freudian novel, *Ulysses,* and then Schnitzler's pre-Freudian *Fräulein Else.* No, Schnitzler is a modern, but a modern whose work has a rare value for the contemporary lover of the drama. For in his regarding the psychological struggles of the individual as essentially dramatic material and in his insistence on sex as the primary interest in men's lives, Schnitzler sounded a note which was to develop into a major theme in the hands of contemporary playwrights.

The last of the great modern dramatists to be considered here is one who, completely integrated not only with his own time but even more specifically with his own country in his own time, has, nevertheless — in a style all his own and in a field remote from the easily recognized currents of modern life — exercised a profound influence on our contemporary theatre. This is Anton Chekhov, born in the Russia of the Czars in 1860, four years after Shaw and two years before Hauptmann and Schnitzler. Like Schnitzler, Chekhov was a practising physician who found his work as a doctor of inestimable value to him in his writing. He practised among the bourgeoisie and the peasants, the latter often getting his services free, in spite of the fact that he had always to earn his own livelihood. This intimate contact with his fellow men furnished his observant mind with those revealing details which make his characters so appealing and so real. But it is false to stress Chekhov as predominantly a creator of character and of a perfected technique of dramaturgy — his famous technique of untheatricality and understatement — and to neglect those essentials of his work which made him a great modern.

For Chekhov's subject matter and the underlying social philosophy that dominates his plays transcend his character delineations and his technical achievements as completely as Ibsen's play content and social concepts transcend his technique. *The Cherry Orchard, The Three Sisters,* and *Uncle Vanya* constitute the most damning picture of prerevolutionary Russia painted by anyone, with the possible exception of Dostoievsky. If these plays evoke laughter, it is the laughter that ends in a groan of pity for those who are struggling so desperately in the chaotic confusion of the death pangs of one era and the birth pangs of another. And if Chekhov does not portray those social dregs, who shriek at us from his friend Gorky's *The Lower Depths,* it is because Chekhov reveals himself as a social revolutionary chiefly by indirection. What better evidence could we have of the essential Chekhov than the words of the incomparable Stanislavsky, director and actor of the Moscow Art Theatre in his *My Life in Art:*

There are plays written on the simplest of themes, which in themselves are not interesting. But they are permeated by the eternal and he who feels this quality in them perceives that they are written for all time. Chekhov is a writer of such plays. . . . There you will understand that Astrov and Uncle Vanya are not simple and small men but ideal fighters against the terrible realities of the Russia of Chekhov's time. . . . When he and his heroes forget the sad reality of life, he is normal, healthy and courageous. But when the plot of the play drags him and his heroes into the sad and dark life of the eighties of the last century, then the happy laughter of the men in love with life serves but to make clearer the hardships that were borne in Russia by the great men who became heroes in the days of revolution. I cannot believe that a man like Astrov would remain unrecognized in a moment of national uplift in Russia. Sonia and Uncle Vanya came to life and the Serebriakovs and Gaievs perished together with that epoch which no one could criticise and condemn like the same Chekhov. . . . I know of no greater idealism than that which believes in a better future although it is surrounded by hopeless circumstances. And all the plays of Chekhov are permeated and end in a faith in a better future on the part of the fatally ill, talented and life-loving poet, whose own life was as hard as that of his heroes.

In the Moscow Art Theatre's unforgettable production of Chekhov's plays in New York (1923), Stanislavsky played the part of Gaiev in *The Cherry Orchard,* that lovable, irresponsible, dull-witted, spendthrift parasite, one of the last of the helpless, feudal landowning class, falling like chaff before the wind as the new rich merchant class, virile and acquisitive (typified in the play by the *nouveau riche* Lopakhin), gets possession of their age-old estates to transform them into lucrative "real estate." But *The Cherry Orchard* is also here for the play-reader. No actor is needed to overwhelm one with the poignancy of those last moments when Gaiev and his sister, the volatile and equally irresponsible Mme. Ranevskaya, sob in each other's arms before leaving forever their beloved cherry orchard, symbol of their life and of a social class and a social epoch whose *Finis* is here written. In the finale they have all gone and the sound of the departing carriages gradually ceases. Then in comes the old retainer, feeble, eighty-six-year-old Firs, "liberated" by law but still in his heart the serf of his adored master Gaiev, who has now deserted him, the symbol of a social relation and a social type that have ceased to exist. Sick and alone, old Firs lies down on the floor, and we read: *He lies motionless. The distant sound is heard, as if from the sky, of a string breaking, dying away, melancholy. Silence ensues, broken only by the sound, somewhere in the distance, of the stroke of the axe on the trees, in the cherry orchard. Curtain. . . .*

This moving depiction, in terms of individualized characters, of the passing of long-established social groups is, of course, highly characteristic of Chekhov's work, but what is usually strangely lacking in a so-called critical estimate of his plays is the other side of the picture: Chekhov's equal stressing of those characters who express directly his faith in the new life that is coming to his beloved Russia. These characters, who not only utter their hopes for the new social order but announce also their determination to work for it, are not Chekhov's stepchildren, but are at least as beautifully drawn as the showier representatives of the old order. For instance, Peter Trophinov, the poor, shabby student in *The Cherry Orchard,* who has been more interested in studying the problems of his vast country than in getting his university degree, is Chekhov's mouthpiece when, in the outdoor scene of Act II, he begins a long indictment of Russia's intelligentsia:—

Mankind marches forward, perfecting its strength. Everything that is unattainable for us now will one day be near and clear; but we must work; we must help with all our force those who seek for truth. At present only a few men work in Russia. The vast majority of the educated people that I know seek after nothing, do nothing and are as yet incapable of work.

And later when Anya — lovely, eager, seventeen-year-old Anya, symbol of the new generation, finished with the idle, unregenerate past of her family and her class, determined to study and become a worker for the future envisioned by her beloved Peter — says to him

What have you done to me, Peter? Why is it that I no longer love the cherry orchard as I did? I used to love it so tenderly; I thought there was no better place on earth than our garden —

Trophinov replies:

All Russia is our garden. . . . Think Anya, your grandfather, your great-grandfather and all your ancestors were serf-owners, owners of living souls. Do not human spirits look out at you from every tree in the orchard, from every leaf and every stem? Do you not hear human voices? . . . Oh! it is terrible. Your orchard frightens me. When I walk through it in the evening or at night, the rugged bark on the trees glows with a dim light, and the cherry-trees seem to see all that happened a hundred and two hundred years ago in painful and oppressive dreams. Well, well, we have fallen at least two hundred years behind the times. We have achieved nothing at all as yet; we have not made up our minds how we stand with the past; we only philosophise, complain of boredom, or drink vodka. It is so plain that, before we can live in the present, we must first redeem the past, and have done with it; and it is only by suffering that we can redeem it, only by strenuous, unremitting toil. Understand that, Anya.

And to the rich Lopakhin who offers him money, Trophinov flings back:

Shut up, shut up . . . If you offered me a hundred thousand, I would not take it. I am a free man; nothing you value so highly, all of you, rich and poor, has the slightest power over me . . . I can do without you. I can go past you; I'm strong and proud. Mankind is marching forward to the highest truth, to the highest happiness possible on earth, and I march in the foremost ranks!

Lopakhin sneeringly asks: "Will you get there?"

Peter Trophinov quickly replies: "Yes." Then he pauses and adds: "I will get there myself or I will show others the way!"

This is indeed the very essence of Chekhov, who aligned himself with the forces of the "Left," as we say today, and who regarded the theatre as a place in which the harmful outworn must be exposed and the beneficent new heralded with faith.

By the same sign is *The Three Sisters* so often falsely described as a play depicting a group of the groping intelligentsia buried in a provincial town, longing pathetically for the superior attractions of Moscow. But actually this play is a scathing indictment of the Russian "educated" class, ignorant, eaten up with petty egotism, selfish, futile, which we have already seen so mercilessly exposed by the student Trophinov. Yet even among these aimless beings are again the exceptions, the moving characters who express Chekhov's own social vision. First and foremost there is the noble figure of Vershinin, Lieutenant-Colonel of a battery stationed in the provincial town. Doomed to repeated frustrations of his personal happiness, Vershinin nevertheless glows with his vision of the future happiness of mankind. That promise, he believes, is the only compensation for all that is lacking in his own life and in his own time.

"How can I put it?" asks Vershinin thoughtfully—

It seems to me that everything on earth must change, little by little, and is already changing under our very eyes. After two or three hundred years, after a thousand — the actual time doesn't matter — a new and happy age will begin. We, of course, shall not take part in it but we live and work and even suffer today that it should come. We create it — and in that one object is our destiny; and, if you like, our happiness.

Besides Vershinin, there are also the Baron, who is a Lieutenant in the army, and Irina, youngest of the three sisters. A great truth has dawned upon Irina which she proclaims to the Baron with passionate conviction: —

When I awoke this morning . . . I seemed to grasp the meaning of life. . . . Everyone must toil in the sweat of his brow, whoever he may be. In this alone is the aim of his life, his happiness, his ambition. How splendid it is to be a workman who gets up at daybreak and breaks stones in the street, or a shepherd, or a schoolmaster who teaches children, or a railroad mechanic! . . . My God, if I can't be a man who works, I would rather be an ox, or a horse, or any work animal than a young lady who wakes up at noon, has her coffee in bed, and then spends two hours dressing. . . . Oh, it's awful! Sometimes I crave work as a thirsty man craves water on a hot day!

To which the Baron replies: —

I can understand that craving for work. God! I've never worked in my life. I was born of a family that never needed to work nor ever had to worry. . . . They shielded me from work; they almost succeeded; almost! But the day of reckoning is here. Something formidable is threatening us; a strong cleansing storm is gathering; it is coming nearer and nearer; it will soon sweep our world clean of laziness, indifference, prejudice against work and wretched boredom. I shall soon work, and within twenty-five or thirty years everyone will work! Everyone!

It was in 1901 that Chekhov wrote these prophetic words. In January, 1904, *The Cherry Orchard* had its premiere in Moscow, and in July of that year Chekhov succumbed, at the early age of forty-four, to the illness that had long kept him an exile from that city. That same month the ruthless Minister of the Interior, Plehve, was assassinated; and six months later, in January, 1905, came the workers' trusting demonstration before the Czar's palace that was to go down through history as "Bloody Sunday." The Russian Revolution had begun.

Thus our brief survey of the modern dramatists demonstrates that they are great because they consistently considered their convictions more important than their plays and their plays more important than productions in the theatre. In other words, the outstanding modern dramatists were concerned first, last and all the time with *life;* and the art of playwriting and the art of the theatre were to them a means of bettering life. Nor was it anything so vague as life-in-general that drove them into the arduous task of playwriting. No, it was *life-in-particular* that interested them, the life of their own time, which, because they were each an integral and intensely aware part of it, they understood at first hand. And the deductions they drew — each from those aspects of his age which most vitally concerned him — could not be other than significant, not only for the people of their own time but for us of today who have to meet the contemporary versions of the vital questions raised by them. Only the play-lovers who are steeped in the work of these moderns are qualified to evaluate the plays and the theatre of today.

Chapter 3 Contemporary Drama: The Individual in Conflict with Changing Sexual Standards

When we inquire into the drama of our own contemporary era, our standards of judgment must differ from those determining the values of the modern dramatists. In considering the moderns, we have two standards. The first is the general verdict of fame — the recognition that time has already bestowed on them. Thus the permanent values of Ibsen, Chekhov, and of certain plays of Hauptmann are no longer in doubt. The second standard is the selection of new subject matter so vital that its significance can be fully judged only by the succeeding age. According to this standard I apply the term *great* to the modern dramatists previously discussed.

Obviously we cannot apply these standards of evaluation to the dramatists of our own age, because the element of time is lacking. We may have valid reasons for believing that the work of certain contemporary playwrights will live, but we cannot know. To playwrights of today we must apply another standard, summed up in the question: *What does their work mean to us living today?* Are they writing about subjects of interest and importance to the contemporary world? Are they treating these subjects with vision, with courage? Do their plays illumine matters of moment to us, both as individuals and as members of society? Are they carrying forward in their turn the pioneer work of the great moderns? It is this standard which I shall apply to them here.

In the preceding chapter I showed that even those great moderns, like Galsworthy, who actually experienced the change from the modern to the contemporary world were unable to become completely integrated with the new age. The exception we found to be Shaw, whose interests, however, have always been social and who never expended on the individual any of the intense and brooding devotion that characterizes the work of Ibsen, of Schnitzler, of Galsworthy.

And therein lies the explanation of Shaw's contemporaneousness, because social changes are never realized until long after the rebelling individual has protested against the havoc wrought upon his life by outworn social usages. Galsworthy's "fugitive," the helpless individual enslaved by marriage, must struggle and die long before Shaw's liberating social theories on the enslaving economic basis of marriage can be practically realized by society as a whole. So Shaw remains a prophet still, even though the numbers of individual women today trained to find economic support outside of marriage are legion. But we cannot overestimate the importance of playwrights who record the conflict of the individual with oppressive social traditions. For just as soon as this individual conflict contains clearly defined general implications, the problem reveals itself as not, in its essence, an individual conflict at all. True, Nora does not actually call a mass meeting of wives and mothers and organize them into "The Society of Women Opposed to Dolls' Houses," but in effect she does just that when she slams the door of her own doll's house and departs. Although her conflict with the established status of woman as an inferior sex is shown by Ibsen as a purely individual one, the condition against which Nora revolted was universal in all countries where a similar level of social development prevailed. Thus the individual conflict serves as the focus of attention for the universal conflict and becomes its rallying-point.

But since we are all ourselves individuals, it is the presentation of individual conflicts that most deeply moves the majority of people in the theatre. "There, but for the grace of God, go

I," says the audience, or more often, alas, "There go I, without the grace of God." In this way the expression of an individual protest provides the crucial first step toward the formulation of a protest consciously directed against the causes of conflicts affecting people generally.

Although the individual is likely to encounter his most intensely personal conflicts in the search for sexual happiness, these conflicts are largely the result of the special sex relation of two specific individuals, while the only sex problems to have validity in the theatre are those that illuminate aspects of the subject important to the happiness of people generally in a given time. Let us see what our contemporary dramatists have done to bring into the theatre such problems, and to discuss taboos which have become anachronisms in our age of radically changed sexual standards.

One of the tenets of sexual morality most tenaciously adhered to since the beginning of monogamic marriage is "the double standard," which, toward the end of the modern era, was first subjected to sharp attack. This is the code which demands complete chastity on the part of all members of the female sex who expect to be admitted into the sacred bonds of marriage, but permits the male to roam at will, on the theory that woman is by nature asexual and "pure," while man is a creature of sex and therefore inevitably impure. The true scientific explanation of the superimposition of chastity on woman is that monogamic marriage was established to insure, as far as possible, the legitimacy of a man's heirs to his property. Thus monogamy had nothing to do with the higher erotic life, but was actually the first form of the family in which woman was reduced to complete economic and sexual subjection. The revolt against the "double standard" could therefore come only when industrial evolution necessitated woman's economic emancipation.

The first of the four plays I have selected, to illustrate how this passing of the "double standard" has been treated in the theatre, just antedates our contemporary period. But it is the first play to deal frankly and robustly with what in 1912, the year of its production in England, was decidedly a taboo subject; and if ever a dramatist created a young heroine contemporary in point of view and behavior, she is that sturdy and breezy precursor of a better day, Fanny Hawthorn. The play in which Fanny takes her stand for the single standard of sexual morality is the famous *Hindle Wakes,* written by the young English playwright, Stanley Houghton, who died in 1913, at the age of 32. Houghton, however, not only was thoroughly integrated with his own time, but also, like Shaw and Chekhov, understood its social and economic defects and visioned the future that was to come. The reader of the highly original *Hindle Wakes* will understand why I not only place Stanley Houghton among contemporary playwrights, but also in that company which carries forward from one age to the next with candor and with courage the good fight for men and women who shall be equal, unafraid and free.

Fanny Hawthorn is a Lancashire lass, a weaver in the Jeffcote Mill at Hindle. Ostensibly spending the Bank Holiday week-end, locally known as Hindle Wakes, at a seaside resort with a girl-friend, Fanny is actually spending it with young Alan Jeffcote, son of Hindle's industrial magnate. Because of the girl-friend's drowning, Fanny's parents discover the truth, and her shrewd mother determines that Jeffcote's son must now "make an honest woman" of the "ruined" Fanny. And so firmly ingrained is this moral code, that, despite the fact that young Alan is betrothed to another magnate's daughter with whom he is sincerely in love and that the breaking-off of this match shatters his parents' dearest hopes, his father now insists that there is only one girl whom Alan can "honestly wed," and that girl is the "wronged" Fanny Hawthorn. But they have all reckoned without Fanny; and the final scene in which, after disrupting the combined family conclave by flatly refusing to be thus disposed of, Fanny privately tells Alan why she has no thought of marrying him, is not only delightful, but also far-reaching in its implications. I shall quote its quintessential lines, although every word of the entire play is precious. It is after Fanny and he have discussed his broken engagement that Alan says: "I know why you won't marry me."

FANNY: Do you? (*She smiles.*) Well, spit it out, lad!

ALAN: You're doing it for my sake.

FANNY: How do you make that out?

ALAN: You don't want to spoil my life.

FANNY: Thanks! Much obliged for the compliment.

ALAN: I'm not intending to say anything unkind, but of course it's as clear as daylight that you'd damage my prospects, and all that sort of thing. You can see that, can't you?

FANNY: Ay! I can see it now you point it out. I hadn't thought of it before.

ALAN: Then, that isn't why you refused me?

FANNY: Sorry to disappoint you, but it's not.

ALAN: I didn't see what else it could be.

FANNY: Don't you kid yourself, my lad! It isn't because I'm afraid of spoiling *your* life that I'm refusing you, but because I'm afraid of spoiling *mine*. That didn't occur to you?

ALAN: It didn't. . . . But you didn't ever really love me?

FANNY: Love you? Good heavens, of course not! Why on earth should I love you? You were just someone to have a bit of fun with. You were an amusement — a lark.

ALAN (*Shocked*): Fanny! Is that all you cared for me?

FANNY: How much more did you care for me?

ALAN: But it's not the same. I'm a man.

FANNY: You're a man, and I was your little fancy. Well, I'm a woman, and *you* were *my* little fancy. You wouldn't prevent a woman enjoying herself as well as a man, if she takes it into her head?

ALAN: But do you mean to say that you didn't care any more for me than a fellow cares for any girl he happens to pick up?

FANNY: Yes. Are you shocked?

ALAN: It's a bit thick; it is really!

FANNY: You're a beauty to talk!

ALAN: It sounds so jolly immoral. I never thought of a girl looking on a chap just like that! I made sure you wanted to marry me if you got the chance.

FANNY: No fear! You're not good enough for me. The chap Fanny Hawthorn weds has got to be made of different stuff from you, my lad. *My* husband, if ever I have one, will be a man, not a fellow who'll throw over his girl at his father's bidding! Strikes me the sons of these rich manufacturers are all much alike. They seem a bit weak in the upper story. It's their father's brass that's too much for them, happen! They don't know how to spend it properly. They're like chaps who can't carry their drinks because they aren't used to it. The brass gets into their heads, like!

ALAN: Hang it, Fanny, I'm not quite a fool.

FANNY: No. You're not a fool altogether. But there's summat lacking. You're not a man enough for me. You're a nice lad, and I'm fond of you. But I couldn't ever marry you. We've had a right good time together, I'll never forget that. It has been a right good time, and no mistake! We've enjoyed ourselves proper! But all good times have to come to an end, and ours is over now. Come along, now, and bid me farewell.

ALAN: I can't make you out rightly, Fanny, but you're a damn good sort, and I wish there were more like you!

When the waiting parents now hear her decision, Fanny's mercenary mother in furious disappointment tells her that she can "fetch her things and . . . pack off." And to Alan's eager

"I'm not going to see you without a home," Fanny replies, smiling:—

It's right good of you, Alan, but I shan't starve. I'm not without a trade at my finger-tips, thou knows. I'm a Lancashire lass, and so long as there's weaving sheds in Lancashire I shall earn enough brass to keep me going. I wouldn't live at home again after this, not anyhow! I'm going to be on my own in future. (*To her father.*) You've no call to be afraid. I'm not going to disgrace you. But so long as I've to live my own life I don't see why I shouldn't choose what it's to be.

In these simple words lies a new philosophy of life for women. Here we have a young working woman clearly conscious that the basis of her self-respect and of her freedom of action is her ability to earn her own bread. Through her direct statement of her point of view, Houghton proves his thesis: that women's subjection to a double standard of sexual morality is an economic subjection.

It was well over a decade later that another English dramatist carried the same subject right into the drawing-rooms of London's socially elect. In *The Constant Wife,* W. Somerset Maugham created, in the guise of one of the wittiest of comedies, a satire of deep import. Maugham, I fear, is not sufficiently appreciated as a penetrating social analyst. This misunderstanding is undoubtedly due to his lack of the superficially recognizable earmarks of the "social playwright," as that term is glibly used. Maugham is essentially interested in individuals, not in social groups, and specifically in the individuals of his own class, the upper middle class, whose qualities and difficulties he dissects with an imperturbable knife. Very likely it is his own emotional involvement with his subject matter which often gives his work an astringence that seems to repel the merely theatre-conscious. But the play-conscious will surely respond to his bitter anti-war play *For Services Rendered* and to *The Breadwinner,* an acute picture of a typical upper middle-class family in which the husband and father finally revolts against his life of perpetually earning the wherewithal for his wife's and children's spending. True, it is individuals whom Maugham depicts, but it is individuals conditioned by social and economic forces which create the situations in which they find themselves.

This underlying social basis of Maugham's more important work is especially dominant in *The Constant Wife.* But, alas, just as with the plays of Shaw, the laughter it evokes in the theatre too often causes the significance of Maugham's most scintillating lines to be missed. It is, therefore, to the play-reader that *The Constant Wife* is a joyous revelation, that Constance, the play's dazzling heroine, becomes unforgettable—a woman whom her more somber and tragic sisters of the modern age would welcome into their midst with genuine pride. The vital question which Maugham not only asks in *The Constant Wife,* but answers with complete candor, is: *How does the economic basis of the "double standard" affect not only the women of the upper classes today, but their husbands, their marriage-relation, in fact, the whole institution of monogamy?*

Constance is thirty-six and has been married to the eminent London surgeon, John Middleton, for fifteen years. She has borne him a child, she and John delight in each other's society and generally offer every evidence of a successful marriage. When the play opens we find Constance's mother, her sister, and her close friend, Barbara, upset and indignant because there can be no doubt that John is having an affair with one of Constance's married friends, Marie-Louise, the wide-eyed, pretty and clinging type of femininity. But Constance, handling this, like every other situation, deftly and firmly, refuses to make an issue of it or to consider divorcing John, and she tells why in a succession of provocative discussions in which she argues the subject of marital infidelity. Finally, in a highly effective scene, determined that there shall be no scandal, Constance, with great presence of mind, persuades Marie-Louise's jealous and irate husband that John's cigarette case found compromisingly in his wife's bedroom is one she herself uses and had left there. This crisis safely over, she proceeds illuminatingly to explain her action and to discuss their marriage relation with John himself. No, Constance is not outraged at John's conduct, because, as she now makes him also honestly admit, it is some years since they have no longer been *in love* with each other, during which years she has been fully aware of his various "infidelities," even though they had not come before the public eye like the present one. Oh yes, they are still "devoted" to each other, the best of companions, bound together by their common interests, by genuine affection and by their home, but they are not *in love;* so, why, asks Constance, should she play the dog in the manger and break up a comfortable, congenial, nay, happy home? Indeed she has even persistently rejected the eager offer repeatedly made her by her concerned friend, Barbara, to become a partner in the latter's successful business of antiques and decoration.

But now a new situation develops which causes Constance to plumb more deeply the subject of upper-class marriage and marital infidelity. There has just arrived from Japan for a visit in England, Bernard, a rejected suitor of her youth, a bachelor, who loves and desires her still. When he learns of John's behavior, he promptly assumes that now he can ask for Constance's love, her divorce and marriage to him. And Constance's response to Bernard in the following scene is the most trenchant expression in contemporary drama of the thinking wife's new understanding and changed point of view.

BERNARD: There's no reason now why I shouldn't tell you of the love that consumes me. Oh, Constance, come to me. You know that if things were as I thought they were between you and John nothing would have induced me to say a word. But now he has no longer any claims on you. He doesn't love you. Why should you go on wasting your life with a man who is capable of exposing you to all this humiliation? You know how long and tenderly I've loved you. You can trust yourself to me. I'll give my whole life to making you forget the anguish you've endured. Will you marry me, Constance?

CONSTANCE: My dear, John may have behaved very badly but he's still my husband.

BERNARD: Only in name. You've done everything in your power to save a scandal and now if you ask him to let himself be divorced he's bound to consent.

CONSTANCE: Do you really think John has behaved so very badly to me?

BERNARD (*Astonished*): You don't mean to say that you have any doubts in your mind about his relationship with Marie-Louise?

CONSTANCE: None.

BERNARD: Then what in God's name do you mean?

CONSTANCE: My dear Bernard, have you ever considered what marriage is among well-to-do people? In the working classes a woman cooks her husband's dinner, washes for him and darns his socks. She looks after the children and makes their clothes. She gives good value for the money she costs. But what is a wife in our class? Her house is managed by servants, nurses look after her children, if she has resigned herself to having any, and as soon as they are old enough she packs them off to school. Let us face it, she is no more than the mistress of a man of whose desire she has taken advantage to insist on a legal ceremony that will prevent him from discarding her when his desire has ceased.

BERNARD: She's also his companion and his helpmate.

CONSTANCE: My dear, any sensible man would sooner play bridge at his club than with his wife, and he'd always rather play golf with a man than with a woman. A paid secretary is a far better helpmate than a loving spouse. When all is said and done, the modern wife is nothing but a parasite.

BERNARD: I don't agree with you.

CONSTANCE: You see, my poor friend, you are in love and your judgment is confused.

BERNARD: I don't understand what you mean.

CONSTANCE: John gives me board and lodging, money for my clothes and my amusements, a car to drive in and a certain position in the world. He's bound to do all that because fifteen years ago he was madly in love with me, and he undertook it; though, if you'd asked him, he would certainly have acknowledged that nothing is so fleeting as that particular form of madness called love. It was either very generous of him or very imprudent. Don't you think it would be rather shabby of me to take advantage now of his generosity or his want of foresight?

BERNARD: In what way?

CONSTANCE: He paid a very high price for something that he couldn't get cheaper. He no longer wants that. Why should I resent it? I know as well as anybody else that desire is fleeting. It comes and goes and no man can understand why. The only thing that's certain is that when it's gone it's gone forever. So long as John continues to provide for me what right have I to complain that he is unfaithful to me? He bought a toy and if he no longer wants to play with it why should he? He paid for it.

BERNARD: That might be all right if a man had only to think about himself. What about the woman?

CONSTANCE: I don't think you need waste too much sympathy on her. Like ninety-nine girls out of a hundred when I married I looked upon it as the only easy, honourable and lucrative calling open to me. When the average woman who has been married for fifteen years discovers her husband's infidelity it is not her heart that is wounded but her vanity. If she had any sense, she would regard it merely as one of the necessary inconveniences of an otherwise pleasant profession.

BERNARD: Then the long and short of it is that you don't love me.

CONSTANCE: You think that my principles are all moonshine?

BERNARD: I don't think they would have much influence if you were as crazy about me as I am about you. Do you still love John?

CONSTANCE: I'm very fond of him, he makes me laugh, and we get on together like a house on fire, but I'm not in love with him.

BERNARD: And is that enough for you? Isn't the future sometimes a trifle desolate? Don't you want love?

(*A pause. She gives him a long reflective look.*)

CONSTANCE (*Charmingly*): If I did I should come to you for it, Bernard.

BERNARD: Constance, what do you mean? Is it possible that you could ever care for me? Oh, my darling, I worship the ground you tread on.

(*He seizes her in his arms and kisses her passionately.*)

CONSTANCE (*Releasing herself*): Oh, my dear, don't be so sudden. I should despise myself entirely if I were unfaithful to John so long as I am entirely dependent on him.

BERNARD: But if you love me?

CONSTANCE: I never said I did. But even if I did, so long as John provides me with all the necessities of existence I wouldn't be unfaithful. It all comes down to the economic situation. He has bought my fidelity and I should be worse than a harlot if I took the price he paid and did not deliver the goods.

As soon as Bernard leaves, Constance takes up the telephone and we hear her say:

Mayfair 2646. . . . Barbara? It's Constance. That offer you made me . . . is it still open? Well, I want to accept it . . . No, no, nothing has happened. John is very well. He's always sweet, you know. It's only that I want to earn my own living. When can I start? The sooner the better.

Between this curtain speech of Act II and the last act, a year has elapsed. When we see Constance again she has been working like a beaver. She has proved herself invaluable to Barbara and she is now about to depart on a six weeks' holiday. That is the length of time she has told the rather surprised Barbara she must have off. So we come to the final scene, that of her farewell with her husband, and we shall let this scene, in part, speak for itself:—

JOHN: . . . By the way, do you want any money? I'll write you a cheque at once.

CONSTANCE: Oh, no, thank you. I've got plenty. I've earned fourteen hundred pounds during this year that I've been working.

JOHN: Have you, by Jove! That's a very considerable sum.

CONSTANCE: I'm taking two hundred of it for my holiday. I've spent two hundred on my clothes and on odds and ends and the remaining thousand I've paid into your account this morning for my board and lodging during the last twelve months.

JOHN: Nonsense, darling. I won't hear of such a thing. I don't want you to pay for your board and lodging.

CONSTANCE: I insist.

JOHN: Don't you love me any more?

CONSTANCE: What has that to do with it? Oh, you think a woman can only love a man if he keeps her. Isn't that rating your powers of fascination too modestly? What about your charm and good humour?

JOHN: Don't be absurd, Constance. I can perfectly well afford to support you in your proper station. To offer me a thousand pounds for your board and lodging is almost insulting.

CONSTANCE: Don't you think it's the kind of insult you could bring yourself to swallow? One can do a lot of amusing things with a thousand pounds.

JOHN: I wouldn't dream of taking it. I never liked the idea of your going into business. I thought you had quite enough to do looking after the house and so forth.

CONSTANCE: Have you been less comfortable since I began working?

JOHN: No, I can't say I have.

CONSTANCE: You can take my word for it, a lot of incompetent women talk a great deal of nonsense about housekeeping. If you know your job and have good servants it can be done in ten minutes a day.

JOHN: Anyhow you wanted to work and I yielded. I thought in point of fact it would be a very pleasant occupation for you, but heavens knows, I wasn't expecting to profit financially by it.

CONSTANCE: No, I'm sure you weren't.

JOHN: Constance, I could never help thinking that your determination had something to do with Marie-Louise.

(There is a moment's pause and when Constance speaks it is not without seriousness.)

CONSTANCE: Haven't you wondered why I never reproached you for your affair with Marie-Louise?

JOHN: Yes. I could only ascribe it to your unfathomable goodness.

CONSTANCE: You were wrong. I felt I hadn't the right to reproach you.

JOHN: What do you mean, Constance? You had every right. We behaved like a couple of swine. I may be a dirty dog, but, thank God, I know I'm a dirty dog.

CONSTANCE: You no longer desired me. How could I blame you for that? But if you didn't desire me, what use was I to you? You've seen how small a share I take in providing you with the comfort of a well-ordered home.

JOHN: You were the mother of my child.

CONSTANCE: Let us not exaggerate the importance of that, John. I performed a natural and healthy function of my sex. And all the tiresome part of looking after the child when she was born I placed in the hands of much more competent persons. Let us face it, I was only a parasite in your house. You had entered into legal obligations that prevented you from turning me adrift, but I owe you a debt of gratitude for never letting me see by word or gesture that I was no more than a costly and at times inconvenient ornament.

JOHN: I never looked upon you as an inconvenient ornament. And I don't know what you mean by being a parasite. Have I ever in any way suggested that I grudged a penny that I spent on you?

CONSTANCE (*With mock amazement*): Do you mean to say that I ascribed to your beautiful manners what was only due to your stupidity? Are you as great a fool as the average man who falls for the average woman's stupendous bluff that just because he's married her he must provide for her wants and her luxuries, sacrifice his pleasures and comfort and convenience, and that he must look upon it as a privilege that she allows him to be her slave and bondman? Come, come, John, pull yourself together. You're a hundred years behind the times. Now that women have broken down the walls of the harem they must take the rough-and-tumble of the street.

JOHN: You forget all sorts of things. Don't you think a man may have gratitude to a woman for the love he has had for her in the past?

CONSTANCE: I think gratitude is often very strong on men so long as it demands from them no particular sacrifices.

JOHN: Well, it's a curious way of looking at things, but obviously I have reason to be thankful for it. But after all you knew what was going on long before it came out. What happened then that made you make up your mind to go into business?

CONSTANCE: I am naturally a lazy woman. So long as appearances were saved I was prepared to take all I could get and give nothing in return. I was a parasite, but I knew it. But when we reached a situation where only your politeness or your lack of intelligence prevented you from throwing the fact in my teeth I changed my mind. I thought that I should very much like to be in a position where, if I felt inclined to, I could tell you, with calm, courtesy, but with determination, to go to hell.

JOHN: And are you in that position now?

CONSTANCE: Precisely. I owe you nothing. I am able to keep myself. For the last year I have paid my way. There is only one freedom that is really important and that is economic freedom, for in the long run the man who pays the piper calls the tune. . . .

JOHN: You know, I would sooner you had made me scenes for a month on end like any ordinary woman and nagged my life out than that you should harbour this cold rancour against me.

CONSTANCE: My poor darling, what are you talking about? Have you known me for fifteen years and do you think me capable of the commonness of insincerity? I harbour no rancour. Why, my dear, I'm devoted to you.

JOHN: Do you mean to tell me that you've done all this without any intention of making me feel a perfect cad?

CONSTANCE: On my honour. If I look in my heart I can only find in it affection for you and the most kindly and charitable feelings. Don't you believe me?

(*He looks at her for a moment and then makes a little gesture of bewilderment.*)

JOHN: Yes, oddly enough, I do. You are a remarkable woman, Constance. . . . (*With an affectionate smile*) I wish I could get away. I don't half like the idea of your travelling by yourself.

CONSTANCE: Oh, but I'm not. Didn't I tell you?

JOHN: No.

CONSTANCE: I meant to. I'm going with Bernard.

To this news John responds in the time-honored manner of the outraged husband; then, during a scene of which the play-reader cannot afford to miss a word, Constance's mother enters, saying in her emphatic disapproval of her daughter's intentions:—

We all know that unchastity has no moral effect on men. They can be perfectly promiscuous and remain upright, industrious and reliable. It's quite different with women. It ruins their character. They become untruthful and dissipated, lazy, shiftless and dishonest.

That is why the experience of ten thousand years has demanded chastity in women. Because it has learnt that this virtue is the key to all others.

To which Constance replies: —

They were dishonest because they were giving away something that wasn't theirs to give. They had sold themselves for board, lodging and protection. They were chattel. They were dependent on their husbands and when they were unfaithful to them they were liars and thieves. I'm not dependent on John. I am economically independent and therefore I claim my sexual independence. I have this afternoon paid into John's account one thousand pounds for my year's keep.

After Constance has admitted to her husband that Bernard is a little dull and that he really can't measure up to him in any respect, John bursts forth: —

Then in Heaven's name why do you want to go away with him?

CONSTANCE: Shall I tell you? Once more before it's too late I want to feel about me the arms of a man who adores the ground I walk on. I want to see his face light up when I enter the room. I want to feel the pressure of his hand when we look at the moon together and the pleasantly tickling sensation when his arm tremulously steals around my waist. I want to let my head fall on his shoulders and feel his lips softly touch my hair.

JOHN: The operation is automatically impossible, the poor devil would get such a crick in the neck he wouldn't know what to do.

CONSTANCE: I want to walk along country lanes holding hands and I want to be called by absurd pet names. I want to talk baby-talk by the hour together.

JOHN: Oh, God.

CONSTANCE: I want to know that I'm eloquent and witty when I'm dead silent. For ten years I've been very happy in your affections, John, we've been the best and dearest friends, but now just for a little while I hanker for something else. Do you grudge it me? I want to be loved.

JOHN: But, my dear, I'll love you. I've been a brute, I've neglected you, it's not too late and you're the only woman I've ever really cared for. I'll chuck everything and we'll go away together.

CONSTANCE: The prospect does not thrill me. . . . Oh, my poor John, I didn't work so hard to gain my economic independence in order to go on a honeymoon with my own husband.

JOHN: Do you think I can't be a lover as well as a husband?

CONSTANCE: My dear, no one can make yesterday's cold mutton into to-morrow's lamb cutlets.

JOHN: . . . But of course you don't care two straws for me any more, that's quite evident.

CONSTANCE: Oh, don't be unjust, darling. I shall always care for you. I may be unfaithful, but I am constant. . . . Won't you say good-bye to me?

JOHN: Go to the devil.

CONSTANCE: All right. I shall be back in six weeks.

JOHN: Back? Where?

CONSTANCE: Here.

JOHN: Here? Here? Do you think I'm going to take you back?

CONSTANCE: I don't see why not. When you've had time to reflect you'll realise that you have no reason to blame me. After all, I'm taking from you nothing that you want.

JOHN: Are you aware that I can divorce you for this?

CONSTANCE: Quite. But I married very prudently. I took the precaution to marry a gentleman and I know that you could never bring yourself to divorce me for doing no more than you did yourself.

JOHN: I wouldn't divorce you. I wouldn't expose my worst enemy to the risk of marrying a woman who's capable of treating her husband as you're treating me.

CONSTANCE (*At the door*): Well, then, shall I come back?

JOHN (*After a moment's hesitation*): You are the most maddening, wilful, capricious, wrong-headed, delightful and enchanting woman man was ever cursed with having for a wife. Yes, damn you, come back.

(*She lightly kisses her hand to him and slips out, slamming the door behind her.*)

Curtain.

Thus, once again, does a wife's slamming of the door, with its sharp reminder of Nora's classic departure, symbolize the closing of another chapter of woman's subjection to outworn codes. And, as the playwright brilliantly demonstrates, the economic independence of the wife not only causes her own rejection of the double standard of sexual morality, but her new freedom imposes on the husband his rejection of the outworn code as well. Nor does Maugham forget to state that such economic independence is achieved by the working-class wife through "giving good value for the money she costs." And finally this subject in no way loses its fundamental importance because Maugham treats it through the medium of satiric comedy.

Let us observe now how different are a French and an Italian treatment of the same theme. For, as we have seen in the widely divergent approaches to similar sexual subjects by a Norse Ibsen, a German Wedekind and an Austrian Schnitzler, the integrated play reflects also specific national and racial reactions to these questions. Thus while the English Houghton and Maugham treat their theme rationally and directly, our Gallic and Latin playwrights treat it emotionally and indirectly. With the economic cause of the passing of the double standard these playwrights are not concerned, but with the result — the changed attitude toward a wife's infidelity — they are, as contemporary dramatists responsive to the changing currents of their time, very actively concerned.

The French play is *Mr. & Mrs. So and So* (*Monsieur et Madame Un Tel*), by the author of many Parisian successes, Denys Amiel, who like Maugham has chosen comedy for presenting a contemporary solution to a sexual problem. The play takes the inevitable Gallic form of the triangle, but gives it a new aspect into which the concept of the single standard of sexual morality has perhaps almost unconsciously entered.

The title is unusual for a French title, because it is deliberately general and reveals at once the author's intention to tell you about a very usual sort of married couple. Therefore, when the quite expected Gallic situation of the wife's infidelity arises, the new angle of the old triangle is the unexpectedly civilized behavior of the husband. For this quite usual Mr. So and So has come to understand that his wife may have a profound need of emotional experiences with which he is unable to supply her, and that such experiences do not render her unfit for his further respect and devotion. For this wife, Suzanne, is another Nora — spoiled, mendacious, pretty, seductive and intensely physical, but basically fine. She is apparently happily married to George, solid, meticulous, kindly. Then Robert comes into their life. Robert is what the dramatist interestingly describes as a "postwar type," a well-built male, devoted to sport, elegant, exhaling the sensuality of a handsome animal; and when the first act curtain falls, poor George realizes that his adored Suzanne has been bowled over by the superior physical attractions of Robert.

Six weeks later we see Suzanne, in a highly hysterical state, about to depart on a feigned visit to an aunt, but actually preparing to go off with Robert. This George discovers, although he has been aware of her passion for Robert for over a month. For being intrinsically fine, Suzanne has not concealed it from him; and George, being the new type of civilized husband, has tried with patient devotion to help her conquer this passion, but in vain. And now Suzanne is in real anguish; she cannot bear to hurt the husband whom she loves, but neither can she resist Robert's call to her flesh. Once more George meets the situation with conduct revealing how far the husband has traveled since another George, depicted by Galsworthy, did exercise his property rights upon his wife, Clare, thus driving her to escape from her home, a helpless fugitive. For our present George is capable of regarding his wife, Suzanne, objectively as another human being and not merely subjectively as a legal wife who is "wronging" him. Therefore he understands that it would be quite futile for him to force her to stay and that such an act could never restore happiness to their marriage.

So we come to a rare comedy scene, rich with human implications, in which our sympathetic laughter turns to unashamed tears as we watch the distressed George face this crisis according to his convictions. Summoning Robert on a pretext, he hustles Suzanne off on the pretended visit to her aunt before Robert can have time to reach the house. When the much-startled Robert does arrive, George promptly reassures him that he is not going to behave in the manner of the classic husband in a romantic novelette and asks him, with touching seriousness, if he realizes the gravity of his responsibility toward this young creature whose life he is uprooting. Then, breaking down completely, George, in a ridiculously human and moving speech, tells Robert, between sobs, that he must take the most watchful care of Suzanne, that she really isn't very strong, that she insists on wearing the most preposterously thin clothing and on eating the most utterly indigestible food, especially fresh, hot rolls, which always make her violently ill. . . . Even the hard-boiled and quite amoral Robert, to whom this is only just another amorous adventure, is touched at this exposure of a George he had not dreamed of, and he offers to put an end to the affair then and there and disappear. To which George cries in reply: "What? Now? When you have promised her everything I cannot give her — travel, excitement, passion!

What? Have her stay with me now to hate me? No, no, I would rather see her dead!" And he pushes Robert quickly out of the door. . . .

When the last act opens, fifteen months have passed, and we find George — who is not in the least a superman but just a Mr. So and So running quite true to Gallic form — ensconced, comfortably enough, in the flat of his mistress. And thither comes a much worn and disillusioned Suzanne, because, as she explains, she just had to see George again while in Paris on a purchasing trip with the dressmaker who now employs her in Nice. Yes, Robert left her after three months, and now the whole affair with Robert is just as if it had never really been. But George knows what Suzanne has come for and he has no intention of losing again the woman he loves. In fact all he has been waiting for, in his serene, ordered way, is her return. He even has ready the itinerary of a second honeymoon trip, confidently labeled "When Suzanne shall return," which he shows her with quiet joy. And the play ends with George and Suzanne leaving together for "home."

Less, even, than in a French play, would we expect to see this changing attitude toward the double standard find its way into an Italian play. For if there is one thing that seems immutable in this changing world it is the Latin attitude toward sex in its most primitive aspects. The French take sex and turn it into a sophisticated divertissement; the English take it and turn it into a not quite decent difficulty, while the Germans turn it into a harrowing social problem. But the Italians do not *take* sex at all — they leave it where it was in the days of antiquity when they set up statues to Priapus in their gardens. As one of their own Italian critics, Guido Ruberti, expresses it: "The currents of modern thought make little impression on the primitiveness of the Italian people." This persistingly Latin quality of "primitiveness" we naturally find reflected in the entire field of Italian drama, even in much of Pirandello's work. But I include here an Italian play as evidence that changing concepts important to human happiness do find their way even into contemporary Italian drama. *The Mask and the Face* by the distinguished Italian dramatist, Luigi Chiarelli, is again a satiric comedy presenting a husband's attitude toward a wife's infidelity, in sharp and often brilliant dialogue, occasionally turning into farce. This type of tragi-farce the young postwar Italian group, of which Chiarelli was one, descriptively named a "grotesque" (*grotesco*).

A group of friends are gathered at the villa of Savina and Paolo on Lake Como. Their conversation reveals the typical attitude of their race and class toward love and passion—a cynical laissez-faire of deceive and be deceived, of jealousy and revenge. The exception is Paolo, who announces with savage conviction that, if his wife deceived him, "I should kill her without the slightest hesitation!" Savina, a spirited and intelligent woman, resents her husband's high-handed, primitive, male code; and so, when we hear her arrange with one of their friends, Luciano, that he shall later return and slip into her bedroom while the rest are engrossed at cards, we realize that it is a mixture of this resentment, bravado and the whole murky sex atmosphere about her, and not in the least any love for Luciano, that makes her commit this folly.

Luciano's jealous fiancée, however, has guessed what is happening, and in revenge she now so arouses Paolo's suspicions that when, on rushing to Savina's bedroom, he finds the door locked, he breaks it down. By this time Luciano has escaped through a window undiscovered. Paolo is beside himself with rage and his first speeches show clearly that it is not grief but wounded vanity and pride that cause him to shout: "You all knew. It was only I who was blind. Like any other damn fool of a husband, I am ridiculous; that's what I am, ridiculous." And he continues half-inarticulately in this strain until his friends finally depart. Then, as he strides up and down in excitement, with gestures of despair, Savina appears. She tells him she has come to humble herself and that if he has ever loved her . . . "Love you — love you!" shouts Paolo. "I'll show you how I love you!" Poor Paolo has no idea of the real significance of those words, because, when he now rushes at Savina and seizes her throat to strangle her, he cannot do it. And what is more he realizes that he never will be able to kill his wife, because he loves her, and the face of the man who loves has taken the place of the mask of the conventionally outraged husband.

But Paolo is still at the mercy of his fear of being ridiculous; before the world he must stand as the husband who has "avenged his honor" and who lives up to the established code of sexual morality. So when Savina pleads with him — "Paolo, be sincere with yourself. Don't let yourself be taken in by words and prejudices. Tear off that mask of make-believe . . . don't do anything irreparable. We can still save something of our lives" — Paolo cannot rise to this plea of reason. He cannot kill her, but he tells her that he will that night take her over the border, commands her then to go on to Paris, change her name and never return — "Be dead to everyone" — in other words be *as if he had killed her*. And to the worried Luciano, who later arrives to ascertain what has happened, Paolo gives a dramatic account of how he killed Savina by pushing her off the terrace into the lake, where she drowned. Then, to add to Luciano's horror, he promptly engages him as his lawyer and his friend to defend him at his coming trial for murder.

Between Acts I and II six months have passed. It is the day of Paolo's acquittal on the plea of the "unwritten law," and we see his villa filled with flowers, sent not only by his friends, but also by dozens of ardent "women admirers," tragically unconscious of the depth of their sexual degradation. Paolo, revolted by this perverse and disgusting demonstration, is especially furious at Luciano who, in his "great" speech to the jury, painted Savina as the lowest harlot in order to insure Paolo's acquittal. Crowds now come to seek Paolo's autograph; he is invited to a banquet arranged by the Mayor in his honor, when, at the height of these sardonically farcical scenes, the awful news comes that Savina's long-drowned body has just been found! Paolo, who knows that Savina is alive and well, frantically tries to persuade them all that it is not her body. But the servants and others identify it; and seeing no way out, Paolo finally does the same. A moment later a veiled lady appears to see Paolo alone. It is Savina, who has been following the trial at the nearest frontier point and who has now come "home" to congratulate Paolo. The scenes between them that now follow are the finest in the play. Savina is fighting for the man she loves and for her life's happiness, while Paolo, obviously loving and longing for her, is still fighting to maintain the conventional code which holds that because she has "betrayed" him, she must therefore be dead to him. Savagely he orders her to go, but when, in despair, she is about to do so, he cannot bear it and tells her to stay "until nightfall." In deepest understanding and pity for his anguished struggle, Savina says tenderly: "Until nightfall, my dear one, my darling."

By the last act nightfall has come and gone, and in Savina's arms, at first shaken by sobs and torment, Paolo has finally realized exactly what Mr. So and So did, with much less commotion and anguish — namely, that this is the woman he loves and who loves him and that in the face of this supreme value, her petty infidelity counts as less than nothing. At last the civilized face has thrust aside forever the barbarous mask. . . . But Paolo has yet to learn that while the law may be "a ass," it will not be made an ass of. A man may be acquitted for killing his wife, but he will surely be sent to prison for having reported a living person as dead and for having falsely identified a dead body. Now their joint safety lies in both getting over the border as quickly as possible. So we come to the last scene, the extreme of satiric comedy. The hour set for the supposedly dead Savina's funeral has arrived and just as they are beginning their hasty preparations for departure, "suddenly in the street are heard the notes of Chopin's funeral march. Paolo stops and listens. Savina moves up to the terrace window, hardly turning her head toward the street. She steadies herself by holding the curtain. She is seized with a sudden pain. The drama they have lived through lives again in their minds. They look at each other with passionate anguish. Then she quickly goes to Paolo with her arms outstretched in a supreme gesture of love. He takes her and presses her to his heart, kissing her tenderly on her hair. The sound of the funeral march grows fainter and fainter. Curtain."

I cannot leave Chiarelli's play without mentioning another character in it who reflects the new sexual tolerance of his age. This is the philosopher of the play, the mellow and understanding Cirillo. Married to an avid young thing, twenty years his junior, he does not blame her for constantly "deceiving" him. He blames himself for their "unnatural" marriage and pities her. He knows that she is not in the least evil and that the day will come when she will turn to him for companionship and affection. . . .

I hope someday to see a production of *The Mask and the Face* that will bring out all of its values. But perhaps, as in the case of Shaw and other satirists, this is too much to ask of the theatre. The laughter evoked by the "grotesque" treatment will, I fear, continue to drown out the significance of the content.

Our survey of these four diversified plays on fundamentally the same contemporary theme furnishes full evidence that our drama is an accurate barometer of the changing attitude toward matters vital in our own time. We should expect, therefore, to find other individual conflicts in the sexual field; if not more revolutionary than the struggle for the single standard, then at any rate even more shocking to the conventional concepts of the compact majority. If we can show that the taboo against some of these vital sexual subjects has been lifted in our theatre, then we shall know that our contemporary playwrights are performing something of the great service rendered by the modern dramatists.

Perhaps if the world had continued along the road of orderly, peaceful progress, another Wedekind might have arisen to ask what parents and teachers are doing today to help solve the sexual problems of young people in a society in which, through economic causes, early marriages are impossible and in which, through other causes arising out of this basic economic factor, marriage is no longer regarded as either a permanent or a monogamic bond. But before pioneer playwrights could help clarify these problems of youth, the young were driven to help themselves by that most brutal of teachers, war. For in the young, war arouses only one cry: "Let us love today, for tomorrow we may lose both love and life!" As a result, during the war period the young took sexual satisfaction where and when they could. When the war was over, with this new moral code added to the even more acute economic factors, premarital sex experience had become a more or less openly accepted fact.

In America, for the more privileged young people, various solutions have been offered by those eager to give the benefit of clergy to the premarital relations they realize they cannot prevent. The best-known among these are the "trial" and the "companionate" marriage, and there are many parents today who, if they can afford to do so, finance or help to finance an early marriage of their economically dependent sons and daughters, although all parties to the arrangement are agreed that it may turn out to be only a "trial" marriage. The almost universal knowledge of methods of birth-control today makes the fear of conception no deterrent to such experimental sex-relations. But outside of these rational endeavors on the part of a constructive minority stands the still unchanged majority with hands up in horror, hypocritically refusing to admit that youth is not premaritally virginal. And, of course, for the theatre such a subject as a new sex orientation for youth must, in their opinion, be taboo!

No doubt because it has always been characteristic of the Germans to treat serious subjects seriously, and also because the postwar condition of European youth was especially tragic, Ferdinand Bruckner's play about youth's encounter with sex, called *Sickness of Youth,* is bitter and devastating tragedy. Bruckner, one of Germany's leading contemporary dramatists, belongs to the distinguished company of exiles, for whom, under Nazi ideology, there is no room in their native land. He is also the author of a play on anti-Semitism in Nazi Germany, which tells no typical pattern-story of atrocities but shows that the persecution of the Jews is a boomerang which destroys Aryans also, even driving the leading young Aryan of the play to suicide as the result of his own self-loathing. This play is the ill-fated *Races,* produced by the Theatre Guild and presented out of town, but never brought to New York. Bruckner's approach is always psychological, as in *Criminals,* in which he shows how the law, in its cruel convictions, takes no account of the psychological motivation for acts which should not properly be classed as crimes at all.

In *Sickness of Youth* Bruckner expresses his conviction that, while sex is obviously a sort of sickness through which all youth must pass, it is for the disillusioned, insecure youth of this cynical age a grave sickness indeed. His purpose is to show that while it is normal for youth to regard sex as the most important thing in the universe, the attitude toward sex manifested by youth today is often not normal. Sex too often becomes an obsession, leading to promiscuity or to satisfaction through abnormal channels. Finally, the healthy frankness in sex matters, so valiantly fought for by the moderns, is often perversely expressed today in terms of a decadent exhibitionism and the rejection of all inhibition.

In Bruckner's play we meet seven young people: three girls and three men who are students, and a fourth girl, a maid servant. The young men are somewhat older than the girls. The action takes place in Marie's room, in a students' boarding house. Marie is about to graduate from medical school and has for two years been happy in the love of Petrell, whom she has mothered and even supported by giving lessons, so that he could be free to write. Insanely jealous of Marie is Irene, also in love with Petrell. Insidiously she wins Petrell away from Marie by taunting him with the fact that Marie, who always calls him by a diminutive pet name, treats him like a little child and by further accusing him of not being a man in love at all, but a small boy suffering from a mother-complex. To Marie the rupture with her lover is a terrible blow, combining erotic frustration with humiliation.

Opening out from Marie's room is that of Desirée, who at seventeen ran away from the corrupt ménage of her father, a Baron, only herself to plunge into the depths of sexual excess. Brilliant mentally, passing the most difficult medical examinations with ease, she is devoid of faith or hope, and finds in the excitement of physical sex her only surcease from complete disillusionment. The only lover she remembers is Freder, another medical student, as brilliant, cynical and sadistic as herself, of an overpowering sexuality which has rendered other men tasteless to her. So when Marie, in her frantic grief and yearning for her lost lover, turns to her in friendship, Desirée seizes this opportunity to satisfy her Lesbian cravings and the heartsick

Marie, hungry for love, overcoming her natural distaste, responds. But after a week, Desirée, realizing that she can never make a satisfactory lover out of the sexually normal Marie, rejects her with savage cruelty. This she does in the presence of the third male character, Alt. Alt has passed far beyond the sickness of youth, and has already had a savage encounter with the realities of life. While an intern he ended the agony of an incurably diseased child by administering morphine. For this he was sent to prison, his medical career forever ruined. But "I would do the same thing over again," says Alt, who has come out of this shattering experience morally whole. Desperately he tries to rout the antisocial, ruthless spirit of negation which dominates Freder and Desirée and which threatens even the healthy and normal Marie. And in the scene in which the once more frustrated Desirée taunts the suffering Marie, Alt shrewdly suspects that Desirée is looking toward suicide as the only release. Sternly Alt says to her: —

> One does not become a deserter.
>
> DESIRÉE: What do I care about moral principles?
>
> ALT: That is not a moral principle. It is the only social duty we owe our fellow beings.
>
> DESIRÉE: Now you're getting sentimental.
>
> ALT: You can do with yourself what you like. But the very premise on which life is based, the only denial that life is mad, is that every one must live his life to the end. Better even to murder someone else. But he who murders himself becomes a menace to the life of all the rest.
>
> DESIRÉE: For the first time I hear you utter phrases.

To which Marie, expressing her own intrinsic and potential capacity for positive living, replies:

> That is no phrase. It is the only God-like feeling that exists in us. . . .

In the meantime, however, Freder has been conducting a sadistic experiment with the little housemaid, Lucy. Having reduced her to complete sexual bondage to him, he wants to see if he can actually get her to commit a crime in order to retain his favors. Finally he even persuades her to go on the street, which she does, half in a trance, to please him. Excited by this adventure of Lucy, Desirée cynically decides to try the still untasted experience of the streetwalker. But this Marie will not permit, and by physical force she prevents Desirée from leaving the house, after which, in her self-disgust and despair, Desirée does commit suicide by quietly taking an overdose of veronal. Completely unnerved by this second emotional shock, Marie, half-crazed and desperate, now wildly calls on the loathed Freder to take her. Pathetically she calls him by the pet name she had called her lover Petrell. In a frenzy of self-destruction, she goads him to ferocity; and as he seizes her in the darkened room, while the curtain falls, Marie cries out of the depths of her sick soul: "Murder me! Murder me. . . ." About the sexual crisis through which youth is passing, Ferdinand Bruckner has unflinchingly written the truth, as he sees it.

Let us turn now to an American play in which the seriousness, even the imminence of tragedy, as in *The Mask and the Face,* is implicit rather than explicit, because the medium is satiric comedy. This, one of the most delightful of contemporary plays, is *Young Love* by Samson Raphaelson. Produced in New York in 1928, it caused most of those mouthpieces of the compact majority, the drama reviewers, to report the play as shocking and to pretend that its experimental young lovers were monstrous exceptions in the otherwise solid phalanxes of conventionally moral youth. But while frightened hypocrites fumed, and half-shocked and titillated audiences laughed, the play presented its warm and revealing picture not only of a changed code of sexual morals for youth but also of a new approach to marriage.

Spending the week-end on nothing more revolutionary than the Long Island estate of an older married couple, young David and Fay appear upon the scene at dawn, starry-eyed over the wonder they have just lived through — their first night of love. Fay is now ready to promise David that she will marry him, because it was she who had insisted that *first* they must find out if they really love each other. "What use is it," asks Fay, "living in an enlightened age if we don't take advantage of all the enlightenment?" But now they know that their love is the greatest love in the world, even more wonderful than that of their so devoted host and hostess, Peter and Nancy, married for ten years. Within the next hour, however, the inquiring young Fay learns from Peter that he and Nancy both indulge in extramarital adventures, and that for two years he has been desiring her, Fay. These disillusioning discoveries raise new doubts in Fay about the enduring quality of her and David's love, and when she later mournfully confesses to David that the thought of Peter's "seducing" her gave her a "kick" and David in turn confesses that when a moment ago Nancy goaded him into kissing her, that kiss "meant something" to him, the agony of doubt of their young love is complete.

But Fay is not the child of her scientific age for nothing. With relentless logic, she announces that now only another test can help them. Both must see if their love will emerge triumphant after an "affair" with Peter and with Nancy respectively. And the first-act curtain descends on their facing this new problem with young despair. How Fay, like a Joan of Arc, as Nancy later describes her, stoically goes through with her end of the experiment, Peter willingly but bewilderedly assisting; how David, however, balks at his end, and then, in very human jealousy and pain, savagely condemns the unhappy but furious Fay because she did keep to their agreement;

how a rupture between the hurt young lovers is healed only because of the depth of their mutual passion—all this the playwright tells divertingly, but with sympathetic understanding of the changing morals of the youth of his time. Love may be an eternal verity, but youth is bringing new verities to its concept of love and of its outward form, marriage. Groping and bungling, the girl and the boy of *Young Love* are sublime in their desire for the truth about their relation at all costs. And, finally, if the habitants of a future age desire to know how Americans of this day expressed themselves, they have only to study the pungent dialogue of Raphaelson's *Young Love.*

Another enchanting comedy, treating from an original angle youth's new sexual code, is *Yes, My Darling Daughter* by Mark Reed, produced in New York in 1937. Young Ellen is the finest type of American college girl, intelligent, studious, interested in and critical of the world in which she finds herself, courageous, sexually eager, but not in the least "sexy." Her graduation has been spoiled because the young man whom she loves, although no love has yet been expressed on either side, a "broke" and jobless architect (an accurate picture of the young of that profession in 1937), could not afford to attend her graduation and in wounded pride returned to her the twenty-five dollars which this 1937 young woman quite naturally wired him, as a "friend," for his expenses. Now he appears suddenly at the country home of her parents to tell her that, in despair at his economic condition, he has accepted a job to sell razor blades in Belgium for a period of two years, and that he is sailing in three days. In this crisis their love is revealed, and they are aghast at the prospect of separation. But Ellen, like Fay of *Young Love,* is also not the child of her time for nothing. She thinks fast and decides that instead of going on the week-end visit for which she is scheduled, she will only pretend to go, and that she and Doug, this young man whom she loves so utterly, will at least have three days to be together in and to plan their future. Doug, as the slower-moving male, has moral scruples at first, but when Ellen declares solemnly "Doug, this is an emergency measure," — he finally agrees.

Their secret plan, however, is suspected by Ellen's aunt, who illustrates the opposite type of woman to Ellen: a restless divorcée, ever on the quest for a permanent love relation but never finding it because love to her is sexual excitement. She promptly imparts her suspicions to Ellen's mother, who believes her because, as she puts it, "an affair" is a subject on which her sister-in-law is "a final authority." Ellen's mother is a well-known writer who, at Ellen's age, as the flaming Ann Whitman, was one of the famous Greenwich Village band who with John Reed, "Jig" Cook, and the rest raised aloft the banner of freedom — social, industrial, sexual. Now, happily married to Ellen's father, a banker, she is still charmingly unconventional, but her days of free love are over. There are few characters more delightful to meet than Ann Whitman. When Ann hears the news of Ellen's intentions, she reacts to them, not as the once free-thinking daughter of Greenwich Village, but as a mother who doesn't want her young daughter to spend a week-end with a young man. But she has reckoned without her 1937 daughter. For Ellen knows about her mother's liberal past, not vaguely, as that lady discovers to her discomfiture in the battle-scene between them — for Ellen has actually written her Senior English thesis on the subject of "The Contribution of Greenwich Village to the Cause of Freedom in American Art and Morals." Her research has caused her to "check up pretty thoroughly" on the activities of her mother, including her quite open "affair" with an English poet. Accused of inconsistency and hypocrisy by her young daughter, so bitterly fighting for her happiness, Ann rises once more to her true self.

"Go quickly," says Ann, "before I regain my common sense. Go. Climb hills. Walk hand in hand under the stars. Make love. This may be your one great hour on earth. Go. I'll stand by you."

How Ellen's conservative father takes the news, how shocked poor Doug is on Monday morning when he finds out that Ellen's mother knew about and connived at her going, how a combined conspiracy gets Ellen a job in Paris, and sends them off on a honeymoon trip across to their new work and a new future, the rest of the play gaily narrates.

But this denouement doesn't matter. What matters is that the theatre has shown how daughters think and act today and that they are splendid young women, not in spite of their new code of sexual morals, but because of it.

After the passing of the double standard and the sex problems of youth had been thus frankly dealt with, other sexual taboos still remained to be discussed in the open forum of the theatre. Ignorance on the forbidding subjects of homosexuality and incest, even today widely regarded as forms of vicious immorality, had to be dissipated in order that the sexually abnormal should no longer be treated as pariahs by their complacently benighted fellow beings. The time had come for the findings of Havelock Ellis and Dr. Sigmund Freud to be brought into the realm of the theatre.

When the first play to deal seriously with homosexuality reached these shores in 1926, our guardians of morality did not rest until New York audiences had been "protected" against the corruption of mental contact with such a subject, just as earlier audiences were considered to need the moral protection of censorship against a public discussion of the sexual problems of adolescents, venereal disease and prostitution.

That play, which suffered a disgraceful fate in the American theatre, was *The Captive,* by the French dramatist Edouard

Bourdet. How, when and where Bourdet decided to write this play on Lesbianism is of interest because of my point of view that *postwar* and *contemporary* must be regarded, for critical purposes, as synonymous terms. For it was during the World War that Bourdet met a young officer who interested the playwright intensely, because he became convinced that this man was determined to get himself killed. Finally, confessing this to be true, he told Bourdet that he was married to and deeply in love with a woman incapable of responding sexually to his love or to that of any other man, and that he could no longer endure the torment of this tragic situation. He won the release of death; and out of this encounter grew Bourdet's decision to write a play on this forbidden theme. Lesbianism is no new discovery of today or yesterday. But it is a discovery on the part of a playwright to realize that the time is ripe for a serious discussion of that subject in the theatre, because it has become essential for people to know that homosexuality is a widespread condition involving not only the happiness of the abnormal but, indirectly, that of the normal as well. No doubt the subject has been copiously discussed by warriors at the front in earlier wars, since the abnormal separation of the sexes caused by war as well as women's enforced entry into masculine occupations always bring active as well as latent sex abnormalities into the open. But only the upheaval caused by the twentieth-century World War, with its resultant breakdown of surviving inhibitions, prejudices and codes of conduct, could have made possible bringing into the theatre a play like *The Captive.*

Irene de Montcel, twenty-five, femininely lovely, intelligent, talented, is the daughter of a French Ambassador just ordered to Rome. When the play opens we find Irene desperately determined not to leave Paris and finally flatly refusing to obey her father's characteristically harsh command that she accompany him. Her father concludes that it is because of some man that she insists on staying, and when she obstinately refuses to discuss her reasons, he tells her he will get the truth from her inseparable friends, the d'Aiguines. We at once see how this threat shocks Irene and realize that the one thing she will prevent is a meeting between her father and these friends. So to avert this crisis Irene informs her father that she does not want to leave Paris because she is sure Jacques Virieu, a distant cousin, is about to propose to her. To this her father replies that he will have a talk with Jacques tomorrow. Realizing that only a desperate measure can now save her, Irene summons Jacques and begs him to help her remain in Paris by pretending that they are secretly betrothed. This is a cruel request because some months before, after giving Jacques hope, Irene suddenly rejected him. But Jacques deeply loves Irene and still hopes to win her, so finally his righteous indignation at her request gives way to her distraught pleas. Throughout these scenes — indeed, from the very rising of the curtain — Bourdet has almost miraculously created the atmosphere of the strange and the sinister around the reason for Irene's desperate need for remaining in Paris, though what it is we do not yet know. Thus, when Jacques asks her quite innocently, "Why not tell the truth?" Irene, looking at him searchingly, asks sharply "What truth?" To which Jacques replies: —

I don't know. But whatever it may be, it's certainly better than this — this lie.

IRENE (*Hopeless. Staring ahead.*): If I had told the truth no one would have understood it.

JACQUES: Why? (*She is silent.*) Tell me! . . . Can't you at least tell *me?*

IRENE: No.

But of course the truth must come out, and it does in a powerful scene in the second act. Dismayed at her sister's troubled state, young Gisele naïvely decides that Jacques must be responsible for her unhappiness and goes to have a talk with him. Carefully questioning the girl, Jacques discovers that Irene sees no one but the d'Aiguines, that she goes, ostensibly, to her painting lessons in the daytime and is rarely out at night. Disturbed, Jacques requests Mr. d'Aiguines to call at once, and he, recognizing in Jacques' name that of an old schoolmate, promptly responds. Jacques is shocked at the sight of d'Aiguines, who, although his own age, looks like a worn, gray shadow. When Jacques mentions the name of Irene, d'Aiguines is visibly upset and coldly insists he knows nothing about her. Finally in his despair Jacques tell d'Aiguines how deeply he loves Irene, and at this information d'Aiguines hesitatingly tells the amazed Jacques that it is no man who is causing Irene such distress, but a woman.

JACQUES: Do you—know this woman?

D'AIGUINES: Yes. (*Looks at Jacques quickly, and sees that the latter is not observing him. A great sadness crosses his face.*) I know her.

JACQUES (*After a moment.*): I am dumbfounded—

D'AIGUINES: And a little relieved . . . aren't you?

JACQUES: Well, good Lord! After what I had feared! . . .

D'AIGUINES: So you'd prefer—? (*Pause*) Well, you're wrong to prefer it!

JACQUES: You'd rather she had a lover?

D'AIGUINES: In your place? Yes! A hundred, a thousand times rather!

JACQUES: Are you mad?

D'AIGUINES: It's you who are mad. If she had a lover I'd say to you: Patience, my boy, patience and courage. Your cause isn't lost. No man lasts forever in a woman's life. You love her and she'll come back to you if you know how to wait. . . . But in this case I say: Don't wait! There's no use. She'll never return—and if ever your paths should cross again, fly from her, fly from her . . . do you hear? Otherwise you are lost! Otherwise you'll spend your existence pursuing a phantom which you can never overtake. One can never overtake them! They are shadows. They must be left to dwell alone among themselves in the kingdom of shadows! Don't go near them . . . they're a menace! Above all, never try to be anything to them, no matter how little — that's where the danger lies. For, after all, they have some need of us in their lives . . . it isn't always easy for a woman to get along. So if a man offers to help her, to share with her what he has, and to give her his name, naturally she accepts. What difference can it make to her? So long as he doesn't exact love, she's not concerned about the rest. Only, can you imagine the existence of a man if he has the misfortune to love — to adore a *shadow* near whom he lives? Tell me, can you imagine what that's like? Take my word for it, old man, it's a rotten life! One's used up quickly by that game. One gets old in no time — and at thirty-five, look for yourself, one's hair is gray!

JACQUES: Do you mean — ?

D'AIGUINES: Yes. And I hope you'll profit by my example. Understand this: they are not for us. They must be shunned, left alone. Don't make my mistake. Don't say, as I said in a situation almost like yours, don't say: "Oh, it's nothing but a sort of ardent friendship — an affectionate intimacy . . . nothing very serious . . . we know all about that sort of thing!" No! We don't know *anything* about it! We can't begin to know what it is. It's mysterious — terrible! Friendship, yes — that's the mask. Under cover of friendship a woman can enter any household, whenever and however she pleases — at any hour of the day — she can poison and pillage everything before the man whose home she destroys is even aware of what's happening to him. When finally he realizes things it's too late — he is alone! Alone in the face of a secret alliance of two beings who understand one another because they're alike, because they're of the same sex, because they're of a different planet than he, the stranger, the enemy! Ah! if a *man* tries to steal your woman you can defend yourself, you can fight him on even terms, you can smash his face in. But in this case — there's nothing to be done — but *get out* while you still have strength to do it! And that's what you've got to do!

JACQUES: . . . Why don't you get out yourself?

D'AIGUINES: Oh, with me it's different. I can't leave her now. We've been married eight years. Where would she go? . . . Besides it's too late. I couldn't live without her any more. What can I do — I love her? . . . (*Pause.*) You've never seen her? (*Jacques shakes his head.*) You'd understand better if you knew her. She has all the feminine allurements, every one. As soon as one is near her, one feels — how shall I say it — a sort of deep charm. Not only I feel it. Every one feels it. But I more than the rest because I live near her. I really believe she is the most harmonious being that has ever breathed . . . Sometimes when I'm away from her, I have the strength to hate her for all the harm she has done me . . . but, with her, I don't struggle. I look at her . . . I listen to her . . . I worship her. You see?

JACQUES (*Pursuing an idea*): Tell me . . . why is Irene suffering?

D'AIGUINES: I don't know. (*Rises.*) You don't suppose I'm confided in, do you? She is suffering, probably, as the weak always do, struggling with a stronger nature until they give in.

JACQUES: You think Irene is weak?

D'AIGUINES: Compared to the other? Oh, yes. (*Pause.*) She is probably still struggling.

And right on the heel of this terrific scene comes the still struggling Irene, unaware of Jacques' discovery, to seek his help in her losing fight against this overpowering force — "this prison to which I must return captive, despite myself." Finally when he declares himself helpless to protect her, Irene, in deep shame, tells the distraught Jacques that he can save her by becoming her lover. Jacques clearly understands that she hopes through giving herself to him to alienate the other woman, thus freeing herself, and he bluntly tells her so. Aghast at his knowledge, Irene sobs in despair: "I want so much to love you . . . and when you will have cured me . . ." Overwhelmed by his passion, Jacques acquiesces.

JACQUES (*Taking her in his arms . . . he starts to kiss her on the mouth. As Irene beholds his face filled with longing, she makes an abrupt movement of aversion. He lets her go.*): You see?

IRENE: No, no—forgive me! (*This time it is she who offers her lips to him. Then, her nerves giving away, she lets her head fall on his shoulder, struggles with herself a moment, and breaks into tears.*)

JACQUES (*In despair*): Irene!

IRENE: No, no!—Pay no attention!—It doesn't mean anything . . . It's all over! You will keep me with you? Always?

JACQUES: I'll try.

Thus ends the second act, subtly preparing us for the inevitable end. For in the last act we learn that after a year of marriage during which Irene has steeled herself to submit to the loathed male embraces, Jacques has suffered equally in a relation devoid of joyous sexual response on the part of his beloved. In this impasse there re-enters into Irene's life the other woman, who has planned a seemingly accidental meeting. And when after this meeting the trembling Irene rushes home to Jacques to implore him to flee Paris with her, he sharply refuses and to her "Why?" replies:

You want to know why? Look at yourself! You're breathless—your eyes are dazed—your hands are trembling—because you've seen her again, that's why! For a year I've been living with a statue and that woman had only to reappear for the statue to come to life, to become a human being capable of suffering and trembling! Well, I give up, Irene, do you understand? I give up! I've loved you more than anything in the world, you know that. I've proved it to you. As long as I hoped that some day you might love me as I loved you, as a man and woman can love each other, with body and soul, I accepted the role of your guardian. But now I've had enough. I resign from a useless and ungrateful task. Protect yourself, if you can. It doesn't interest me any longer. It's over! I'm tired of pursuing a phantom. D'Aiguines knew what he was talking about when he said, "Leave her alone, get out of her way, she isn't for you." He was right.

Yes, he was right, as was Jacques when he said to Irene: "You long to love, just as I long to be loved." Only, alas, for Irene it was imperative to love and to be loved by a woman and not by a man and no power on earth could make it otherwise for her. So the play ends with her leaving to obey this call which, in spite of all self-sacrificing effort, proves irresistible. . . .

Knowing full well that he was attempting to introduce into the theatre a taboo subject, Bourdet invested it with the very quintessence of tact and delicacy. Although he made the other woman's influence powerfully felt, he did not introduce her as a character and deftly aroused sympathetic understanding of the unfortunate type of woman he portrayed. If the shallow critics who expressed their horror at the portrayal of a girl of Irene's feminine charm and breeding as an incurable homosexual had had some familiarity with the writings of Ellis and Freud, not to mention the more popular sexologists and psychologists, the revealing speech of Irene to her father in the very beginning of the play would not have escaped them. To her father's accusation that neither she nor her sister Gisele loves him, Irene quietly replies:—

And you father, do you love us? Have you ever given us a moment's concern, a moment's bother? I may as well say it, since we're on the subject. What has our childhood been? Not a happy one, father. Always alone with servants. If Gisele hadn't had me and I her, there'd have been little enough affection in our lives since mother's death.

Clearly Bourdet wants us to know that Irene's childhood and adolescence have been loveless, filled with a longing for maternal love — that is, for the love of an older woman. This she supplied to her younger sister, but no woman supplied it to her; and so, logically, the need for a woman's love has become the great need of her life. Apparently Bourdet knows well a fact insisted upon by psychologists, namely, that the absence of maternal affection constitutes a powerful impetus towards homosexuality.

La Prisonnière was first produced in Paris in March, 1926. Productions soon followed in Berlin, Vienna, Budapest and other European cities, and in September of the same year the play had its New York première under the title *The Captive*. Because of the nature of its theme there was the inevitable pother of advance excitement, with rumors of impending police interference. As usual the enlightened intelligentsia hoped for the best, while the sensation-mongers hoped for the worst. What happened was an opening night that will remain memorable to all who were present. If ever an audience experienced catharsis, it was that audience. How many had any understanding at the time of the subject presented does not matter. What does matter tremendously is that many received, *in the theatre,* their first impact with a vital subject which they had hitherto regarded not only as taboo, but also as in itself degenerate, now nobly and sympathetically presented to them for public discussion. Even the reviewers rose to the splendor of that occasion.

For nearly five months *The Captive* moved and educated its audiences. But the bigoted and frightened Pharisees, to whom ignorance is security and knowledge jeopardy, were determined to foil this victory of enlightenment, and a weapon was soon placed in their hands. For during these months, encouraged by the unmolested success of a play dealing with a subject previously taboo, the venal elements of Broadway, determined to make hay while the sun shone, offered two tawdry and sensation-mongering theatrical brews on sexual themes, meretricious and disgusting travesties on the serious sex play. This was all the enemies of *The Captive* needed; and on a night early in February, 1927, the police raided all three plays, thus degrading Bourdet's lofty work by placing it on the low level of the other two. The producers and actors of *The Captive* were arrested, charged with "corrupting public morals," with committing the crime of presenting and participating in an "obscene, indecent, immoral, impure drama" in violation of the New York Penal Law. Later the charge was withdrawn on condition that the producers discontinue the play until some court should decide that it was *not* in violation of the law.

Here was a clear-cut issue of theatre censorship, especially flagrant because the play had been so highly commended not only by members of the lay public, but also by physicians, psychologists and even clergymen, and because at that very moment the printed play was legally on sale in bookshops and available in the New York Public Library. Surely the producers should have regarded it as their moral responsibility to secure a court decision on the alleged criminality of *The Captive*. But the producing company, itself owned by a famous motion picture company, did nothing, and promptly returned all its production rights to the author. Hope was revived, however, when the late Horace B. Liveright announced that he had acquired the rights, had leased a theatre, and would at once produce the play. However, as soon as the owners of the theatre learned that it was *The Captive* he intended to present there, they refused permission for its production in their theatre, on the ground that the district attorney had advised them that this would infringe the law, since the play was "indecent, immoral and obscene." Liveright now sought an injunction compelling the theatre-owners to permit the production of

The Captive. But the Court refused to grant this, stating: "We are convinced that a court of equity should not give its mandate to a theatre-owner which would compel him to permit the production of a play which has come under the condemnation of the police and the authorities charged with the enforcement of the criminal law." And now Liveright in his turn carried the issue no further, and *The Captive* disappeared from the New York theatrical scene without ever having been accorded its just and deserved due, namely a trial *on its merits,* in order to secure a court decision on its criminality, as obscene, immoral, indecent, and so on, under the Penal Law. In spite of, or more likely because of, its New York experience, a number of productions in other cities followed. The play was unmolested in Baltimore and enjoyed its longest run of five weeks in Cleveland. But in Detroit and Los Angeles it was once more closed by the police.

Thus ended, ignominiously for the still supine producers, police departments, and courts of America, the brief career of *The Captive*. Its work, however, had been done. The taboo against the discussion of homosexuality in the theatre had been lifted, and when seven years later an American play appeared, dealing with the subject of Lesbianism far more outspokenly, it enjoyed a long run, undisturbed by the threat of censorship.

Before we discuss *The Children's Hour* by Lillian Hellman, however, I wish to call attention to an English play which reached New York during the preceding year, 1933—namely, *The Green Bay Tree* by Mordaunt Shairp. Here, through a masterly use of indirection, is a study of a male homosexual and of his baleful influence on the boy whom he has deliberately moulded to be his life's companion. Not that there is ever a suggestion of a physical relationship or the desire for one. The companionship is based on the older man's inoculation of the younger with his own values of life: his sybaritism, his æstheticism, his super-refined sensuality, his aversion to women. Never in the play is there a mention of what Mr. Dulcimer is, not a suggestion of the well-known vulgar figure of the musical revue, or of the hand-on-hip travesty, through which this type of man has been caricatured and affronted. We recognize the abnormal in Mr. Dulcimer in the exquisite feminine beauty he has created in his home, in his feminine love of arranging flowers, in the embroidery frame which holds the delicate work he does while his adopted son Julian plays the piano, and in all the other indirect evidence the playwright so deftly supplies. Mr. Dulcimer, or "Dulcie," as Julian with unconscious significance calls him, is not only interesting as a study of the male invert of breeding and culture, but also as a character with implications much more far-reaching than the merely sexual, because he is shown as the protagonist in a larger conflict, contemporary in its very essence.

Having adopted the poor boy at an early age because of his beauty and charm, Mr. Dulcimer has fashioned him in his own image. Now, in the early twenties, steeped in luxurious living, untrained for work of any kind, Julian's normal instincts cause him to fall in love with his complete antithesis, a splendid, competent girl of today, successfully earning her living as a veterinary surgeon. To Mr. Dulcimer's horror, Julian is determined to marry her, so he fires his first shot in his relentless battle to win back Julian for himself by using the economic weapon of withdrawing his allowance. The spoiled Julian returns to the crude home of his father and makes a heroic effort, with the help of the girl, Leonora, to become a veterinary surgeon himself and share her work. But he loathes his surroundings and is hopelessly bored by his studies. At the moment in which the shrewdly plotting Mr. Dulcimer is convinced that Julian's discouragement and disgust must be complete, he emerges from the rose gardens of the country home he knows Julian adores, to weave about him once again the alluring web of sybaritic ease and sensuous enjoyment which constitute the be-all and the end-all of his own pathological existence. Leonora puts up a brave fight to save their love and to save Julian's soul, to arouse in him the desire to share the common lot of man, to experience the joy of work, the pride of creative labor. In the course of her desperate, losing struggle with Mr. Dulcimer she says significantly: —

> You get what you want out of life simply because you can pay for it. Your foundations are entirely in the sand. Another convulsion in the world and you might vanish tomorrow.

And Mr. Dulcimer reveals the depths of his diseased egotism, of his anti-social soul, by replying, as he points to a revolver, "If the convulsion comes . . . there is always this." So Julian is lost, not only to the normal erotic experience of man, but — and this is far more fundamental — he is also morally and spiritually destroyed by the corruption of parasitism. And in the last scene we see Julian, the inheritor of Mr. Dulcimer's wealth, his very incarnation, standing there just as "Dulcie" had stood in the first scene, fastidiously selecting a vase and arranging his flowers. . . .

In November, 1934, Lillian Hellman's play bearing the innocuous title of *The Children's Hour* opened in New York. It created immediate and wide discussion which continued during the play's long run of six hundred and ninety-one performances. And, what is most unusual in a world lacking in play-consciousness, where the end of the play *as theatre* almost invariably means the end of interest in it, *The Children's Hour* still lives in the minds of those who saw it. Discussion ranges from doubts as to the fitness of the subject of homosexuality for presentation in the theatre to questions as to the motivation for the behavior of the characters and the logic of the play's denouement. I know that the seeing of *The Children's Hour* was for thousands their first impact with the subject of homosexuality. Breaking through the accumulated darkness with simple, yet illuminating, directness, *The Children's Hour* is a striking example of the vital play, profoundly integrated with its own time. Finally, so far as American audiences are concerned, here is a play that does not deal with an aristocratic Parisian young lady or with a plutocratic London gentleman, but with two ordinary American girls, earning their own living as schoolteachers, exactly like everybody's sisters and cousins and sweethearts, who nevertheless become tragically entangled in a hideous situation. It is to Miss Hellman's credit that she makes the crux of her play not the question of homosexuality itself, but society's savage treatment of the homosexual, arising out of cruelly persisting ignorance. Thus in this play we see again how an individual conflict may serve to focus attention on its crucial social implications.

Karen Wright and Martha Dobie have, through eight years of work and self-sacrifice, established their school for girls near a typical American town. They are progressive college women who thoroughly understand the disturbing behavior of the adolescent girl, and so they have been more than patient with their fourteen-year-old pupil, Mary Tilford. This girl is almost subject enough in herself for a play, although here she is used only as the entirely credible instrument responsible for the drama's catastrophe. Mary is an orphan, spoiled by a grandmother who adores her and whom she dominates. In the world outside, symbolized by the school, which she instinctively senses is hostile to her, she expresses her will to power by trickery and lies so far as her teachers are concerned, and by a sadistic cruelty toward her fellow pupils which makes of them her abject slaves. Last, but not least, her awakening interest in sex takes the form of a prurient pursuit of its abnormal aspects. It is she who secretly circulates a volume of *Mademoiselle de Maupin*. On the fatal day on which the play opens, Mary, in furious resentment at the discipline meted out to her for reprehensible conduct, announces to a few of the pupils that she intends to run away at once to her grandmother. To the astounded question: "What are you going to tell your grandmother?" Mary replied: "Oh, I'll think of something to tell her." And we have little doubt that she will. . . .

At almost the same time Martha, who has, for economic reasons, tolerated, as a teacher in the school, a narrow-minded aunt who is dependent on her and of whose unfitness she is on this disturbed day especially conscious, informs her she must leave; and the aunt, turning on her, blames Martha's action on the fact that "he" is in the house that day. "He" is Dr. Joe Cardin, Karen's fiancé, and the aunt continues:—

> I know what I know. Every time that man comes into the house you have a fit. It seems like you just can't stand the idea of them being together. God knows what you'll do when they get married. You're jealous of him, that's what it is. . . . And it's unnatural, just as unnatural as it can be. . . . You were always like that, even as a child. If you had a little girl friend you always got mad when she liked anybody else. . . .

Startled by a noise at the door, Martha discovers some eavesdropping girls, who promptly report what they have overheard to Mary. And Mary's miserably deformed mind tells her that here she has found her story for her grandmother, her weapon for release from the hated school.

So Mary goes to her grandmother, the respectable Mrs. Tilford, with a whispered tale of horror, detailing the abnormal love-life of the innocent Karen and Martha. And kindly Mrs. Tilford, now hardened by the ignorant repulsion of millions like her, is incapable not only of the shadow of doubt, but also of the shadow of pity. Overcome with disgust, she telephones the shocking news to all the mothers she can reach, so that they may hurry their daughters away from the school.

All her previous knowledge of the two admirable young women is at once blotted out by the mention of what to her uninformed mind is unpardonable moral depravity. Incredulous, Karen and Martha appear; and together with the Doctor they insist on questioning Mary. And when Mary's story is finally shaken, she shrieks that it was another girl who "saw them." Whereupon this child, having been previously terrorized by Mary's threats, corroborates her vindictive lies. But Martha and Karen, determined to be cleared publicly, inform Mrs. Tilford that they will sue her for "libel."

When the last act opens, their "libel" suit has been lost and Karen and Martha, hopeless, have hidden themselves away in their empty school. They are publicly branded, and they feel that wherever they may go they will be pariahs. The Doctor, outwardly cheerful, has a plan for their all going to Vienna, where he studied and can get work; but Karen knows how he longs to stay in his home town with his own practice. And to her bitter grief she knows another thing, too — that in the heart of the man she loves there lurks a doubt, that on his lips there trembles the question she finally compels him to ask. Gently she answers it: "No. Martha and I have never touched each other." But shaken as she is, she feels that he and she can never again believe each other, never again be natural and joyous together. So she sends him away "to think this all over," although she is convinced that their relation is at an end.

It is Martha, however, who is the real victim of the tragedy. Whether she has been shocked by her experiences into a clarifying knowledge of her true nature, or whether she has been so shattered as to believe herself abnormal, Martha now confesses to Karen that she does love her "the way they said" and that she probably always did. And feeling that she has ruined Karen's life and her own, and above all that they can now no longer stay together, Martha steps quietly into the next room and shoots herself.

A few moments later there appears at the school none other than Mrs. Tilford herself. She has come to tell them that, through the other girl, Mary was finally compelled to confess her diabolical lies, and that her grandmother is now here to make amends, including a public apology arranged by the judge who had found them "guilty." But Martha is dead, and to Karen there seems no reason for living. Yet when she sees the remorseful woman, Karen's bitterness falls from her; she understands that Mrs. Tilford, herself a victim of society's ignorance, could not have acted otherwise. Wearily she promises to accept her help, even "perhaps" later to go back to the Doctor. . . . At least we are left with the consolation that Karen will find her way out of this nightmare of medieval torture into a life and love enlarged by new understanding. . . .

This play has broken down, in thousands, their antipathy against its subject and aroused in them the desire for further knowledge. The suicide of Martha, immolated on the altar of cruelty toward the invert, raises the important question of the tragic needlessness of her death and of the right of the homosexual to the fullest personal happiness. *The Children's Hour* is not flawless, but the playwright deals with a subject of grave human import in such a way as to carry the theatre forward and to give it its deepest meaning and significance.

Another age-old sexual conflict of the individual is that arising out of incest. Regarded since classic times as a monstrous thing, the incest theme exhibits a revolutionary metamorphosis when viewed in the light of the post-Freudian theatre. We have only to recall examples in the field of drama dealing with this theme in order to realize that one note, the note of uncomprehending, if pitying horror, dominates the earlier works. That there may be reasons other than the will of just or unjust gods for abnormal sexual attraction between parents and children, brothers and sisters, does not seem to be even faintly surmised.

We do not look for calm, scientific curiosity on the part of Sophocles or Euripides, especially when they were dealing with such dark, distant pre-classical subjects as the incestuous marriage of Œdipus and the, to us, equally incestuous revenge of Electra. The pre-classical attitude of regarding incestuous feelings as inhuman "pollutions" unfortunately, however, persists.

Thus, when we leap from Greece of the fifth century B.C. to seventeenth-century England, we find little change in the playwrights' treatment of incest. John Ford's *'Tis Pity She's a Whore* still presents the subject with passionate violence, portraying the unhappy sister and brother writhing in shame, victims of an inexplicable act of God. Even the winged Shelley advances no further, investing his tragedy *The Cenci* with the usual admixture of pity and abhorrence. He himself writes of it (1819):—

> This story of the Cenci is indeed eminently fearful and monstrous: anything like a dry exhibition of it on the stage would be insupportable. The person who would treat such a subject must increase the ideal, and diminish the actual horror of the events, so that the pleasure which arises from the poetry which exists in these tempestuous sufferings and crimes may mitigate the pain of the contemplation of the moral deformity from which they spring.

Clearly the time was not yet ripe for this seeing spirit to glimpse that the causes of incestuous desires might be other than the traditionally ascribed one of moral depravity; that men and women might be doomed by uncontrollable forces for which they were not responsible. These were understood only when Havelock Ellis and Freud applied to the subject the illumination of their genius.

In the meantime, fascinated by the dramatic possibilities of the incest theme, playwrights continued to exploit it in the traditional vein. In 1898 in Italy, D'Annunzio made it the subject of a characteristically exotic play, *The Dead City,* drenched in all his pseudo-Hellenism and exuding sinister mystery. The doomed characters, consisting of a brother who sinfully loves his sister who sinfully loves a married man who sinfully loves her, as well as the blind, but all-seeing wife, go their tormented way to the fore-ordained tragic end. Even well into the new century, in 1922, when D'Annunzio's complete opposite, the French playwright Claude Anet, presented in *The Lost Girl* an incest theme, he completely failed to interpret the situation he depicted in the light of authoritative psychological findings. This play, subjected to bitter attack when produced in Paris, tells the story of a father and a daughter who meet, ignorant of their relation, and become lovers. When they discover the truth their first reaction is one of horror; but when they realize that the quality of their mutual feeling is unchanged and that they cannot live without each other, instead of walking into the mill-race, they decide that for them the solution of their problem is to remain lovers. Thus while Anet divests the subject of its Homeric horror and approaches it with the reasoned calmness particularly necessary to the consideration of sexual taboos, yet he contributes nothing in his play to a deeper understanding of incestuous emotions.

It was Eugene O'Neill, writer of the greatest psychological plays of our age, who, by treating incest in terms of Freudian interpretation, notably in *Mourning Becomes Electra,* removed the last vestige of the incest taboo from the theatre.

But there is one more contemporary drama dealing with incest which deserves attention — the moving tragedy of an American farmer and his young daughter called *The Earth Between,* by Virgil Geddes. On his farm in Nebraska lives Nat Jennings with his seventeen-year-old daughter Floy, whom he has brought up and who is now the image of her dead mother. When the play opens a dance is in progress in a neighboring farm house. Jake, Jennings' shy, clumsily sensitive young farmhand, awaits Floy's coming, less eagerly than mournfully, because as usual "she's coming with *him.*" Soon Floy arrives, as expected, with her father and coaxes him: "You are going to let me dance with Jake? Just once?" Jennings sternly refuses. She may dance—once—with his nephew, Wilbur, but not with Jake. Wilbur, however, in disgust tells the unhappy Jake he's going home, he doesn't want to dance with Floy "after the way I saw him hugging her around." In lines as simple as these, half-inarticulate as the farm-folk who utter them, we gather that Jennings is too fond of his gentle young daughter, and also that she is interested in Jake as he in her. And so, in what Shelley would indubitably have called "a dry exhibition" of this subject, in a few cautious words feeling their way, or in a few wild words desperate with jealousy or fear, the tragic tale unfolds. "Stark" is the favorite word used with lazy indifference to dispose of this playwright's style. But it is not stark: it is rich with overtones.

Fearful of losing his daughter to Jake, Jennings sends the boy away from the house to sleep in the barn. There, in the damp straw, insufficiently covered, Jake contracts pneumonia. In a tense scene, Wilbur savagely tries to shake Floy out of her almost hypnotic subjection to her father by urging her to save the life of the boy she loves and to let him save her. But Floy desperately replies: "There isn't any way out, Wilbur. It's got to go on. Like this." So Jake dies, actually murdered by Jennings, who has withheld from him the medicines left by the doctor; and Wilbur, filled with loathing, after excoriating Jennings, leaves the farm.

Thus we come to the last scene of the play. It is some weeks after Jake's funeral, and Jennings is alone in the fields, working. He pauses and looks across the fields to the house.

JENNINGS: Here she comes, by golly. She sure is a sweet one to me. Just like *she* always was. (*He sighs tiredly, then rubs his hand over his stomach.*) I can sure drink a gallon or two now.

(*Floy appears in the field, carrying a jug of water.*)

FLOY: I'm coming, Pop.

JENNINGS: So you are, and I'm needing you, too.

FLOY: Done a lot of work, haven't you?

(*She hands him the jug.*)

JENNINGS: A lot for me, I'll say, at my age. (*He takes a long drink.*) We're pretty much alone, don't you think? You and me? (*He looks at her appealingly.*)

FLOY: That's right, Pop. I'm the only hired man you've got now, aren't I?

(*She smiles encouragingly.*)

JENNINGS: You *are* that. And my only woman—er, girl—my little girl.

FLOY: I'm your daughter, Pop.

(*A sudden, frightened timidity comes over her.*)

JENNINGS: That's it. Or the way to say it, maybe.

FLOY (*Almost pleadingly*): Just your little girl. Isn't that enough?

JENNINGS (*Looking away*): Sometimes. Then sometimes it isn't.

FLOY: Pop. I'm not enough? Just me?

JENNINGS (*Heavily*): Yes. But it's not that. There's something in me, that wants more. (*He looks at her questioningly.*) It doesn't hurt you, when I say that, does it?

FLOY: No. But it makes me feel lost.

JENNINGS: You would be lost, without your pop, wouldn't you? (*He looks at her eagerly, for an affirmative answer.*)

FLOY: I don't know. Did you ever think of me away from you?

JENNINGS: Not much. Nobody's good enough for you, except me, I guess.

FLOY (*Wistfully*): Jake was. Don't you think?

JENNINGS (*Excitedly*): Nobody, Floy. Nobody that I've seen. They ought to be strong, those who want you. But they don't grow that way any more, I guess.

FLOY (*Weakly*): Maybe they don't. Maybe that's the reason I'm still with you.

JENNINGS: It is. They never were strong enough to take you from me.

FLOY: Do you wish they had been, sometimes?

JENNINGS (*Frightenedly*): You wouldn't have gone, would you?

FLOY: I don't know, Pop.

JENNINGS (*Forcefully, but appealingly*): I'm your pop. And you're my girl. Almost her. Like a woman, I mean, for me.

FLOY (*With a sudden protectiveness*): But Pop, there's something between us?

JENNINGS: What is it, Floy?

FLOY: I don't know. But I can feel it.

JENNINGS (*Hopefully again*): Yes? Something that you can feel? Now?

FLOY: I don't know. But it's there. Something heavy; so you can't push it away. Like it was the earth, itself.

JENNINGS (*Looking off across the fields to hide his boyish eagerness*): You mean something in common, don't you? We've got lots between us, if that's what you mean.

FLOY (*Searchingly*): What have we got, Pop? That belongs to us two?

JENNINGS: We've got the whole of this farm, Floy, and your seventeen years grown up beside me.

FLOY: Maybe it's that. The seventeen years.

JENNINGS (*Ecstatically*): You *can* feel that, can't you. Those seventeen years?

FLOY: I don't know. (*Then frightenedly*) I think it's something else, Pop.

JENNINGS (*With effort*): And lots of other things we've got between us. We've got your mother, Floy. Her in you.

FLOY: Maybe it's her.

JENNINGS (*Lost in his own ecstasy*): Yes. You're a woman, now. You can take her place.

FLOY (*With sudden defensiveness*): No. Something that isn't in common. It stands between us and I can't move.

JENNINGS (*He gets down on his knees, before her.*): You're her. But stronger. Better than she was.

FLOY: Do you think so, Pop?

JENNINGS: It'll be you and me, Floy, always, side by side.

(*He puts out his arms and draws her to him.*)

(*Curtain.*)

The sacrifice of Floy to her father's incestuous, even if physically restrained, love is undeniably tragic. But this father is no pre-classic or even classic monster. He is a plain American farmer whose wife was taken from him when his entire sexual and emotional life, his entire libido, to use the Freudian term, was centered in her. As a result, he unconsciously transferred his libido to his daughter. When she becomes, as a woman, the very incarnation of the lost wife, his sexual emotions become transferred also. How simple a story of incestuous love when told in the light of contemporary understanding! Tragic and deplorable, but surely no monstrous tale of inhuman "pollution." Today the seeing and reading of O'Neill's drama and of this revealing play of Geddes purge us of terror, but not of pity.

The plays discussed in this chapter offer evidence that our contemporary theatre has done vital work in bringing changed sexual standards to the attention of the slow-moving compact majority. As I have said, our sole test of contemporary drama is the value of these plays for us who need a living theatre today, and since one of the salient expressions of this time is the individual's conflict with changing sexual standards, we can judge the deep significance, for us, of plays that interpret this conflict.

Chapter 4 ❧ Contemporary Drama: The Conflict within the Individual

❧ Of all man's conflicts none has more persistently appealed to the playwright as essentially dramatic than his struggle with himself. Even primitive man, free from the neurotic conflicts engendered by civilization, manifested inner disturbance, and resorted to exorcism as the means of freeing the individual from an evil spirit that was destroying him. Rites of exorcism continued among the Greeks and Romans, throughout the history of early Christianity, and are to this day retained in the Roman Catholic Church. All of which shows that from his earliest days the individual has been beset by forces battling within himself and that inner harmony is a consummation which he must fight to attain.

Nor is there any assurance that the struggle will result in victory. It often ends in tragedy, as for example in the strange Chassidic legend utilized in *The Dybbuk*. Here an erotically frustrated girl, convinced that a dybbuk, the soul of her lost lover, is inhabiting her body, speaks with his male voice and later dies when the dybbuk is exorcised. In *The Strange Case of Dr. Jekyll and Mr. Hyde* the end of the symbolic conflict is again tragic. Literature supplies endlessly variegated material to demonstrate that the human soul is a house divided against itself.

Actually, however, we need no further evidence than that furnished by our own lives. In each one of us there exist diametrically opposed qualities constantly warring with each other, causing difficulties in our behavior, in our relations with other human beings and in reaching decisions that may change our lives. Ambition wages war with inertia, courage with cowardice, agnosticism with religion, radicalism with conservatism, altruism with selfishness. There may be a respite for the individual in his conflict with the external world, but respite in the conflict with himself there is none.

It is not, therefore, by accident that two of the greatest dramatic works, Shakespeare's *Hamlet* and Goethe's *Faust,* both deal with that basic inner struggle, referred to as the struggle between man's "higher" and "lower" self. We see the Hamlet, of high purpose, go down in tragedy before the Hamlet made indecisive and futile by his unstable emotions. We see Faust, the learned scientist, the positive philosopher, succumb again and again to Mephistopheles, symbolizing the spirit of negation.

So powerfully intrenched in the consciousness of the creative artist is the age-old dramatic device of depicting man's "lower" or negating self as an amoral spirit taking on human form and engaging in visible struggle with him that the contemporary dramatist Franz Werfel uses this theme again in his brilliant Faust-drama of today: *Mirror-Man.*

Mirror-Man, a symbolic drama, most of it written in rhymed verse, is so vast in scope and so rich in philosophic content that it is no more a work for the theatre than its classic prototype, Goethe's *Faust.* It takes place in an unnamed region that we soon recognize as our contemporary world. Thamal, a young man, weary of his empty existence, decides to enter a monastery. But the Abbot tells him that he can reach spiritual harmony only after experiencing the dirt and the blood of life. Apparently the old doctrine of finding oneself through losing oneself is regarded by Werfel as still sound. Thamal persists, however, and so the Abbot leaves him. Soon he notices a curtain and, sensing that something of import to him lies beyond, he draws it and finds himself face to face with a large mirror. At the sight of his own image, his old self-loathing seizes him and he shoots, *not at himself,* but at his image in the mirror. And out of the shattered glass leaps Mirror-Man, the embodiment of the self Thamal has been trying to escape, his destructive, his "lower" self. Alive now with energy and power, Mirror-Man promises Thamal the realization of all his ego can possibly crave: wealth, love, adventure, fame. For an instant Thamal has a premonitory shudder, then together they start out into the world.

First they return to Thamal's home, where follows a scene that could exist only in post-Freudian drama. Thamal is oppressed by the father-son relation, by the survival of his childhood fear and hate of his father as God and by Mirror-Man's taunting him that to his father he is a schoolboy still. When his father commands Thamal, as his heir, to accept a high position, he refuses with the revealing words "I am no heir. I myself am a beginning!" and his father disinherits him. But Mirror-Man is helpless without wealth. He persuades Thamal to employ his magic and rob his father while he sleeps. Thamal is worried, but Mirror-Man reassures him with the warning that, as he takes the key from his father's neck, he must keep the murder-wish out of his mind, or else his father will die. The money secured, Thamal and Mirror-Man make their escape.

Under the influence of the amoral self that seeks only ego-satisfactions, Thamal now lives through the varied experiences of a contemporary Faust. Urged on by Mirror-Man, he seduces Ampheh, the bride of his closest friend, who yields because she recognizes in Thamal the one great love of her life. But soon, irked by Ampheh's constant criticism of Mirror-Man, he allows the latter to persuade him that her approaching motherhood will prove a burden to him and so he deserts her. He reaches the land of slimy snakes and deadly indifference — symbolic of the contemporary political state — where he suddenly develops a social conscience and longs to be a Messiah, to achieve a sense of his own worth through an act of sacrifice. Mirror-Man, knowing that only he whose purpose is clean can become a Messiah, proceeds to wreck Thamal's social usefulness by soiling it with personal ambition. So Thamal allows the people to bow down and worship him as a god — the ego's supreme wish-fulfillment. But at the height of his power he is accused of his father's murder and finally brought to judgment.

The judge presiding over his trial tells him that he will have to pronounce sentence on himself, since no other person can know the hidden causes of one's actions. Those whom Thamal has so deeply wronged appear and one by one forgive him — his father, his friend who was Ampheh's husband, and Ampheh herself. The last witness called against him is his child. Hardly able to drag itself along on its crutches, the syphilitic child tries weakly to speak but collapses. Then Thamal rises and says: "My crimes against the past and the present I could in anguish expiate. But I have wrought deeper evil. Oh child! I have poisoned mankind's future. . . . Ah, I am ready to pronounce my own sentence — death!" And the judge repeats as he records it: "Death." In his cell awaiting execution Thamal is once more confronted by Mirror-Man, who tempts him anew and magically opens the cell-door. But Thamal realizes that death alone can free him from Mirror-Man, and so he chooses to die. He seizes the goblet the guard brings him and, as he drinks the potion, Mirror-Man, in an agony of fear, disappears into the mirror.

The last scene brings us back once more to the monastery. Thamal lies upon a bier and when the Abbot bids him rise, asks: "Am I dead?" For answer the Abbot leads him before the mirror and commands him to touch it. Thamal does so and instantaneously it changes into a gigantic window, beyond which is visible a sunlit landscape drenched in color. Crying "I see — I see — I see!" Thamal understands that he has been reborn, freed at last from cynicism and egotism. And the splendor of the world, in which he now understands how to live and work, is almost more than he can bear.

Thus does Werfel interpret the conflict within the individual and state his faith in the affirmative spirit of man. Negation, the denial that life is a positive good, means decadence and death. Only in affirmation grounded in invincible spiritual strength can there be life and the struggle for human advancement and freedom.

It is in the plays of Eugene O'Neill, however, that we find an interpretation of the inner conflicts of the individual expressed in terms so completely contemporaneous that their significance for the audiences and readers of this age is at once recognized. This response to O'Neill is noteworthy because he is a man to whom life seems essentially tragic and who therefore must portray it in terms of tragedy. And he does this consistently despite the fact that audiences, so deficient in play-consciousness, as a rule recoil from tragedy in the theatre.

Wide admiration, in Europe as well as in America, for the work of this dramatist, who is in no sense a popular playwright, is all the evidence required to establish the fact that O'Neill possesses the two great elements of genius: irresistible power and the quality of universality. These are readily recognizable as the elements of Shakespeare's genius, making him at the same time the idol of the cultured intellectual and of the common man, today exemplified in the working-class audiences who applaud his plays at the Old Vic Theatre in London. It is not, however, the question of O'Neill's genius that occupies us here, but the extent to which his work is integrated with his own age. We must again ascertain, as we did in the case of *Hindle Wakes, The Sickness of Youth, The Children's Hour,* whether or not the individual conflicts he portrays are sufficiently general in their revelations to possess a universal significance for his time.

O'Neill has been severely criticized by commentators of the left as a dramatist of genuine substance who lacks any definite social point of view or social philosophy and who therefore treats his characters as if they lived in some sort of social vacuum. This criticism of O'Neill is identical with that which they direct at Freud himself, namely, that he sees the individual conditioned by every force under the stars except the basic one, the economic force, which dominates the life of the individual under the existing industrial world order. They accuse O'Neill of being blind to the social conflicts of his time and therefore of failing to understand—and this is the quintessence of their criticism—that the psychological maladjustments of his characters have their origin in a system of society based on a savage struggle for existence.

Whether this social point of view is sound is not the issue here. What does concern us is whether or not it is sound to apply this criterion of judgment to O'Neill. In my opinion it is unsound, just as it is unsound to hold that there is an inherent contradiction between the tenets of Freudism and those of the most advanced social philosophy. Freud asserts that the inner conflicts of the individual began when the "curbs of civilization" forced man to inhibit his instincts and to restrict his ego-satisfactions. It is not Freud's function to be concerned with the causes, economic or otherwise, responsible for the fact that those "curbs of civilization" took the form of oppressive social institutions. The important thing is that the institutions of organized society, such as marriage, the family, the church, did develop in the individual conflicts and difficulties of adjustment to life which only in our contemporary age Freud was scientifically to analyze. Thus, far from being contradictory, his contribution is an invaluable supplement to the Marxian interpretation of the individual's problems.

What is true of Freud must be true of his disciple, O'Neill. A great artist may reveal almost clairvoyantly, as O'Neill seems often to do, the psychological conflicts in the souls of his fellow men, interpreting them according to Freud's doctrines, without himself understanding how future processes of civilization can be changed so as to free the individual from these consequences of his past. Perhaps O'Neill is "the final cry of a decadent and dying epoch," as I once heard a speaker of the left describe him. Even if this be true, what can be more revelatory to us than to listen to the voice of our outstanding dramatic genius and to let it help us to an understanding of our time? Whatever verdict the future may pronounce on the creative artists of today, I believe that the genius who wrote *The Emperor Jones, The Hairy Ape, Lazarus Laughed, Strange Interlude,* and *Mourning Becomes Electra* is sure of his place.

Very few dramatists are as interesting to follow chronologically as Eugene O'Neill. For his plays reveal logical development, both in choice of subject and method of treatment, from his early work through *Mourning Becomes Electra,* which at this writing marks the end of his important contribution. Between *Strange Interlude* and its successor *Mourning Becomes Electra,* both contemporary to the core, came *Dynamo,* the first manifestation of the schism in O'Neill's philosophy of life, which in *Days Without End,* his latest play to date, brought him to religious orthodoxy as the solution of the problem of faith. Despite this ominous change, so contradictory to the free spirit of his other work, and despite his enormous output, the result of which shows in the varying quality of his work, there are actually no plays, even the minor ones, that do not reward the play-reader.

Concerned always with the interior conflicts of the individual, O'Neill is not interested in the conflict of the individual with a hostile society. Were he, for example, to write *The Children's Hour,* we should have no battle royal between the Philistine world on the one side and two of its maltreated victims on the other. Instead we should have a portrayal of the inner anguish of two women through which O'Neill would reveal their unconscious reactions to their experience and the importance of those reactions for their behavior. To Miss Hellman the events of the play are the all-important factors; to O'Neill the psychological reactions of the characters to those events would be the all-important factors. O'Neill's approach is never objective. Always completely identified with his characters, he must look out from them into life. The problems that move him as themes for drama are inevitably fought out within the microcosm of the individual. Yet because the universal implications of his portrayal are immediately recognizable, the individual in his plays takes on the larger proportions of a symbol, representing a group, a class, a sex, a race.

That this approach constitutes the essential O'Neill may be seen in his first important play, *The Emperor Jones*. Though six of its eight scenes present the hallucinatory experiences of an individual Negro, the play is uniformly described as an "epic of the American Negro." And it is just that; because O'Neill here re-creates the tragic history of a race by exhibiting the race-memories of one of its individuals made sentient through terror.

On an island in the West Indies, Brutus Jones, an American Negro convict, escaped from a chain gang, has ruled as "Emperor" for two years. He has compensated for his fear and hatred of his hereditary enemy, the white man, by employing the latter's methods, learned during his years as a Pullman porter. Thus by "big stealin' " and the domination over his inferiors, the ignorant "bush-niggers" of the island, the Emperor Jones has made his pile and is planning soon to depart and enjoy life elsewhere. But even these primitive creatures revolt against his ruthless bleeding of them, and when the play opens they have withdrawn to the hills to whip themselves up into the battle-courage necessary to go out to "get" the Emperor.

Contemptuously defiant of them, his first sense of apprehension seizes him when, according to O'Neill's stage directions, "*from the distant hills comes the faint steady thump of a tom-tom, low and vibrating*" — which "*continues at a gradually accelerating rate . . . uninterruptedly to the very end of the play.*" This use of the tom-tom by O'Neill is a stroke of genius in the theatre, for it keeps the audience conscious during every moment of the play of primitive forces and of impending doom. Genuinely alarmed now, Jones determines to leave at once, cross the forest to the other coast and board a boat for Martinique. His fear is mitigated by the fact that he has made the credulous blacks believe that only a bullet made of silver, which they do not possess, can kill him. He has six bullets in his gun — five lead ones for the natives, the sixth and last of silver — "to cheat 'em out o' gittin' me."

There follow the six scenes of Jones's imaginary experiences in the Great Forest, where the only spoken words are those uttered by him to express his visions, thoughts and fears. Observe that in this, one of his earliest plays, O'Neill's purpose already is to let a character reveal his *unconscious* self, although he accomplishes this here with far less subtlety and through a different technique from that which he was to employ later.

Entering the forest, Jones makes for the spot where he has hidden food; but it is not there. Frantic at having lost his way, he becomes aware of black, shapeless figures creeping toward him, their "low, mocking laughter like a rustling of leaves." These are the Little Formless Fears that are attacking him, and with a yell of terror Jones shoots at them. They scurry away, but in the silence, hearing nothing but the "quickened throb of the tom-tom," Jones realizes his error in having by his shot given his pursuers a clue to his whereabouts, and he plunges more deeply into the forest. There he suddenly sees before him the image of Jeff, his fellow Pullman porter whom he had killed with a razor "in an argument ovah a crap game." Shouting in terrified rage "Nigger . . . Has I got to kill you ag'in?" he shoots—and then, in fear at the nearer sound of the tom-tom, leaps into the underbrush. Now he notices a road along which marches a familiar chain gang. Hypnotized, Jones joins it. Soon the phantom Prison Guard lashes him with his whip, and when Jones discovers that this time he has no shovel in his hands with which once more to slay the vicious white guard, he fires his revolver at him and flees. He reaches a clearing, and is paralyzed with horror to find himself surrounded by men and women in the costumes of the prewar South. They are examining batches of slaves presented to them by the Auctioneer, who soon orders Jones to the auction-block. Shaken with hate and fear, shouting to the apparitions before him, "What? . . . Is you sellin' me like dey uster befo' de war?", Jones fires again, twice.

Now he has no bullet left save the silver one. But the nightmare of his remembered racial fears is not yet over. In the moonlight he imagines he sees two rows of black galley-slaves, swaying to and fro as though in a moving ship. As if under compulsion, Jones joins them, sways and wails with them, finally running from them deeper into the forest. But the Negro race has experienced terrors even more primitive than these, and Jones is now confronted by the Congo Witch-Doctor who calls on him to offer himself as a sacrifice to the crocodile that appears on the riverbank. Fascinated, almost yielding, Jones suddenly remembers his silver bullet, which he fires at the beast while the tom-tom pulsates more and more strongly. But the Emperor Jones has underestimated the craftiness of his enemies. With bullets moulded from melted silver coins, his black brothers now avenge his exploitation of them. In this primeval world, the white man's "tricks" avail him nothing. He remains as ever their dupe and victim.

Although O'Neill was destined to rise to greater heights, he has never written anything more characteristic of himself, more artistically complete within the limits of its form, or sharper with contemporary meaning, than *The Emperor Jones.* Placing his audience directly within the consciousness of this American Negro, O'Neill enables us, with an inner vision, to understand his racial history. The ability thus to create individual characters who at the same time fulfill the larger function of symbols constitutes the essence of O'Neill's genius.

Such a tragic symbol is O'Neill's next creation, Yank in *The Hairy Ape*. His is the tragedy of emerging man, in whom the conflict arises out of his inability any longer to "belong" to his brute past and his incapacity, as yet, to "belong" to a reasoned world. Yank is a stoker, and we first see him in the forecastle of an ocean liner. O'Neill describes him and his fellows thus: "The men . . . resemble those pictures in which the appearance of Neanderthal Man is guessed at. All are hairy-chested, with long arms of tremendous power and low, receding brows above their small fierce, resentful eyes. All the civilized white races are represented. . . ." Among them Yank is the most highly individualized, the most capable of self-expression. He glories in his brute strength. Violently silencing the Cockney Socialist for his drunken animadversions against "the damned Capitalist clarss,' Yank holds forth: "What's dem slobs in de foist cabin got to do wit us? One of us guys could clean up de whole mob wit one mit. . . . Who makes dis old tub run? Ain't it us guys? Well, den we belong, don't we? We belong and dey don't. Dat's all. . . ."

But Yank is soon to learn what the "slobs in de foist cabin" have to do with him. The bored daughter of an American steel-magnate comes to have a look at the stokehole. As she enters escorted by a ship's engineer, Yank, who is working with his back to the door, does not see her and launches into an especially foul-mouthed tirade. Suddenly turning, he glares into her eyes and reads there her loathing. Shutting out the sight of him with her hands she cries: "Take me away. Oh, the filthy beast!"—leaving Yank in bewildered fury at this insulting concept of himself. So we next see Yank, just off duty, seated, brooding "in the exact attitude of Rodin's 'The Thinker.'" "Lemme alone," he says. "Can't youse see I'm tryin' to tink?" His comrades are puzzled and incredulous. His abortive "tinking," which takes the form of rage against the girl who treated him as if he were a hairy ape, results in a vow of revenge. What! This "white-faced skoit" who "don't belong"! He'll show her who's a hairy ape . . .!

Three weeks later, on a Sunday morning on Fifth Avenue, unwashed and bitter, Yank seeks to assuage the wound in his soul which self-doubt has inflicted, by behaving like a hooligan among the church crowd, bumping viciously into the men and insulting the women. In this scene, O'Neill exhibits his effective use of symbolism. Describing this Fifth Avenue crowd as "a procession of gaudy marionettes, yet with something of the relentless horror of Frankensteins in their detached, mechanical unawareness," he shows them treating the bewildered Yank as if he did not exist. *They* are not jarred—"rather it is he who recoils after each collision." But finally one Gentleman irritably calls: "Officer! Officer!" and in an instant "a whole platoon of policemen rush in on Yank from all sides." This is a picture of the society against which an emerging brute, who thinks he "belongs," essays to pit himself!

Thrown into jail, Yank hears for the first time about "a tough gang" called the I.W.W., who "blow up tings." It offers a way to get even with her—through "her old man, president of de Steel Trust." Released from jail he makes for the I.W.W. local on the waterfront. Here he expresses his astonishment that the door is not locked, that he has been permitted to walk in, unquestioned. His suspicions aroused, the Secretary questions him and Yank replies with a wink, "Aw, can it! Yuh wanter blow tings up, don't yuh? Well, dat's me! I belong!" And he further explains his readiness to blow the steel works "offen de oith." At which, denounced as a spy and scorned as "a brainless ape," the stupefied Yank finds himself thrown out by the workers present. Brooding, he replies to the policeman who asks him what he has done: "Enuf to gimme life for! I was born, see? Sure, dat's de charge. . . . I was born, get me!" Yank has evolved to the point of questioning the good of life itself.

The last scene, with its original symbolism, is the monkey house at the Zoo. In one cage crouches a gorilla, "himself in much the same attitude as Rodin's Thinker." Yank comes to see him, not understanding that he has been drawn by the unconscious hope that in the world of brutes, to which he has been consistently relegated by the world of men, he may find welcome and the assurance that he belongs. "Ain't we both members of de same club — de Hairy Apes?" he bitterly asks the gorilla. This scene, in the form of a long monologue addressed to the gorilla, must be read in its entirety, to get both the measure of Yank's inner confusion and the fullness of O'Neill's symbolism. Gropingly Yank tries to understand the ape's place and his own: "Yuh don't belong with 'em and yuh know it. But me, I belong wit 'em — but I don't, see? . . . It beats it when you try to tink it or talk it — it's way down — deep — behind — you 'n me feel it. Sure! Bot' members of dis club!" With a wild feeling of affinity for the brute, he "jimmies" open the door of the cage and when the ape is out he holds out his hand to him with a "Come on, Brother. . . . Shake — de secret grip of our order." The enraged animal, however, springs on Yank with a murderous hug and then throws his crushed body into the cage, shutting the door. But Yank manages to open his eyes and mutter painfully: —

. . . Even him didn't tink I belonged. (*Then with sudden passionate despair.*) Christ, where do I get off at? Where do I fit in?

(*He grabs hold of the bars of the cage and hauls himself painfully to his feet—looks around him bewilderedly—forces a mocking laugh.*) In de cage, huh? (*In the strident tones of a circus barker.*) Ladies and gents, step forward and take a slant at de one and only—(*His voice weakening*) one and original—Hairy Ape from de wilds of—(*He slips in a heap on the floor and dies. The monkeys set up a chattering, whimpering wail. And perhaps the Hairy Ape at last belongs.*)

Curtain.

The meaning of this play is clear. Terrible is the struggle of man to emerge from the brute. But once his soul has been born, he can never return to the satisfactions of his origin, even though he is tortured by his efforts to understand where he belongs.

The Hairy Ape is often referred to as the one *social* play written by O'Neill. Those who so describe it are deceived by the fact that an alleged Socialist rails against capitalism, that the daughter of a steel-magnate is portrayed as a decadent, that Fifth Avenue churchgoers are depicted as shallow, purblind marionettes, and that the I.W.W. is presented sympathetically, as the real answer to a groping Yank. But all this is only the material selected for his play by a genius sensitive to the living issues of his day. Even a casual reading will show that O'Neill has no interest in his caricature of a Socialist. As for his stereotyped daughter of wealth, she is only the necessary spark with which to ignite Yank. Finally, as a creative artist, O'Neill despises the conforming Philistines and Pharisees and he also has sufficient intelligence to know that the I.W.W., very much in the public eye in 1920, were not dynamiters. No, if *The Hairy Ape* were social drama, O'Neill's purpose would have been to show that Yank's need was to discover his place in the social organism as a worker. But O'Neill is not in the least concerned with the social problems of Yank. He is really not concerned with Yank at all. His interest is with the inner conflicts of *man,* midway between the hairy ape he has left behind him and the evolving human race to which he is not yet conscious that he belongs.

To follow the evolution of O'Neill's dramatic work is to admire the incorruptibility of his approach to his art. Refusing to give the slightest heed to accepted shibboleths of "success" in the theatre, O'Neill has written solely about subjects that impressed him with their significance, and has created new forms of dramatic treatment whenever his subject matter seemed to him to demand them. No clearer evidence can be adduced of this indifference to the prejudices of the compact majority, especially in America, than *All God's Chillun Got Wings,* his first major play to follow *The Hairy Ape.*

This tragedy goes to the heart of one of America's most violent taboos: miscegenation. Now O'Neill is not interested in miscegenation as a social problem. His concern is with the inner conflicts that destroy the lives of a young Negro and a white girl when they marry in a land whose assumption of white superiority is one of its persisting prejudices. Ella, an Irish-American product of the tenements, after high school runs off with the local bully and prize fighter, Mickey, bears his child, and is later deserted by him. Ever since school days Ella has been worshiped by her playmate, Jim Harris, a gentle, ambitious young Negro of superior family, whose sister has become a schoolteacher. Alone, and in desperate need of help, Ella agrees to marry Jim. But when Jim, obsessed by a feeling of race inferiority, tells Ella how he has repeatedly failed in his Bar examination, because, when he sees the white men "so sure," his own mind becomes a blank, Ella remains strangely indifferent. Jim, however, cannot stop, he must persist, he must manifest his mental equality with the white man.

The play becomes the tragic story of this marriage. Ella, half-crazed by the humiliation of her position as the white wife of a Negro, clings madly, for compensation, to the myth of white superiority. This makes her not only wound to the depths of his soul the patient, adoring Jim, but it drives her deliberately to undermine his morale, so that he cannot pass his Bar examination. His failure to do so has become for her the symbol of his inferiority, which she must preserve at all costs. Jim tries to study while he nurses the malicious yet pitiful Ella, but in the heartbreaking last scene of the play he learns that once more he has failed to pass. In wild despair he hears Ella crying, as she dances up and down: "Oh Jim, I knew it! I knew you couldn't! Oh, I'm so glad, Jim! I'm so happy! You're still my old Jim—and I'm so glad!" Jim's rage dies down as he realizes that she is no longer responsible for this racial hate that dominates her to madness. And when, in a moment of contrition, she asks him, like a child, "Will God forgive me, Jim?" Jim answers: "Maybe He can forgive what you've done to me; and maybe He can forgive what I've done to you; but I don't see how He's going to forgive—Himself."

All God's Chillun Got Wings is one of O'Neill's finest achievements. Psychologically sound, alive with dramatic intensity, clearly implying the menace of these ingrained racial complexes, it is a play to which America should have risen in grateful response. Instead, the play's content and purpose were sensationally exploited in the press, especially in the South, and the New York City police authorities attempted to stop the play on the evening of its first performance. The District Attorney, himself a Southerner, outraged at the report that the play treated with serious dignity the marriage between a white woman and a Negro, influenced the Mayor to refuse acting permits to the children, Negro and white, who appear in the first scene. This first scene is essential to the remainder of the play, because it shows the warm friendship between black and white children who are neighbors, undisturbed by any race antagonism, and it establishes the beginnings of the relationship between Ella and Jim. The police authorities were, however, no match for the intrepid Provincetown Playhouse. With the vociferous approval of the audience, the opening scene was read by the stage manager, after which, in the face of the police lined up at the theatre entrance, the play went on. This reading of the first scene continued until practically the end of the play's run, when the children were permitted to act for a few nights. O'Neill himself, threatened by letters from the ignorant in all sections of the country, bitterly resented the "unwelcome notoriety" which, as he said, "put the whole theme of the play on a false basis and thereby threw my whole intent in the production into the discard."

In his next play, produced during the same year, O'Neill was again to see the intent of his work distorted. For the District Attorney, defeated in his effort to close *All God's Chillun Got Wings,* saw an opportunity for revenge in the production of *Desire Under the Elms.* This play is without doubt one of O'Neill's most effective works in the theatre. Dealing with the most elemental of passions, presented at a high pitch of theatricality, *Desire Under the Elms* possesses an irresistible appeal to the essentially theatre-conscious. It is, with the exception of *Marco Millions,* the least interior of O'Neill's important plays, its conflicts arising out of the struggles of the characters with each other to satisfy exterior physical desires, rather than out of inner struggles. The theme is lust — lust of the flesh and lust of possessions. And it is interesting to note that the theme of *Marco Millions* is also acquisitiveness, which goal sums up the philosophy of the materialist.

To the New England farmhouse in *Desire Under the Elms* comes Abbie, who has married Cabot, over twice her age, because she hopes thereby to secure his farm as her own property. Soon, however, Abbie finds herself "lusting" for Eben, his son, who desires her but at the same time hates her for threatening his property rights, especially since he and his father are bitterly hostile to each other. But Abbie seduces him, driven by her plan of bearing a son whom she can pass off as the child of old Cabot, senilely eager for an heir. All goes according to calculation except that out of the lust of Eben and Abbie for each other is born a deeper passion. In one of their constant flare-ups of hatred, Cabot taunts Eben with Abbie's deliberate plan to bear the old man a son so that Eben will be "cut off." Eben, furious at Abbie's trickery, tells her he is leaving for the West forever. Abbie cannot endure parting from Eben. How shall she prove to him that her passion for him now outweighs all desire for the property? She solves her dilemma without a moment's hesitation—with no conflict of inner forces—by murdering the newborn baby, the symbol of her guilt toward Eben. Sick with repulsion, Eben informs the police, but he returns, broken, to tell Abbie that he loves her and to beg her to forgive him. Ecstatic now, Abbie is ready to take her punishment; but when the Sheriff comes, Eben tells him: "I helped her do it. Ye kin take me, too."

To this violent tale of lust, O'Neill applies his dazzling gifts for the theatre. But even these cannot supply the lack here of the universal implications which inform his greater plays. The emotional change which occurs in Abbie is imposed on her from without. Her resultant psychological experiences do not emanate from her unconscious, as they do in *The Great God Brown,* or *Strange Interlude.* For all its dramatic intensity, *Desire Under the Elms* fails to reveal those inner values which constitute the essential O'Neill.

However we may rank it, the fact remains that the interference of censorship perverted the values of this play. The District Attorney's efforts to close the play, after a run of four months, failed, because outraged citizens and leading newspapers rallied to its defense. But the mischief was done; and when the play moved uptown to become a Broadway success, it drew sniggering audiences who charged the theatre with the atmosphere of their prurience. And as the result of its New York experience, difficulties with the censor pursued it elsewhere. In Los Angeles the company was arrested, and, after giving a performance of the play in the courtroom itself, acquitted. In Boston and in London production of the play was forbidden. Contrary to popular belief, the threat of censorship to a serious play, especially one dealing with a sexual theme, is no asset to its reputation, but a distinct liability.

The next play of O'Neill to be considered is *Lazarus Laughed,* his allegory of man's faith in life. And since we are following his major work chronologically, it is interesting to note how his next three plays overlap in the writing. Early in 1925 O'Neill wrote in its entirety *The Great God Brown,* and later in that same year he began *Lazarus Laughed.* But the latter was not completed until 1927, and in 1926 part of *Strange Interlude* was written. Thus the organic bond that exists between *The Great God Brown* and *Strange Interlude* remains unbroken, and we are not deviating from our course by considering first *Lazarus Laughed* and then the inseparably linked *The Great God Brown* and *Strange Interlude.*

Almost as important as sex to man's inner life is faith. In our analysis of Werfel's *Mirror-Man* and of the recurrent Faust-Mephistopheles theme, we met the conclusion that man's faith in life *must* conquer his doubt, his negation of life, or he is lost. For us of this scientific age to "know" that the sun will rise on the morrow is as complete an expression of faith as the same conviction in the breast of the savage. And we carry this faith in the behavior of physical phenomena even further, into the realms of the spiritual and the social. We believe in the potential power of man to *rise* also, which means that we have faith in life as the manifestation of an often tragic, but somehow positive, good. Yet such faith is apparently not enough.

Men have allowed themselves to be distracted by another conflict: the question of the form or dogma their faith shall take.

After the World War, the deep-rooted inner compulsion of men to mould faith into dogmas once more expressed itself in the religious controversy between Fundamentalism and Modernism, which arose in America as a reaction to the cynical materialism of the postwar period. In the Scopes case of 1925, a teacher of science in a Tennessee high school, charged by Fundamentalists with having violated a state law prohibiting the teaching of the theory of evolution in the public schools, was convicted. The controversy over this trial served many as a basis for a revaluation of the entire question of religion and faith. And it is evidence of O'Neill's integration with his time that in that year he stated his own faith, his philosophy of life, death and immortality, in *Lazarus Laughed.*

O'Neill designates this drama as "A Play for an Imaginative Theatre." It presents such difficulties of production that so far only the indefatigable Gilmor Brown has presented it, in his famous Pasadena Community Playhouse. The play begins in Bethany, at the home of Lazarus, shortly after his resurrection and the departure of Jesus. There are present a crowd of men and women. Of these, O'Neill gives the following description:—

All of these people are masked in accordance with the following scheme: There are seven periods of life shown: Boyhood (or Girlhood), Youth, Young Manhood (or Womanhood), Manhood (or Womanhood), Middle Age, Maturity and Old Age; and each of these periods is represented by seven different masks of general types of character as follows: the Simple, Ignorant; the Happy, Eager; the Self-Tortured, Introspective; the Proud, Self-Reliant; the Servile, Hypocritical; the Revengeful, Cruel; the Sorrowful, Resigned. . . .

Lazarus, freed now from the fear of death, wears no mask. . . .

O'Neill uses masks here for two reasons. The first is merely to distinguish diversified human types and their degrees of physical maturity. The second, however, is one of inner revelation. *All* wear masks—even as you and I—to hide their constant fear of death; that is, all except Lazarus. In awe the people gaze at him, while his father proposes a toast to his son "brought back from death." Then Lazarus, "suddenly laughing softly out of his vision . . . and speaking with strange, unearthly calm in a voice that is like a loving whisper of hope and confidence," says:

No! There is no death!

Incredulous, the people repeat after him:—

There—is—no—death?

And then they continue: "Why did you laugh? What is beyond there? What is beyond?" To which Lazarus answers "in a voice of loving exaltation":—

There is only life! I heard the heart of Jesus laughing in my heart; "There is Eternal Life in No," it said, "and there is Eternal Life in Yes! Death is the fear between!" And my heart reborn to love of life cried "Yes!" and I laughed in the laughter of God!

(*He begins to laugh, softly at first—a laugh so full of a complete acceptance of life, a profound assertion of joy in living, so devoid of all self-consciousness or fear, that it is like a great bird-song triumphant in depths of sky, proud and powerful, infectious with love, casting on the listener an enthralling spell. The crowd in the room are caught by it. Glancing sideways at one another, smiling foolishly and self-consciously, at first they hesitate, plainly holding themselves in for fear of what the next one will think.*)

CHORUS

(*In a chanting murmur*)

Lazarus laughs!
Our hearts grow happy!

Laughter like music!
The wind laughs!
The sea laughs!
Spring laughs from the earth!
Summer laughs in the air!
Lazarus laughs!

LAZARUS

(*On a final note of compelling exultation*)
Laugh! Laugh with me! Death is dead!
Fear is no more! There is only life! There
is only laughter!

CHORUS

(*Chanting exultingly now*)
Laugh! Laugh!
Laugh with Lazarus!
Fear is no more!
There is no death! . . .
There is only life!
There is only laughter!

Thus O'Neill allegorically declares death to be nonexistent, since it is nothing but the fear between differing manifestations of the life of the universe. This concept he clarifies as we proceed with the play. For even after Jesus is crucified and the Nazarenes slaughtered, and his father and mother and his sisters, Martha and Mary, are dead, Lazarus nevertheless cries out, "in a great triumphant voice": —

Yes! Yes!! Yes!!! Men die! Even a Son of Man must die to show men that Man may live! But there is no death!

Lazarus, joyous apostle of the deathless life of Man, is now called upon to measure the strength of his faith against its antithesis, personal material power, which must, of its own inner necessity, crush all that is fearless and free in the spirit of man. Here the destructive, the negating, is symbolized in the combined persons of Tiberius Cæsar and his heir, Caligula. Cæsar summons Lazarus to Rome, and the rest of the play presents the conflict between two opposing philosophies of life.

Surrounded by worshiping crowds who follow him chanting, "There is no Death," Lazarus encounters first the self-obsessed, cruel Caligula, and replies to his terror-stricken cry: "I must kill him!" with a laughing: "Death is dead, Caligula!" To which Caligula responds:—

I say there *must* be death! . . . You have murdered my only friend, Lazarus! Death would have been my slave when I am Cæsar. He would have been my jester and made me laugh at fear! . . . Then if there is no death, O Teacher, tell me why I love to kill?

LAZARUS

Because you fear to die! But what do you matter, O Deathly-Important One? Put yourself that question—as a jester!

(*Exultantly*)

Are you a speck of dust danced in the wind? Then laugh, dancing! Laugh yes to your insignificance! Thereby will be born your new greatness! As Man, Petty Tyrant of Earth, you are a bubble pricked by death into a void and a mocking silence! But as dust, you are eternal change, and everlasting growth, and a high note of laughter soaring through chaos from the deep heart of God! Be proud, O Dust! Then you may love the stars as equals!

Later Caligula, recognizing in Lazarus and his philosophy the mortal enemy of Cæsar, has the followers of Lazarus murdered. And when Miriam, his wife, symbol of those who cannot rid themselves of the horror of *personal* death, asks, in anguish:

. . . How could you laugh when they were dying?

Lazarus replies, with passionate, proud exultation:—

Did they not laugh? That was their victory and their glory! Eye to eye with the Fear of Death, did they not laugh with scorn? "Death to old Death," they laughed! "Once as squirming specks we crept from the tides of the sea. Now we return to the sea! Once as quivering flecks of rhythm we beat down from the sun. Now we re-enter the sun! Cast aside is our pitiable pretense, our immortal egohood, the holy lantern behind which cringed our Fear of the Dark! Flung off is that impudent insult to life's nobility which gibbers: "I, this Jew, this Roman, this noble or this slave, must survive in my pettiness forever!" Away with such cowardice of spirit! We will to die! We will to change! Laughing we lived with our gift, now with laughter give we back that gift to become again the Essence of the Giver! Dying we laugh with the Infinite. We are the Giver and the Gift! Laughing, we will our own annihilation! Laughing, we give our lives for Life's sake!"

In the same vein he addresses the terror-obsessed Caligula:—

You are so proud of being evil! What if there is no evil? What if there is only health and sickness? Believe in the healthy god called Man in you! Laugh at Caligula, the funny clown who beats the backside of his shadow with a bladder and thinks thereby he is Evil, the Enemy of God! Believe! What if you are a man and men are despicable? Men are also unimportant! Men pass! Like rain into the sea! The sea remains! Man remains! Man slowly arises from the past of the race of men that was his tomb of death! For Man death is not! Man, Son of God's Laughter, IS!

Finally the fear-ridden Tiberius himself, having warned Lazarus that "there shall be death while I am Cæsar," orders him to be burned at the stake. Exultant, Lazarus enters the flames. Tiberius and the crowd, as ever, have turned against the Saviours. For, as Lazarus had said earlier: "The greatness of

Saviours is that they may not save. The greatness of Man is that no god can save him — until he becomes a god!" The crowd jeers at the dying man, and Tiberius taunts him, crying: —

> What do you say now, Lazarus? You are dying!
>
> LAZARUS
>
> (*His voice a triumphant assertion of the victory of life over pain and death*)
> Yes! . . . O men, fear not life! You die — but there is no death for Man!

As in the beginning of the play, the crowds and Tiberius now plead: —

> What is beyond there, Lazarus? What is beyond?

And Lazarus replies: —

> Life! Eternity! Stars and Dust! God's Eternal Laughter!

The crowds laugh with him in frenzied joy and Tiberius himself joins them, shouting: —

> I have lived long enough! I will die with Lazarus! I no longer fear death! I laugh! I laugh at Cæsar! I advise you, my brothers, fear not Cæsars! Seek Man in the brotherhood of the dust! Cæsar is your fear of Man! I counsel you, laugh away your Cæsars!

At which prophetic words, Caligula screams: —

> You give him your laughter? . . . You make him laugh at Cæsars — at me!

And springing on Tiberius, he kills him. Then, while the new Cæsar, although hailed by the crowds, grovels in terror, Lazarus compassionately utters his last words: —

> Fear not, Caligula! There is no death!

In this drama O'Neill reaches the highest spiritual concept of our age, the concept of immortality as the living progress of the race. He regards life as the arena of man's struggle to liberate himself from fear, as the deathless adventure of man in the universe of which he is an inseparable part. *Lazarus Laughed* stands as the positive expression of a faith unconcerned with either forms or dogmas. Too overwhelming in its demands on even the "imaginative" theatre, O'Neill's poetic allegory can be appreciated only in the theatre-of-the-armchair.

Coming now to *The Great God Brown, Strange Interlude* and *Mourning Becomes Electra,* we reach those plays in which O'Neill's use of the Freudian interpretation of the conflicts of the individual identifies him with his own age as nothing else could. Not that he had failed to make earlier use of Freudian psychology, for it forms the basis of all his full-length plays even when it does not actually permeate them. This basis is unmistakable in one of his most characteristic, if minor plays, *Diff'rent,* written as early as 1920.

In *Diff'rent* the Freudian doctrine that the urge for sex fulfillment, if repressed, takes its revenge on the individual through some form of psychological disturbance, is demonstrated in the character of Emma. A New England girl of twenty, in the year 1890, Emma is betrothed to Caleb, a sailing captain. Obsessed by a false ideal of chastity, she has persuaded herself that Caleb is in that respect "diff'rent" from other men, and when she inadvertently learns that he yielded to the lure of a "brown gal" on an island near "the Line," she refuses to marry him. Thirty years later, in 1920, when we see Emma again, she presents a pitiful figure. Incongruously dressed and clumsily made up to look like a young girl, the repressed spinster is in a dither of sexual excitement over Caleb's nephew Benny, a doughboy, one of the war's offscourings, back from overseas. He is a coarse, low cad, who pretends to be attracted to her in order to extort money from her. His mother, Caleb's sister, angrily remonstrates with him:—

> You ought to be 'shamed to take advantage of her condition, but shame ain't in you.

To which Benny replies:—

> . . . Honest, Ma, this here thing with Aunt Emmer ain't my fault. How can I help it if she goes bugs in her old age and gets nutty about me? (*With a sly grin—in a whisper*) Gee, Ma, you oughta see her today. She's a scream, honest. She's upstairs now gettin' calmed down. She was gettin' crazy when your callin' stopped her. Wait till she comes down and you git a look! She'll put your eye out—all dolled up like a kid of sixteen and enough paint on her mush for a Buffalo Bill Indian . . .

When Caleb returns from a voyage to find himself confronted with this horrible creature called Emma, whom he still hopes to wed after waiting thirty years, and hears from her own lips that she is planning to marry the scheming Benny, he goes quietly out to the barn and hangs himself. But before Emma learns of this, Benny elatedly informs her that Caleb has promised him more money than she can give him if he refuses to marry her. He humiliates and tortures her further by viciously expressing his physical loathing of her. So, after she learns that Caleb has hanged himself, whispering "Wait, Caleb, I'm going down to the barn" Emma joins him at last —in death . . . Today we know, through the psychological discoveries of Freud, that if we do thus violate the inner laws of our being, life "punishes" us as inexorably as did the outraged gods of the ancients.

Five years later O'Neill attempted to portray exceedingly subtle and complicated inner conflicts in *The Great God Brown*. Chronologically this play is significant because it leads on directly to *Strange Interlude* and thence to *Mourning Becomes Electra.* Judged per se, it is one of his least realized dramas, confused in thought, in symbolism and in technique.

This technique consists in the use of masks by the leading characters as a defense mechanism for hiding from the world their true selves, as well as to indicate changes going on in their personalities. During the course of the play the characters put on, take off, and change their masks, often in haste, so that the unexpected appearance of one character will not find another unmasked or improperly masked. The result of all this hocus-pocus—for it *is* hocus-pocus in spite of the fact that O'Neill never intended it as such—is to *add* to the confusion portrayed instead of clarifying it. Even worse is the fact that this business of the masks becomes a "stunt," which the audience watches with childish interest. Those who recall that *The Great God Brown* ran in New York for over nine months need not deceive themselves in the belief that its audiences understood the subtleties of its psychological revelations. Here was a *novelty,* by Eugene O'Neill, whose worst was usually more powerful than most other playwrights' best. I saw the production twice and I remember, on my second visit, hearing a young woman say to her escort: "I couldn't get those masks at all, could you? But it was awfully exciting!"

The masks certainly did not supply the technique through which to differentiate visually *on the stage* a character's secret from his revealed self. But they did furnish to O'Neill, himself, determined to present *in terms of the theatre* the inner conflicts of the individual, a necessary experiment that resulted in the clear technique of the *utterance* of hidden thoughts and emotions he later used in *Strange Interlude.*

Nor does the symbolism of *The Great God Brown* possess that clarity which alone justifies its use as a method of literary expression. Indeed it is the only one of his many works in which the symbolism is not beautifully right, but forced and tortured. Let us glance at O'Neill's own explanation of his portrayal of one of the characters, Dion, taken from a letter sent by him to the press soon after the production of the play: —

> I had hoped the names chosen for my people would give a strong hint of this. (An old scheme, admitted — Shakespeare and multitudes since.) Dion Anthony — Dionysus and St. Anthony, — the creative pagan acceptance of life, fighting eternal war with the masochistic, life-denying spirit of Christianity as represented by St. Anthony — the whole struggle resulting in this modern day in mutual exhaustion — creative joy in life for life's sake frustrated, rendered abortive, distorted by mortality from Pan into Satan, into a Mephistopheles mocking himself in order to feel alive; Christianity, once heroic in martyrs for its intense faith, now pleading weakly for intense belief in anything, even Godhead itself. (In the play it is Cybele, the pagan Earth Mother, who makes the assertion with authority: "Our Father, Who Art!" to the dying Brown, as it is she who tries to inspire Dion Anthony with her certainty in life for its own sake.) . . .
>
> Dion's mask of Pan which he puts on as a boy is not only a defense against the world for the supersensitive painter-poet underneath it, but also an integral part of his character as the artist. The world is not only blind to the man beneath, but it also sneers at and condemns the Pan-mask it sees. After that Dion's inner self retrogresses along the line of Christian resignation until it partakes of the nature of the Saint while at the same time the outer Pan is slowly transformed by his struggle with reality into Mephistopheles. It is as Mephistopheles he falls stricken at Brown's feet after having condemned Brown to destruction by willing him his mask, but, this mask falling off as he dies, it is the Saint who kisses Brown's feet in abject contrition and pleads as a little boy to a big brother to tell him a prayer.

If this is the best O'Neill himself can do by way of explaining his symbolism and masks, then it is obvious that he did not succeed in illuminating his theme. *The Great God Brown* is not a major work, but possesses major importance because of its effort to present through the medium of the theatre an interpretation of hitherto baffling manifestations of behavior.

O'Neill's next work, for which *The Great God Brown* may be regarded as experimental preparation, is from every point of view unique in contemporary drama. Indeed I am convinced that the play on which the greatest variety of persons would agree as the outstanding drama of our time is *Strange Interlude*. I have seen all sorts of faces glow with the memory of the Theatre Guild's production, which, in spite of the play's nine acts, held its audience spellbound for four hundred and twenty-six performances in New York City alone. In addition several road companies achieved extraordinary runs for a play making such demands upon its audiences —for example, nine weeks in Los Angeles and seventeen weeks in Chicago. Nor did *Strange Interlude* escape the distinction of censorship. The City of Boston decided that it could not endanger the morals of its citizens by exposing them to the influence of an immoral play, and so *Strange Interlude* was banned there. Promptly the New York Theatre Guild rented a theatre in the near-by town of Quincy, Massachusetts, arranged special train service for those Boston citizens who refused to accept the Boston city administration as their moral and cultural guardian, and kept the play running there for a month.

In *Strange Interlude* O'Neill evolved a new psychological technique utilizing *speech alone,* whereby each character used *two* different types of expression. One is the everyday speech of human intercourse wherewith we carry on the necessary business of life, curbing our ego, adjusting ourself to the external world. The other is the speech revealing the true ego, whose desires and motives must be kept hidden because of those "curbs of civilization" which Freud found everywhere thwarting the ego-satisfaction of the individual. These hidden thoughts of the characters, *inaudible* of course to their fellow men (the other characters in the play), are meant only for the audience. Thus O'Neill hoped to reveal his characters *in their psychological entirety,* struggling, as we all do, between inner needs and outer adjustments.

To call those speeches through which O'Neill's characters express their hidden selves "asides," is to give a wrong impression of their import. The purpose of the "aside," practically abandoned by modern drama, was to withhold from other characters *factual* information upon which the "plot" hinged. Thus until the moment of denouement only the audience was to know that Grandfather's will was hidden in the chimney. With revealing the *hidden* in the Freudian sense, the clumsy "aside" had nothing whatever to do. On the other hand, the soliloquy, as used by Shakespeare, is related in spirit and psychological content to O'Neill's technique of the spoken self-revelation. To the reader the two types of speeches offer no difficulty because the regular dialogue appears in larger type than the self-revealing speeches. But in the theatre the speaking by each character of two different kinds of "lines" presents a very real problem. This problem the Theatre Guild solved by reducing it to its simplest terms. Before a character began to utter his hidden thoughts, he waited for the space of a split second while the action almost imperceptibly halted, and then expressed these thoughts quite naturally. The flow of the play was actually uninterrupted. Within a few moments after the curtain rose, the audience swung into the double rhythm and soon differentiated with perfect ease between the characters' ordinary dialogue and the utterance of his inner thoughts— a miracle of directing and acting.

The question is repeatedly asked, Does O'Neill regard this

as the ideal technique for the psychological play of today? Obviously he does not, since he fails to use it again in *Mourning Becomes Electra,* a play at least as complicated psychologically as *Strange Interlude.* The answer, however, is that O'Neill is an experimental artist, interested in evolving techniques only for his own use. Besides, there is more than one technique for presenting psychological conflicts, as Clifford Odets, for example, has demonstrated in his play *Golden Boy.*

The characters of *Strange Interlude* are typical of the great middle class which forms the majority of theatre audiences everywhere. Audiences, therefore, could identify themselves with the college professor, his daughter, the minor novelist, the doctor-scientist and the successful businessman, all satisfyingly recognizable. These characters underwent no experiences that are not the common lot of all, even though for purposes of drama such experiences had to be intensified. And not content with depicting a cross section of life at a given moment, O'Neill brings his characters from youth to the beginning of age, and so conveys another experience common to all — the passing of life.

Finally, although audiences who only heard the lines in the theatre could get little more than a suggestion of the drama's symbolism, they were carried away by the impact of its leading character, Nina. For Nina is Woman Incarnate in her struggle to attain fulfillment in an androcentric world. In this struggle lies Nina's tragedy, which is the universal tragedy of woman, namely, that her true fulfillment can be attained only through her femaleness, that she can realize her essential self only through the male element, through men. But she has learned that it is not enough, in a world in which the male is driven by his nature to realize his creative urge quite apart from sex, to function solely as a female. This contradictory nature of woman's essential self is the source of an inner conflict, intensified in this contemporary age by the fact that our social mechanism for living lags behind the dual demands of woman for human as well as female fulfillment. In Nina, however, O'Neill stresses with powerful emphasis woman's struggle to satisfy her supreme need of female fulfillment. If future generations desire to discover what was the postwar, the post-Freudian concept of woman, — not of the working woman, or the feminist, or the surviving parasite woman, but of this age's concept of the essence of woman, — they will turn, I think, to *Strange Interlude*.

When the play opens, Nina is already the victim of the erotic frustration which was to condition her life. Gordon, the aviator, her betrothed, has perished in flames in the World War. Nina's psychotic condition is due not so much to his death as to the fact that he left her without the consummation of their passion, and the possibility of bearing his child to fulfill and comfort her. For this Nina blames her father, Professor Leeds. And justly so, since the Professor, having unconsciously transferred his libido from his dead wife to his daughter, was filled with a jealous hatred of the young man she loved and had extracted a promise from Gordon that he would not jeopardize Nina's whole future by marrying her just before he left for the front. Gordon was a man of "honor" and so he left Nina virginal, to be obsessed by her image of him all her life. As the result of her frustration, the lover who never attained reality now becomes transmogrified into the *ideal* lover who would have given her everything body and soul desired. So Nina, almost insane, begins to seek in life compensation for the loss of this ideal lover of her dreams. At the beginning of the play when we meet Nina's father, soon to die, we also meet the first of the men who are to be bound up in Nina's compensatory demands to satisfy her woman's needs. This is Charles Marsden, "good old Charlie," from the Freudian point of view especially, one of O'Neill's most successful characters. There is nothing in the whole of *Strange Interlude* more brilliant than the long speech of hidden thoughts with which Charlie opens the play. Before quoting it in its entirety, I shall preface it with O'Neill's description of the room we see as the curtain rises: —

The library of Professor Leeds' home in a small university town in New England. This room is at the front part of his house with windows opening on the strip of lawn between the house and the quiet residential street. It is a small room with a low ceiling. The furniture has been selected with a love for old New England pieces. The walls are lined almost to the ceiling with glassed-in bookshelves. These are packed with books, principally editions, many of them old and rare, of the ancient classics in the original Greek and Latin, of the later classics in French and German and Italian, of all the English authors who wrote while s was still like an f and a few since then, the most modern probably being Thackeray. The atmosphere of the room is that of a cosy, cultured retreat, sedulously built as a sanctuary where, secure with the culture of the past at his back, a fugitive from reality can view the present safely from a distance, as a superior with condescending disdain, pity, and even amusement. . . .

There is one entrance, a door in the right wall, rear. It is late afternoon of a day in August. Sunshine, cooled and dimmed in the shade of trees, fills the room with a soothing light.

The sound of a Maid's Voice — a middle-aged woman — explaining familiarly but respectfully from the right, and Marsden enters. He is a tall thin man of thirty-five, meticulously well-dressed in tweeds of distinctly English tailoring, his appearance that of an Anglicized New England gentleman. His face is too long for its width, his nose is high and narrow, his forehead broad, his mild blue eyes those of a dreamy self-analyst, his thin lips ironical and a bit sad. There is an indefinable feminine quality about him, but it is nothing apparent in either appearance or act. His manner is cool and poised. He speaks with a careful ease, as one who listens to his own conversation. He has long fragile hands, and the stoop to his shoulders of a man weak muscularly, who has never liked athletics and has always been regarded as of delicate constitution. The main point about his personality is a quiet charm, a quality of appealing, inquisitive friendliness, always willing to listen, eager to sympathize, to like and to be liked.

MARSDEN

(*Standing just inside the door, his tall, stooped figure leaning back against the books—nodding back at the maid and smiling kindly*)

I'll wait in here, Mary.

(*His eyes follow her for a second, then return to gaze around the room slowly with an appreciative relish for the familiar significance of the books. He smiles affectionately and his amused voice recites the words with a rhetorical resonance.*)

Sanctum Sanctorum!

(*His voice takes on a monotonous musing quality, his eyes stare idly at his drifting thoughts.*)

How perfectly the Professor's unique haven! . . .

(*He smiles.*)

Primly classical . . . when New Englander meets Greek! . . .

(*Looking at the books now*)

He hasn't added one book in years . . . how old was I when I first came here? . . . six . . . with my father . . . father . . . how dim his face has grown! . . . he wanted to speak to me just before he died . . . the hospital . . . smell of iodoform in the cool halls . . . hot summer . . . I bent down . . . his voice had withdrawn so far away . . . I couldn't understand him . . . what son can ever understand? . . . always too near, too soon, too distant or too late! . . .

(*His face has become sad with a memory of the bewildered suffering of the adolescent boy he had been at the time of his father's death. Then he shakes his head, flinging off his thoughts, and makes himself walk about the room.*)

What memories on such a smiling afternoon! . . . this pleasant old town after three months . . . I won't go to Europe again . . . couldn't write a line there . . . how answer the fierce question of all those dead and maimed? . . . too big a job for me! . . .

(*He sighs—then self-mockingly*)

But back here . . . it is the interlude that gently questions . . . in this town dozing . . . decorous bodies moving with circumspection through the afternoons . . . their habits affectionately chronicled . . . an excuse for weaving amusing words . . . my novels . . . not of cosmic importance, hardly . . .

(*Then self-reassuringly*)

but there is a public to cherish them, evidently . . . and I can write! . . . more than one can say of these modern sex-yahoos! . . . I must start work tomorrow . . . I'd like to use the Professor in a novel sometime . . . and his wife . . . seems impossible she's been dead six years . . . so aggressively his wife! . . . poor Professor! Now it's Nina who bosses him . . . but that's different . . . she has bossed me, too, ever since she was a baby . . . she's a woman now . . . known love and death . . . Gordon brought down in flames . . . two days before the armistice . . . what fiendish irony! . . . his wonderful athlete's body . . . her lover . . . charred bones in a cage of twisted steel . . . no wonder she broke down . . . Mother said she's become quite queer lately . . . Mother seemed jealous of my concern . . . why have I never fallen in love with Nina? . . . could I . . . that way . . . used to dance her on my knee . . . sit her on my lap . . . even now she'd never think anything about it . . . but sometimes the scent of her hair and skin . . . like a dreamy drug . . . dreamy! . . . there's the rub! . . . all dreams with me! . . . my sex life among the phantoms! . . .

(*He grins torturedly*)

Why? . . . oh, this digging in gets nowhere . . . to the devil with sex! . . . our impotent pose of today to beat the loud drum on fornication! . . . boasters . . . eunuchs parading with the phallus! . . . giving themselves away . . . whom do they fool? . . . not even themselves! . . .

(*His face suddenly full of an intense pain and disgust*)

Ugh! . . . always that memory! . . . why can't I ever forget? . . . as sickeningly clear as if it were yesterday . . . prep school . . . Easter vacation . . . Fatty Boggs and Jack Frazer . . . that house of cheap vice . . . one dollar! . . . why did I go? . . . Jack, the dead game sport . . . how I admired him! . . . afraid of his taunts . . . he pointed to the Italian girl . . . "Take her!" . . . daring me . . . I went . . . miserably frightened . . . what a pig she was! . . . pretty vicious face under caked powder and rouge . . . surly and contemptuous . . . lumpy body . . . short legs and thick ankles . . . slums of Naples . . . "What you gawkin' about? Git a move on, kid" . . . kid! . . . I *was* only a kid! . . . sixteen . . . test of manhood . . . ashamed to face Jack again unless . . . fool! . . . I might have lied to him! . . . but I honestly thought that wench would feel humiliated if I . . . oh, stupid kid! . . . back at the hotel I waited till they were asleep . . . then sobbed . . . thinking of Mother . . . feeling I had defiled her . . . and myself . . . forever! . . .

(*Mocking bitterly*)

"Nothing half so sweet in life as love's young dream," what? . . .

(*He gets to his feet impatiently*)

Why does my mind always have to dwell on that? . . . too silly . . . no importance really . . . an incident such as any boy of my age . . .

(*He hears someone coming quickly from the right and turns expectantly. Professor Leeds enters . . .*)

How could we possibly know more about Charlie if a psychological novelist devoted a volume to him! All that Charlie says and does during the play are only variations upon the theme here presented with such clarity. It has always distressed me, however, that O'Neill, with his instinct for what is right in the theatre, should have opened his play with this extraordinary speech, giving it to his audiences before the flow between actors and audience has been established and before audiences have been able to master his technique of the utterance of hidden thoughts. For the play-reader it is perfect as an opening speech and O'Neill's own devotion to play-reading, which he prefers to the theatre, furnishes an interesting commentary on the point of view of this book, that the ephemeral life of a work of art in the theatre is of little consequence in comparison with its immortality on the printed page.

For the unhappy Nina, longing for love, the sexless Charlie could have no erotic interest. But even while her father is lying dead, Charlie assumes his place in her life: she makes compensatory use of him by substituting him for the father-element she has now lost. Seeking comfort she slips onto Charlie's lap like a little girl, and as she confesses to him her tortured efforts to adjust to life, after the loss of Gordon, she unconsciously calls him "Father." And it is Charlie, the mother-bound, himself so afraid of life, who perfectly understands Nina when she says to him:—

> The mistake began when God was created in a male image. Of course, women would see Him that way, but men should have been gentlemen enough, remembering their mothers, to make God a woman! But the God of Gods — the Boss — has always been a man. That makes life so perverted, and death so unnatural. We should have imagined life as created in the birth-pain of God the Mother. Then we would understand why we, Her children, have inherited pain, for we would know that our life's rhythm beats from Her great heart, torn with the agony of love and birth. And we would feel that death meant reunion with Her, a passing back into Her substance, blood of Her blood again, peace of Her peace! Now wouldn't that be more logical and satisfying than having God a male whose chest thunders with egotism and is too hard for tired heads and thoroughly comfortless? Wouldn't it, Charlie?

To which Charlie answers "with a strange passionate eagerness": —

Yes! It would indeed! It would, Nina!

Charlie, torn between his love for her and his impotent fear of life, persuades Nina to marry Sam Evans, a former friend of Gordon, kind, boyish, with the potentiality of success, who worships her. She does not love him but, as she says, "No more depths, please God!" and above all she wants children, "so I can give myself." But when she is happy at last in her pregnancy, she is told secretly by Sam's mother that she dare not bear this child because of the "curse" of insanity in Sam's family. She urges Nina to pick "a healthy male to breed by," so that Sam shall not succumb to worry over not giving her the child he knows she so desires. When Sam nearly does succumb and is no longer able to work and her own longing for her lost child and for motherhood will not be stilled, she turns to young Dr. Ned Darrell, another friend of the dead Gordon and of Sam. Knowing that physical attraction exists between them, she makes her plea to him in the name of science, in the name of Sam's happiness and sanity and her own, and Darrell, his desire for her growing, rationalizing as the scientist dealing with "guinea pigs," superior to moral scruples, agrees: —

Yes — yes, Nina — yes — for your happiness — in that spirit!

But his hidden thoughts express themselves "fiercely triumphant": —

I shall be happy for a while!

Yes, Ned is happy and so is Nina, who in those "dear, wonderful afternoons of happiness" with him at last knows the ecstasy of passion.

Her love for Ned becomes so strong that she threatens to tell Sam the truth and ask for a divorce. But this shocks the doctor in Ned—he is here to help Sam, not to destroy him—so he tells Sam that Nina is going to have a baby and departs for Europe without seeing Nina again. At first her anguish at the loss of her lover, "gone forever, like Gordon," seems greater than she can bear, but Sam's rapture and new vitality together with her own deep sense of the fulfillment of motherhood at last help to still the pain.

When next we see Nina over a year has passed. Although the mere mention of Ned still shakes her to the depths, contentment has come with the birth of her son, significantly named Gordon. The unsuspecting Sam, filled with paternal pride and happiness, is on the high road to success. Charlie, plunged into grief over the death of his adored mother, more and more seeks his solace in the orbit of Nina. Ned has been wasting himself in Europe, for he can no more get Nina out of his blood than she can cease longing for him. He returns, and this time it is he who wildly demands the divorce and the possession of Nina and his child. This, Nina now realizes, can never be. Sam must keep the child they gave him and the child must keep Sam as his father. But Nina knows too that she could not endure losing her lover again and that he desires her too much to leave her. After Ned has found it impossible to carry out his threat of telling the truth to Sam, Nina knows she has won the victory, that she has successfully established the pattern of her life. And with this we reach that climactic scene which will always live for those who saw it as one of the unforgettable experiences of the theatre. It begins when Nina realizes that Ned will never be able to tell Sam the truth.

NINA

(*With a strange triumphant calm*)

There! . . . that's settled with for all time! . . . poor Ned! . . . how crushed he looks! . . . I mustn't let Sam look at him! . . .

(*She steps between them protectingly*)

Where's Charlie, Sam?

MARSDEN

(*Appearing from the hall*)

Here, Nina. Always here!

(*He comes to her, smiling with assurance.*)

NINA

(*Suddenly with a strange unnatural elation — looking from one to the other with triumphant possession*)

Yes, you're here, Charlie — always! And you, Sam — and Ned!

(*With a strange gaiety*)

Sit down, all of you! Make yourselves at home! You are my three men! This is your home with me!

(*Then in a strange half-whisper*)

Ssshh! I thought I heard the baby. You must all sit down and be very quiet. You must not wake our baby.

(*Mechanically the three sit down, careful to make no noise — Evans in his old place by the table, Marsden at center, Darrell on the sofa at right. They sit staring before them in silence. Nina remains standing, dominating them, a little behind and to the left of Marsden*)

DARRELL

(*Thinking abjectly*)

I couldn't! . . . there are things one may not do and live with oneself afterwards . . . there are things one may not say . . . memory is too full of echoes! . . . there are secrets one must not reveal . . . memory is lined with mirrors! . . . and he was too happy! . . . to kill happiness is a worse murder than taking life! . . . I gave him that happiness! . . . Sam deserves my happiness! . . . God bless you, Sam! . . .

(*Then in a strange objective tone — thinking*)

My experiment with the guinea pigs has been a success . . . the ailing one, Sam, and the female, Nina, have been restored to health and normal function . . . only the other male, Ned, seems to have suffered deterioration. . . .

(*Then bitterly humble*)

Nothing left but to accept her terms . . . I love her . . . I can help to make her happy . . . half a loaf is better . . . to a starving man . . .

(*Glancing over at Evans — bitterly gloating*)

And your child is mine! . . . your wife is mine! . . . your happiness is mine! . . . may you enjoy my happiness, her husband! . . .

EVANS

(*Looking at Darrell affectionately*)

Sure good to see Ned again . . . a real friend if there ever was one . . . looks blue about something . . . oh, that's right, Charlie said his old man had kicked in . . . his old man was rich . . . that's an idea . . . I'll bet he'd put up that capital . . .

(*Then ashamed of himself*)

Aw hell, what's the matter with me? . . . he's no sooner here than I start . . . he's done enough . . . forget it! . . . now anyway . . . he looks pretty dissipated . . . too many women . . . ought to get married and settle down . . . tell him that, if I didn't think he'd laugh at me giving him advice . . . but he'll soon realize I'm not the old Sam he knew . . . I suppose Nina's been boasting about that already . . . she's proud . . . she's helped me . . . she's a wonderful wife and mother . . .

(*Looking up at her — solicitously*)

She acted a bit nervous just now . . . queer . . . like she used to . . . haven't noticed her that way in a long time . . . suppose it's the excitement of Ned turning up . . . mustn't let her get overexcited . . . bad for the baby's milk . . .

MARSDEN

(*Glancing furtively over his shoulder at Nina — broodingly thinking*)

She's the old queer Nina now . . . the Nina I could never fathom . . . her three men! and we are! . . . I? . . . yes, more deeply than either of the others since I serve for nothing . . . a queer kind of love, maybe . . . I am not ordinary! . . . our child . . . what could she mean by that? . . . child of us three? . . . on the surface, that's insane . . . but I felt when she said it there was something in it . . . she has strange devious intuitions that tap the hidden currents of life . . . dark intermingling currents that become the one stream of desire . . . I feel with regard to Nina, my life queerly identified with Sam's and Darrell's . . . her child is the child of our three loves for her . . . I should like to believe that . . . I should like to be her husband in a sense . . . and the father of a child, after my fashion . . . I could forgive her everything . . . permit everything . . .

(*Determinedly*)

And I do forgive! . . . and I will not meddle hereafter more than is necessary to guard her happiness, and Sam's and our baby's . . . as for Darrell, I am no longer jealous of him . . . she is only using his love for her own happiness . . . he can never take her away from me! . . .

NINA

(*More and more strangely triumphant*)

My three men! I feel their desires converge in me! . . . to form one complete beautiful male desire which I absorb . . . and am whole . . . they dissolve in me, their life is my life . . . I am pregnant with the three! . . . husband! . . . lover! . . . father! . . . and the fourth man! . . . little man! . . . little Gordon! . . . he is mine too! . . . that makes it perfect! . . .

(*With an extravagant suppressed exultance*)

Why, I should be the proudest woman on earth! . . . I should be the happiest woman in the world! . . .

(*Then suppressing an outbreak of hysterical triumphant laughter only by a tremendous effort*)

Ha-ha . . . only I better knock wood . . .

(*She raps with both knuckles in a fierce tattoo on the table*)

before God the Father hears my happiness! . . .

In this extraordinary scene O'Neill uses his technique for the expression of hidden thoughts not only with intense dramatic effectiveness but also at its most revelatory. What every woman desires is a perfect mating: to find united in one man the passion or lover-element, the friendship or husband-element, and the protection or father-element. This consummation which Nina was convinced she would have realized in Gordon, she now gathers for herself out of three men. And out of these three male elements grows the ultimate female completion: to be the mother of a man-child. No dramatist of today has probed the psyche of woman with so seeing an eye.

From this climax we gradually descend. Eleven years later we see how Nina's and Ned's passion has died down, although it still at intervals brings them together, through the bond of their son. But their tie now exacerbates, instead of rejoicing them. Ned, without a centre for his life, has become a frustrated scientist. Desultorily he works in a biological experimental laboratory in the West Indies, to the head of which a younger man has risen. And young Gordon, his son, brings him pain, not only the pain of seeing him Sam's adored and adoring son, but also of knowing that the boy hates him because he senses a bond between Ned and his mother which he regards as an affront to Sam. And Nina, too, sees this son, on whom the libido of approaching middle age has fastened itself tenaciously, turn away from her to companionship with Sam, whose counterpart he seems destined to become. Sam, a contented Babbitt, stands as the one seeming justification for Nina's arrogating to herself the right to dominate other lives for her own fulfillment. And good old Charlie? Already he feels with joy that Nina, near the end of her active sex-life, turns more and more to him for sympathy and understanding.

The end comes as presaged. Ten years later Ned has finally broken the destructive bond that held him to Nina. He can never now be the great scientist he once dreamed of, but he can and will selflessly devote the rest of his life to biological research. Before he passes out of Nina's life forever, he performs one act of vital import for his son. Nina, maddened by the possessive mother's jealousy of the girl her son loves, is about to tell her the lie that she dare not marry Gordon because of the insanity in his "father's" family. Ned prevents this by asking the girl to discredit whatever Nina may say to her because "she is morbidly jealous and subject to queer delusions." But Sam's last illness purges Nina, and after his death she no longer struggles to keep the life-cycle from completing itself. Quietly she gives her son up to his own love-life, and as the airplane bearing him and his bride away circles high over her, she calls to him "with tortured exultance": —

> Fly up to Heaven, Gordon! Fly with your love to heaven! Fly always! Never crash to earth like my old Gordon! . . .

So the woman loses her man-child. And can the lover, lover no more, turn into husband? No, Ned and Nina know the impossibility of that — "Our ghosts would torture us to death," says Nina, and Ned kisses her hand tenderly in farewell. So Charlie comes into his own as Nina turns to him for the protecting father-love in which she will find peace at last. And the curtain descends on Nina "so contentedly weary with life," her head on Charlie's shoulder, fallen quietly asleep while "he watches with contented eyes the evening shadows closing in around them."

Not to have read *Strange Interlude* is to have missed a superlative experience in contemporary play-reading. It reads like a novel, and for months held its place as a national best-seller. It has been translated into many languages and produced in various foreign countries. Breaking new ground in its subject matter and defying all conventions of the theatre, *Strange Interlude* has nevertheless already established itself as a classic.

Before O'Neill wrote his second great psychological drama, *Mourning Becomes Electra,* he turned again to the question of faith, in the play *Dynamo,* which, marking a schism in his philosophical outlook, leads to the religious absolutism of his latest play, *Days Without End.* Unless his future work should change its status, *Mourning Becomes Electra* must be regarded as the high point of his achievement.

This strikingly conceived play is a tragedy in which the Greek concept of fate is re-stated by O'Neill in terms of its contemporary analogue. For enlightened people to believe today that human beings behave as they do because they *must,* in no way implies a reversion to fatalism. On the contrary, it implies enhanced understanding of the truth that the individual's behavior is conditioned by inescapable influences. To our knowledge of the laws of heredity and environment there has been added, thanks to Freud, new knowledge of psychological laws — which are quite as important in shaping human life. The great Greek tragedies all depict the inexorable working-out of laws of fate that drive even the greatest among men to a doom decreed in advance by the gods. In man's struggle to assume control of his fate he realized more and more that the all-important factor was to acquire an understanding of the *nature* of the forces dominating his destiny. We see now that the great laws of life control us just as completely as they did the Greeks. But because we understand their nature, we know further that unless we direct these laws and rob them of their destructive influences on the individual, they will continue to provide a fate that, like the Greek prototype, ends in tragedy. What could bring this truth before audiences of today more forcefully than a drama in which our contemporary psychological interpretation of fate would be portrayed?

This is the importance of O'Neill's drama, based on the legend of the House of Atreus, on the unescapable fate of its daughter, Electra. How closely, in his American tragedy, O'Neill follows Æschylus or Euripides or how far he departs from them, is quite unimportant, as is the fact that there is a resemblance between the names of some of his American characters and those of their Greek originals. And while the use of a group of gossiping New England townspeople in the guise of a metamorphosed Greek chorus may be interesting technically, this, too, is devoid of basic importance. Immediately significant, however, is O'Neill's evocative title. At once we know that mourning becomes Electra because it *must* become her, because she is pre-destined to mourning. Her very name, A-lektra, according to legend, signifies the Un-mated. The gods have decreed for her a tragic fate.

Unerring psychologist that he is, O'Neill selects as a time for this play of contemporary significance the close of the Civil War. Why does he do this? Because the identification audiences would have to make, if they were listening to characters of our day, would be so intensely subjective as to lose all objectivity. But by placing us in a period not too remote from, yet not actually, our own, and by confronting us with men and women in costumes different from ours, O'Neill enables us to retain sufficient emotional detachment not to be completely engulfed by what might seem devastating exposures of our own lives. We know by the terms in which O'Neill refers to war in the play that he has not the slightest concern with the Civil War, but is here indicting all war. We know that he has learned from what he saw after the World War how men disintegrate morally through participation in war, and that Orin Mannon, changed by his Civil War experiences from a happy and gentle boy into a nerve-shattered and brutalized creature, is none other than the postwar "hero" of our time. There is a sound psychological principle utilized by O'Neill in providing us with emotional protection so that we may observe with a calmer and therefore with a more seeing eye the unfolding of his tragedy.

In *Mourning Becomes Electra* O'Neill uses neither masks nor the technique of the utterance of hidden thoughts. As a result he makes tremendous demands on the art of the theatre, calling for such effects as striking facial resemblances between mother and daughter, between father, son and distant cousin, and for psychologically revealing physical changes in individual characters almost beyond the power of make-up. In addition, the descriptions of the characters, of their appearance, their reactions, the inner basis for and outer expression of their behavior, as well as his directions for every aspect of the production, are worked out with painstaking care. Once more it is beyond the power of the theatre to realize more than a fraction of the subtle detail which fills almost every page of the printed play. No more understanding production of this play could be expected than that given it by the Theatre Guild. But if ever a play abounds in riches for the reader, it is *Mourning Becomes Electra.*

O'Neill calls his drama "A Trilogy" and divides it into three parts: "Homecoming"; "The Hunted"; "The Haunted." Its great length, manifesting no compromise with conventional Broadway standards, again necessitated the arrangements required by *Strange Interlude.* The first part of the trilogy was played between 5:30 o'clock and the dinner interval; the second and third parts took up the remainder of the evening. And in spite of the unusual demands which it makes upon audiences, *Mourning Becomes Electra* had a run of one hundred and fifty-seven performances in New York and its two companies equaled the same number on the road. That this play, uncompromising in treatment, and above all a tragedy, should achieve popular success can be attributed only to the genius of O'Neill in illuminating those dark causes of our behavior which dominate our lives.

In a small New England seaport lives the family of Ezra Mannon, the town's most prominent citizen, a rich shipowner, who has been its judge and Mayor and is now a General fighting with Grant. The play opens after Lee's surrender. General Mannon is expected home any day. The prospect of his return fills both his wife and his daughter with horror, although for different reasons. Christine, his wife, with her French blood and voluptuous beauty, is alien in every instinct to the New England heritage of the Mannons. Having suffered since her wedding-night from the emotional torture of this marriage, she has, at the age of forty, at last found ecstasy with a lover who has become her whole existence. Lavinia, the daughter of her marriage — the Electra of the play — is twenty-three. But while her facial resemblance to her mother is marked, her body is flat, her look is hard, and she wears her beautiful, copper-colored hair pulled back, so that it shall in no way resemble her mother's similar crowning splendor. Lavinia is filled with violent hatred of her mother, hatred that began in her earliest childhood when Christine, unable to feel affection for this child who symbolized the disgust of her wedding-night, repulsed her little daughter's proffers of love. But by the time her son, Orin, was born, Christine had become resigned. Her husband had long been away in the Mexican War, this boy seemed *her* child only and she expended upon him all her starved emotions.

Thus the Mannon family constellation, the counterpart of which we may behold anywhere, established itself. Lavinia, hungry for love, turned to her father, who became the sole object of her devotion. But jealousy consumes her, jealousy of the beautiful mother, whom her beloved father, for all his Mannon repression, so clearly adores, and whom the younger brother passionately worships. "I know you, Vinnie!" cries Christine, in a terrible scene of accusation between mother and daughter. . . . "You've tried to become the wife of your father and the mother of Orin! You've always schemed to steal my place!" To which Lavinia replies: "No! It's you who have stolen all love from me since the time I was born!" When we add to this Ezra's dislike of his son, because of the too close relation between the boy and his mother, and Orin's antipathy for his father who stands between him and his mother, we have completed the psychological family picture. The entire play may be said to consist of the logical working-out of the family's fate, as the result of this psychological conditioning to which Freud first discovered the deciphering key.

Over Christine's protest, the Mannon concept of duty prevails, and Orin is sent off by his father to the war. Fearful for his life and loveless once more, Christine is attracted to a man who looks like Orin. This is Captain Adam Brant, the unknown son of Ezra's uncle, who had been disinherited because he loved and married a French Canadian nursemaid. Adam, bitterly resentful of the Mannons' treatment of his mother, vows vengeance on them, but his vow collapses when he finds himself loving and loved by Christine. Behaving with the folly of a woman desperately in love, Christine invites Brant to the Mannon home, in the absence of Ezra and Orin, where he is to avert suspicion by pretending to court Lavinia. But if Christine was sexually attracted to the unknown cousin because he looks like her son Orin, Lavinia is equally attracted to him because he looks like her father! And her perceptions, sharpened by ever-present jealousy, soon arouse in her suspicions of the relation between her mother and this man whom she could love and who is so cruelly betraying her. Following her mother to an assignation with Brant, she hears their kisses and their words of love behind a closed door. How can she protect her father against this infamous blow, the Mannon name against scandal? Confronting her mother with the truth, Lavinia extracts the lying promise from the desperate Christine that she will never see Adam Brant again.

Realizing that there can be no future for her and Adam while Ezra lives, this frustrated woman, for whom love has now become everything, determines to administer poison to her husband in such a way as to create the impression that he died during one of his heart attacks. On the very night of his homecoming, goaded beyond endurance by his physical possession of her, as well as by his suspicions, Christine, after deliberately inducing a heart attack by telling Ezra that Brant is her lover, gives him the poison in place of his medicine. He utters a whispered "Help! Vinnie!" and at once Lavinia appears, dazed with sleep, answering the beloved father's need that had penetrated to her unconscious. After directly accusing Christine, Ezra dies and when, her strength gone, she faints at the foot of the bed, the inculpating box slips out of her hand and is found by the horrified Lavinia.

On the day of her father's funeral Orin returns. His loathing of war, his agony of fear, for which he has overcompensated by stupid acts of "heroism," have turned the boy into a pitiful neurotic. There is no more shocking indictment of war in contemporary drama than Orin's hysterical disclosures of how it has destroyed him, physically, emotionally, spiritually. Orin is unmoved by his father's death, but when he learns from Lavinia that his mother has murdered him because of a lover, he is crazed with jealousy. The impulse to kill, which war has made easy for him, urges him to vengeance upon Brant. So he carries out with Lavinia, also driven on by thwarted emotions, her carefully laid plan to kill Brant at night on his own ship, in such a way as to make it appear that he has been robbed and murdered by waterfront thieves. No better example can be found of O'Neill's extraordinary dialogue in this play than the lines immediately following Orin's killing of Brant:—

ORIN: By God, he does look like Father!
LAVINIA: No! Come along!

Orin: (*as if talking to himself*) This is like my dream. I've killed him before—over and over.

Lavinia: Orin!

Orin: Do you remember me telling you how the faces of the men I killed came back and changed to Father's face and finally became my own? (*He smiles grimly*) He looks like me too! Maybe I've committed suicide!

Lavinia (*frightenedly—grabbing his arm*): Hurry! Someone may come!

Orin (*not heeding her, still staring at Brant—strangely*): If I had been he I would have done what he did! I would have loved her as he loved her—and killed Father too—for her sake!

Lavinia (*tensely—shaking him by the arm*): Orin, for God's sake, will you stop talking crazy and come along? . . .

After he brutally tells his mother that he has murdered her lover, and Christine in hopeless anguish kills herself, Orin again reveals himself and the truth when he cries:

Why didn't I let her believe burglars killed him? She wouldn't have hated me then! She would have forgotten him! She would have turned to me! (*In a final frenzy of self-denunciation*) I murdered her!

The third part of the play, "The Haunted," makes clear how the fate that finally closes in upon this sister and brother moves with the same logic which, given their family constellation, led to the tragic events already witnessed. A year has passed since the violent deaths of Ezra Mannon, Adam Brant and Christine. In an effort to make Orin forget, but also because of her terror lest he confess the truth to Peter and Hazel, a normal brother and sister who have been their lifelong friends, Lavinia has taken Orin on a long sea voyage. Orin and Hazel are unofficially betrothed, but Peter has received only cold rebuffs from the repressed Lavinia, whose impulses were always those of hatred, not love. During this year away, an extraordinary change has come over Lavinia. Freed by her mother's death from the necessity of repressing her likeness to Christine, Lavinia has let this likeness develop into complete identification. She acquires her mother's physical voluptuousness, she affects her favourite color of rich green set off with her now softly worn masses of copper-colored hair. And she has also released her inherited desire for love. During the voyage Lavinia was determined to make a stay on some South Sea Islands—those Islands which all through the play are used by O'Neill to symbolize the land of heart's desire, of wish-fulfillment, whose happiness and security will still the tortured soul of man. It was to such Islands that Brant planned to take Christine. It was on such Islands that Ezra hoped he might at last break down the wall between Christine and himself. It was of such Islands that Orin dreamed on the battlefield, identifying them with his incestuously desired mother: "The breaking of the waves was your voice. The sky was the same color as your eyes. The warm sand was like your skin. The whole island was you. . . ." These Islands finally set Lavinia free. The simple love of the natives, "without knowledge of sin," banishes her obsession with hate and death. The feeling that men desired her at last seemed right and beautiful. Become her mother's very self, Lavinia, on her return, responds to New England Peter with an ardor that thrills but also shocks him, when she passionately kisses him and says:—

> We'll be married soon, won't we. . . . We'll make an island for ourselves on land, and we'll have children and love them and teach them to love life so that they can never be possessed by hate and death!

In this affirmation of life Lavinia has momentarily forgotten her brother. Orin has not been able to recover from all the emotional shocks to which he has been subjected and has disintegrated until his condition is now hopelessly psychotic. "Forget the dead!" commands Lavinia as he shudders and cannot enter the Mannon house. But Orin, crushed with the guilt of having murdered his mother, cannot forget the dead. Lavinia lives in terror lest he ruin her chance of happiness by making good his threat of confession. So she dares not marry Peter, because she dares not leave Orin out of her sight.

If Lavinia has become her mother incarnate, Orin has, even in physical resemblance, become identified with his father, because, having transferred to his changed sister the incestuous feelings that bound him to his mother, he now stands in the same emotional relation to Lavinia in which Ezra had stood to Christine. Orin understands this and he understands too that in Lavinia's heart there is the same death-wish that drove his mother to murder his father. So, impelled by his fear of separation from Vinnie as well as by his inner need for expiation, Orin writes a history of the "crimes" of the Mannon family, which he hands in a sealed envelope to the bewildered Hazel to be given by her to Peter on the day before his and Vinnie's wedding. When Lavinia, in desperation, promises to do anything he wants to if he will only take this envelope away from Hazel, Orin extracts as the price her giving up Peter for him. All her loathing is driven into the open by this incestuous plea, with which Orin insanely hopes to bind her to him, and Lavinia at last gives overt utterance to her death-wish:

> I hate you! I wish you were dead! You're too vile to live! You'd kill yourself if you weren't such a coward! . . .

Stricken by these words, Orin suddenly realizes that "Death is an Island of Peace too," and as Peter enters the room he casually announces that he is going "to clean his pistol." Lavinia clings madly to Peter, her one hope of life, talking volubly to drown out the sound she wants to hear, the sound she knows will come. It comes; and as Peter rushes out, she turns to the portraits of the Mannons on the walls, saying defiantly: "I'm Mother's daughter — not one of you! I'll live in spite of you!"

And desperately Lavinia still tries to live. On the day of Orin's funeral, in black once more, looking strangely like the old Lavinia, she fills the Mannon house with flowers for Peter, as Christine had once filled it for Adam. Peter comes, troubled by all that Hazel has told him, and his suspicions grow when Lavinia implores him to marry her that very evening. To his shocked response: "I can't see why you're so afraid of waiting," Lavinia retorts with desperate, wild pleading:

> . . . Listen, Peter! Why must we wait for marriage? I want a moment of joy — of love — to make up for what's coming. I want it now. Can't you be strong, Peter? Can't you be simple and pure? Can't you forget sin and see that all love is beautiful? (*She kisses him with desperate passion.*) Kiss me! Hold me close! Want me! Want me so much you'd murder anyone to have me! I did that — for you! Take me in this house of the dead and love me! Our love will drive the dead away . . . (*At the topmost pitch of desperate, frantic abandonment*) Want me! Take me, Adam! (*She is brought back to herself with a start by this name escaping her — bewilderedly, laughing idiotically.*) Adam? Why did I call you Adam? I never even heard that name before — outside of the Bible! (*Then suddenly with a hopeless, dead finality*) Always the dead between! It's no good trying any more!

No, there is no use in Lavinia's trying any more. All her past deeds burst from her in that unconscious, revelatory cry: "Take me, *Adam!*" That past, those deeds and the dead, must always be between. So, after repelling Peter still further by lying to him about her chastity, Lavinia deliberately drives him from her forever and, turning back to the house of the dead, utters her famous last speech:

. . . There's no one left to punish me. I'm the last Mannon. I've got to punish myself! . . . I'll live alone with the dead and keep their secrets and let them hound me until the curse is paid out and the last Mannon is let die! . . . I know they will see to it I live for a long time! It takes the Mannons to punish themselves for being born!

So the Electra of today — the un-mated — meets her doom. What could be clearer than the meaning of those words: "I've got to punish myself!" They are Lavinia's words of fate: "I do what I do because I must, because the laws of life which made me what I am, now preclude for me any other future.". . . O'Neill's analysis of the causes of this tragedy, presented in the light of contemporary psychological knowledge, gives to *Mourning Becomes Electra* the purging quality which is the essence of all great tragedy; it lifts its audiences *beyond tragedy* into the realm of a new and enlarged understanding of life. Men will no longer need to punish themselves, if they utilize their knowledge of the laws that dominate their lives so as to thwart their *destructive* powers and make them *constructive* forces for the attainment of individual fulfillment. Toward this goal, *Mourning Becomes Electra* points the way. To control and direct these laws, instead of being controlled and directed by them, means the end of the old Greek concept of fate and the beginning of that new concept of fate by which we purpose to live today.

Were O'Neill a lesser dramatist it would be unnecessary to comment on that change in his religio-philosophic attitude which excludes his latest plays from the category of vital drama. This change first manifests itself in *Dynamo,* the play immediately preceding *Mourning Becomes Electra,* continues to reveal itself by indirection in *Ah, Wilderness!,* and leads directly to *Days Without End,* the frank expression of his faith in Catholicism, which thus far constitutes O'Neill's solution of life's problems. Yet while plays indicating such a solution no longer represent the O'Neill who has contributed drama of high import to our age, it is impossible to leave the dramatist suspended in mid-air, as it were, without a final note of critical interpretation.

When O'Neill announced *Dynamo* as the first of a trilogy that was to probe into the failure of science to find a meaning in life and a substitute for faith in a personal God and a personal immortality, there could be no doubt as to the significance of such a project. It meant that the affirmation of life, based upon a scientific concept of the universe, which he had promulgated in *Lazarus Laughed* and which seems so harmonious to our epoch, had not proven for the playwright himself a satisfying faith. Therefore he proceeds from a point of view entirely alien to that to find a faith that he believes will comfort the confused soul of contemporary man.

In *Dynamo,* O'Neill shows how the faith of an adolescent boy in the Protestant God of his fathers is shattered at the same moment of emotional upheaval in which he loses his faith in his adored mother and in the girl whom he has invested with all his erotic idealism. Forsaken by what to O'Neill symbolizes the good in its various expressions, the disillusioned boy, typifying O'Neill's conception of the floundering youth of today, turns to Electricity, as the God of this scientific age. But, so great, according to O'Neill's changed attitude, is man's need of a God to worship, that the groping boy soon finds in the Dynamo, which generates the mysterious life-force, electricity, a substitute for the Protestant God of his fathers who has betrayed him. He now worships the purring, powerful dynamo as an idol, even swearing to it the old vow of chastity, if it will only tell him "the secret . . . what electricity is . . . what life is . . . what God is"—if it will only "give him the secret of truth" so that he may "become the new saviour who will bring happiness and peace to men." But the boy fails in his vow of chastity. Having killed the girl whose love has tempted him, in order to prove to his Dynamo-God that he will never again thus fail it, maddened by remorse and pleading for release for his tortured spirit, he throws his arms about the electrically-charged dynamo and meets annihilation at the hands of his new God.

We can read O'Neill's meaning clearly: Science—including any philosophy of science such as that expressed in *Lazarus Laughed*—has no answer for man seeking to solve the riddle of life and can only bring him spiritual destruction.

Where then does the answer lie? While O'Neill was writing a final expression of his faith, he paused to produce a play that came as a complete surprise—*Ah, Wilderness!* That O'Neill, the tragic poet, should write a light, humorous comedy delighted the theatre-conscious public. But to the discerning it was rather a cause for sorrow. For here is O'Neill already in a "God's in his heaven: all's right with the world" mood, which clearly presaged his reversion to conventional faith. In *Ah, Wilderness!* the adolescent's struggle to adjust to the adult world is no longer tragic—it is funny. His groping for intellectual enlightenment, for sexual enlightenment; the fact that his parents are bungling incompetents, incapable of helping him, all this is now enormously funny. Even the tragedy of a man and woman forever deprived of erotic fulfillment because of moral weakness in the one and undue moral severity in the other, which would once have given O'Neill the tragic content for a play like *Diff'rent,* now serves as material for "comic" scenes. In a divinely ordained, best of all possible worlds, God knows best. A lesser dramatist than O'Neill, one who does not trail clouds of tragic glory, may give us an *Ah, Wilderness!* and we may smile perhaps at its nostalgic portrayal of youth remembered, of home and family now seen through a glass brightly. But only an altered O'Neill could offer this to us, an O'Neill no longer integrated with the temper of his age.

On the jacket of the printed play *Days Without End,* which bears the subtitle "A Modern Miracle Play," is a picture of the interior wall of an old church on which hangs the life-size figure of Christ on the cross. Rightly does the jacket depict this as the play's crucial scene, in which the hero, a man of forty named John Loving (clearly none other than O'Neill himself), wins, at the foot of the cross, his final victory for the Catholic faith over the doubting self that has kept him in tortured conflict since his fifteenth year. These conflicting selves are shown by O'Neill on the stage as two separate characters. *Loving,* the God-denying self, pessimistic and destructive, *invisible* to the other characters in the play, is *visible* to the audience and gives utterance to the evil philosophy by means of which he is determined to prevent the noble self, *John,* from realizing his "yearning to go back" to his old Catholic faith. The use of two characters in the play, one invisible to the other characters, to depict the divided personality of John Loving, is as confusing as was the use of the masks in *The Great God Brown.* O'Neill's altered ideal of spiritual power is expressed in his description of John Loving's uncle, a Catholic priest: "His appearance and personality radiate health and observant kindliness — also the confident authority of one who is accustomed to obedience and deference — and one gets immediately from him the sense of an unshakable inner calm and certainty, the peace of one whose goal in life is fixed by an end beyond life." This priest, while recounting how his nephew has run the gamut of all the "isms," in his search for a satisfying philosophy of life, becomes O'Neill's mouthpiece in jauntily disposing of such contemporary trifles as Socialism, Karl Marx and the Russian Revolution:

> . . . First it was Atheism unadorned. Then it was Atheism wedded to Socialism. But Socialism proved too weak-kneed a mate, and the next I heard Atheism was living in free love with Anarchism, with a curse by Nietzsche to bless the union. And then came the Bolshevik dawn, and he greeted that with unholy howls of glee and wrote me he'd found a congenial home at last in the bosom of Karl Marx. He was particularly delighted when he thought they'd abolished love and marriage, and he couldn't contain himself when the news came they'd turned naughty schoolboys and were throwing spitballs at Almighty God and had supplanted Him with the slave-owning State — the most grotesque god that ever came out of Asia!

Thus the changed O'Neill, now beholding his world only with the unseeing eyes of blind faith. . . . After John Loving's destructive self has brought his wife to the point of death by a combination of his unchastity and his unconscious death-wish, the crisis of the play is reached, and the priest says to John: "Human science has done all it can to save her. Her life is in the hands of God now." It is then that John, still mocked by his doubting self, Loving, staggers to the crucifix and, after a final struggle, proclaims that the Cross has conquered. At this, Loving falls dead, for with his return to Catholicism, John Loving, no longer a divided soul, is finally at peace. Significantly O'Neill has him utter, as the last words of the play, the exultant words of Lazarus: —

> . . . Death is dead! . . . Life laughs with God's love again! Life laughs with love!

But with what a difference of connotation are the words used here!

Whether this reversion to faith indicates a passing phase of O'Neill's emotional adjustment to a world in whose social problems he has never been interested, or whether it indicates a permanent regression of the independent thinker back to the religious conformist, we shall be able to judge only when a new work sees the light. If this return to the faith of his fathers should be permanent, the tragedy would be greater than any presented in his dramas. But whatever the nature of his future work, it can never decrease the values of his intellectual prime any more than Hauptmann's decline can detract from the values of *The Weavers* and of *Hannele.* O'Neill's great plays will still stand as a revelation of the inner conflicts of the individual such as no other dramatist has even approached.

Chapter 5 Contemporary Drama: The Social Conflict

Our study thus far has demonstrated that dramatists, like other creative artists, fall into two main groups. Those whose interest centers in the individual, and who therefore take him as the starting point for their interpretation of life's problems, constitute one group. The other consists of those who consider the social organism, of which the individual is an inseparable part, the only sound basis for their analysis of both society's and the individual's problems. Between these two divergent points of view there usually, though not necessarily, lies the difference between the absence and the presence of a positive social philosophy. Hauptmann was influenced to write his plays by the new Socialist concepts of economic justice that were beginning to permeate European thought. Shaw's Socialist convictions animate his dramas. Elmer Rice, Paul Green and others now to be discussed must also be placed in this second group because, while indicating no positive social philosophy, they nevertheless clearly relate whatever conflicts they present to a responsible social basis.

On the other hand, Schnitzler and O'Neill, lacking a social philosophy, interpret life in terms of the psychological conflicts of the individual and integrate these conflicts with their time. Artists for whom all the events of life emanate from individual behavior are repelled by the opposite method, for temperamental reasons which keep them from reaching a definite social philosophy, and from interpreting, in its light, subjects undeniably social.

The social conflict is as old as the institution of private property. And the conflict between those who have and those who have not has finally reached the proportions of the world crisis that now confronts us. Society, like the individual, is seen to be a house divided against itself. If any still doubted this fact, the economic forces unleashed by the World War have brought it plainly into the foreground and revealed the supreme importance of the social conflict to our postwar world.

Since our contemporary age has been one of violent upheaval, and therefore one of sharpened social awareness, we should expect to find dramatists to whom only the social approach appears tenable in considering the problems of life today. They see that the workers, *as such,* are condemned to their common lot by economic forces stronger than any other influence in their lives. They feel, as the great modern dramatists did before them, that they must use the theatre as a medium through which to utter their protest against conditions which seem to them reprehensible.

Now the fact that I am discussing the plays of certain dramatists in terms of the social conflict does not necessarily mean that they express themselves directly in terms of that conflict, or of any positive social philosophy. It means simply that this conflict is implicit in their treatment of their subjects and that their plays, for this reason, are integrated with our age. These subjects may represent various expressions of the conflict: the race problem, the labor union problem, the Fascist menace, the question of war. On the other hand, the playwright's attitude may be explicit, his social philosophy unmistakable. Because war is an antisocial phenomenon unique in its nature and scope, the vital antiwar plays of our time will be discussed in a separate chapter.

There could exist no more striking evidence of the effect of the World War and its revolutionary aftermath upon disillusioned youth than that offered by the German poet and playwright Ernst Toller. In 1914, at the age of twenty-one, he volunteers "to defend his attacked fatherland," but when at the front he is first spattered with the blood of a French soldier, he is suddenly overwhelmed by the realization that this blood is exactly like his own and he begins to feel like "a murderer whose hands can never again be clean." In 1917, invalided, he organizes a federation of German youth whose purpose is to unite with the "enemy" youth to end the war. During this period, reading along political and economic lines, he becomes a revolutionary Socialist. In 1918 he takes an active part in a strike of munition workers, called as a protest against war, and is arrested and confined in a military prison where his studies in social and economic science continue. Here too, while walking in the prison yard, he conceives his first drama, *The Transformation,* a subjective account of the change in himself, expressionistic in form and interesting for its implications and promise rather than for its artistic fulfillment. In the Revolution of 1919 he is elected to a prominent office in the first German Soviet Republic of Bavaria, even though he inveighs against this premature step and against more shedding of workers' blood. After Prussian troops have suppressed the first workers' republic he is arrested and condemned by the Munich Court Martial to imprisonment in a fortress for five years. And during these years in prison he writes three vital plays: *Masses and Man, The Machine-Wreckers* and *Hinkemann.* Later, when a dictator came to power in Germany, these and his other works were publicly burned and their author uprooted to carry his passion for peace and freedom into exile.

Masses and Man is described by Toller himself as "A Play of the Social Revolution" and it is dedicated "To The Workers." Poetic in form, symbolic in treatment, the drama consists of seven "Pictures" or scenes. Four of these are scenes of real life—three taking place in a revolutionists' meeting hall and one in a prison. The remaining three scenes are called "Dream Pictures." They take place within the psyche of The Woman (one of the two leading characters), and they reflect her inner reactions to the experiences through which she is living, presented in the shape of dreams. These dream pictures, while experimentally interesting, are, on the whole, confused and add little to the material presented with such power in the scenes of actual life.

The story *Masses and Man* tells of an abortive revolutionary uprising in our time is slight, but the questions it raises are of immediate import. The main question is suggested by the title. Man lives in a dual capacity: as an individual and as an inseparable part of the social organism. In the struggle of the masses for freedom, is it right to sacrifice the individual to the mass? Shall *men* be eternally slaughtered in the hope that *communal man,* the masses, may advance toward the goal of social liberation? In the play, the character who opposes the attainment by bloodshed of the revolutionary cause of the workers is the symbolic figure of The Woman. Although of the bourgeois class, she is opposed to the industrial system, which keeps the working masses sunk in poverty, and has broken with her class, even with her beloved husband, to espouse the cause of the workers. Her husband, called The Man, symbolizes the capitalist State which condones the workers' lot because it upholds the profit system and the State's "sacred" right to maintain the *status quo* by war against its "enemies" within, as well as without. When she tells him that she will attack the State and tear down its mask that hides murder, he warns her that this is treason. But next day in a crowded meeting-hall, while The Woman is urging the workers to demonstrate their power by a general strike, there leaps on the platform the character called The Nameless One who shouts: —

I call more than a strike!
I call: a war!
I call: the Revolution!

Here is The Woman's adversary, who symbolizes violent and bloody revolution, at any cost. Opposing, The Woman pleads:

I will not have fresh murder . . .
Masses are helpless.
Masses are weak.

To which The Nameless One replies: —

Masses are master!
Masses are might! . . .
The individual, his feelings or his conscience,
What do they count?
The Masses count!
Consider this
One single bloody battle; then,
Forever peace.
No mockery of peace, as formerly,
Concealing war —
War of the strong upon the weak,
The war for loot, the war for greed!
Consider this
An end to misery. . . .
The dawn of freedom for all peoples.
Think you I counsel lightly?
War is necessity for us.
Your words will split us —
For the Cause
Be silent.

And carried away emotionally, in spite of herself, The Woman repeats, half in a trance:—

> You . . . are . . . the Masses
> You . . . are . . . right.

But the revolution turns into a shambles. Working men, women and children by the thousands are butchered. And when in the meeting hall a workman reports that he has ordered half of the bourgeois prisoners to be shot, the other half to be used as shock-troops, The Nameless One shouts triumphantly:

> The Masses are revenge!

At this the conflict between the two opposing points of view blazes out again:—

THE WOMAN. Stop! You are crazed with battle.
I bar your path.
The masses should be people bound together
By love.
Masses should be community.
Community is not revenge.
Community destroys the ground
And the foundation of all wrongs
And plants a seed of justice.
Humanity, taking revenge,
Shatters itself. . . .
Half of them shot?
That was not self-defence—
Blind rage—not service to the Cause!
Do you kill men
In the same spirit as the State
Killed men?

Those men outside
Are under my protection!
I was prepared to silence
My conscience, for the Masses.
I cry:
Shatter the system!
But you would shatter
Mankind.
No, I cannot keep silence, not today!
Those prisoners are men,
Born in the blood of groaning mothers—
Are men, immutably our brothers—

THE NAMELESS. For the last time: Silence, comrade!
Force! Force!
They do not spare our bodies:
This bitter battle is not to be won
By pious sentiments—
Pay no attention to this woman—
It is the idle babble of her sex.

THE WOMAN. I call a halt!
And you . . . who are you?
Does lust of power, caged for centuries,
Impel you?
Who . . . are you?
O God . . . who are . . . you?
Slayer or Saviour?
Slayer . . . or . . . Saviour?
Nameless—your face?
You are . . . ?

THE NAMELESS. The Masses!

THE WOMAN. You . . . Masses! . . .
Revenge is not the will to new and living forms,
Revenge is not the Revolution;
Revenge is but the axe that splits

The crystal, glowing, angry, iron will
To Revolution.

THE NAMELESS. How dare you, woman of your class,
Poison this hour of fate?
I find another meaning in your words:
You shield your friends and first companions.
That is your deeper motive:
Treason! you betray.

(*The Masses in the hall crowd angrily round the Woman.*)

A SHOUT. Intelligentsia!

A SHOUT. Stand her
Back to the wall!
Let her be shot!

THE NAMELESS. To shield the prisoners is treason.
This is the hour for action,
For ruthless action.
Who is not for us, is against.
Masses must live.

THE MASSES IN THE HALL. Must live!

THE NAMELESS. I arrest you.

THE WOMAN. I shield . . . my friends . . . my first companions?
No, I am shielding you!
You, who yourselves
Have lined yourselves up to be shot.
I shield our souls!
I shield mankind . . . to all eternity, mankind!
Insane denouncer—
You read fear into my words?
I never chose so basely—
Oh, you lie . . . you lie . . .

Into her prison cell comes The Man, her husband. Powerful in the State, his name has saved her, proved her "guiltless." Reproachfully he says:—

I warned you of the Masses.
Who stirs the Masses, stirs up hell.

THE WOMAN. Hell? who created hell—
Conceived the tortures of your golden mills
Which grind, grind out your profit, day by day?
Who built the prisons? Who cried "holy war"?
Who sacrificed a million lives of men—
Pawns in a lying game of numbers?
Who thrust the masses into mouldering kennels, . . .
Who robbed his brothers of their human face, . . .
Forced and abased them to be cogs in your machines?
The State! You! . . .
THE HUSBAND. I came to you . . .
Do you sit here in judgment?
THE WOMAN. Yes, here, a court of judgment
Comes to be.
I, the accused, I am the judge,
I prosecute, I pronounce guilty
And I absolve. . . .
For in the end, this guilt—
Oh! do you guess who bears the final guilt?—
Since of necessity,
Man must desire to do:
And deeds grow red with blood of men—
Man must needs will to live:
And seas of blood rise round him—
Oh! do you guess who bears the final guilt? . . .
Give me your hand,
Beloved of my blood,
For I have overcome myself—
Myself and you.

The woman refuses to be exonerated and saved by the guilty State. And now The Nameless One, too, comes to her cell to help her escape, for the Masses do not want her to die — they know they have need of her. But when he tells her:

> Two warders have been bribed.
> The third, him at the gate, I shall strike down —

his words at once reveal the abyss that separates them. She denies her right, or even the right of the Cause, to murder this man and will not be swayed to forsake her convictions, even to live:

THE WOMAN. If I took but one human life,
I should betray the Masses.
Who acts may only sacrifice himself.
Hear me: no man may kill men for a cause.
Unholy every cause that needs to kill.
Whoever calls for blood of men,
Is Moloch.
So God was Moloch,
The State Moloch,
And the Masses —
Moloch.

THE NAMELESS. Then who is holy?

THE WOMAN. One day . . .
Community . . .
Free people, freely working together.
Mankind, fulfilling its measure of deeds
Freely.
Work. People.

THE NAMELESS. You lack the courage
To take upon yourself
Action — hard action.
Only by ruthless action
Can this free people
Come to be.
Atone then, by your death.
Perhaps your death is useful to us.

THE WOMAN. I live eternally.

THE NAMELESS. You live too soon.

(*The Nameless leaves the cell.*)

THE WOMAN. And you lived yesterday;
You live today;
Tomorrow you will die.
But I—
Turning and circling—
I
Come into being
Eternally.
I shall become
Cleaner, more guiltless,
I shall become
Mankind.

So The Woman is shot for treason to the State and The Nameless One is free to lead the Masses. It is this basic question of the *justifiability of means* that today separates even those who are united on the question of *ends*. And humanity may well ask: Is there never to be a *present* for men in which they will not be sacrificed on the altar of "principle"? Are there no bloodless roads to progress?

Toller saw that despite war, despite political revolution, despite economic collapse, the old system of exploitation was taking firm root again, unchanged. Above all he realized how the most valuable invention of man, the labor-saving machine, destined to serve the workers, becomes, under capitalism, their relentless enemy. This theme of the injustice of the system of private ownership in the means of life, Toller uses in the second of his plays written while in prison: *The Machine-Wreckers*. He calls it a "Drama of the English Luddites," and it is a historical parable play in which the industrial conditions leading to the riots organized by the weavers of Nottingham, between 1812 and 1815, suggest parallel conditions existing to-day. The Luddites got their name from their leader, Ned Ludd, one of the characters in the play. In selecting weavers as typifying the workers in his drama, Toller establishes historic continuity with his precursor, Hauptmann. The weavers, the textile-workers, become a symbol of all exploited workers, and Toller's parable, pointing our present-day technological tragedy, stands as a projection of Hauptmann's *The Weavers* and stresses human exploitation as the constant factor in capitalist production.

In *The Machine-Wreckers* Toller's contemporary analogue is clear. The weavers of 1812 are suffering the after-effects of war. We hear that "all Europe is crippled by a load of debt." The market for textiles has shrunk, causing widespread reduction of wages and employment. Granaries are full and the workers starve; coal is piled mountain-high and the workers freeze. And when on top of this, the new weaving machines are installed, causing the permanent dismissal of men weavers and the substitution, at starvation wages, of women and even little children, able to perform the simple mechanical work required by the new machinery, the workers organize and proceed to destroy the new machines which they, in their ignorance, regard as responsible for their undoing. Severe repressive legislation was then actually passed, forbidding workers' organizations, a feature which Toller uses very effectively. And in the Prologue he quotes Lord Byron's famous speech in the House of Lords against the proposed law, which was nevertheless promptly passed by the Lords, rendering the destruction of machinery punishable by death. Mark the pertinency of Byron's words:—

> Let us consider well this rabble, lords:
> It is the rabble digging in your fields,

It is the rabble serving in your halls,
It is the rabble whence your soldiers spawn,
It is the strong arm that sets you in power
To bid defiance to an enemy world,
And it will bid defiance to its masters
If it be driven madly to despair. . . .

Just when the weavers of Nottingham have decided to wreck the machines, Jimmy Cobbett, himself a weaver, returns. He has been out in the world to learn what the workers are doing elsewhere. He tells the men their plan is madness: "I know that this machine is our inevitable lot — our destiny," that "in London we have founded a League that shall embrace every workman in the Kingdom." He exhorts them:

. . . Brothers, join hands! Begin! Begin! . . . And the tyrant of machinery . . . will be your tool, your servant! . . . What if you labored to produce for all and not for Mammon — for service, not for profit? What if instead of sixteen hours, you worked but eight? With the machine no more your enemy, but your helper? What if your children, freed from drudgery, grew up in sunny schoolrooms, gardens, play-grounds? . . . Begin brothers! Unite! . . .

The weavers, aroused, choose Jimmy as their leader and agree to "take service at the machine" and thus "serve the cause." But their displaced leader turns traitor. Denouncing Jimmy to the employer "as a Communist . . . in the pay of France," — Toller's current parallel is clear, — he offers to play the *agent provocateur,* to goad the workers into destroying the machines, by persuading them that Jimmy, who happens to be the brother of an overseer, is "in the master's pay." He succeeds in his scheme; and when Jimmy, rushing into the factory just after the weavers have hacked the machine to bits, tries to tell them the truth, to make them see their deed as "a deed of slaves," they fall upon him and beat him to death. Only after he is dead and the police come to arrest them do the machine-wreckers realize that they have been duped. And it is the symbolic figure of the Old Reaper, searching everywhere for God and finding him in the machine, who has the last words, as he looks down on the body of Jimmy:

> . . . I've shot him — I, a bondsman's son . . . There he lies. Our Son, upon the earth, all bruised and broken . . . You poor dear Son of Man . . . (*He bends weeping over Jimmy's body and kisses it*) And I will pray the Father, and he shall give you another Comforter, even the Spirit of Truth; whom the world cannot receive because it seeth him not, neither knoweth him. Ah, poor dear Son! We must bury him. We must be good to one another.

Workers' uprisings in Nottingham, 1812, in Munich, 1919, in Chicago, 1937, are all the same social conflict, the essence of which Toller has here set forth with dramatic effectiveness.

The parallel between the revolutionary modern, Hauptmann, and the revolutionary contemporary, Toller, continues. For, after having dealt with the exploited masses and their exploiters in general symbolic terms (both always depict the adversaries in the social conflict not as individuals, but as symbols), each proceeds to create an individualized character around whom he centers his most moving play. Hauptmann did this in his tragedy of the child of poverty, Hannele, and Toller does it in his drama of the worker, misused by the brute force of war and by the brute spirit war leaves as its heritage. *Hinkemann* is a difficult title to translate. Literally it means "He Who Limps," but to say in German about a person "*es hinkt*" means things are going badly with him. Thus, when Toller calls his chief character Eugene Hinkemann, the symbolism is clear. Eugene means "born well," so it must be life which has turned him into a Hinkemann, for whom living has become an ill.

Hinkemann, a healthy young worker, is sent to the war and returns seeming quite as sound as before. The shrapnel that struck him left him visibly whole, but destroyed his sexual potency. Tender and gentle, he might have adjusted himself to his tragedy and found his place in a world made in his own image, rather than in the image of the brute. But his young wife, Maggie, torn between her love for him and her starved sexual needs, betrays her plight to her husband's friend, Paul Grosshahn, a pursuer of women. Grosshahn is again a symbolic name, meaning "large rooster," and Paul represents the male who knows nothing higher than the sexual instincts of the barnyard. He greets the information about his friend with ribald laughter and regards it as ample justification for seducing the wife. Believing in her loyalty to him, Hinkemann is determined to prove to her that at least he can bring money into the house, despite the postwar unemployment crisis. In despair, he takes the only job offered to him, although it sickens him with horror. He who, as Maggie puts it, "wouldn't hurt a fly," has to do a "turn" in a traveling show, that consists of taking a rat and a mouse out of a cageful, biting a hole in their throats and sucking their blood. "Brings the house down," adds the showman and he explains further:—

> Listen to me. The public is fed up with sob-stuff. Only pacifists fall for it nowadays. That's not my idea of business. The public likes *blood*. Plenty of it. Christians or no Christians. . . .

So Hinkemann, impotent victim of the brute in men, panders to their blood-lust by himself playing the potent brute. One day, Maggie and Paul, pleasure-bent, accidentally come upon the sight of Hinkemann doing his bloody turn. Paul roars with laughter at the "fraud," at the screamingly funny fact that "his country's hero," as the showman describes him, is in reality a "eunuch." But Maggie, in a flash of insight, turns in shame and loathing from Paul and leaves him. Unconscious of having been discovered, Hinkemann, finished for the day and eager to drown the taste of blood, joins his friends in a workmen's café. Ever-brooding, he tells them the story of his own tragedy as that of a mythical friend and asks how such a one is to be helped. At this point Paul enters, drunk, and taunts Hinkemann as a "bloody swindle," a powerful hero who isn't even a man. Hinkemann goes to pieces completely when Paul tells him the sadistic lie that Maggie *laughed* when she beheld him at the show. The thought of this laughter brings him intolerable torment. But he has still to hear the laughter of the men present, as Paul regales them with the story of the blood-sucking eunuch. He interrupts Paul, to say simply: "That man was Hinkemann," and warns them that they will never build the better world they are always theorizing about, on such hate as theirs.

At home with Maggie, he can forgive her everything except her laughter; even when finally convinced that she did not laugh, he is too broken to go on. She insists that she will never leave him, that henceforth it will be "you and me — me and you." But even her need of him, her plea not to leave her alone among the "wild beasts," fails to move him. Realizing that he no longer has the faith to live, Maggie slips from the room and throws herself into the tenement house yard. And the curtain falls on Hinkemann brooding over the dead body, still asking questions as to the cruelty of man's fate on earth. . . .

Made a social revolutionary by the war, Toller saw his age as the scene of a mighty conflict breeding all elements of war. Prophetically he spoke through his war-maimed worker: —

> I see what the world is. It's the war again.
> Men murdering men and laughing. . . .

It is in seeing that the contemporary world is "the war again" and in regarding the theatre as a part of the arena in which the social conflict must be fought, that Toller's contribution to drama lies. These three plays, so full of pain and pity, and of the playwright's social philosophy, must be read in order to get their full impact.

Out of the World War was born another play, which carries revolutionary problems from the realm of poetic symbolism into the world of contemporary events, leaving no doubt of the convictions of its German author, Friedrich Wolf.

The Sailors of Cattaro is based on a mutiny in the Austrian fleet stationed in the Bay of Cattaro, an inlet of the Adriatic, in the year 1918. The names of its chief characters are not fictitious. Boatswain's Mate Franz Rasch, Able Seaman Anton Grabar, and the two Gunner's Mates, Jerko Sisgoric and Mate Bernicevic, all of the battleship *St. George,* are shown by the court-martial records to have been shot near Cattaro as the ringleaders of a revolt that began as a mutiny to stop the war, but soon took on a social revolutionary character. Thus, while from one point of view *The Sailors of Cattaro* might be called an antiwar play, it nevertheless cannot be placed in this category, because the subject of the play is not war, but, as in Toller's *Masses and Man,* the problem of revolutionary behavior and tactics — one might even say of revolutionary theory and practice. Wolf prefaces his play (in the German edition) with a quotation from Lenin, written in the storm and stress of November, 1917: "Never play with revolution; but once it has begun, know that it must be carried through to the end."

We meet the sailors of the *St. George* when their leader, Rasch, back from leave, brings them news of strikes for peace and democratic control all over Europe. Elated, the men frame resolutions, voicing demands which are to be secretly submitted to all the crews of the Cattaro fleet and then presented to the officers. These demands run all the way from

"Immediate overtures for world peace" and "Eight-hour day in the State workshops" to "Same rations for officers and enlisted men." When a Lieutenant baits the sailors, a hot-headed visitor from another ship resents his insolence. To make matters worse, a page of the illegal newspaper, the Vienna *Arbeiterzeitung,* is discovered during inspection. The whole section is punished for this, and the Lieutenant tightens his discipline, which leads to the discovery of the resolutions. The arrest and threatened court martial of Toni (Anton), who desperately tries to swallow the incriminating paper, bring matters to a head. The sailors take control of the battleship, and while they shout "Hurrah for peace and freedom!" the news comes that "six thousand sailors on forty units of the Royal Imperial Navy have hoisted the red flag. . . ."

Now we learn why Wolf quoted as his text Lenin's words — that once a revolution is begun, it must be carried through — for we see it collapse before our eyes and are shown the reasons from the playwright's point of view. First, the goal is lost sight of and immediate, individual desires substituted. The older men want only one thing: any agreement that will permit them, after these years of privation and separation, to go home to their families. Those lower in the scale are satisfied to see the officers forced to eat their own vile rations and no longer want anything that will endanger their getting out of the mess with a whole skin. But of primary importance is the fact that Rasch, having organized a Sailor's Council, refuses to take even the most urgent action without debate, discussion and a vote. Implored to act by one of his comrades, who sees, as does Rasch himself, that a certain strategic step is immediately necessary if all is not to be lost, Rasch refuses to resort to "autocratic rule." To the playwright this failure to discriminate between democratic theory and revolutionary practice represents not only the crux of his play, but the crux of the dissension which divides the revolutionary forces of the world today. A play that presents as effectively as does this one the problem that is, in one form or another, now troubling the entire world, must be regarded as vital.

The strategic moment thus lost, the revolting sailors must either resign themselves to slaughter, or come to terms with their officers. Promised immunity by the Captain if they surrender at once, they turn a deaf ear to the pleas of Rasch and two gunner's mates to risk all for the revolutionary cause. Even Toni cannot bear the thought of never again seeing his little boy. But when the Austrian war flag goes up once more, after the red flag has been hauled down, he cannot endure it and, rushing forward, he seizes the red banner and waves it high. So he is the fourth to die for the cause, and Franz Rasch's simple words: "Comrades! Next time better!" became a slogan for revolutionary workers. When Friedrich Wolf, in exile from Nazi Germany, arrived in Moscow he was greeted with a banner inscribed: "Comrades! Next time better!" For there many thousands had been thrilled by the production of *The Sailors of Cattaro.*

Looking southward from the social-revolutionary theatre of pre-Hitler Germany, we find that even the highly individualized theatre of France could not remain entirely immune to the social conflict that had become an integral part of European consciousness. Dictatorship was already established in Italy, in Germany a weak pseudo-Socialist government was breeding reaction. What subject, then, could seem more vital than that of dictatorship? Analyzing it with the cool detachment of a Frenchman, the eminent writer, Jules Romains, chose for the subject of his drama the evolution of a dictator. When he submitted *The Dictator* to the Comédie Française in 1925 it was rejected on the ground that its controversial theme would rouse political passions. In response to protest, the Minister of Education, at that time none other than M

Daladier, announced he would take responsibility for any incidents that might result from the play's production. The Comédie Française now agreed, "*avec joie*," to produce it, but by this time the play was already in rehearsal at the Comédie des Champs-Elysées.

During those years, *The Dictator* was also produced in several other European countries, including pre-Hitler Germany!

The leading characters in *The Dictator* are Denis and Féréol, two labor leaders at the head of a strongly organized revolutionary movement in the capital of a great modern state, a constitutional monarchy. The men have been close friends since school days and comrades in their life work, without ever realizing that the differences between them are fundamental. Féréol is wary of politics. He has refused to go into parliament and confines himself to agitating among industrial workers, whose organization he regards as essential for revolutionary action. Denis, on the other hand, believes that a revolution, to be successful, must take complete political control. Entire scenes are devoted to ideological discussions between these two friends, as responsible leaders—discussions rich in import and sharp as a knife's edge. For, as the play-conscious know, there is nothing so dramatic as *the conflict of ideas,* when they are presented with the mastery of an artist. Both men trust each other, neither is conscious of the menacing fact that what Denis actually sees in political control is the means to personal dominance.

When their labor party proves itself strong enough to overthrow the cabinet, Denis has risen so high politically that the King offers him the post of Prime Minister. The King is a most democratic gentleman, progressive and well-informed on both revolutionary theory and practice. Above all, he is a judge of character. He has watched Denis and knows he is not the man to plunge the country into revolution.

As the King anticipated, Denis accepts the post, and the workers, freshly confident because their own leader is now prime minister, hasten to perfect their revolutionary plans, urged on by Féréol. But Denis is now the Government, his fingers control the lever of the political machine, and every law of his being cries out against the shattering of this machine, against the menace of revolution, with which his ego has never been really identified. Realizing that he cannot persuade his former comrade to call off the revolutionary plans and trust to political reform, Denis asks the King for the powers of a dictator. The scenes between the King and Denis, like those between Denis and Féréol, flash with the impact of mind against mind, and are packed with meaning for contemporary audiences. As Dictator, Denis is not filled with a lust for power, but rather with a sense of exaltation at being actually able to control the great social forces which he has unconsciously desired to direct for so long. And when Féréol refuses to countermand the order for the public display of posters calling on the army to join the workers in their revolt, the Dictator places him under arrest. . . . Thus does Denis fulfill his destiny, for, according to Romains, character is character, temperament is temperament, and when these are pitted against acquired convictions, the passage from revolutionary to dictator psychology may not be so very strange and incomprehensible. For if the convictions of a revolutionist can go down before his ego's will-to-power, then it is of such incalculable human factors as this that social revolution must beware.

While Romains, the dramatist, has been, temporarily at any rate, obscured by Romains the novelist, it is only a few years ago that he enjoyed the distinction of having four of his plays running simultaneously in Paris. Each of them dealt with some aspect of the antinomies inherent in our present social order. Even his satiric farce, *Dr. Knock,* repeatedly played in little theatres in America, and *Donogoo,* a rollicking satire on the unscrupulous acts committed by acquisitive man in the name of science and civilization, place his audiences squarely in the theatre of social criticism. Unique among his own confrères as Brieux was among the moderns, Romains carries forward, for France, drama whose content is integrated with the life of the people of his time.

Far removed from the embattled European scene, geographically, historically and ideologically, the young nation known as the United States of America did not really exist, dramatically speaking, before our contemporary era. There was an American theatre, to be sure, but its shallow offerings made the term American drama a misnomer. For anyone before the World War to have made the plea for *play-consciousness* which I am making in these pages, would have been futile, because no American drama had been written worthy of the serious attention of audiences. The reasons for this phenomenon are clear. America is, even today, no nation in the European sense of that term, that is, a people speaking a common language and possessing common cultural and historical traditions. America never possessed the unified national background out of which, in European countries, art, including of course the art of the drama, developed. The various national entities which made up what was called America had first to merge, to evolve an equivalent for a unified national consciousness, before articulate self-expression could develop in the realm of art. Indeed, American painting and sculpture as national arts are even now only in their beginnings, while native drama worthy of the name began but a few years earlier.

Therefore we can actually place with exactness the arrival of a serious, integrated American drama as the date of the production of O'Neill's *The Emperor Jones* at the Provincetown Playhouse, New York, in the year 1920. Evidently the time was ripe at last for the rich material of the American scene to be utilized by a new, postwar type of young American playwright. The spuriously romantic America of William Vaughn Moody's *The Great Divide* and the meretriciously "daring" America of a Eugene Walter's *The Easiest Way,* gave way to an America honestly depicted by Elmer Rice, Paul Green, John Howard Lawson and others. Finally, as the result of the World War, the European scene did at last impinge on the intellectual provincialism of America, and the Theatre Guild of New York seized the psychological moment to present what was most vital in European drama to awakening American audiences. Under the circumstances it was inevitable that this emerging American drama should begin to pay attention to the various aspects in which the social conflict reveals itself in America.

It is to the credit of Elmer Rice that he was the first American dramatist to choose, as subject for a play, a typical and unspectacular aspect of the social conflict because he recognized not only its inherent drama but also its tragedy. This subject is the low level of existence to which a machine civilization dooms millions of the little human machines it exploits. The play Rice calls: *The Adding Machine.* Like Hauptmann in *The Weavers* and Toller in *The Machine-Wreckers,* Rice knows that such a play is not concerned with the individual. He selects as his chief character a member of the large class so aptly dubbed in America "white-collar slaves," and gauges the quality of his bookkeeper hero by naming him "Mr. Zero." As an individual Mr. Zero is nothing, he assumes proportion only as a symbol of the countless millions who have been, and are being, made in his pitiful image. He stands in contemporary American drama as the classic portrayal of the ignorant, inhibited, slave-soul produced by capitalist civilization; and Elmer Rice has told his story in one of the most imaginative of contemporary plays. For

Rice not only understands the social conflict, but also its relation to individual conflicts as interpreted in the light of Freudian analysis. *The Adding Machine* therefore has the distinction of being sound in both its social and its Freudian interpretation.

We first meet Mr. Zero in an unusual opening scene — the bedroom of his dingy flat; and stage directions tell us that "*Mr. Zero is lying in the bed, facing the audience, his head and shoulders visible. He is thin, sallow, undersized and partially bald. Mrs. Zero is standing before the dresser arranging her hair for the night. She is forty-five, sharp-featured . . . shapeless in her long-sleeved cotton nightgown.*" The entire scene consists of a bitter monologue directed by Mrs. Zero at her husband. Through it we get a picture of their drab lives. Petty drudgery has turned this woman into a nagging harridan: —

An' what have I got to show for it? — slavin' my life away to give you a home. What's in it for me, I'd like to know? . . . You was goin' to do wonders, you was! You wasn't goin' to be a bookkeeper long — oh, no, not you. Wait till you got started — you was goin' to show 'em. There wasn't no job in the store that was too big for you. Well, I've been waitin' — waitin' for you to get started — see? It's been a good long wait, too. Twenty-five years! An' I ain't seen nothin' happen. Twenty-five years in the same job. Twenty-five years tomorrow! You're proud of it, ain't you? Twenty-five years in the same job an' never missed a day! That's somethin' to be proud of, ain't it? Sittin' for twenty-five years on the same chair, addin' up figures. . . . An' me at home here lookin' at the same four walls an' workin' my fingers to the bone to make both ends meet. Seven years since you got a raise! An' if you don't get one tomorrow, I'll bet a nickel you won't have the guts to go an' ask for one. . . .

We learn one more revealing thing about the Mr. Zeroes of the world before Mrs. Zero turns out the light. She has caught him watching the "goin's-on" of a streetwalker living across the narrow court. Since every normal impulse toward self-realization and happiness has had to be steadily repressed in Mr. Zero, a furtive sensuality that will not down remains the symbol of all his unsatisfied yearnings. . . . Next day in the office, we see Mr. Zero sitting at his high desk facing Daisy, the faded, sex-starved spinster, who for years has been tortured by her longing for him, as he once had longed for her. This is a brilliant scene psychologically. These two frustrated creatures snap at each other querulously in their joint work, and utter aloud, unheard by each other, their secret thoughts, much in the manner which O'Neill was later to perfect. The woman toys with her desires for love and death; the man with his desires for sex and economic advancement.

Later, on this day of his twenty-fifth anniversary in the office, he is surprised by a visit from the Boss. In tense anticipation he listens for news of the "raise" which he is certain must be coming. Instead, he gradually realizes the Boss is telling him that, in the interest of efficiency, adding machines are to be installed, which a lower-salaried girl can operate, and that he is to be fired. Mr. Zero is lashed into fury by the violence of the shock. That something serious and fearful is happening to him was conveyed to the audience by the impressionistic finale given this scene in the Theatre Guild production. The room, while the Boss talks on and Zero listens, begins to spin round and round. The figures, seared for years on Zero's brain, appear on the ceiling, on the walls, dancing, confused, gigantic. Then, while the spectator's own head grows dizzy watching them, a huge red splotch suddenly bursts out among them, and as the curtain descends rapidly we know that a maddened creature has broken through his inhibitions at last. . . .

Back home, Mr. Zero, silent, as his wife scolds him for being late, lives through an evening of "company." Here Rice presents a picture of the mental milieu of the white-collar slave class by showing us Mr. Zero's "friends." They arrive for the evening, Mr. and Mrs. One, Mr. and Mrs. Two, and so on — six couples, the men as identical with Mr. Zero as possible, the women identical in appearance, save that their dresses and their hair are of different colors. Just as O'Neill in *The Hairy Ape* used this symbolic stylization to expose the interior and exterior uniformity of the Fifth Avenue churchgoers, so Rice uses it to portray that of this "lower" social stratum. And as we listen to the "conversation" at the Zeros' party, we hear all the benighted ignorance that is today the backbone of a nascent American Fascism. The scene closes with the arrival of a policeman, whereupon Mr. Zero quietly informs his friends as well as the audience that he has killed the Boss. . . . Next, in a court of justice, we hear Zero's final speech to the jury. This must be read in its entirety, for it is as keen a piece of Freudian revelation as anything ever penned by James Joyce. But in addition it serves to indict a social system which produces the psyche, the character, the life of the millions who are Zero. And by a master stroke, the jury consists of the same six standardized couples of the previous scene, his peers and judges. Incapable of understanding the causes of his criminal act, which Zero is so fumblingly attempting to make clear to them, they finally interrupt him to rise in unison and shout "*GUILTY!*"

But although Zero is now executed, Elmer Rice, alive to all the implications of his subject, is by no means done with him. We follow Mr. Zero into the Elysian Fields, "a scene of pastoral loveliness." Here he meets Daisy, who, in her loneliness and grief for him, had turned her constant death-wish into a reality. She wears "a much-beruffled white muslin dress," too small and much too youthful for her. Under the trees, to the sound of the music of the spheres, freed from the shackles of respectability and from their own repressions, they confess how they longed for each other and never dared to reach out for their happiness together. At last they embrace and, aware of the ethereal music heard only by the happy, they dance until they can dance no more. Yet Zero is still the creature of the earthly codes that destroyed him. They must watch their step, they can't have people talking, they must find a minister to marry them. But when he learns that the two most "beloved" ministers here in the Elysian Fields are Dean Swift and Abbé Rabelais, both famous for what Zero calls "smutty stories," and that this "dump" is also inhabited by vagabonds and adulterers, he rushes away, shocked and outraged, from such low surroundings, leaving Daisy to eternal loneliness.

Even now we have not yet finished with Mr. Zero or with the author's presentation of the bitter truth that something like eternity is apparently required to evolve the Zero-soul into a positive human factor. For we see him once more, this time in a symbolic purgatory, working a gigantic adding-machine, on which he walks as on a treadmill. The ribald person in charge, called Lieutenant Charles, informs Zero, perfectly contented with his treadmill existence, that it is time for his soul to return to earth again. And when Zero protests that, if anyone has done his bit on earth, he has, Charles asks him in scorn if he thinks a soul has been created to be used only once. Bewildered, Zero questions further about the past of his own soul, and Charles replies that he began as a monkey and has been growing worse ever since.

Zero offended says:—

A monkey! . . . That musta been a long time ago.

CHARLES

Oh, not so long. A million years or so. Seems like yesterday to me.

ZERO

Then look here, whaddya mean by sayin' I'm gettin' worse all the time?

CHARLES

Just what I said. You weren't so bad as a monkey. . . . But even in those days there must have been some bigger and brainier monkey that you kow-towed to. The mark of the slave was on you from the start. . . . If there ever was a soul in the world that was labeled "slave" it's yours. Why, all the bosses and kings that there ever were have left their trademarks on your backside.

ZERO

It ain't fair, if you ask me.

CHARLES

(*Shrugging his shoulders*): Don't tell me about it. I don't make the rules. All I know is you've been getting worse — worse each time. Why, even six thousand years ago you weren't so bad. That was the time you were hauling stones for one of those big pyramids in a place they call Africa. Ever hear of the pyramids?

ZERO

Them big pointy things?

CHARLES

(*Nodding*): That's it.

ZERO

I seen a picture of them in the movies.

CHARLES

Well, you helped build them. It was a long step down from the happy days in the jungle, but it was a good job — even though you didn't know what you were doing and your back was striped by the foreman's whip. But you've been going down, down. Two thousand years ago you were a Roman galley-slave. You were on one of the triremes that knocked the Carthaginian fleet for a goal. Again the whip. But you had muscles then — chest muscles, back muscles, biceps. (*He feels Zero's arm gingerly and turns away in disgust*): Phoo! A bunch of mush! . . . And then another thousand years and you were a serf — a lump of clay digging up other lumps of clay. You wore an iron collar then — white ones hadn't been invented yet. Another long step down. But where you dug, potatoes grew and that helped fatten the pigs. Which was something. And now — well, I don't want to rub it in —

ZERO

Rub it in is right! Seems to me I got a pretty healthy kick comin'. I ain't had a square deal! Hard work! That's all I've ever had!

CHARLES

(*Callously*): What else were you ever good for? . . .

ZERO

Why can't they stop pickin' on me? I'm satisfied here—doin' my day's work. I don't want to go back.

CHARLES

You've got to, I tell you. There's no way out of it.

ZERO

What chance have I got—at my age? Who'll give me a job?

CHARLES

You big boob, you don't think you're going back the way you are, do you?

ZERO

Sure, how then?

CHARLES

Why, you've got to start all over.

ZERO

All over?

CHARLES

(*Nodding*): You'll be a baby again—a bald, red-faced little animal, and then you'll go through it all again. There'll be millions of others like you—all with their mouths open, squalling for food. And then when you get a little older you'll begin to learn things—and you'll learn all the wrong things and learn them all in the wrong way. You'll eat the wrong food and wear the wrong clothes and you'll live in swarming dens where there's no light and no air! You'll learn to be a liar and a bully and a braggart and a coward and a sneak. You'll learn to fear the sunlight and to hate beauty. By that time you'll be ready for school. There they'll tell you the truth about a great many things that you don't give a damn about and they'll tell you lies about all the things you ought to know—and about all the things you want to know they'll tell you nothing at all. When you get through you'll be equipped for your life work. You'll be ready to take a job.

ZERO

(*Eagerly*): What'll my job be? Another adding machine?

CHARLES

Yes. But not one of these antiquated adding machines. It will be a superb, super-hyper-adding machine, as far from this old piece of junk as you are from God. It will be something to make you sit up and take notice, that adding machine. It will be an adding machine which will be installed in a coal mine and which will record the individual output of each miner. As each miner down in the lower galleries takes up a shovelful of coal, the impact of his shovel will automatically set in motion a graphite pencil in your gallery. The pencil will make a mark in white upon a blackened, sensitized drum. Then your work comes in. With the great toe of your right foot you release a lever which focuses a violet ray on the drum. The ray playing upon and through the white mark, falls upon a selenium cell which in turn sets the keys of the adding apparatus in motion. In this way the individual output of each miner is recorded without any human effort except the slight pressure of the great toe of your right foot.

ZERO

(*In breathless, round-eyed wonder*): Say, that'll be some machine, won't it?

CHARLES

Some machine is right. It will be the culmination of human effort — the final triumph of the evolutionary process. For millions of years the nebulous gases swirled in space. For more millions of years the gases cooled, and then through inconceivable ages they hardened into rocks. And then came life. Floating green things on the waters that covered the earth. More millions of years and a step upward — an animate organism in the ancient slime. And so on — step by step, down through the ages — a gain here, a gain there — the mollusc, the fish, the reptile, then mammal, man! And all so that you might sit in the gallery of a coal mine and operate the super-hyper-adding machine with the great toe of your right foot!

ZERO

Well, then — I ain't so bad, after all.

CHARLES

You're a failure, Zero, a failure. A waste product. A slave to a contraption of steel and iron. The animal's instincts, but not his strength and skill. The animal's appetites, but not his unashamed indulgence of them. True, you move and eat and digest and excrete and reproduce. But any microscopic organism can do as much. Well — time's up! Back you go — back to your sunless groove — the raw material of slums and wars — the ready prey of the first jingo or demagogue or political adventurer who takes the trouble to play upon your ignorance and credulity and provincialism. You poor, spineless, brainless boob — I'm sorry for you!

Thus does Rice sum up the processes of civilization, in which the age-old supine Zero finally evolves as the least important cog in the machine, the human cog, still preponderantly a slave-soul. While not advancing a positive social philosophy such as that of Toller or Wolf, Elmer Rice nevertheless presents the picture of an economic class conditioned by the fact that the social conflict dominates its whole existence. Outspoken and provocative, *The Adding Machine* stands not only as a pioneer milestone in American drama, but also as a contemporary play which has already won its place as a classic in dramatic literature.

At last the evolution of America as a nation, and the influence of European events and ideas brought home by the World War, had created an articulate advance-guard of young playwrights critical of their America and convinced, as the European moderns were before them, that the theatre must be used as a medium for self-criticism. Under the protecting ægis of the Theatre Guild, another playwright, more intransigeant than Elmer Rice, held the mirror up to America, making it shrink in angry resentment from the reflection of itself which it saw there. The playwright was John Howard Lawson, and the play *Processional.* To the socially sensitive American looking across his country in the years following the World War the picture offered was not a pleasant one. The vigilante spirit, fanned into flame by the professional patriots of the war days, continued to display the burning crosses of the Ku Klux Klan and to flourish in the guise of "Law and Order" committees organized on the assumption that no strike is justifiable and the only good striker a dead one. The two bitter industrial conflicts of Lawrence and Herrin were still bleeding memories. Wall Street was beginning to climb toward the dizzy apex of 1929. And the accompanying national rhythm of these years was that of jazz, to which post-war America was intoxicatedly swaying. The scene was brutal, menacing, but given the turbulence that was and still is America, it was also promising and full of beauty. Something of all this Lawson strove to fuse into what he called "A Jazz Symphony of American Life." *Processional* is a violent picture of the American scene, in terms that have become intensified during the years of sharpening social conflict that followed its production. To audiences seeing it in the recent Federal Theatre revival for the first time, twelve years after its original production, its story was still the story of America today.

The scene of *Processional* is the "Outskirts of a large town in the West Virginia coal fields during a strike," which Lawson describes as follows: —

A drop curtain, like those used in the older vaudeville theatres, represents a town street painted with brick buildings, signs of CEN-

TRAL HOTEL, PALACE MOVIE, QUICK LUNCH, *etc. In center of curtain is the door of Cohen's General Store with show window painted on curtain and this sign:* ISAAC COHEN THE CUT-RATE STORE, GREEN-GROCER, ANTISEPTIC BARBER, KOSHER DELICATESSEN, MINING TOOLS *. . . The tone . . . of the drop . . . is startlingly crude . . . blaringly American. . . . Down the aisle of the theatre comes a newsboy selling papers, shouting as he comes . . .*

Extry! Extry! Trouble in West Virginia! . . . Jazzin' up the big strike! . . . Soldiers an' miners clash! . . .

We know at once that this is no drawing-room comedy, that grim reality lurks behind the vaudeville tone deliberately taken by the playwright. What follows is not so much a clear-cut story as a kaleidoscopic picture of those violent aspects of American life, those "lower depths," which hitherto had not been thought of as material suitable for the theatre. The characters, as in Rice's *The Adding Machine,* were not individuals, but social types, and expressed themselves in graphic idiom, pronouncing truths to which the ears of theatregoers were entirely unaccustomed.

The miners on strike are a typical group of polyglot "Americans," bored with the Marxian exhortations of a Polish worker. A vaudevillian Sheriff and an equally vaudevillian Man in a Silk Hat, "President of the Law and Order League," bolstered up by deputies and soldiers, are on hand, under martial law, to "prevent" violence. The typical young newspaperman has come to get a big story. And Isaac Cohen, the typical little Jewish merchant, is there, upset by the violence of this labor struggle and by his inability to control his motherless, adolescent daughter, Sadie.

In Sadie, Lawson has portrayed with insight the American-born offspring of the underprivileged immigrant. With the warm blood of her race and of youth beating in her veins and the American rhythm of jazz tingling in her feet, with her neglected mind and her lack of opportunities to realize a creative urge to dance, little Sadie Cohen is threatened, in a hostile and brutal world, by the undirected, whipped-up emotions that drive her on. It is inevitable that she should come to grief and that her nemesis, in the atmosphere of industrial violence which surrounds her, should be a wild young striker, Dynamite Jim.

Jim is an example of the American pioneer stock that has gradually deteriorated with the advance of capitalist industrialization. His mother and his worn-out grandmother are living in a dilapidated barn. As the result of a drunken blunder, Jim is thrown into jail, escapes, kills a soldier sent to recapture him and hides out with his mother. Inadvertently he learns that she has spent the night with a crowd of drunken soldiers in the hope of making enough money to get him away to safety. This scene in the old barn, where all the divergent, antagonistic social elements in the play come together, presents, for all its luridly colored treatment and its jazz trimmings, an authentic microcosm of their America with which Lawson intended to shock smug theatregoers into awareness.

After condemning his mother for her "dirty sin," Jim goes out to fight for his life with reckless indifference, and it is Sadie Cohen who pays the price for his disillusionment. Among the miners and soldiers shooting each other like enemies, in a scene lit up by a Ku Klux cross, little Sadie stumbles about, mud-spattered and forlorn, but strangely excited. When Jim, having come upon her, hears the approaching soldiers, he callously hurries into a dark mine, carrying her in his arms. . . . But Lawson has still a finale to add to his symphony in jazz. It begins with a grotesque portrayal of the Ku Klux Klan performing a solemn denunciation of two immoral women, Jim's mother and Sadie, soon to be the mother of Jim's child. Swaying in the rhythm of jazz, King Kleagle ("another incarnation of the Man in the Silk Hat") and his Goblins condemn Sadie as "a Jazz Kid." But Sadie with shining eyes tells them she's not ashamed, she's glad!

> I'm agonna raise my kid . . . sing to him . . .
> show hlm the moon. . . .

Six months after the horrible night of the man-hunt, Jim suddenly turns up. Strung to a tree, with his eyes gouged out by the Klan, he had been cut down by a farmer, sent to jail and later discharged for lack of evidence. Besides, "they" judged, being blind he "can't do no harm no more." Jim has remembered Sadie's voice "like a bell ringin'," and when the brisk young reporter suggests marriage, Jim is ready. But before the final scene of the jazz wedding takes place, the Man in the Silk Hat appears, bearing "good tidings." Shaking the revolutionary Polish striker warmly by the hand, he announces: —

> We want to open up the mines, make concessions, boom business, sign contracts, all that sort of thing . . . a lasting agreement, everybody fully pardoned . . . all around you the shining faces of loyal workmen!

But to the Sheriff he says in a low voice: —

> Make a list of the marked men and we'll get them in their beds tonight! . . .

The closing chords of this American symphony are those of the jazz wedding. When the blinded Jim shouts,

> Shake a leg, ma!

his mother replies harshly:

> We can dance with our hearts breakin'.

And as in the beginning of the play, the newsboy shouted: "Extry! Extry! . . . Soldiers and miners clash!" so now he shouts: "Extry! Extry! Big peace!" Thus we watch the conclusion:—

Jim stands center smiling blindly. Sadie at a little distance from him swaying wildly, while the whole crowd marches round them, the Jazz Band and all the other characters. Then the Procession marches down through the audience. With an increasing noise and rhythm, the Procession disappears at the rear of the Theatre. Then there is silence. . . .

SADIE

They're gone, we're alone.

JIM

(*Feeling his way toward her*) Where are you now?

SADIE

(*Swaying and singing softly*) I'm agonna raise my kid, sing to him soft. . . .

(*Curtain.*)

Thus another pioneer milestone in American drama integrates the universal social conflict with its American equivalent and translates it into the native rhythm and argot of American life.

During those early postwar years, when a new type of American playwright came to understand that the antagonisms engendered during the war period were actually, in a capitalist society, permanent concomitants of the social conflict, a *real* drama of this conflict was being enacted in America and the entire world became its audience. This was the Sacco-Vanzetti case, which, after having been in the Massachusetts courts for seven years, terminated in the execution of two men.

Calling themselves "anarchists" and branded as "foreign labor agitators," Nicola Sacco and Bartolomeo Vanzetti were accused of the murder of a factory paymaster in April, 1920. Their trial degenerated into a trial of opinion in which these

Italian workers, revealing themselves as unusually fine human beings, were branded as dangerous "radicals." In July, 1921, they were convicted of murder in the first degree. For six years more Sacco and Vanzetti languished in prison while their counsel and aroused protagonists of justice made every possible attempt to secure a new trial for them. All efforts to secure a new trial, in which additional evidence of innocence could be introduced, failed, and this in the face of a world-wide demand that two manifestly innocent men should not be judicially murdered. On August 3, 1927, the Governor of Massachusetts stated his "conviction" that Sacco and Vanzetti had had a fair trial, and that he found "no justification for executive intervention." On August 23d they were executed. . . .

A little over a year later, a play was produced in New York called *Gods of the Lightning,* the authors of which were Maxwell Anderson and Harold Hickerson. Although Anderson's career as a playwright at that time had little more than begun, he had, in collaboration with Laurence Stallings, already written a courageous new type of play about war, *What Price Glory.* A few inconsequential plays followed, after which Anderson once more seized a living subject, hewn from the material of the Sacco-Vanzetti case. In *Gods of the Lightning* Anderson showed sound theatrical judgment (he is understood to have been technically the playwright in the case, utilizing Hickerson's well-prepared material) by changing the actual characters sufficiently so as to spare the audience a too oppressive contact with reality. The substance of the case is retained, and in the trial scene some of the actual testimony is offered almost verbatim just as Dreiser used similar detail in his *An American Tragedy.* The characters are a quiet young Italian, Capraro, and a fiery young Irish-American, Macready, an I.W.W. organizer from California. Macready represents the new type of

American workingman. He understands the capitalist system and the conflicts it breeds, and he expresses himself in a breezy vernacular that is a joy to the ear. Indeed, Macready is one of the unforgettable characters of contemporary American drama.

The first act takes place in a restaurant in the Labor Lyceum of an Eastern seaboard city. The usual types of polyglot American workers come in and out. A strike is on and from the hall back of the restaurant we catch sentences of the speakers at a strike meeting. A labor spy urging violence is unmasked and thrown out, which we know bodes no good for the strike leaders. Soon the audience alone learns, in a short and furtive scene, that Suvorin, the restaurant keeper, an old revolutionary worker embittered by years spent in American prisons for labor activity, has just stolen a huge sum from the paymaster on his way to pay the strikebreakers, and that Suvorin's confederate has murdered the paymaster. Thus for the audience the identity of the criminals is at once established, and with this knowledge we now watch the "framing" of two innocent men. Rosalie, Suvorin's daughter, and Macready's sweetheart, arrives in alarm with an evening paper reporting that warrants are out for his arrest and for that of Capraro for having "instigated a riot" in connection with the strike. She implores "Mac" to keep out of things for a while, since the police persistently fasten all blame on him. He refuses, believing that with his efforts the strike may yet be won. But at this moment the news comes to him over the telephone that the police have wrecked the strikers' hall and apparently broken the strike. Soon thereafter a policeman and a sergeant enter, accompanied by the labor spy, armed with warrants for the arrest of James Macready and Dante Capraro, charging them with the murder of the paymaster.

In the second act the playwrights make effective use of the material taken from the testimony in the Sacco-Vanzetti case to show how those who control the machinery of law and government, even in a democracy, use that power against any groups or individuals who seem to them to threaten the existing order. For as we listen to the District Attorney, to a prominent businessman, and others, we realize that, to the conservative governing class, anyone who protests against the evils of the capitalist system is, in their own words, a "Bolshevik," or a "red," who should be exterminated. We are further illumined by hearing the District Attorney, Salter, browbeat his witnesses into giving false evidence. One of these, for example, is a widow whose only son is ignorant of the fact that she has been supporting them both by keeping what the District Attorney delicately refers to as "a certain type of house." Under threat of revealing this to her son, he forces her to swear that from the window of her home she saw Macready fire the shot that killed the paymaster. If we recall the evidence in the Mooney case, we know that Anderson has here not drawn upon his imagination.

From District Attorney Salter's office we pass to the courtroom, where the judge, described by the District Attorney himself as "dead from the neck up for twenty-five years and from the neck down for about forty," is trying the case. The witnesses perjure themselves, his own counsel questions Macready, and the District Attorney cross-examines him. I quote from the courtroom scene of this trial of opinion:

JUDGE VAIL. Does the State wish to question?

SALTER. Yes, your Honor. So you believe, Mr. Macready, that you are going to be convicted?

MAC. If it can be fixed it will be.

SALTER. What makes you so pessimistic, Mr. Macready?

MAC. I've been around in this country some, and I've seen the courts work. When you get a red or an agitator in court the custom is to soak him.

SALTER. Have you ever been convicted of a crime?

MAC. Well, I've been convicted of belonging to the I.W.W. out in California, if you call that a crime.

SALTER. Were you guilty?

MAC. I was of being an I.W.W.

SALTER. What are the principles of the I.W.W.?

MAC. One big union, organized to break the capitalistic strangle-hold on natural resources.

SALTER. Does the I.W.W. advocate violence?

MAC. Only when expedient, which is seldom.

SALTER. When does it consider violence expedient?

MAC. Listen, we're taking up time here. If you're interested in the I.W.W. I've got a book I'd like to lend you. You can read it in fif-teen minutes, and when you get through, you'll know something about economics.

SALTER. Thank you. But do you advocate violence?

MAC. I never have.

SALTER. You would if you thought it expedient?

MAC. I would. So would you. So does everybody.

SALTER. And you don't think the workers get justice in this country?

MAC. No. Do you? Did you ever hear of a policeman hitting a capi-talist over the head?

SALTER. Do you believe in our Constitution?

MAC. I believe it was made by a little group of hogs to protect their own trough. Anyway, why bring up the Constitution when you don't even enforce the bill of rights? The whole damn thing's a dead letter except the eighteenth amendment, and the only reason we make a play for enforcing that is because there's graft in it! You use the courts and the Constitution and the flag and the local police to protect capital and keep the working man in his place! Whenever there's a law that might be to the working man's ad-vantage, you forget that one! That's why you forget the bill of rights! And when some law gets passed by accident that might hamper capital, you forget that! You forgot the Sherman Act till some of you figured out how you could apply it to the Labor Unions! And then, Jesus Christ, how quick you put it on 'em!

(*Judge Vail's gavel falls.*)

JUDGE VAIL. Have you no respect for the courts, sir?

MAC. Certainly not. The courts are the flunkies of the rich.

JUDGE VAIL. You realize that you are on trial in this court for your life?

MAC. Do you think you can scare me into respecting you?

JUDGE VAIL. I merely wish to warn you sir, that in this frame of mind you make an exceedingly poor witness in your defense.

MAC. It's my usual frame of mind.

SALTER. So you don't advocate violence?

MAC. No. If I did I wouldn't work through the unions.

SALTER. Isn't it true that you and Capraro and a man named Nick Bardi, who was killed, organized the attack on the police on the afternoon of the murder?

MAC. We didn't attack the police. They attacked us. We did nothing we didn't have a right to do under that Constitution you're talking about.

SALTER. But you knew there would be violence?

MAC. We knew the police could always be trusted to start something.

SALTER. You had been warned not to try to re-establish your picket lines?

MAC. We had. By a corporation judge.

SALTER. Now, Mr. Macready, isn't it true that you and Capraro started this riot to draw the police and make it easy to get away after robbing the payroll?

And so on until Salter questions Capraro. The young Italian takes the stand:—

ATTENDANT. Do you swear to tell the truth, the whole truth, and nothing but the truth?

CAPRARO. As near as I can.

JUDGE VAIL. There are two possible answers to that question: I do, or I do not.

CAPRARO. You must excuse me. I do.—As near as I can.

JUDGE VAIL. Do you mean that you will tell the truth to the best of your knowledge and belief?

CAPRARO. If you like that phrase better—yes, I do. But I would not wish you to believe that I would know the truth better than other men, for it seems to me that no man would know the truth exactly.

(*Judge Vail smiles frigidly.*)

SALTER. Do you believe in capitalism?

CAPRARO. No.

SALTER. You believe that all property should belong to the workers?

CAPRARO. Property should belong to those who create it.

SALTER. You are a communist?

CAPRARO. I am an anarchist.

SALTER. What do you mean by that?

CAPRARO. I mean, government is wrong. It creates trouble.

SALTER. You would destroy all government?

CAPRARO. It will not be necessary. I would rather wait till it was so rotten it would rot away. That would not be so long now. (*He smiles.*)

SALTER. You are an anarchist?

CAPRARO. Yes.

SALTER. You are against this government of ours?

CAPRARO. Against all governments.

SALTER. Have you ever thrown a bomb?

CAPRARO. No, I would leave that for the other side.

SALTER. In 1917 you left your home to avoid the draft, didn't you?

CAPRARO. Yes.

SALTER. You opposed the war?

CAPRARO. It was a war for business, a war for billions of dollars, murder of young men for billions.

SALTER. You broke the law in evading the draft?

CAPRARO. Yes.

SALTER. You don't mind breaking the law?

CAPRARO. Sometimes not.

SALTER. Who decides for you what laws you will break and what laws you'll keep?

CAPRARO. I decide it.

SALTER. Oh, you decide it!

CAPRARO. Every man decides for himself.

SALTER. There was nothing to prevent you from deciding to kill a paymaster and putting the money in the bank?

CAPRARO. No, only I. I would decide against it.

SALTER. Do you honor that flag?

CAPRARO. I did before I came to this country. Now I know it is like all the other flags. They are all the same. When we are young boys we look on a flag and believe it is the flag of liberty and happy people—and now I know it is a flag to carry when the old men kill the young men for billions. Now I look at that flag and I hear it saying to me, "How much money have you? If you have plenty of money—then I promise you paradise—I will give you more—I will give you the justice and freedom of your neighbors! But if you are poor I am not your flag at all."

SALTER. What is your religion, Mr. Capraro?

CAPRARO. I have none.

SALTER. You are an atheist?

CAPRARO. Yes.

SALTER. You are then an outlaw, bowing neither to the standards of God nor men?

CAPRARO. I have committed no crime.

SALTER. And do you expect us to believe that, Mr. Capraro? What, in all solemnity, in the name of God, prevents you from committing a crime?

CAPRARO. Myself. My own heart.

SALTER. You set yourself above God, above all law, above all control?

CAPRARO. I have met nobody I would trust to decide for my own soul.

SALTER. Your Honor, we have stumbled here upon a subject more serious than robbery, more serious than murder. If I had known where my questions were leading, I should have hesitated before asking them. Perhaps I should apologize—

MAC. You're goddam right you should! (*The gavel falls.*)

CAPRARO. Is there any reason in your Constitution why I should not believe as I think? Is there any reason in your Constitution why I should worship your God or your flag?

SALTER. That is all, your Honor.

MAC. For Christ's sake, Amen.

(*Capraro leaves the stand.*)

The surprise of the trial comes when Suvorin, a witness for the defense, is cross-examined by Salter and virtually accused of various crimes committed by him while working under assumed names. Seeing that he cannot save himself, but expecting to save Macready and Capraro, Suvorin confesses to the robbery of the paymaster and admits that his accomplice, recently killed by a Federal officer, committed the murder. But Salter is too clever a hand at his game to let even a confession spoil this case for him. His orders are to convict these men and to knock the fear of capitalist power into the hearts of insurgent workers from the Atlantic to the Pacific. At once he is on his feet:—

SALTER. This man's confession is an obvious fraud. He is under sentence of death. He has nothing to lose. His daughter is to marry Macready. The man on whom he fixes the crime is dead. This story has been concocted to save the defendants. . . .

So, as was to be expected, the jury, saturated with prejudice and fear, found the two guilty of murder and the judge, refusing to grant a new trial, pronounces the sentence of death. But before he does so, let us listen with him to Dante Capraro pleading against the imposition of the death-sentence upon him: —

What I say is that I am innocent, not only of this crime but of all crimes. I have worked, I have worked hard, and those who know these two hands will tell you they have never needed to kill to earn bread. I have earned by labor what I wanted to live, and I have refused to be a member of any class but the working class, even when it could have been, because to be in business is to take profits, to be a parasite, to take what you have not deserved and that I could not do. All my life I have worked against crime, against the murder of war, against oppression of the poor, against the great crime which is government. Do not do this thing, Judge Vail. It has been a long time and I have suffered too much to be angry. I know that you have been an unjust judge to us, that you have fear for us, and therefore hate for us — that you have wanted us dead and have taken advantage to kill us. You have ruled to help us in the little things so that you could safely rule against us at the last. But you are an old man, and wearier than we, even if we have been in prison; and you too will die sometime, even if you kill us first. So I say to you, do not do this thing, not because the world looks at us and knows that you are wrong, but because if you do it you will prove that I was right all the time. If you kill us in this one-time free city, in this one-time free country, kill us for no wrong we have done but only for passion of prejudice and greed, then there is no answer to me, no answer to the anarchist who says the power of the State is power for corruption, and in my silence I will silence you.

In the last act we are back again in the restaurant. It is 11:30, the electrocution has been set for midnight. There is an air of impending tragedy about the place. Most of the workmen we have already met are gathered, asking each other in low tones if this horror is actually going to happen. The clock moves relentlessly toward twelve. Rosalie returns from a last attempt to get a stay of the execution from the Governor. She sobs, the men whisper, the crowd murmurs outside. The hands point to a minute to twelve, then "click to midnight." Wildly Rosalie asks what it says on a bulletin board across the street erected to keep the anxious crowd informed. One of the men reads: "Capraro Murdered." Soon a cry, a woman's shriek, tells her that now it says "Macready Murdered" and as Rosalie speaks agonized and bitter words of protest the curtain falls.

That this dramatization of an international *cause célèbre* should have proved a Broadway failure is no reflection on the play's values. The long list of significant plays which have met a similar fate testify to that absence of *play-consciousness* which is not only the most serious obstacle to the existence of a vital theatre but the most destructive enemy of the serious playwright. *Gods of the Lightning* should have met a response that would have sent this stirring play across the country. To explain its failure, as some commentators have done, by saying that the American people wanted to forget the whole affair, substantiates the charge against them. For it is just because our audiences go to the theatre in order to forget the great questions of life that we have, with infrequent exceptions, a theatre cluttered with the paltry and the futile, that is preponderantly a theatre of escape.

Nor could there be a more thought-provoking commentary on this basic weakness of our theatre, than the fact that no American dramatist has, in recent years, more consistently made himself the representative of this theatre of escape than Maxwell Anderson, who began his career by expressing such a constructive integration with his time. Less than two years after *Gods of the Lightning* Anderson fled from immediate reality all the way to Elizabethan England and enchanted Broadway audiences with an historical pastiche, partly in verse, toying with the relation between Elizabeth and Essex: *Elizabeth the Queen.* These audiences usually discussed the play in terms of Lynn Fontanne's make-up as the Virgin Queen, but in this case the usual mental confusion between play and production didn't much matter. Anderson followed this with a glib, shallow, muck-raking play about political intrigue and corruption in Congress, called *Both Your Houses.* The same year, escape again, this time to *Mary of Scotland,* which caused much admiring comment on the ability of such a short little lady as Helen Hayes to seem every foot a Queen.

Anderson's escape from the realities of his own age to the love-life of distant queens is far less meaningful, however, than the more insidious forms of escape, which serve as the basis of his most recent plays. The first of these, *Winterset,* is a distorted wraith of *Gods of the Lightning,* swathed in layers of poetic disguises. What has Anderson, for all his hope expressed in a preface to this play, that "now is the time for our native amusements to be transformed into a national art of power and beauty," made of what he vaguely refers to as "a contemporary tragic theme"? That event, growing out of world-wide clashes of social and economic convictions, becomes in *Winterset* the private quest of a boy to clear the name of his father, wrongly executed for the murder of a paymaster. In his quest the son finally tracks down, and in one spot, too, all the guilty men involved: the gangster who had committed the murder, the young member of the gang who had borne false witness, the judge, now mad from brooding over his responsibility for the unjust death sentence. The play vaporizes over an unreal theme instead of coming to grips with a real one and remains a fable for audiences, who do not get even a glimmer of its awful, factual basis. What has become of the flesh-and-blood Macready and Capraro, uttering intolerable truths? They have escaped into the son called Mio, a working-class boy of seventeen who explains in this wise to a pal he meets: —

> . . . Fell in with a fisherman's family on the coast and went after the beautiful mackerel fish that swim in the beautiful sea. Family of Greeks — Aristides Marinos was his lovely name. He sang while he fished. Made the pea-green Pacific ring with his bastard Greek chanties. Then I went to Hollywood High School for a while. . . . Jeez, I'm glad we met up again! Never knew anybody else that could track me through the driven snow of Victorian literature. . . .

Apparently, at the Hollywood High School, Mio learned all Maxwell Anderson knows, including a familiarity with Freud that would make the average college graduate pea-green as the Pacific with envy. . . . Finally, after the audience, or the reader, has floated over this poetic sea of unreality, Mio and his love are mowed down by the gangster's machine gun, and the play ends with a long speech in blank verse, expressing the utter defeatism that has supplanted the playwright's former responsive understanding of the implications of the Sacco-Vanzetti case.

Winterset represents an escape into an unreal world where such manifestations as legal injustice, venality, and inequality are no longer related to their social sources. And this loss of a real integration with his age, by a contemporary playwright who has achieved the reputation of Anderson, must be understood just as clearly as O'Neill's escape into Catholicism. For this reason, therefore, we must refer briefly to three of his most recent plays in which Anderson makes evident that the only answer he has for his age is a negative one.

In *The Wingless Victory* Anderson selects as his subject: race prejudice. But he removes this issue from all current reality to the New England of 1800, where at that time it was perfectly logical that a proud Colonial family should feel outraged when their sea-captain son and brother brought home to them a Malay wife and their two brown children. The world was vast and practically unknown in those days, and America a country in which Negro slavery was accepted as a God-ordained institution. Why, therefore, should a Malay princess seem other than a black woman from the jungle, with whom a marital alliance would be nothing but a disgrace and a scandal? And what has all this to do with the race-superiority myth manifesting itself today in America, in Great Britain, in Germany, in Austria and elsewhere? A parable may be an excellent art form, as, for example, Werfel's *Goat Song,* but its application to the current scene must be unmistakable, completely sound, and always illuminating the contemporary parallel. What light does a primitive princess, an escape on a stolen ship, personal hatreds, revenges and betrayals, hemlock poison, and suicide throw on the tragedy of race prejudice as it is now affecting the lives of millions of our fellow beings? When O'Neill in *All God's Chillun Got Wings* places his race tragedy in the heart of New York City today, integrating it with the life we know and are a part of, he comes to grips with his problem. As a result, his audiences, psychologically identified with it, come to grips with it also. But Anderson escapes from the living problem of race prejudice, actually flees from it in distaste, saying a shuddering "No" to his age instead of a responsible "Yes." And in his escape he of course takes his bewildered audiences with him.

In his next play, *High Tor,* the escape element is more pernicious, for here it is offered as a solution to the youth of today contemplating, with a disgust that is clearly the playwright's, the industrial evils, the sordid acquisitiveness bred by our present economic order. The art form is a fantasy, involving ghosts of the Dutchmen who first explored the Hudson River on whose shores the scene is laid. These phantoms of a bygone age are again totally unrelated to the conflict presented by the play and only confuse the issue. Anything rather than life *as it is,* seems to be the tune of Anderson's inner compulsion. The penniless young hero of the play refuses to sell the Hudson peak he owns to a trap rock company, because he loathes commercialism. He also refuses a steady job in the town below because he loathes the treadmill existence necessitated by working for one's living. So he works a few weeks at a time and then off he goes, to hunt deer or track a bear. This is escapism with a vengeance. Let those of our youth who loathe capitalism run away from it, if they can, and the devil take the hindmost.

When our young hero finally awakens to the fact that his rugged individualism will not change the tenor of his age, how does he resolve his conflict? Or rather, how does Anderson effect youth's economic and spiritual adjustment to his age? The solution seems incredible in a dramatist who once stood in the heart of the fray. Capitulating to the trap rock company, our hero announces that, after selling for what he can, he'll "move out farther west, *where a man's land's his own.*" Is there, then, between him and the capitalist world he despises, any difference other than that of degree? We have in *High Tor* the picture of a genuine personal dilemma arising out of the social conflict, resolved in terms of individual escape that is not only blind but spurious.

It is in *The Masque of Kings,* however, that Anderson's social negativism finally bursts forth. Here he uses the tragic figure of the Crown Prince, Rudolf of Habsburg, as a peg on which to hang his own loss of hope and faith. We see Rudolf rejecting his high purpose of establishing in his country a liberal government, and reduced to the blackest cynicism. Listen to Anderson speaking through his character: —

> I have been taken up on a crest of time and shown the kingdoms of the world, those past, those present, those to come, and one and all, ruled in whatever fashion, king or franchise, dictatorship or bureaucrats, they're run by an inner ring, for profit. It's bleak doctrine, it's what the old men told us in our youth, but it's savagely true. . . .

And again in Rudolf's last speech before he escapes into death: —

> . . . Now the earth boils up again and the new men and nations rise in fire to fall in rock, and there shall be new kings, not you or I, for we're all past and buried, but a new batch of devil-faces, ikons made of men's hope of liberty, all worshiped as bringers of the light, but conquerors, like those we follow. I leave the world to them, and they'll possess it like so many skulls grinning on piles of bones. To the young men of Europe I leave the eternal sweet delight of heaping up their bones in these same piles over which their rulers grin. To the old and dying I leave their dying kingdoms to be plowed by the new sowers of death — fools like myself who rush themselves to power to set men free and hold themselves in power by killing men, as time was, as time will be, time out of mind unto this last, forever. . . .

If Anderson believes — for manifestly these sentiments are his — that all governments, even "those to come," will be "run by an inner ring, for profit," and that greed and violence will continue "unto this last, forever," then what avail his talents? One can only hope, as in the case of Eugene O'Neill, that such retrogressive thinking represents merely a phase, that the affirmation of life as a positive good will reassert itself in the work of Anderson. In any case I believe that the readers of the future, seeking in drama, a commentary on our America, will find it, not in Anderson's confused escape plays, but in *Gods of the Lightning,* his transcript of an actual tragedy of the social conflict.

It was inevitable that the protagonist of one of America's major social problems, the Negro, should at last appear in the American theatre as something other than the laugh-provoking shuffling servant or the nimble song-and-dance man. The pioneering Provincetown Playhouse had produced O'Neill's psychological portrayals of the Negro: *The Emperor Jones* and *All God's Chillun Got Wings.* But the drama of the Negro as a race just emerging from slavery, discriminated against in every field of endeavor, struggling for security and equality against the hostile, dominant white world—that drama had still to be portrayed. It is in the South that the Negro's struggle takes on its most violent aspects. Thus it is the Negro of the South who logically becomes the focus for the play that most truthfully describes his race, its hopes and fears, its injustices, its slow awakening to its peculiar position in the social conflict and the part it is being called upon to play by feudal employers on the one hand and aroused workers on the other.

Once more, the Provincetown Players demonstrated their understanding of what constitutes important American drama by producing, in 1926, *In Abraham's Bosom.* It had as a subtitle "The Biography of a Negro," and was the first full-length work, as well as the first professional production, of a young man from North Carolina named Paul Green. The son of a farmer, Green had worked in the fields with Negroes since childhood, feeling himself one of them, loving them, understanding them. Indeed, later, in referring to his "own folks," Green is careful to explain that he means both "black and white." And so when he writes for us the tragic story of an aspiring Southern Negro, the victim not only of the Southern white man's prejudice but also of his own inadequacies, we know that this story is authentic, written out of the playwright's heartfelt devotion to this submerged people. Abraham is a completely individualized character, but he stands, nevertheless, in his strength and his weakness, as a symbol of his race.

We first meet Abraham McCranie as a young turpentine worker of twenty-five in the woods of Eastern North Carolina. His surname he has from his white father, Colonel McCranie, once a slave-owner, and so, as a mulatto, Abraham starts with the troublesome mixture of white and black in his bosom. Abe has one goal, which a primitive bully of a Negro describes in the first scene: "Wanter rise him up wid eddication" — to which he adds the significant words: "Give a nigger a book and des' well shoot him. All de white folks tell you dat." We see Abe using his lunchtime to grapple with an arithmetic problem his untrained mind cannot solve. Finally he gets it: —

> I got it, folkses, I got it . . . Dat white man know whut he doing, he all time git dem answer right.

As he eagerly looks up, he observes that all the other Negroes have fallen into a heavy sleep. His face takes on a look of hopeless brooding: —

> Yeh, sleep, sleep, sleep yo' life away. I figger foh you, foh me, foh all de black in de world to lead 'em up out'n ignorance. Dey don't listen, dey don't heah me, dey in de wilderness, don't wanta be led. Dey sleep, sleep in bondage. (*He bows his head between his knees.*). . .

But we soon see that it is not only against the inertia of his own people that Abraham has to fight, but against those Southern whites who hate and fear the Negro, who are determined to use all their traditional power to keep him in bondage. Such is Lonnie McCranie, the Colonel's son, filled with a venomous hatred of Abe, both because of their relationship and because he resents Abraham's daring to aspire to the status of a self-respecting human being. The decayed Colonel is at heart a kindly person, genuinely concerned for the welfare of his black son, Abraham. But when it comes to Abraham's exhibiting any threat to white supremacy, even the Colonel treats him like the slave he in his heart holds him still to be.

We understand this attitude from the beginning of the play when the Colonel and Lonnie come to the Negro workers in the woods and Lonnie begins to bait Abraham. Nevertheless Abe presses the Colonel not to neglect asking the school board if he may start the Negro school that is his dream. When Lonnie silences him like a dog, and Abe, half-mad with resentment, protests, Lonnie strikes him across the face with his whip. At this Abraham seizes Lonnie and hurls him into a thicket. Although his father had earlier endeavored to check Lonnie, this striking a white man is an act of black insubordination which, even today, the white Colonel cannot tolerate. Seizing the whip and shouting: "Git down on your knees, you slave!" he horsewhips Abe. . . . This is the setting for Abraham's aspirations, this world of hostile whites and primitive blacks against which he dares to pit himself.

We now follow Abraham's struggle to help his people rise through "eddication." Three years later he is still in abject poverty, reading, studying. His undernourished wife, who loves him devotedly but has no understanding of his quest, has just borne him a son. His wife's mother, still mentally in the jungle, hates him and injures his books when she can. The Colonel, about to die and wanting to make amends, gives Abe a deed to a plot of land and in addition tells him he is at last to have his school for Negro children. Ecstatic, Abraham lifts up his manchild and baptizes him "Douglass.". . . But less than a year later the precious school is already doomed. Abraham, in his zeal a hard teacher, has savagely thrashed a lazy, lying pupil. His enemy, Lonnie, seizes this opportunity to get rid of him, and his own people, who are not only afraid to fight for him but who also in their hearts resent his superiority, desert him.

Fifteen years later, in the Negro section of a North Carolina city, Abraham seems to have struck bottom. Refusing to be a servile black, he has lost job after job. His wife is disfigured with toil. His only son, so proudly named Douglass, loathes books and school. He is a guitar-strumming ne'er-do-well, who steals from his mother when he can and hates his father because Abraham, in his disappointment and his pain, beats him. Again Abe loses his job, explaining as always: "I didn't do nothing but stand up foh my rights. A white man sass me and I sass back at him. And a crowd of 'em run me off. Won't be able to git no other job in dis town. . . ." So he yields to his wife's pleading to go back "home," rent some land from Lonnie, and "start all over."

Once more three years have passed. Back on the land, things have gone only slightly better, but Abraham justifies himself: "I ain't a farmer. My business is with books. . . ." So indomitable is he in his purpose that he is again attempting to launch a school, larger, more ambitious, to grow into "a great center of learning." We hear him rehearse the speech he is to make at the meeting that night:—

> Looking over the country . . . we see eight million souls striving in slavery, yea, slavery, brethren, the slavery of ignorance. And ignorance means being oppressed, both by yourselves and by others—hewers of wood and drawers of water . . . We want our children and our grandchildren to march on to full lives and noble chareckters, and that has to come, I say, by education. We have no other way. . . .

But the white men will have none of this meeting to plan a Negro college, and after driving off those of his own people who have come to hear Abraham, they beat him and order him to leave the district. As Abe, clothes torn and bloody, crawls along the road, he meets Lonnie, now stout and middle-aged, and in wild indignation tells him what has been done to him. Lonnie profits by the situation to defraud Abe of his cotton crop and tells him to look for other land. At this outrage all the years of abuse and frustration burst from Abe in rage, and in the physical combat that follows between the two men, Abraham kills Lonnie. Pursued by all the agony of fear experienced by a black man who has killed a white, he stumbles back to his cabin. It is only a matter of moments, however, before he and his terror-stricken family hear the posse of white men approaching. Angelic in his faith, Abraham still hopes that perhaps, if "I go talk to 'em, I go meet 'em . . ." As he bravely opens the door a roar of guns greets him and he falls while we hear voices saying: —

> Quit the shooting. He's dead as a damned door! Now everybody get away from here — no talking, no talking. Keep quiet — quiet. . . . Yeh, mum's it. He won't raise no more disturbances! . . . What a bloody murder he done! He's still now, by God! It's the only way to have peace, peace. Peace, by God!

And in Abraham's bosom, too, there is peace at last — but it is the peace of annihilation.

No story can more than suggest the poignancy and beauty of this tragedy of the Southern Negro's struggle for emergence as told by Paul Green. Strangely enough, however, when the play was first produced some of the most prominent among Abraham's own people resented its outcome and called it "defeatist." But surely, telling the truth about the difficulties facing any emerging class or race is not defeatist. The sailors of Cattaro met defeat and their leaders met death, but there was no defeat in their living slogan: "Comrades! Next time better!" Like them, the beaten Abraham points the way of his people's task, pleads through his example that efforts like his own must not continue solitary and misdirected. There is no romantic success-story in Paul Green's play. Between that and his tragedy lies all the difference separating easy fiction from that clarifying truth which is always defeatism's most redoubtable enemy. There are no easy victories in the social conflict.

Chapter 6 The Social Conflict in American Drama of the "Left"

We have seen how drama dealing with postwar aspects of the social conflict ranges all the way from such explicitly revolutionary European plays as those of Toller and Wolf, to the first American plays of Rice, Lawson and others in which social antagonisms are implicit in the bitter discord between groups of opposing economic interests which they depict. As the political changes in Europe obtruded more and more inescapably on our American consciousness, and, in addition, a shattering economic crisis at home brought America into the arena of social upheaval, it was inevitable that all this should serve not merely as a stimulus to the writing and production of plays of the social conflict but that these plays should become more sharply positive in their point of view.

A definitely "left" orientation of social drama may be observed in the difference between the type of play dealing with the American Negro which we have already discussed and the two plays we shall now consider. To go from O'Neill's Negro plays, which are essentially not social at all, but psychological, and Paul Green's treatment of the Negro, in which the social conflict looms in the background of the race conflict, to such plays as John Wexley's *They Shall Not Die* and Paul Peters' and George Sklar's *Stevedore,* with their calls for organized action against the racial-economic injustice of the white South, is to move from one economic epoch into another within the postwar period.

In 1927 the Sacco-Vanzetti case impelled Maxwell Anderson to write a play about its tragic injustice. Seven years later another trial, conducted according to the super-legal code of Southern race-prejudice, namely, the Scottsboro case, drove John Wexley, in his play *They Shall Not Die,* to help arouse the nation to the defense of nine Negro boys, patently innocent of the crime of rape for which eight had been convicted and condemned to electrocution. As the court proceedings in this again internationally prominent case, begun in March, 1931, have only just been concluded, I must assume that my readers are familiar with its essentials. Except for the use of fictitious names, Wexley's play is largely a transcript of the case, both in the utilization of actual testimony and court proceedings, and in the vivid re-creation of the atmosphere of that deepest South in which the case was tried.

The scene of the first act is the county jail of "Cookesville," in "a Southern state." It is divided into three parts: the white prisoners' cage, the office, and the "Pen" or large steel cell for "niggers." The dilapidated aspect of it all, with deputy sheriffs spitting into dirty cuspidors, conveys to the audience the caliber of a community which permits such a scene to represent the forces of constituted authority. This atmosphere of lethargy gives way to one of excitement, however, when news comes over the telephone: ". . . seems like a half-dozen white kid hoboes was thrown off the freight from Chattanoogie by some *niggers.*" We also learn that there were

two white gals on the train dressed like boys, with overalls. . . . No, they didn't say what the niggers done to 'em. . . . Mebbe they did and mebbe they didn't. . . .

But the immediate assumption is that the "niggers" *did,* and while a deputy sheriff exclaims, "Now we're gonna see some fun" and orders rifles in readiness, we hear voices outside:—

Hi, theah, Hillary!
What's up heah?

We heerd of some rape.
Who raped 'em?
How many?
Where're the niggers, Fred?
They'll be along.
I'm gittin' my gun.
Where're them gals?
Whut's up, Jeff?
They musta near killed 'em.
Theah's be'n a rape.
A rape?
A rape!
A rape!

And so, with no more knowledge or evidence of crime committed than this, the black man hunt is on. . . .

When the two white girls are brought into the jail, it is obvious that the hard, sharp-tongued young woman, called Virginia Ross in the play, is no better than she should be and that her badly frightened companion, called Lucy Wells, is a different type of girl who has gotten into bad company. We learn that both girls are cotton spinners, but we already have an idea of their earnings from a remark made earlier in the scene: "No wonder 'em gals'll lay down with niggers. They kin make mo'in five minutes than workin' all night.". . . After Solicitor Mason, the prosecuting attorney, has taken a good look at the girls and questioned Virginia, he says firmly to Sheriff Trent: —

Just hold on, Trent . . . These heah girls don't look to me like they've been attacked.

TRENT (*with amazement and somewhat hurt*): Whut yuh tryin' tuh say to me, Luther . . . ?

MASON (*firmly*): I'm trying to say this. . . . If these girls had been assaulted against their will, they wouldn't be acting the way they are. They would be crying all over the place. They would be all hysterical and nervous. Their clothes would be torn. . . .

TRENT (*angered, annoyed*): You ain't sayin', Luther, that them niggers were left alone with these white gals and didn't try to . . . ?

MASON (*interrupting with some scorn*): No! They didn't need to try. These whores just took them on for whatever they could get. . . .

TRENT: Luther, you ain't goin' to let them black bastards get away with somethin' like that?

MASON: No . . . I'm not letting them get away. . . . (*He seems to be listening to Trent only with one ear and to be thinking of a plan of procedure.*)

TRENT (*in a rage*): I don't keer if they are whores . . . they're white women! You think I'm gonna let them stinkin' nigger lice get away from me? Like hell I am! They're gonna git whut's comin' to 'em long as I'm the law round heah. . . . (*He is at the height of his temper and his feelings run away with him.*) What the hell will folks heah say of us . . . ? Why, they'll spit on us if we don't git them niggers when we got the chance. . . . The hull county, the hull State, the hull South'll be down on our haids. . . .

This the shrewd Solicitor knows, and he also sees here a sensational case which, if cleverly handled, should bring him political advancement. Therefore when the Sheriff suggests that "It wouldn't be sech a bad idea to let the boys . . . save the county money . . . with a coil of rope," he reminds him that "This county has got a bad lynch reputation already . . . What we want is just a nice speedy trial. That's all."

His first step is to have a doctor make a physical examination of the girls. When the reasons for this are explained to Virginia, she denies categorically that any "nigger" has raped her. And while the doctor reports evidence that the girls "have both consorted with a man," he refuses to go so far as to assert that there is evidence of rape, and certainly will not say there is evidence of rape by *nine* Negro boys, which happens to be the number caught on the freight train and brought to the Cookesville jail. Disgusted with the doctor's scruples, the Solicitor now sees his only hope for evidence in the testimony of the girls, and correctly assumes that Virginia can be readily corrupted into committing perjury on the witness stand. With an appeal to race-prejudice, with the promise of newspaper notoriety and above all a job, a new dress and three dollars a day as an accommodating witness, there is nothing this ignorant girl, all her normal instincts and desires perverted by her underprivileged life, will not swear to.

The Solicitor meets a rebuff, however, in the person of one of the captured white hoboes, young Collins, who insists, even in the face of threats, that he saw no rape on the train and is convinced that there wasn't any. "I don't have tuh swear 'way the lives of nigger kids fo' yo' benefit," he says shrewdly to the Solicitor, adding to the threatening Sheriff: "I ain't no nigger. I'll talk my haid off." . . .

The final scene of the first act is a portrayal of white "law" in the darkest South, and of what everyone familiar with the Scottsboro case knew had actually transpired there. The Theatre Guild's realistic production of the play made the nine Negro boys in the cast seem the Scottsboro boys in the very flesh. Kicked and horsewhipped by the Sheriff and his deputies when they deny their guilt, the innocent young Negroes, broken by physical torture and terror, "confess" to the rape of the two white girls. And while some of the soldiers whom the careerist Solicitor has cunningly asked the Governor to send to Cookesville, for the maintenance of "law and order," jab with bayonets the terror-stricken Negro boys huddled in their pen, the curtain falls.

When the second act opens a few weeks have passed and the trial is over. Eight of the boys — all but the youngest — have been found guilty and sentenced to death. In her poverty-stricken home in a section known as "Niggertown," helping to support her family by furtive prostitution, Lucy Wells bitterly repents her part in the trial. Not only is she deriving none of the economic benefits promised her for her perjury, while the "smart" Virginia is cashing in, but also remorse is gnawing at her. It is romance that serves as the motive power impelling Lucy to confess the truth. Heartbroken because a young traveling salesman, with whom she is genuinely in love, leaves her when he learns of her connection with the Cookesville case, Lucy, ill for months, suffers nights of torment—"thinkin' of them po' nigger kids, goin' tuh burn any day on that 'lectric chair. I dream of them screamin' an' yellin' in pain . . . I see myself, always lightin' fires and helpin' tuh burn them. . . ." Finally she manages to see the young man when he is again in town, for he also cares too much to be able to forget her, and she informs him that a letter she wrote telling him the truth about the young Negroes' innocence and her perjury has been intercepted by the prosecution and that the Cookesville prosecuting attorney is coming to see her that night. Quickly the young man hurries her into his car and carries her out of further harm's way.

Meanwhile other matters of great importance to the condemned boys have occurred which Wexley presents in a scene in the Negro death-house of the prison where the boys now are. Treadwell, a representative of the A.S.P.C.P.—the American Society for the Progress of Colored Persons (the name in the play for the N.A.A.C.P.), comes to inform them that the Society has engaged the services of the distinguished Southern lawyer, Mr. Lowery, whom he has brought with him, to conduct an appeal for them. The young Negroes are not impressed by what they instinctively sense as the perfunctoriness of this offer; and when, impatiently pressed for their signatures of authorization, they explain that they promised a "white man . . . from the No'th . . . to give his N.L.D. [the name in the play for the I.L.D.—the International Labor Defense], man a chance to talk wid us befo' we sign anything at all . . ."

In this situation lay the critical turning-point in the Scottsboro case, and our "left" playwright presents it with eloquent conviction. For while other groups had been protesting, the International Labor Defense had been acting. From their point of view, the Scottsboro case represented just another flagrant incident in the omnipresent class struggle, and the Scottsboro boys were nine black workers against whom the economic oppression of the South was arrayed—a symbol of its determination to continue master in what it regarded as its own house. The I.L.D. intended to save these Negro working boys by rallying to their defense the united workers of America and by demonstrating that for awakened labor, at any rate, no color-line exists. Small wonder then that the I.L.D. regarded the N.A.A.C.P. as "bourgeois" and lacking in a determined dedication to their cause, while the conservative N.A.A.C.P. "viewed with alarm" the entry of the "radical" I.L.D. into the case.

Wexley makes the introduction of this new element of the social conflict the dramatic crux of the scene in the Negro death-house. There now enters the New York lawyer of the N.L.D., called Rokoff in the play, to secure, in his turn, the authorization of the boys for his organization to represent them on their appeal. To the horror of the Southern warden, Rokoff begins by shaking hands with the Negro boys who have been let out of their cells at his request. He offers them cigarettes, he talks to them, and they become completely absorbed by what he is saying:—

Now, you boys are in a jam but there are a lot of other fellers, black and white, all over this country and they're in jams, too. And we're an organization that tries to get these fellers out and free. Now you just saw how this boy here . . . refused to give his buddy any of those cigarettes I gave him. You've got to understand right away that that's the wrong idea to have. Men should stick together. Now, I'd like to show you what I mean and how we work. Just suppose there are two men on this side of me (*He demonstrates with gestures his meaning.*) fighting against a certain thing and they're being licked. And on this other side, are three men fighting against almost the same kind of thing and they're being beaten, too. But if these two fellers and these three fellers would get together . . . (*He holds up two fingers on one hand and three on the other.*) . . . then there would be five . . . and nobody could lick 'em! That's what we work for. You see, up North and out West and here in the South there are white workers fighting for liberty and justice and a right to live happy. And down here in the South you black workers are fighting for the same thing. But you're all fighting apart. Now, if you will fight for the white workers in the North and the South and the East and West, then they'd get together and fight for you black fellers down here. Now you know as well as I do that it's going to be very hard for you boys to get a fair trial down here. I don't have to tell you that. I can't fool you with promises and fine words. You know you didn't get a fair trial at Cookesville.

PARSONS (*with feeling*): No, we didn't . . .

TREADWELL (*somewhat excited, unable to contain himself*): Listen to me, boys! I'm one of you and God-willing, I'd like to be darker than I am if that would help my people. And therefore I want to warn you against this dangerous N.L.D., this radical organization which only wants to use you boys as a cat's paw to pull their chestnuts out of the fire. You poor children are too young to know it but they are about the worst, insidious group of traitors to this country. . . . They not only want to spread rebellion and revolt through your case but they also want to destroy and ruin the great, benevolent A.S.P.C.P.

WARDEN (*to Lowery, in a low voice*): That high yaller ain't sech a bad talker.

PARSONS: Well, whut do yuh want tuh do fo' us?

TREADWELL: We have only one object. *One object.* And that is to get you boys a fair trial. We have no ideas of overthrowing the government as they have.

PARSONS: How . . . how yuh gonna git this fair trial?

TREADWELL (*annoyed*): We . . . we will not spare any effort to protect you from the death penalty. . . .

ANDY: Well. . . . We don't want no lip-talk.

ROKOFF: And I'm not going to give you any lip-talk. I'm not going to say you're going to get that fair trial that these high-sounding organizations will try to get. And you know why you can't get it. You can't get it because the South wants you to burn. They want to teach you blacks a lesson, they want to frighten you blacks with the burned-up bodies of nine negro boys. They want to make you shut up and keep quiet. They want to keep the nigger in his place . . . that's why. . . . And so . . . the only thing fair that you'll ever get will be a fair amount of electric juice to burn you alive on the chair in there. . . . (*Points to the door leading to electrocution chamber.*)

LOWERY (*striding forward, angrily*): Now, don't you pay attention to this talk. You better be white man's niggers, or . . .

ROKOFF: I object to these interruptions, Warden Jeffries . . .

WARDEN: Well. . . .

LOWERY (*simultaneously with Warden*): But Mr. Jeffries. . . .

ROKOFF: I'm an attorney, Warden, and I'd like to finish what I have to say! . . .

LOWERY (*interrupting*): I never heard sech kind o' talk to niggers. . . .

ROKOFF (*with some irony*): But I've heard of Southern courtesy. . . .

WARDEN: Well, make it quick-like, Mist' Rokoff. . . .

ROKOFF: I will. (*To the boys.*) Now you're thinking if things are as hard as I say they are, what can be done? What can the N.L.D. do? I'll tell you what we can do. First, we'll get the finest lawyers in this country to fight the courts at their own game . . . but more important than that, we'll go to the workers of America, to the workers of the world. We have proof that you're innocent of these rape charges. We'll show them this proof. Then we'll say to them: Black and white workers of the world! Workers of America! Down in the South nine innocent boys are being put to death because they have black skins. Are you going to stand for that? And they will answer with a shout that will ring around the whole world. . . . NO. We will not. Yes, we will force the South and those in the South who are trying to murder you . . . we will force them to free you. Yes, they will. They'll be afraid to keep you, afraid to kill you . . . they'll be afraid of fifteen million black workers who will stand shoulder to shoulder with fifty million white workers and who will roar . . . Don't you touch those boys! Don't you dare touch those black children workers . . .!

And after Rokoff further divulges that he has not only gotten permission for the boys to see their parents, for the first time since their arrest, but has actually brought them to the prison with him, there seems little doubt left that they will "sign wid the N.L.D." Still they ask to be allowed to talk it over alone, and after debating the question, they decide to sign. The scene ends as the most intelligent of them says with feeling:—

> NO . . . No, niggers! We ain't gonna die. No. No. . . .
> NO . . . NO!

The last act takes place after the United States Supreme Court had twice set aside the death sentences of the Negroes and sent the case back to the Alabama courts on the ground that the constitutional rights of the defendants had been violated by the exclusion of Negroes from jury service. In the first scene we meet, in New York, one of the country's most successful criminal lawyers, called Rubin in the play, and hear Rokoff enlist his services to try the case, which is to be held once more in an Alabama court. He agrees and we move on with him to the last scene of the play, the trial scene, reproduced, in many of its speeches and incidents, with almost complete fidelity, from the records of the actual case.

The illegality of the procedure causes Rubin to declare again and again that in all his years at the bar he has never heard or seen anything like the conduct of this trial. Not only is the expected Negro race prejudice rampant, but in addition the prosecution shamelessly incites Jewish race prejudice, when the Solicitor himself utters his notorious appeal: "Gentlemen of the jury, tell 'em, tell 'em that Southern justice cannot be bought an' sold with Jew money from New York . . ." No account of it here can convey to the reader an idea of the quality of this scene, which must be read in its entirety as John Wexley wrote it. . . . The great surprise for the prosecution is, of course, the appearance on the witness stand of Lucy Wells and her recantation of her perjured testimony at the first trial. But instead of this having any salutary effect on those present in the courtroom, Lucy is hissed and threatened as she leaves the witness stand. Finally, after appeals to the lowest passions have been expressed, after Rubin has made his summation and the judge has charged the jury, the play ends thus:—

(The Jury stands, turns and crosses to the jury-room, in silence. The court-audience is silent too. The Guard shuts the door on them. A pause. Silence. Then suddenly from the jury-room, a sound of loud laughter, raucous and derisive. As he hears this, Rubin is startled for a brief instant and turns slowly, not knowing where the sound is coming from. Then with a half-audible sound and an expression of mixed astonishment and dismay, he rises slowly and speaks.)

RUBIN: If the court please. . . . I have seen and heard of many strange and crazy things in my time, but I have never heard of anything like that . . . in there. (*He gestures toward jury-room.*) But I'm not through yet. Let them laugh . . . let 'em laugh their heads off . . . this case isn't ended yet. . . .

ROKOFF (*rises and stands at Rubin's side*): No . . . and our fight isn't ended either. . . .

JUDGE (*rapping his gavel*): This . . . this is out of order . . .

ROKOFF (*continuing over the interruption*): You have the jurisdiction to stop us in this court . . . but there are hundreds of thousands of men and women meeting in a thousand cities of the world in mass protest against the oppression and ownership of man by man . . . and over them, you have no jurisdiction. . . .

RUBIN (*inspired and fired by Rokoff*): No . . . we're not finished. We're only beginning. I don't care how many times you try to kill this negro boy . . . I'll go with Joe Rokoff to the Supreme Court up in Washington and back here again, and Washington and back again . . . if I have to do it in a wheel-chair . . . and if I do nothing else in my life, I'll make the fair name of this state stink to high heaven with its lynch justice . . . these boys, *they shall not die!*

(*Laughter from the jury-room dies down and the court-audience stare at him with eyes and mouths agape . . .*)

Curtain.

After seven years of battle, the court proceedings were finally concluded, and in spite of the sentences hanging over four of these Negro boys, *they did not die,* thanks chiefly to the efforts of radical labor and its friends on their behalf. Six years after the opening of the case, the rape charges were dropped against five of the defendants (one having been held on an entirely unrelated charge), and now the five still in prison continue to hope that pardons will be granted them. True, this is hardly justice, but—they did not die. . . . And what prouder function can a playwright have than to utilize his own medium so that it will play its part on that greater stage where the battles for human emancipation are being fought!

However, not even the Theatre Guild's supposedly play-conscious and "superior" audience responded to John Wexley's play. Indeed, the North evidenced prejudices of its own, as well as the usual timorous refusal of audiences to face life and its problems in the theatre and to be stimulated to thought there. A notice issued by the Theatre Guild announcing a forthcoming play on the Scottsboro case, brought objections from irate subscribers. The general tenor of these was that so "unpleasant" and "controversial" a subject had no place in the theatre, and that, as one gentleman put it to me, saying more than he probably meant to: "The theatre's no place for dynamite!" Others informed me that they had no intention of using their tickets for such a play. Thus does Ibsen's compact majority merely change its blind spots in each succeeding age.

But sad as it is that the prejudiced theatre-conscious who had the privilege of seeing *They Shall Not Die* should refuse to attend, it is at least as sad that for thousands to whom this play would have presented a genuine experience, Broadway theatregoing is entirely prohibitive. Some colored persons at one of my lectures asked me if the Theatre Guild did not intend reducing prices for the "Scottsboro" play, or possibly giving it on certain nights at special rates "so that our people will be able to see it." Obviously a discussion of this problem, crucial as it is, has no place in this volume, but it must be mentioned here as a retort to the airy dismissal of such a play as *They Shall Not Die* as having been "no success." It cannot be repeated too often that a play's success in the theatre is not determined by its values as a dramatic work of art. The question of producing plays in such a way as to attract psychologically responsive audiences, at prices within their means, is of basic importance in the building-up of a play-conscious theatre — a truth which has been demonstrated by the splendid results achieved by the Federal Theatre.

Two months after *They Shall Not Die,* a totally different type of play also dealing with the black worker in the South, was produced in New York. This was *Stevedore,* the collaborative work of Paul Peters and George Sklar, two young playwrights with a thorough knowledge of their subject and with positive economic convictions. The Scottsboro case revealed the constant danger in which the Negro of the deep South lives. To relate this danger to the social conflict and make clear its economic aspects, to show that race-prejudice not only is the white employer's weapon for Negro exploitation but also acts as an economic boomerang for the prejudiced Southern white worker who refuses to make common cause with his black fellow-worker — that is the theme of *Stevedore.* And if this does not sound like a dramatic subject for a play, a perusal of the enthusiastic reviews of *Stevedore* by some of New York's Broadway-conditioned critics, notoriously unresponsive to social drama, will convince my readers that this is one of the most stirring examples of contemporary drama.

Stevedore takes us to the wharves and Negro section of New Orleans. The first scene, however, which at once places the black man as the scapegoat for the white, takes place at night in the back yard of a house. The lover of a married white woman of low caliber, named Reynolds, is breaking with her. When, stung by his insults, she threatens to "fix" him, he "beats her up." As she falls to the ground, shrieking, her awakened husband rushes out and finds her. Several neighbors appear. How is she to explain her condition? How answer the questions: "What happened? Who was it? Who did it?" She finds the always credible lie "Somebody just jumped out of the dark and grabbed me. . . . It was — a nigger!"

Almost at once we hear a voice from a police radio car repeating: "Woman attacked. . . . Pick up all suspicious Negroes . . . Pick up all suspicious Negroes." And in a police station we see a group of Negroes lined up for identification by the white woman. In the line we first meet young Lonnie

Thompson, the only Negro who dares protest against the treatment to which they are being subjected:

> . . . You know none of us ever touch dat woman. She say she don't recognize nobody. What you holdin' us here fo'? Why don't you let us go?

This is enough to make Lonnie a marked man. The Sergeant asks him his name, his place of work and inquires about his police record. Released, we hear him again voice his indignation in Binnie's lunchroom in the Negro section near the wharf. Ruby, the girl who adores him and whom he loves, is sobbing with relief at seeing him free. The other Negroes try to calm Lonnie's rage with a "You better forget it, boy . . ." "You talk too much . . . you heading straight fo' trouble," as he blazingly asks: —

> . . . What dey think I am? Do I look like some kind of animal? Do I look like somebody who'd jump over a back fence and rape a woman? . . . What right dey got to treat us dat way? Line up nigger. Step out, nigger. Get back in yo' cage, nigger. . . . Dat's de whole trouble wid de black man. Always crawling, crawling on his belly.

To which Binnie, the shrewd, capable Negress who runs the lunchroom, retorts: —

> Well, crawling on yo' belly's better dan hanging by yo' neck.

The Negroes, in their racy vernacular, discuss how they are constantly being "gyped" by Walcott, the Superintendent of the company for whom they work as stevedores. Presenting the argument of one of them that "Black man dat don' want to get in no trouble got to be a good nigger," Lonnie replies: —

> Well, here one black man ain't satisfied being just a good nigger. . . . You wo'k like a mule, dey cheat you on pay, and all you

can do is hush up and be a good nigger. Well, by God, I ain't gwine hush up. I gwine to Walcott and tell him we work twenty-four hours and we want to get paid fo' it.

And roused by Lonnie's "We don't lose no job if we all stick together," all but the cringing gang-captain and one other join to go to Walcott.

So we come to one of the most important scenes in the play, in Walcott's office. He has been bossing blacks for years, and he reveals himself when, after granting them two hours' more pay, he says to Sam, Ruby's father, who has been working for him for fifteen years, but clearly addressing himself to Lonnie: —

Guess I know how to treat my niggers. That is providing they're good niggers. None of my old men ever complain to me about anything. But you take some of these young fly niggers who get uppity notions and think they can hold down a white man's job; well, I reckon they're looking for trouble and I reckon I can help them find it. . . .

LONNIE: I reckon dat mean me, Sam.

WALCOTT: Nobody's talking to you. Keep out of this.

LONNIE: You been talking to me all dis time, ain't you?

(*A pause.*)

WALCOTT: You're a fresh nigger, aren't you? (*Pause.*) I understand you've been hanging around with Lem Morris, Thompson.

LONNIE: I been talking to him, yes.

WALCOTT: Well, you take my advice and steer clear of him.

LONNIE: I reckon I can use my own judgment, Mr. Walcott.

WALCOTT: You know he's a Red, don't you?

LONNIE: I know he talk mighty good sense.

WALCOTT: So you think he talks good sense, do you?

LONNIE: Yes.

WALCOTT: What do you call good sense? Organizing? Equality? The nigger's as good as a white man, huh? Is that what you call good sense? (*A pause.*) I've been watching you for a long time, Thompson. You're too god damn uppity. You shoot off your mouth too much.

SAM: He don't mean no harm, Mr. Walcott.

WALCOTT: You keep out of this. You start any funny business on *this* wharf, Thompson, and you'll get something you're not looking for. I haven't any use for you, Thompson. You're a trouble-maker. You're a bad nigger.

LONNIE: You mean I'm a nigger you can't cheat.

WALCOTT: What'd you say to me?

LONNIE: You heard what I said. You mean I'm a nigger you can't cheat. (*Walcott hits him in the face and knocks him down.*)

WALCOTT: You black son-of-a-bitch, you can't talk to me that way. (*Lonnie starts to rise; Sam takes a restraining hold of his arm.*) Now get out. (*Lonnie gets up and looks at him steadily.*)

SAM: Come on, Lonnie. (*They go out.*)

WALCOTT: Hey Mike! (*Mike enters.*) First thing in the morning get hold of Mitch and tell him to keep an eye on that Thompson nigger. (*He goes back to his desk, moves the chair as if to sit down; then pushes it aside and paces the floor in a fury.*) That god damn shine's been hanging around with Reds, that's where he gets those notions! Organizing! Equality! Christ, those coons are just running riot! This country won't be fit to live in any more. Look at all the rapes they've been pulling in this town. Look at what they did to that Reynolds woman. And did they catch anybody for it? No! Where the hell are the cops? . . . If they don't do something about it, I'll organize a posse and go after them myself. It's high time those niggers were put in their place. . . .

Again we hear the voice of the police car radio: "Renew search for Reynolds case assailant. Pick up all suspicious Negroes . . ." and then we see the stevedores in their noon lunch hour on the wharf. Between singing and jesting they talk desultorily about Lonnie's new ideas: black and white getting together in one union, better pay, no night work. . . . Lonnie now rushes in, cut and bruised, attacked as he came out of the union hall by a hoodlum white gang that has nothing to fear from the police. He exhorts the longshoremen to arm themselves and, aroused, they seize shovels, crowbars and ax handles. But the whistle blows, they falter, and soon Walcott comes roaring out, with two men. Subdued, the Negroes start back to work, but the two men approach Lonnie, and when Walcott says: "That boy's a trouble-maker. He's a bad nigger," they arrest him. Lonnie loudly protests and struggles to free himself, but, his black friends not daring to come to his aid, the men drag him off.

So far we have only been hearing about this new kind of union that believes white and black workers must organize and fight together in order that the white employer will no longer be able to use the unorganized, underpaid Negro as a whip with which to hold back the economic advancement of the white worker. Now we are at last to see this union in action, in the scene which is, ideologically, the crux of the play. We are shown a corner in the Union Hall, where there is a table with a mimeograph machine. On a blackboard is announced a mass meeting for the following night. Lem Morris, described as "a simple, rugged white longshoreman of about forty" is handing out leaflets to two Negroes and is trying to get Al, a typical, lazy white Southerner, to take some leaflets to the docks. At this moment Charlie, also white, rushes in excitedly waving a newspaper, and the scene continues:

CHARLIE: Hey, Lem! You know that Thompson boy who's been coming up here?

LEM: Yeah?

CHARLIE: Well, they pulled him in this afternoon.

LEM: What for?

CHARLIE: Rape.

MARTY: Rape?

LEM: Well, for Christ's sake!

CHARLIE: Yeah, in the Reynolds case. Here, they got it plastered all over the front page.

(*They crowd about him and look at his newspaper.*)

MARTY: My God, he got away!

CHARLIE: Yeah, he jumped off the viaduct.

LEM: Wonder where he is.

CHARLIE: Nobody seems to know.

LEM: God damn it. Wait till those lynch mobs get going. There's going to be hell to pay.

AL (*whistling*): There'll be a hot time in the old town tonight.

MARTY: What's this going to do to our meeting?

AL: I'm for calling that meeting off.

CHARLIE: So am I.

LEM: What do you mean, call it off? We can't call it off. We got to go through with it. And what's more we've got to help them. We've got to hit the ball on this Thompson business right away.

MARTY: What you going to do?

LEM: Well, the first thing we can do is to turn this meeting into a protest meeting. (*Picking up a leaflet.*) Look, Marty, there's some space up there. You got another stencil?

MARTY: Sure.

LEM: All right. We can run these through again, and put a couple of lines across the top. How about using a stylus on it?

MARTY: O.K., Charlie, run out and buy a can of ink, will you? (*Charlie leaves.*)

LEM: Say, Al. You got that tin can of yours downstairs?

AL: Yeah. What do you want it for?

LEM: Well, I want to take a run over to Binnie's and see what we can do.

AL: What do you mean, see what we can do?

LEM: Well, he's a member of the union and we've got to help him get away.

AL: Well, I'll be god damned if you can use my car to help a rape nigger.

LEM: Christ Almighty! You going to start that up again. Rape nigger. Where do you get that noise?

AL: That's what they arrested him for, didn't they?

LEM: You mean, that's what they framed him for.

AL: Aw nuts. You're always yelling about frame-ups. How do you know he didn't rape her?

LEM: Listen, you know damned well, the only reason they arrested him was to keep him from organizing the Stuyvesant Dock.

AL: That's your idea.

LEM: Well, you don't think old man Walcott would sit around and let him get away with it, do you? For Christ sake, Al, put two and two together, will you?

AL: Well, by God, some nigger raped her.

MARTY: Rape, my eye!

AL: Yeah, rape. You let 'em get away with it, and no white woman will be safe on the streets any more. Christ, if a nigger raped your woman in your back yard, how would you feel if we helped him?

LEM: Listen, Al. I don't stand for rape any more'n you do. But when anything smells as fishy as this does, I just know better, that's all.

MARTY: Quit your beefing, Al, and let him have the car.

AL: Now wait a minute. You help that rape nigger, and I'm going to pull out, and I won't be the only one either.

LEM: What the hell you trying to do, bust up this union?

AL: If anyone's trying to bust it up, you are.

LEM: Aw, bushwah. If we listened to you, we'd drive every black man out of the union.

AL: Well, I never did savvy the idea of blacks and whites in one union anyway.

LEM: Listen, Al. We've had this out before. The only way we can tie up this river front is by organizing these black boys, and you know it. There are three of them to every white man on these docks. And if you think you're going to pull a strike in two weeks without them, you're crazy. Now, what do you want them to do? Stick with us, or scab for Walcott?

AL: They'll scab on you anyway. You can't trust those dirty niggers.

LEM: That's it! That's the stuff! You call them dirty niggers, and they call you low white trash. If you'd cut that out, if you'd get together and fight the Oceanic Stevedore Company for a change, maybe we'd get somewhere.

AL: Aw, you're talking through your hat.

LEM: Don't be such a god damned fool. You work for the Oceanic Stevedore Company just the same as they do. You get your wages cut just the same as they do. And every time they get it in the neck, you can be pretty damned sure you're going to get it in the neck too.

AL: You talk just like a nigger-lover.

LEM: Aw, for Christ's sake, Al.

AL: Yeah. Like a god damned nigger-lover.

LEM: Nigger-lover! We've been working day and night to build up this union. If we're ever going to get anywhere — if we're ever going to get a decent living wage, it's going to be through this union. And if fighting for this union makes me a nigger-lover, all right: that's what I am!

MARTY: The hell with him, Lem. We can get Chuck Walker's car. (*Showing Lem the new leaflet.*) Here, how's this hit you?

AL: Wait a minute. You're not going to pass out those leaflets!

LEM: Why not?

AL (*angrily*): Well, we've got something to say about that, too.

LEM: There's no Jim Crow in this union, and you knew it when you joined up.

AL: All right, then, go ahead, go ahead! Help that rape nigger. Distribute your god damned leaflets. But you're not going to rope me in on it. (*He seizes the leaflets and throws them on the floor.*)

MARTY: What the—
LEM: Pick 'em up.
AL: Who says so?
LEM: Pick 'em up.
AL: The hell I will.
LEM: Then get out of here. Go on, get out! (*He pushes Al out.*)
AL (*offstage*): You god damned nigger-lover.
LEM (*after a pause*): All right, Marty! Let her rip.
(*Marty turns the crank of the mimeograph machine.*)

Thus is the reality of labor's common interests obliterated by the dividing issue of race prejudice, so deeply ingrained in Southern psychology that it has itself taken on the aspect of a formidable reality.

Lonnie has managed to escape during his arrest and the stevedores are hiding him under the wharf until they can get him away. The moment comes when he gives way to the terror of lynching that is in his very blood: "Oh Sam, every black man dat was ever lynched, I know how he feel, I know how he feel!" The other Negroes, including the franctic Ruby, cannot overcome their distrust of the white Lem Morris, who arrives to help Lonnie escape. "Dar ain't no white man you can trust," says Sam, "dat dangerous, white man hiding black." While Lem goes for a car, the white gang appears and in the fight that ensues Lonnie once more manages to get away. Now follows a dramatic scene in Binnie's lunchroom. We hear over the radio:—

New Orleans: Two white men have just been assaulted and severely beaten on the municipal docks near Napoleon Street by four Negroes, one of whom was identified as Lonnie Thompson, escaped Negro charged with the rape of Mrs. Florrie Reynolds. According to information just received, the two white men, employees of the Oceanic Stevedore Company, were set upon by the Negroes without provocation. One of them was knocked unconscious by a blow from an ax handle. The Negroes escaped and are still at large. Posses, which have been combing the Negro district for Thompson all afternoon, are now centering the pursuit around the wharf area. Race feeling on the riverfront has grown extremely tense.

The Negroes are filled with foreboding. What is going to happen next? A brick crashes through the window as the white mob goes down the street. And then, to the alarm of his friends, Lonnie enters. Binnie feeds him and he is just about to leave with Lem Morris in his car, when the mob returns. Hiding Lonnie behind the counter, they turn the radio on in a blare of jazz. Furious at finding a "white guy" . . . in a "nigger joint," some in the mob identify Lem as that union organizer, the "nigger-lover," manhandle him, and throw him out. The Negroes try to keep calm under the insults of the mob and of the police officer. But when the policeman proceeds to step behind the counter, Ruby utters an involuntary cry. But Lonnie once more escapes, shots ring out, and gentle Sam drops dead with a bullet wound in his temple. . . .

Next we see an attic in the Negro section. While the funeral services are being held and the Negroes are singing their spirituals, those tragic wish-fulfillments of a disinherited people, Lonnie appears. Almost at once news is brought him that the white gang is coming to "clean up" the "wharf niggers" and burn down their homes. Lonnie urges them to defend themselves, "to stay right hyar and fight." This is such a startling concept that the timid "good niggers," such as the gang captain on the wharf and the preacher, are aligned against him. But Lonnie knows the truth and speaks it: —

The lowest animal in the field will fight fo' its home. And all you can think of doing is running away. And supposing you do run away? Whar you gwine go to? Baton Rouge? Mississippi? Is it gwine be any different dar? Dey gwine treat you better dar? You gwine find jobs? You gwine get yo'self a home? Nassuh. You got black skin. You can't run away from dat. Make no difference whar you are, dey hound you just de same. . . . Nassuh, you can't run away from yo'self, black man. You been running away fo' two hundred years. . . . We can't wait fo' de judgment day. We can't wait till we dead and gone. We got to fight fo' de right to live. Now — now — right now.

So we come to the final scene, when, with the courtyard entrance to their homes barricaded with the poor possessions they have dragged together, — furniture, mattresses, an old wagon, — and armed with baseball bats, bricks and a rabbit gun, they await the white mob. It comes and when its leader commands them to come out or be killed, Lonnie answers: "We staying hyar." A shot rings out and the Negroes see Lonnie fall. But his lessons in solidarity have not been in vain and they rally, just as Lem Morris with a band of white union men arrive to help them. The fight goes on and finally there is a cry: "They're running! They're running! They're running!" Yes, black workers and white workers have fought together, and for once the white mob has been beaten. . . . But Ruby sobs over the dead Lonnie in her arms, and as the others gather mournfully about his body, the curtain falls. . . .

When *Stevedore* was announced, its producing organization, the Theatre Union, having established its theatre away from Broadway, was not in the least concerned over the possible antagonism of Broadway theatregoers, because it knew in advance that the play was being awaited by a huge audience, sympathetic with its ideology, to whose incomes the scale of ticket prices had been adjusted so far as this was possible. The Theatre Union, which began its career in 1933, with the anti-war play, *Peace on Earth,* described itself as "the first professional social theatre in America, incorporated as a non-profit-making, membership organization." It stated that "it was founded on three main principles which . . . differentiate it from all other theatres in America": —

> (*1*) We produce plays that deal boldly with the deep-going social conflicts, the economic, emotional and cultural problems that confront the majority of the people. Our plays speak directly to this majority, whose lives usually are caricatured or ignored on the stage. We do not expect that these plays will fall into the accepted social patterns. This is a new kind of professional theatre, based on the interests and hopes of the great mass of working people.
>
> (2) We have established a low price scale so that masses of people who have been barred by high prices can attend this theatre. A scale of thirty cents to a dollar and a half (no tax), with more than half the seats priced under a dollar, is bringing thousands of people into the theatre who have never seen a professional play, or who have not gone to the theatre for years.
>
> (*3*) In order to exist we organize our own audience through benefit theatre parties and subscribing members.

Before the opening of *Stevedore,* one hundred and thirty-eight organizations, including teachers', workers', political, peace and cultural groups, eager to welcome a theatre producing plays that deal boldly with the "deep-going social conflicts," had bought in advance enough seats to guarantee a six weeks' run for the play. This beginning launched *Stevedore* on a successful run of twenty-four weeks, in contrast to the Theatre Guild's six weeks' subscription run of *They Shall Not Die,* presented before audiences who, if not actually prejudiced, were largely resentful or bored.

Why the Theatre Union was unable to continue its valuable work is again a subject outside the scope of this book. But the reasons may be summed up in a single phrase: the seemingly insuperable difficulties of conducting such a theatre in the midst of the anti-social, anarchic conditions under which the commercial theatre today functions. The economic basis of the theatre, from the problems of the playwright and actor to those of the electrician and stagehand, is unsound. All of which shows that the only possible *people's* theatre, save for small workers' theatres functioning within their own ranks, must be a theatre permanently endowed by the Government, Federal and local.

The all-important truth that no such entity as *a* theatre audience exists, but that there exists *a variety* of audiences with tastes as divergent as their interests, is one which the commercial theatre, compelled to cater always to the lowest common denominator of audiences, must ignore. That plays must find their own audiences was again made clear by the fate of another outstanding drama of the social conflict, *Let Freedom Ring,* a play by Albert Bein, from the novel by Grace Lumpkin, *To Make My Bread.* Once again we are taken into the contemporary South, described by Franklin D. Roosevelt as constituting "the nation's number 1 economic problem." This time, however, we are concerned chiefly with the submerged white workers swallowed up by the South's particular brand of feudal industrialism.

Let Freedom Ring tells the story of the metamorphosis of Carolina mountain folk, American pioneer stock, into textile workers, finally driven by the unendurable conditions of their life into taking part in a labor battle. It opened on Broadway, perfectly cast and directed, with sympathetic care lavished on every detail. But escape-seeking audiences who want nothing of the theatre save a few hours of forgetfulness, and who are able to pay for this, would have none of a play that says: "Fellow-Americans it is *your* America that is like this — look at it!" After two weeks on Broadway *Let Freedom Ring* was compelled to close, and it would have been a tragic waste so far as the theatre is concerned, had not the Theatre Union taken it over and presented it to play-conscious audiences, responsive to problems from which they well knew there was no escape. It now played for ten weeks, and an eight weeks' tour followed.

Nowhere will the reader find a more authentic picture of human exploitation than in this drama of the industrial South. We remember the play in terms of its characters, notably those of the McClure family, headed by Ora, the mountain-born mother, who, fighting against poverty in the mill-town, awakens, at first against her will, to active participation in labor's struggle. There is a scene in the second act in which Ora listens to the opposed arguments of her two sons: the elder, Kirk, a fighting labor organizer, in and out of jail, "beat up and run outa towns," long regarded as the family black sheep, and the younger, John, a "wizard of a mechanic," the mill-owner's pet, rejoicing at his personal rapid advancement, as yet indifferent to the lot of his fellow-workers. As Ora, torn between them, deeply affected by Kirk's account of the workers' struggle, slowly begins to respond to his point of view, we experience one of the most beautiful scenes in contemporary drama. . . . Born of another age and country, of outspoken "left" convictions, *Let Freedom Ring* carries forward the drama's battle for the emancipation of the workers, begun by Hauptmann's *The Weavers*.

We turn now to the work of the most outstanding of the young "left" playwrights, namely, Clifford Odets, and find ourselves confronted with an unusual talent. While both their gifts and their outlook on life exhibit a complete disparity, Odets is the only American dramatist who may be said to challenge the position of Eugene O'Neill. I have no intention of measuring a young man just beginning against a genius whose work first appeared two decades ago. But if we compare the earlier plays of O'Neill with the plays thus far written by Odets, we find evidence of unusual gifts in both. Also both are essentially concerned with the inner conflicts of the individual, with his struggles for fulfillment against external forces that dominate and crush him. Odets' plays, like O'Neill's, paint for us a gallery of frustrated, psychologically maladjusted men and women. But at this point the comparison ceases and their fundamental difference comes into view. For unlike O'Neill, Odets knows that the inner conflicts of the individual have as their basic cause the *social* conflict, that every life is conditioned by the economic struggle. He interprets, therefore, even the most personal problems of his characters in the light of this social conditioning, thus placing himself, in distinction from O'Neill, not only in the general category of *social* dramatist, but also in the special position of "left" dramatist. And as a "left" dramatist, though many of his characters are doomed, his interpretive note is always one of hope for humanity.

What are the earmarks of this exceptional talent that struck so forcibly those hearing it for the first time? The first is a dynamic quality which at once absorbs the listener. You may disagree with Clifford Odets, you may be annoyed, or even repelled by him. But you cannot be indifferent to him. Until the last word is spoken, you are almost literally on the edge of your seat. This dynamic quality derives much of its power from Odets' second extraordinary gift, his flair for pungent, evocative dialogue. This dialogue is the ultimate in contemporary idiom, but it has nothing in common with the currently popular "clipped" speech, described by some one as made up of a grunt and a hiatus. It consists in the ability to find the *mot juste,* the word or phrase packed with suggestibility, with an instantaneous appeal to the imagination of the audience. When Ralph, in *Awake and Sing,* earnest, hard-working boy, says of life

It's crazy—all my life I want a pair of black and white shoes, and can't get them. It's crazy!

the sentence is an explosive, bursting with a hundred implications. Even the most inarticulate, the most shoddy of his characters is enabled, by means of the supremely right expression, to give to the audience, in his own language, the essence of himself. Add to these elements Odets' unerring sense of dramatic values, of making visible the inner drama of his characters, and we understand why we listen to an Odets play compelled by the intensity of an impact with life itself. Completely individualized as his characters are, they all fulfill Odets' deeper purpose in creating them, namely, to serve as symbols of various aspects of a social order whose hurtfulness for humanity he is indicting. If the Emperor Jones is a symbol of the Negro race, and Yank, the hairy ape, of emerging man, then Joe Bonaparte, the Golden Boy, is a symbol of youth today, destroyed by the conflict between the need for self-realization and the possessing demon of materialist success, and Jacob, the grandfather of *Awake and Sing,* a symbol of man's eternal revolutionary idealism.

The defects of Odets' work are the defects of his qualities. They make him far less valuable for the reader than he should be in the light of his play content and his underlying point of view. Relying on his dynamic dialogue for purposes of the theatre, he fails to give the reader enough of the interpretive and descriptive matter which makes the reading of an O'Neill play or a Shaw play so satisfying. O'Neill's descriptions of his scenes—Professor Leeds's study in *Strange Interlude,* the New England house of the Mannons in *Mourning Becomes Electra*—are projections of character and environment and furnish the reader with material of inestimable creative value. Obviously, for the play's short life as theatre, this extra-dialogue material is not necessary, because the characters are there in the flesh and describe themselves, as does the scenery. But the reader is entitled to all the dramatist can possibly give him. This the other dramatists discussed in these pages have all recognized, but Odets has thus far failed in responsibility to his greatest permanent audience, his readers, and thereby detracted from the value of his work as dramatic literature. This defect is one which a deeper insight into the function of drama, beyond theatre, should speedily remedy in a playwright of Odets' importance.

No play has ever had so turbulent a career as Odets' first work to reach the public, the one-act play *Waiting for Lefty*. With its first nonprofessional showing before an audience sympathetic to social drama, the play became the talk of the town overnight. New York had just been experiencing a violent and finally successful strike of taxi drivers. In this strike the public was vouchsafed intimate knowledge of the methods with which strikes are fought, including the employment of gangster strikebreakers. Odets' drama about taxi drivers, with a strike meeting as the center from which the various episodes of the play radiate, thus achieved an immediate integration with its informed audiences, especially since the characters on the stage, representing the head of the union and some committeemen, address the theatre audience directly. And this integration was furthered by the fact that the Group Theatre, which produced *Waiting for Lefty* and with which Odets was affiliated, was ideologically sympathetic with the play's point of view.

On a bare stage, the porcine racketeer and union head, who knows which side butters his bread, is trying to persuade the men *not* to strike. In the audience voices begin calling for their chairman: "Where's Lefty?" As one of the men seated on the platform rises and steps forward to speak to the crowd — the theatre audience — a gunman stationed at the proscenium slowly moves forward. But the head of the union says insolently: —

Sure, let him talk. Let's hear what the red boy's gotta say!

The speaker is Joe:

You boys know me. I ain't a red boy one bit! Here I'm carryin' a shrapnel that big I picked up in the war. And maybe I don't know it when it rains! Don't tell me red! You know what we are? The black and blue boys! We been kicked around so long we're black and blue from head to toes. But I guess anyone who says straight out he don't like it, he's a red boy to the leaders of the union. What's this crap about goin' home to hot suppers? I'm asking to your faces how many's got hot suppers to go home to? Anyone who's sure of his next meal, raise your hand! . . . And that's why we're talking strike — to get a living wage!

VOICE: Where's Lefty?

JOE: I honest to God don't know, but he didn't take no run-out powder. That Wop's got more guts than a slaughter house. Maybe a traffic jam got him, but he'll be here. But don't let this red stuff scare you. Unless fighting for a living scares you. We gotta make up our minds. My wife made up my mind last week, if you want the truth. It's plain as the nose on Sol Feinberg's face we need a strike. There's us comin' home every night — eight, ten hours on the cab. "God," the wife says, "eighty cents ain't money — don't buy beans almost. You're workin' for the company," she says to me, "Joe! you ain't workin' for me or the family no more!" She says to me, "If you don't start . . ."

At these words the lights fade and a spotlight thrown on the space between the men seated on the stage indicates a room. Joe's wife, the mother of his two young children, enters, drying her hands on her apron. There follows the first Episode between Edna and Joe, in which the more intelligent and courageous woman rouses her man to belief in the urgent necessity for a strike. Fired by her convictions, Joe leaves her joyous; and we see him finishing his speech at the strike meeting: "You guys know this stuff better than me. We gotta walk out."

Five other Episodes show, as with Joe, the critical incident in each of the committeemen's lives responsible for their participation in this labor struggle. In the first, an industrialist tries to corrupt Miller, a young laboratory assistant, by promise of a large increase in salary, to spy on the progress of the chemist who is working on a new type of poison gas for the next war. Miller loathes war only a little more than he loathes spies. So when on his prompt refusal he loses his job and the industrialist suavely smiles: "No hard feelings?", Miller ends the Episode with:

> Sure hard feelings! . . . Nothing suave or sophisticated about me. Plenty of hard feelings. Enough to want to bust you and all your kind square in the mouth! (*Does exactly that*) . . .

And that is why Miller is no longer a "lab" assistant, but a taxi driver.

The next Episode is called "The Young Hack and his Girl." For three years Sid and Florence, deeply in love, have been "engaged," without even a room to sit in alone. What could better sum up their long frustration than Sid's rationalization: "I'm glad we never got together. This way we don't know what we missed." They try to be gay by dancing to a tune on a cheap phonograph. Sick with longing, he whistles and "soft shoes" for her. But it's no good. She buries her face in her hands, he falls on his knees and puts his face on her lap. . . . So Sid is now a committeeman on the platform in the strike meeting.

Back at the meeting, we next witness the unmasking of a labor spy, brought in by the racketeer union head to tell the boys how the taxi strike in Philadelphia failed and how he, a former driver, has been blacklisted ever since. But it so happens that one of the boys at the meeting is his brother. He rises in the audience to recite the company spy's record, and orders him loudly to "scram." The spy "scrams."

The next scene is a New York theatrical producer's office. A young actor, in need of a job, with his wife about to have a baby, tries in vain to impress his ability on a commercial producer who is, after all, only the other side of the shield that is the commercial theatre. But the young woman stenographer, who is a "militant," gives him a dollar and also a copy of something to read, called *The Communist Manifesto.* From actor to militant taxi driver is not so strange a transformation in these days.

The last Episode shows the hospital intern, young Benjamin, "top man" on the staff, learning two facts about the society which he had hoped to serve as a doctor. The first is that not ability, but political pull or financial pressure gives the young doctor his chance, even if some charity patients die because the incompetent nephew of an influential Senator operates on them instead of the able Dr. Benjamin. The second fact he learns is that when the hospital has to economize, it is he, the "top man," who is let out. Why? The distinguished Gentile physician, Dr. Barnes, sickened by the chicanery to which his profession has descended, tells him why. It is because of "an old disease, malignant, tumescent," explains Dr. Barnes angrily. "We need an antitoxin for it." That disease is anti-Semitism, and Benjamin is a Jew. . . . So the Episode ends thus:—

BENJAMIN: Lots of things I wasn't certain of. Many things these radicals say . . . you don't believe theories until they happen to you.

BARNES: You lost a lot today, but you won a great point.

BENJAMIN: Yes, to know I'm right? To really begin believing in something? Not to say, "What a world!" but to say, "Change the world!" I wanted to go to Russia. Last week I was thinking about it — the wonderful opportunity to do good work in their socialized medicine —

BARNES: Beautiful, beautiful!

BENJAMIN: To be able to work —

BARNES: Why don't you go? I might be able —

BENJAMIN: Nothing's nearer what I'd like to do!

BARNES: Do it!

BENJAMIN: No! Our work's here — America! I'm scared. What future's ahead, I don't know. Get some job to keep alive — maybe drive a cab — and study and work and learn my place —

BARNES: And step down hard!

BENJAMIN: Fight! Maybe get killed, but goddam! We'll go ahead! (*Benjamin stands with clenched fist raised high.*)

The Episodes are over and on the platform one of the committeemen rises. In racy idiom he describes the conditions of their lives and of their venally controlled union, and urges them to action. Just as he pleads: "What are we waiting for. . . . Don't wait for Lefty!" — a man dashes forward through the audience and up on the stage to tell his fellow workers that they have just found Lefty, behind the car barns, with a bullet in his head. . . . So when the speaker cries: "Hear it, boys, hear it? . . . Well, what's the answer?" the entire audience seems to shout: STRIKE! and again and louder: STRIKE, STRIKE, STRIKE!!! — as the curtain falls.

This play of fighting workers, exposing almost every evil inherent in the present economic order, met a barrage of censorship wherever an attempt to produce it was made. Its experience in New Haven will, I think, be of special interest. At the annual Yale Drama Tournament (spring, 1935), the George Pierce Baker Cup had been awarded to the Unity Players for their production of *Waiting for Lefty*. They then received permission to repeat the play in a public school building. But, apparently frightened by the upheaval in Boston over police interference with the play, the New Haven Board of Education rescinded this permission, whereupon a police edict was promptly issued banning the play from being presented anywhere in New Haven. Aroused by this attempt at theatre censorship, the American Civil Liberties Union, the International Labor Defense, students of the Yale Law School, and Professor Walter Prichard Eaton of the Yale School of Drama all joined with the Unity Players in an effort to secure an injunction against this police interference. Yale students and others joined picket lines at Police Headquarters and at the Board of Education, while a newspaper in a neighboring town, the *Bridgeport Sunday Herald,* printed the play in its entirety, carrying a banner headline: "New Haven Police Won't Let You SEE Prize Winning Play, READ It In This Issue of the Herald And Judge For Yourself." The determined stand in New Haven, with consequent notoriety for the censors, caused the ban to be lifted, and *Waiting for Lefty* opened in a leading theatre, where it played to large audiences. Elsewhere, however, lacking the distinguished support received in New Haven, the outcome of theatre censorship was not so happy.

All censorship is rooted in one purpose: the determination of those controlling the machinery of government to prevent the public from seeing or reading any matter of which they disapprove. But it is important for the reader to distinguish between the censorship of plays dealing with sex themes, such as *Desire Under the Elms* and *The Captive,* and the censorship of plays dealing with aspects of the social conflict. The banning of plays like *Waiting for Lefty, Stevedore* and *They Shall Not Die* is in itself an expression of the social conflict, a weapon deliberately used by those dominant economically, to resist the advance of an ideology hostile to their power.

Censorship in this field is closely bound up with the great social issues of our time, and is, therefore, far more serious and fundamental than that relating to so-called moral matters. The suppression of *Waiting for Lefty, Stevedore* and other plays on "moral" grounds, because of their alleged "offensive profanity," is in reality a subterfuge for banning them on account of the social and political ideas they present. All censorship must be fought, but, in this age of sharpened social conflict, censorship in the field of social protest is to be regarded as especially sinister.

One month before the Group Theatre offered to Broadway the already famous *Waiting for Lefty,* this organization had given theatregoers a memorable experience in their production of Clifford Odets' first long play, *Awake and Sing*. The title uses the opening words of the phrase from *Isaiah* which Odets prefaces as the text for his play:—

Awake and sing, ye that dwell in dust.

In a flat in the Bronx lives the Berger family, always on the edge of poverty, always struggling to realize the unattainable standards of bourgeois respectability. Only a writer who knows the lives of such families intimately, could reveal with so true and tender an understanding their desires and frustrations. Only one who had lived among them could know every nuance of their feelings, of their expressive idiom, and the humor which is their constant safety-valve against grief and pain. The family includes, first, the father, Myron. Myron is American born, a sober, hard-working, and kindly man. He has been for thirty years a clerk, and never received enough pay to lift his family above the line of always doing without. Interested in the better things, but without an education, Myron's brain is a jumble of useless information. He is one of the millions oppressed by the sense of being a failure without understanding that all the cards of the social structure in which he yearned to be a success were stacked against him. Second, there is the mother, Bessie. A life in which every thought has by necessity been concentrated on stretching out the dollar has bred in this naturally devoted wife and mother a hard acquisitiveness. When she fights tooth and nail against her son's marrying a penniless orphan, partly because she dreads the loss of the weekly money he is contributing, and the boy accuses her: "You never in your life bought me a pair of skates even — things I died for when I was a kid," Bessie retorts:

. . . He didn't have skates! But when he got sick, a twelve-year-old boy, who called a big specialist for the last $25 in the house? Skates!

And later in another argument over some insurance money left by the grandfather, poor Bessie sums herself up to her son:

Ralphie, I worked too hard all my years to be treated like dirt. . . . Summer shoes you didn't have, skates you never had, but I bought a new dress every week. A lover I kept — Mr. Gigolo! Did I ever play a game of cards like Mrs. Marcus? Or was Bessie Berger's children always the cleanest on the block?! Here I'm not only the mother, but also the father. The first two years I worked in a stocking factory for six dollars while Myron Berger went to law school. If I didn't worry about the family who would? On the calendar it's a different place, but here without a dollar you don't look the world in the eye. Talk from now to next year — this is life in America.

To which her son Ralph replies: —

Then it's wrong. It don't make sense. If life made you this way, then it's wrong!

The older child of Bessie and Myron is Hennie, in her early twenties. Hennie, too, is a family wage-earner, avid for the glory of the life she sees all about her, but self-contained and proud. She has never forgiven the vigorous but acrid Moe, now a boarder with the family, for taking her, a virgin, and leaving her "crying on the bed like I was two for a cent!" In truth she and Moe have a genuine attraction for each other; but meanwhile, having responded to the soft words of an absconded stranger, Hennie is "in trouble." The only way out is to follow her mother's unethical but practical suggestion of foisting her unborn child on Sam, a groping, lonely "foreigner" who wants to marry Hennie as a page dreams of marrying a queen.

The boy, Ralph, twenty-one, is a stock clerk in a silk house. Intelligent, sensitive, deprived of the education that should have been his as a matter of course in a land boasting of its opportunity, Ralph is beginning to question the good of the life he and millions like him are compelled to live. But to understand Ralph we must first understand his grandfather Jacob, a frustrated revolutionary, rootless in an alien land, who instinctively senses in the boy his spiritual heir.

The playwright tells us that when the door of Jacob's room is open "one sees a picture of Sacco and Vanzetti on the wall and several shelves of books." At once this man takes form for us, a form which Odets invests with all the admiration he so clearly feels for this idealist, whose Bible is Marx and whose dream of social justice illuminates the darkness of his family life, of his habitation that is no home. Uncompromising and human, Jacob tries to awaken the household to an understanding of the reasons for their unhappy lives. His daughter Bessie's materialism repels him, as does the success of his clothing manufacturer son, Morty, who, by flouting labor's cause, has "risen" out of its ranks to exploit it. Morty is a sensualist. He lives well, drives a big car and contributes the sum of five dollars a week toward the support of his father whom he baits as a "nut." And when Morty asks contemptuously why young Ralph should not attain the same "success" that he has, Jacob replies:

It's an exception, such success. . . . No, Morty . . . economics comes down like a ton of coal on the head. . . . A boy . . . dreams all night of fortunes. Why not? Don't it say in the movies he should have a personal steamship, pyjamas for fifty dollars a pair, and a toilet like a monument? But in the morning he wakes up and for ten dollars he can't fix the teeth. And millions more worse off in the mills of the South—starvation wages. (*Morty laughs loud and long.*) Laugh, laugh . . . tomorrow not. . . . You never heard how they shoot down men and women which ask a better wage? Kentucky 1932? . . . It says in the Bible how the Red Sea opened and the Egyptians went in and the sea rolled over them. In this boy's life a Red Sea will happen again. I see it!

When the others turn on him, it is balm to his heart to hear Ralph shout: "Let him alone—he's right!" For it is Ralph whom Jacob is ever exhorting:—

Boychick, wake up! Be something! Make your life something good. For the love of an old man who sees in your young days his new life, for such love take the world in your two hands and make it like new. Go out and fight, so life shouldn't be printed on dollar bills. . . .

But there is a point at which the cracked heart of even this philosopher must break. Upbraided by Ralph, when the boy in a family crisis learns the truth, for not having prevented Hennie's deception of her husband, insulted by the nerve-shattered Bessie, who in a tantrum smashes his beloved Caruso records, Jacob, quietly taking the little family dog up on the roof, as was his custom, slips off and falls into the snow below. . . .

Not of the family but very much in it, as a boarder, is the vitriolic Moe, whose passion for Hennie, to which he knows she responds, consumes him like a fever. Moe is a brilliantly drawn character, a product of Jacob's hated world order. Life has made him bitter and cynical; he believes in nothing. And he expresses his contempt in language not pleasant for delicate ears. Hear Moe, in his last and successful bout with Hennie, sick at the sight and the touch of Sam: —

> What the hell do you want, my head on a plate? Was my life so happy? Chris', my old man was a bum. I supported the whole damn family — five kids and Mom. When they grew up they beat it the hell away like rabbits. Mom died. I went to the war; got clapped down like a bedbug; woke up in a room without a leg. What the hell do you think, anyone's got it better than you? I never had a home either. I'm lookin' too!

Moe can give Hennie the things she has longed for — a Southern cruise, roses, champagne. For he is beyond good and evil, in that world of racketeering where the big money flows to those whose faith society has early shattered. . . .

Shocked by his grandfather's death, occupying his room and poring over his books, Ralph repeats his very phrases: "It can't stay like this. . . . We don't want life printed on dollar bills, Mom!" And when Bessie answers: —

> So go out and change the world if you don't like it. —

Ralph replies: —

> I will! And why? Cause life's different in my head. . . . "Awake and sing," he said. Right here he stood and said it. The night he died, I saw it like a thunderbolt! I saw he was dead and I was born! . . .

So Ralph, spiritual inheritor of the revolutionary dream of a better world, girds his loins to make that dream come true.

In his second play, *Paradise Lost,* Odets attempted a task far more difficult than that of *Awake and Sing.* His purpose now was to show the lot of the bewildered middle class today as it watches its position of once-established solidity disintegrate. Always dissociating themselves from the working class, with whom they believe they have nothing in common, the distressed members of the middle class cannot understand their inability and, even worse, the inability of their children, to whom they have given an education, any longer to "succeed" in the business and professional world. Turn as they will, they seem unable to find a solution of the difficulties, economic and spiritual, that engulf them.

If, in attempting to deal with so crucial a subject, the symbolism of Odets' characters is not always as completely realized as it might be, he has nevertheless made a contribution to contemporary drama which emphasizes the tragic aspects of his theme and is at the same time highly original.

But, with a characteristic lack of play-consciousness, most of the New York play reviewers rejected *Paradise Lost* because it did not once more offer them the theatrical excitement of *Awake and Sing*. Is the audience, then, to make no mental effort to meet the earnest, challenging effort of the dramatist? For audiences and readers eager to make this effort, *Paradise Lost* offers a rich reward.

Leo Gordon, liberal, idealistic, is a leather-goods manufacturer, who has left the running of the business to his aggressive partner, Sam Katz. Leo's wife, Clara, mother of his three grown children, typifies the middle-class woman who takes it for granted that there will always be the wherewithal for tomorrow, one maid-of-all-work, good and ample food, successful careers for the children. Shrewd and intelligent, although understanding nothing of the world she lives in, she is fine enough to appreciate her husband's qualities and to love him for them. The Gordons' older son is Ben, a former Olympic champion, now out of the running because of a bad heart and unable to find a job to compensate for this deflation of his infantile ego. Ben symbolizes the pursuit by middle-class youth of the treacherous values of headline worship, of seeing life in terms of personal exhibitionism. He is the hero of his home, spoiled by his mother; when the falsity of the standards by which he has lived becomes clear to him, his world collapses like a bubble. Incapable of judging either woman or man, he is deceived by both, and when he finally agrees, in a last effort to gain a financial foothold in his slipping world, to participate in a hold-up, he cannot face life on such degrading terms. As his gangster friend, Kewpie, puts it: "He stood there soaking up cops' bullets like a sponge. . . . Ben Gordon wanted to die!"

The Gordons' second son is Julie. Julie is slowly dying of sleeping-sickness. Every ounce of his energy, every waking thought, is expended on feverish calculations as to how he may make a fabulous fortune in Wall Street. If the symbolism of this middle class tragedy is not clear, nothing I can add will make it clearer. And finally there is the Gordons' daughter, Pearl. A fine musician, for years an indefatigable worker at her piano, she has been brought up in the belief that there is a place in the world for the artist. Now she not only realizes that her career as a concert pianist is a mirage, but she must endure seeing her fiancé, a violinist, unable to get a job anywhere. Pearl, however, cannot compromise her ideal: an artist's marriage, soaring to the heights. She prefers to send her lover from her, "free" to scour the country for a job, if that is, today, society's response to the artist's gift and need. In thus isolating herself from life, Pearl symbolizes the artist who refuses to see his struggle in terms of the general social conflict.

The Gordons live in an American city in a house they have owned for seventeen years. An upper portion of it is occupied by Leo's partner, Sam Katz, with his wife, whom he mistreats and publicly abuses for her childlessness — "a man like an ox can't have a son." Sam is a violent neurotic at the point of collapse. For years now he has been trying to save the business, by terrorizing the workers into signing false statements of hours and wages, by shady financial schemes, even by robbing and ruining his partner, Leo. And at the end, when all is lost, his pitying and devoted wife, breaking her silence, tells the truth: it is poor Sam who is impotent, and it is this impotence which has destroyed him. The symbolism of this impotence is clear, especially in the light of recent economic history. For have we not seen the middle class industrialist, powerless to create a future, completely impotent in the face of a collapsing capitalism?

In the Gordon household, too, there is Gus Michaels, a typical Odets character, formerly a small businessman, now a "failure" being helped by his old friend, Leo Gordon. Gus voices all the nostalgia for the paradise the middle class has lost:—

> I can't explain it to you, Mr. G., how I'm forever hungerin' for the past. It's like a disease in me, eatin' away . . . some nights I have cried myself to sleep—for the old Asbury Park days; the shore dinners at old Sheepshead Bay. In those days every house had its little dog—we was no exception, as you well remember, with our Spotty, the fire dog—it was a common sight to see them out walkin' of a summer night, big ones and little ones. How beautiful the summer nights before the Big War! We would sit out there . . . and the streets fulla laughin' playin' children. I had Mrs. Michaels with me in those days. Oh, yes, the pleasant laughin' talk, when we went around to Schoemacher's Ice Cream Parlor. Oh, it was so beautiful in those days! Wasn't it, Mr. G.?

And there are two other characters who, "before the Big War," would never have impinged on middle-class life. One is Kewpie, Ben's childhood friend, driven by his acquisitive lust into becoming a gunman. His continued friendship with Gordon's son would have been unthinkable before 1914. But

Kewpie's ill-gotten wealth turns to dust when he realizes that in destroying Ben he destroyed the symbol of all the values of life society had never permitted him to make his own. The other is Pike, the Gordons' furnace man, an American of pioneer stock, whose sons were "blown to hell" in the war. As a migratory worker, his descent into the working class has given him economic understanding and a social philosophy to which he gives picturesque expression. There is no obscurity about the symbolic meaning of this character.

In the last scene, about to be evicted from the house they have lost, just as the local politicians are staging a "prosperity block party," the high-minded Leo Gordon takes his last step in the spiritual pilgrimage along which we have been following him during the three years which the play covers. It is "a typical homeless man," hired to help evict him, once a businessman and a house owner like himself, now among the economically awakened, who completes Leo's transformation. As he stands there, to all appearances a broken man, let us listen to Leo Gordon's last ringing speech: —

That was the past, but there is a future. Now we know. We dare to understand. Truly, truly, the past was a dream. But this is real! To know from this that something must be done. That is real. We searched; we were confused! But we searched, and now the search is ended. For the truth has found us. For the first time in our lives — for the first time our house has a real foundation. Clara, those people outside are afraid. Those people at the block party whisper and point. They're afraid. Let them look in our house. We're not ashamed. Let them look in. Clara, my darling, *listen to me*. Everywhere now men are rising from their sleep. Men, men are understanding the bitter black total of their lives. Their whispers are growing to shouts! They become an ocean of understanding! *No man fights alone*. Oh, if you could only see with me the greatness of men. I tremble like a bride to see the time when they'll use it. My darling, we must have only one regret—that life is so short! That we must die so soon. (*Clara slowly has turned from Julie and is listening now to her husband.*) Yes, I want to see that new world. I want to kiss all those future men and women. What is this talk of bankrupts, failures, hatred . . . they won't know what that means. Oh, yes, I tell you the whole world is for men to possess. Heartbreak and terror is not the heritage of mankind! The world is beautiful. No fruit tree wears a lock and key. Men will sing at their work, men will love. Ohhh, darling, the world is in its morning . . . and *no man fights alone!* (*Clara slowly comes down to her husband and kisses him. With real feeling. Everyone in the room, Leo included, is deeply moved by this vision of the future. Leo says:*) Let us have air . . . Open the windows. (*As he crosses to the windows a short fanfare is heard without.*)

Those of the middle class who are ready, as Ibsen might have said, to "open the windows," will feel the air of a new dawn—instead of a "paradise lost," a paradise to be won for all.

Odets' next play, *Golden Boy,* while it excels in those qualities of dynamic theatre which, as in *Awake and Sing,* elicit an immediate response from theatre-conscious audiences, is, in addition, a work of deep symbolic import. Here Odets shows us a psychological conflict within the individual as devastating as anything O'Neill has portrayed, but he relates it clearly to its social causes, to the false standards of life thrust on the individual by a competitive society. Thus the conflict experienced by the young man in Odets' play symbolizes the conflict confronting millions of young people today, torn between the need of doing the thing they love best, and the need of attaining the success that alone will make them "somebody" in the materialistically dominated contemporary world. And if, in addition, a sensitive youth starts out in America as the underprivileged child of an alien, feeling himself an outsider, then the drive of the wounded ego for compensation, the compulsion to conquer a hostile world on its own terms, may well become an obsession.

Such a child was Joe Bonaparte, son of an Italian fruit peddler who has devoted a large share of his earnings to violin lessons for the talented Joe, to whose career as a musician all his veneration for the artist is dedicated. We first meet Joe on the eve of his twenty-first birthday, seething with revolt against his poverty and obscurity and already secretly on the way to win "fame and fortune" for himself in a field that represents the very antithesis of the violinist's art: prize fighting. Why has Odets chosen prize fighting to symbolize the world of competition in which Joe hopes to achieve success? Because it epitomizes the battle for gain shorn of all pretense—at its most brutal and at the same time at its most lucrative and spectacular.

In the opening scene of *Golden Boy,* written in Odets' racy manner, Joe, shabbily dressed, bristling with his sense of inferiority, totally unknown, bursts into the office of Tom Moody, the fight manager. He implores Moody to let him replace in a match that night a professional whom he has just incapacitated in an amateur encounter. Joe's opinion of his own prowess and his insistence infuriate the manager, but apparently he can deliver the goods and so he is taken on for what is actually his first professional fight. The second scene, later that same night, reveals to us all that represents the Joe with whom the aggressive prize fighter is in conflict. In the combination parlor and dining room of his father's flat, where plaster busts of Mozart and Beethoven stand on the sideboard, the fine-feeling father is arguing with his Jewish friend, Carp, owner of a candy and stationery store. Living there, too, are Joe's good-natured, ignorant sister and her bumptious young husband, a taxi driver. And there, just for the night, is his brother, Frank, a labor organizer, en route to the Southern textile mills. "Tex-tiles!" sniffs Mr. Carp. "What's it his business if the workers in tex-tiles don't make good wages!" To which Mr. Bonaparte replies: "Frank, he fighta for eat, for good life. Why not?" And when Mr. Carp retorts "Foolish!" Joe's father says significantly: "Whatever you got ina your nature to do isa not foolish!"

That utterance fills the air after Joe comes home from his victorious fight, the news of which they have already seen in the newspaper, and belligerently announces:—

> Poppa, I have to tell you—I don't like myself, past, present and future. Do you know there are men who have wonderful things from life? Do you think I like this feeling of no possessions? . . . Tomorrow's my birthday! I change my life!

To his father's troubled

> Hey, Joe, you sounda like crazy! You no gotta a nature for fight. You're musician . . .

Joe has no answer, and he leaves the scene abruptly. Now follows the story of Joe Bonaparte's rapid rise as a prize fighter, in a moral underworld, which could exist only in a society that is sick with the most virulent acquisitiveness. The noxious and pitiable creatures who attach themselves to the Golden Boy like leeches must be known by the reader through direct contact with the play. Our interest here is with Joe himself and with his inner conflict. At first the struggle between the sensitive, music-loving Joe and the possession-hungry, success-seeking Joe manifests itself in a way that worries the leeches. The brainiest fighter in the ring is holding himself back—he seems to be afraid of his hands. Only when Joe's father appears at the manager's office, to see for himself his son's "new friends," do they learn to their dismay that Joe plays the violin and that that is why he is afraid to hurt his hands fighting. Tom, his manager, remarks: "I'm beginning to see the light. Joe's mind ain't made up that the fist is mightier than the fiddle."

But Joe's mind must be made up for him, because as Tom puts it to his girl, Lorna: —

> . . . It's our last chance for a decent life, for getting married — we have to make that kid fight! He's *more* than a meal-ticket — he's everything we want and need from life!

Lorna, whom Tom loved when she had sunk as low as the streets, assures him she knows "a dozen ways" to make Joe fight. She doesn't need them, however, because Joe has fallen in love with her, and she with him. It is the prospect of winning her away from Tom, and of making her the princess in his golden success story, that makes Joe fight now with no holding back for the sake of his hands, lulled into the belief that his inner conflict is no more. The scenes between these two, whose love rises between them as only another battle to be fought, are poignant beyond words. For Lorna has her own conflict. Not only has she no longer the courage to expose herself to the inevitable pain of love, but also she cannot bear to deal this blow to Tom, whose devotion has inspired in her a genuine tenderness.

Embittered by the break with Lorna at the height of his emotional involvement with her, Joe plunges recklessly into his career. But he cannot get Lorna out of his blood any more than he can get his father out of his conscience, his father who will take none of his money and to whom he cries: —

> Poppa, I have to fight, no matter what you say or think! This is my profession! I'm out for fame and fortune, not to be different or artistic! I don't intend to be ashamed of my life!

A little later we see him in his dressing room, after winning a fight. As his glove is removed, he holds out his hand in exultation. It is broken. There can no longer be any doubt that

Joe has become—a fighter. Never again can he revert to a "nobody" who plays the violin. Now he is "somebody."...

But, as our "left" playwright sees it, the competition needed to become a "somebody" in our world today, when carried to its logical conclusion, means killing, or, figuratively, destroying, one's fellow creatures for personal gain. When Joe, during a fight, giving his opponent, as he puts it, "the fury of a lifetime," accidentally kills him, the symbolism of the play proceeds irresistibly. The real Joe is the sensitive artist, not the competitive killer. On the night of this crisis, when Lorna, yielding to her love, pleads that together they seek simple happiness somewhere, Joe understands himself:

> ... I see what I did. I murdered myself, too ... Now I'm smashed ... I'm no good—my feet are off the earth!

Yes, Joe is smashed. Now he can neither fight nor make music—neither function in the competitive world nor in the world of satisfying self-expression. Having aligned himself with the destructive forces of society, he has destroyed—himself. Obeying a deep, unconscious realization that he is through, Joe takes Lorna in his car and drives recklessly away. His physical death in a smash-up merely completes for the play the spiritual death already witnessed.

In the last scene, back in his father's flat, we wait with Tom and other fight associates for news of Joe. Once more his brother Frank is there, this time with a bandaged head, for he has been fighting too—in a strike. "You got a good build," says Eddie, the gunman, who "owns a part" of Joe and is as yet ignorant of his fate—"You could be a fighter."

FRANK

I fight....

EDDIE

Yeah? For what?

FRANK

A lotta things I believe in. . . .

EDDIE

Whatta you get for it? . . .

FRANK

I'm not fooled by a lotta things Joe's fooled by. . . . But I get what Joe don't.

EDDIE

What don't he get?

FRANK

(*Modestly*)

The pleasure of acting as you think! The satisfaction of staying where you belong, being what you are . . . at harmony with millions of others!

Thus does Odets in conclusion symbolize for us the difference between the good fight and the bad. . . . Finally over the telephone comes the news of Joe's fatal crash and it is his father who has the last word:—

Joe. . . . Come, we bring-a him home . . . where he belong.

Today there is no dramatist whose work is being watched with greater interest than that of Clifford Odets. The theatre-conscious watch him because of his gift for writing effective theatre. They hope that maturity will gradually eliminate his "left-ness." To the play-conscious, however, such a change would mean the loss of an important playwright who expresses a profound social integration with his age.

It is the young "left" playwrights of America, even those whose work is not outstanding as dramatic art, who are carrying on the efforts of the great modern dramatists and who are building a drama which, in spite of technical changes and startling idiom, the moderns would at once recognize as the legitimate fruit of their own work. Partisan in their espousal of the cause of the exploited, and proud to be so, these playwrights affirm their belief in a theatre that will help humanity to awake and sing.

Chapter 7 Contemporary Drama: Plays against War

From the days of Euripides and Aristophanes to the present, no established institution has ever inspired men and women with such ambivalent emotions as does war. Since tribal days, war and patriotism have been synonymous terms, and the warrior has persuaded himself that the sacrifice or even the risk of his life forthwith made him into a hero. Without this hero myth, the wars of the world, whether frankly acquisitive or engaged in for some supposedly exalted purpose, could never have been fought. For always in conflict with this hero patriot reflex, is man's love of life, his hatred of pain and death. Always men have struggled between their idealization of war as a heroic endeavor to protect their country and their loathing of it as something barbarous. Even in such an indictment of war as *The Trojan Women,* Euripides cannot escape from this ambivalence. He paints a picture of war's insensate cruelty, especially as it affects women, yet cannot escape from investing it with an atmosphere of the heroic and from visualizing the dead as heroes.

This dualistic attitude toward war persisted until the middle of the last century when new economic and historical concepts of the basis of war gave birth to a new principle, that of Internationalism. Internationalism was the logical outgrowth of the theories beginning to spread over Europe, which affirmed that the workers, exploited by the profit system in all countries, were united by the bonds of common interests and must therefore unite to advance those interests. From this it followed that they must also pledge themselves not to slaughter each other for so-called "national" interests which they no longer regarded as their own. During the last decades of the modern period preceding the World War, the International Socialist movement loomed as a bulwark against war, and millions of workers not only ceased regarding themselves as potential heroes, but began to see themselves as potential murderers of their fellow workers. But the new Internationalism was not yet strong enough to win out against the snare of nationalism with its lure of economic security to be won by conquest and its siren call of "patriotism." The first blow to Internationalism and peace was struck by the powerful Social Democratic Party of Germany in voting for war in 1914. And when the majority of the workers in the other countries followed and it became apparent that the brotherhood of man could not prevail in our competitive world, soldiers once more became heroes.

The shock of the World War, and the aftermath which marked the beginning of our contemporary age, placed upon serious creative artists a new responsibility, namely to interpret to the world the significance of the catastrophe which had overtaken it. For on the day the Treaty of Versailles was signed, every thinking person recognized the mockery of the phrase "a war to end all wars." And not long afterwards, we find the dramatist writing a new kind of play against war.

What are the characteristics of this new type of antiwar play which differentiate it from the plays about war written before our contemporary age? First, these postwar plays show a determination to strip the veil of glamour from war and to reveal it as mechanized carnage. The hero myth is shattered by showing the soldier as a helpless pawn, coerced into being destroyed by a war whose true cause he does not understand and which he has had no voice in determining. But the new type of antiwar play goes further and makes it clear that no side ever wins in a war because, due to its destruction of basic values, war not only solves no old problems, but must inevitably create new problems even more acute. Finally, the new type of play against war probes into the causes of war, suggesting means whereby it may be at last abolished. The playwrights integrated with this contemporary age understand that the task of a dramatist writing an antiwar play is not merely to depict the terrors of war, but to show the terrors of the peace that follows war and to arouse the interest of audiences in solving the problem of how to end war.

Here I must pause to consider a very successful play dealing with the World War generally referred to as an antiwar play, which actually is not a true play against war at all. This is *Journey's End* by R. C. Sherriff, produced both in London and New York in 1929. I readily admit all its fine qualities, but it is important for us to understand that *Journey's End* is an old-fashioned play exhibiting the time-honored, ambivalent emotions of loathing war's cruelty while glorifying its victims as heroes. The English playwright does not carry his subject one step forward from the attitude of Euripides. The audience leaves the theatre weeping for dead heroes, but without a single clarifying or provocative idea on the subject of war.

The scene of *Journey's End* is a dugout in the British trenches before St. Quentin in March of 1918. The able commander of the company is Captain Stanhope, whom inordinate drinking alone has kept from nervous collapse in the face of the revulsion war inspires in him. He is a man wrecked for life by the mental torture of war; he dares not show himself on leave to his father, a country vicar, or to the girl to whom he is tacitly betrothed. When a terror-stricken young man in his company pretends illness in order to get away to a hospital, does Stanhope help him? No, he tells him that if he goes, he will have him shot for deserting, threatening to shoot him himself to spare him this disgrace. Stanhope then talks to him in this fashion:

> . . . If you went — and left Osborne and Trotter and Raleigh and all those men up there to do your work — could you ever look a man straight in the face again — in all your life? You may be wounded. Then you can go home and feel proud — and if you're killed, you — you won't have to stand this hell any more. . . . Don't you think it worth standing in with men like that? — when you know they all feel like you do — in their hearts — and just go on sticking it because they know it's — it's the only thing a decent man can do. . . .

In this speech lies the essence of the play, summing up the attitude of the British soldier and gentleman toward any war in which his country is engaged. "Theirs not to question why, theirs but to do and die." This was the soldier's code from the beginning, and Sherriff gives us no word that it will not continue to be so. When Osborne, a middle-aged schoolmaster, tells the young second-lieutenant Raleigh how once a German officer — the German front line was no further away than "the breadth of a football field" — ordered the British soldiers to carry one of their wounded away and "fired some lights for them to see by," he adds:

> Next day we blew each other's trenches to blazes.

And to young Raleigh's comment:

> It all seems rather — *silly,* doesn't it?

Osborne replies:

> It does, rather.

And in this key of well-behaved, unthinking acceptance of war, *Journey's End* comes to its tragic close. Osborne, with his beloved wife and children, and young Raleigh are both killed, in a suicidal raid, after which, the big attack at last begun, we see Stanhope going out to certain death as the curtain falls. It is not at their death that the audience should weep, but at their perishing without vision, without anyone revealing the truth about their futile heroism. No hero-complex blinded Toller at the front, nor Wolf, when he has the doomed sailors of Cattaro cry "Comrades, next time better!" If we compare these sailors with Sherriff's soldiers, we recognize who were the true war heroes and realize that *Journey's End,* based on the old confusion of the hero myth, forfeits all claim to be regarded as a play against war.

In 1924 there appeared in America *What Price Glory?* by Maxwell Anderson and Laurence Stallings. While this cannot be classed among the true antiwar plays, it must be regarded as a first step in that direction. It is interesting to recall that *What Price Glory?* was produced six months after Elmer Rice's *The Adding Machine* and in the same year as John Howard Lawson's *Processional* and Eugene O'Neill's *All God's Chillun Got Wings.* Like these plays, the Anderson-Stallings drama was a pioneer effort to deal truthfully with a subject of vital contemporary significance. This subject is the World War—which still retained its romantic glamour, especially for the stay-at-homes who had sentimentalized at long distance over the "heroes" at the front.

Naturally, the American theatre had offered its quota of "war" plays in the period before the World War. In those plays, the Revolutionary and Civil Wars figured chiefly as the background against which the attachment of young "enemy" lovers moved through fearful difficulties to a happy ending. They were nothing but costume plays that provided their audiences with romantic pictures of uniformed actors and beflounced actresses. On the sterner side there were the classics, in which, if war was treated more sonorously, it nevertheless still affected its audiences as remote, heroic adventure.

Against these romantic traditions, *What Price Glory?* hurled itself like a bomb. Its avowed purpose was to "de-bunk" war, to show in the theatre war as it really is and soldiers as they really are. For Stallings had been at the front with the Marines he portrays. He knew that they were not clean, gentlemanly, well-behaved heroes, but dirty, earthy sons of the people, whose vocabulary must be described as something more than merely "colorful." He knew that they regarded the physical torture inflicted on them by the war with resentment and terror, and looked on its proclaimed purpose with cynicism.

We meet in this play Captain Flagg and First Sergeant Quirt, as well as Corporal Lipinsky, Lieutenant Schmidt, Privates Mulcahy and Lewisohn and the rest of the motley American company. Between the diverting rowdy first and third acts, that take place in the same French village, and reveal the genus soldier off-duty and uninhibited, comes the serious interlude of the second act, with its picture of actual war. This takes place in a cellar, in a town where fierce fighting is going on. We learn that the soldiers are "indescribably dirty and with six or eight days' beard," and we see them in miserable discomfort, half-dead with fatigue, sick with terror. "The whole damned universe is crazy now," comments the worldly-wise Corporal Kiper, after which he proceeds to terrify Corporal Lipinsky by denying the existence of God, heaven and the soul. Captain Flagg appears at the head of the cellar stairs supporting the wounded Lieutenant Aldrich and "easing him gently down the steps." I shall let the authors describe them:—

Aldrich is not groaning. After all, it won't hurt for fifteen minutes or so. But he is weak from loss of blood and soaked through, and is in an indescribable mess of dried blood and dirt, which appears black. Flagg, who is unkempt, has no leggings or laces in his breeches, these flapping in the most disillusioning fashion about his bare legs. His blouse, an old army blouse many sizes too big and without a sign of any insignia, is tied with a piece of twine. He is bare-headed — no tin hat and no accoutrements of any sort. He is a very weary-looking man. . . .

Hardly has Aldrich been placed in his bunk, when "a strange sob is heard at the head of the stairs" and Lieutenant Moore rushes in to his friend, crying: —

Oh, God, Dave, but they got you. God, but they got you a beauty, the dirty swine. God DAMN them for keeping us up in this hellish town. Why can't they send in some of the million men they've got back there and give us a chance? Men in my platoons are so hysterical every time I get a message from Flagg, they want to know if they're being relieved. What can I tell them? They look at me like whipped dogs — as if I had just beaten them — and I've had enough of them this time. I've got to get them out, I tell you. They've had enough. Every night the same way. (*He turns to Flagg.*) And since six o'clock there's been a wounded sniper in the tree by that orchard angel crying "*Kamerad! Kamerad!*" Just like a big crippled whippoorwill. What price glory now? Why in God's name can't we all go home? Who gives a damn for this lousy, stinking little town but the poor French bastards who live here? God damn it! You talk about courage, and all night long you hear a man who's bleeding to death on a tree calling you "*Kamerad!*" and asking you to save him. God damn every son of a bitch in the world, who isn't here! I won't stand for it. I won't stand for it! I won't have the platoon asking me every minute of the livelong night when they are going to be relieved. . . . Flagg, I tell you you can shoot me, but I won't stand for it . . . I'll take 'em out to-night and kill you if you get in my way. . . .

After the audience has caught its breath during an amusing scene between Captain Flagg and Sergeant Quirt, the act ends as follows:

LEWISOHN: (*Screams, outside*) Captain Flagg . . .

FLAGG: Who's that?

LIPINSKY: It's little Lewisohn, sir.

(*Lewisohn is carried in by Gowdy followed by Pharmacist's Mate, and he is crying monotonously for Captain Flagg*)

LEWISOHN: Captain Flagg. Captain Flagg. Stop the blood. Stop the blood.

FLAGG: (*Takes him from Gowdy and puts him on floor*) I can't stop it, Lewisohn, I'm sorry.

(*He examines wound in left side.*)

LEWISOHN: Oh, Captain Flagg, stop the blood.

FLAGG: Fix him with your needle, Mate.

(*Mate gives him needle in arm.*)

LEWISOHN: Oh, Captain Flagg, can't you please, sir, stop the blood?

FLAGG: (*Puts hand behind Lewisohn's head and gently lowers him to floor*) You'll be all right, boy. You'll be all right. You'll be all right.

(*Lewisohn sighs and relaxes his body.*)

Curtain

No wonder New York's first-night audience was shocked by such realism in the portrayal of war, and by such soldiers. But the fact that, for all its seriousness, the play is almost continuously mirth-provoking, brought the audience to its feet with cheers. The deeply serious plays against war, placing grave problems before audiences and asking them to think in the theatre, were yet to come. *What Price Glory?* was their precursor, and the enemies it made proved that it had brought into the open matters which the hushers-up preferred to keep under a veil of silence. Members of the clergy and writers in religious publications uttered their usual protests against such "horrible profanity and blasphemy" and asked that the play be closed "in the name of public decency." The most violent antagonists, however, came from the army itself. Objections were made that the play violated a section of the National Defense Act, which permitted uniforms to be worn on the stage provided nothing was done by their wearers to reflect discredit on the service. *What Price Glory?,* a naval officer reported, holds the United States Marine Corps and the United States Army up to ridicule and therefore curtails enlistments! . . . But after three "objectionable" expressions had been deleted, the play ran for two hundred and ninety-nine performances.

Four-and-a-half years later, when *Journey's End* was produced, a play-reviewer, comparing it with *What Price Glory?,* wrote that the English play is "the more heartbreaking, the more inherently tragic of the two" . . . that it has "a greater capacity for inducing tears." Perhaps, but the tears are only sentimental tears shed for "heroes," and not for the fumbling, war-ridden world.

The first true play against war is an English one: *Wings Over Europe,* by Robert Nichols and Maurice Browne. The high plane of imagination on which it is conceived, together with its intellectual appeal, combine to make it a distinguished achievement. The authors' subtitle is: "A Dramatic Extravaganza on a Pressing Theme." The "extravaganza" consists in their basing the play on the discovery by its hero of what scientists have long known would prove the supreme discovery of all time, namely how to control the energy in the atom. Thus to be able to dominate matter would mean to dominate the earth. Humanity could immediately be freed of all oppressive evils and the world re-created so that need for material supremacy, and hence for war, would automatically cease. How the men who rule the world react to such a discovery the dramatists then disclose.

When the play opens — Time: "Tomorrow morning" — we find ourselves in the Council Room of the British Cabinet, at Number 10 Downing Street. We soon gather that a matter of extraordinary significance is to be discussed at a special meeting of a Cabinet Committee called by the Prime Minister. We learn further that this matter involves a scientific discovery which a young English physicist desires to place before the government of his country. We meet the young man, Francis Lightfoot, during a conversation with the Prime Minister, his uncle, just before the meeting. Francis might be the reincarnation of Shelley, who is his ideal and intellectual and spiritual guide. Like Shelley, he is a combination of artist, scientist, lover of humanity and rebel against injustice. At twenty-five, Francis is slated for the Nobel Prize in physics and regarded as a prodigy by Einstein. Almost the first words he utters to his uncle are:

Think! Today, for the first time in history, Man is free!

And he is shocked when the Prime Minister refers to his coming interview with the Cabinet members as a "battle." "Battle!" he repeats, adding: —

I am going to make a statement, nothing more. You and the Cabinet Committee will then act on it for the public good.

To which his uncle replies: —

But has it ever struck you, Francis, that there's nothing on earth — except religion — on which men are so divided as the public good?

When the Prime Minister tactfully suggests that Francis put on a necktie, the youth replies:

What a lot of preliminaries there do seem to freeing Mankind!

The other leading character of the play now enters alone, the brilliant, suave Secretary for Foreign Affairs, Evelyn Arthur, highly cultured, disillusioned, practical, a "liberal" statesman, who hopes for little and expects less. "Hope," he pronounces—"horrid monosyllable, out of place in the mouth of any really Civilized Man." To which he adds:—

. . . We have had no civilization yet, only civilizations.

It is to Evelyn Arthur that Francis looks for support in the impending encounter.

Now a dozen of the highest Cabinet members come in: the Secretary of War, the Lord High Chancellor, the Secretary of State for the Dominions, every one individualized and made alive for us. The Prime Minister introduces his nephew and Evelyn Arthur adds some impressive words. They do not help much, for Francis begins by saying that at first he wondered to whom to disclose his discovery: "You see, of course, I'm opposed to all governments, for all governments are founded on force"—and he explains that he was "frightfully bothered" whether to tell it to *them,* because "all his life, Shelley was opposed to the British Government." Murmurs are heard from the ministers; Evelyn Arthur smooths things over; and Francis begins a scientific explanation of what he has achieved. After a moment or two, Lord Sunningdale, wealthy owner of race horses, interrupts him to say:—

. . . Now look here, young man . . . we're politicians, God help us, not professors. Be a good feller: have mercy on a lot of old codgers: cut the cackle an' come to the hosses.

Taken aback, Francis checks himself on the advice of his uncle and announces with intense excitement:—

Gentlemen, I can control . . . the energy . . . in the atom.

This news makes no impression and he repeats the words, after which the First Commissioner of Works, an engineer, cries:—

What! Man alive! . . . Gentlemen! D'you realize what that means?

They do not in the least realize what that means, so Francis tries to explain:—

It all seems so elementary to me. Well . . . it means that the present, all this, all that you're accustomed to call civilization, is—is relegated at last to its proper place as the confused remembrance of an evil dream of no more account than a child's nightmare. Yesterday, Man was a slave; to-day, he's free. Matter obeys him.

They are still at sea, so Evelyn Arthur tries to elucidate:

Now, gentlemen, here we have a table made of—let me see—oak, isn't it? Yes, oak. Very well. Now, if Mr. Lightfoot were so vulgar as to wish to turn this table into gold, hey, presto, he could do so. And if he happened to dislike it as much as I do, he could, hey, presto, abolish it. Is that clear?

Decidedly it is not clear, and Francis continues:—

Mr. Arthur has—has put it a little oddly; but—yes, that's what it means. Oh, please, please, don't waste time asking silly questions; consider what you're going to *do*. (*Very earnestly and as if repeating a peroration*) You see—the history of Man up to now has been one long horrible narrative of his slavery to matter. To-day I put into your hands power *over* matter; ultimate power over matter; the power of—of a god, to slay and to make alive. Incidentally it means food, shelter, abundance, for everyone. But that's just incidental. Beyond that—a mere matter of organization—rises the New World, the Summer of Mankind, the Golden Age. Don't you see, gentlemen? It's—Man's free! And now, now, he can live as the sages of all countries have always dreamed he might live—not—not a feebly struggling parasite, not a thing oppressed by needs and fears, with no security, no leisure, but, Man, a Titan, a Prometheus, a Prometheus Triumphant, all his days and nights one long hymn of praise to Beauty and to Truth, the Beauty and the Truth which from hour to hour Man discovers and Man creates! (*Quietly, exhausted*) That's what it means, gentlemen; that's what my discovery means. You're the first—except my uncle—to know. Now I'm going to leave you to organize. That's your job; the new *organization*. I'll come back, a week from to-day, at the same time. Have your plans ready. (*He makes as if to withdraw.*)

At this bedlam breaks loose. Aroused at last, they assail Francis with an onslaught of questions, revealing the effect of this information on men who dominate the world. Not one evidences any interest in the "New World, the Summer of Mankind, the Golden Age." Each is concerned with how his particular interest will be affected. Francis, his uneasiness mounting, explains that, with his discovery, all private interests have ceased to exist. What, he asks the Lord High Chancellor, can his system of law, based on force, avail against man's new power over matter, which by the use of a small mechanism, for example, could cause all the policemen in London, nay, in the world, to disappear? To the Secretary of War exulting that this discovery means "England for ever!" Francis snaps back: "Your army doesn't exist." To the Secretary for the Dominions, worried about the colonies and raw materials, Francis replies: "All colonies are henceforth Humanity. As sources of raw materials, they cease to exist." To the Chancellor of the Exchequer, alarmed about credit, Francis retorts: "Credit? Credit in units of what? Your system, which is founded on gold, has ceased to exist." And to the question: "What about Labor?" Francis answers that *as it is now,* Labor has certainly ceased to exist. Aghast, the First Lord of the Admiralty asks about "Empire." "Empire?" asks Francis in turn. "What Empire? I'm talking about Mankind."

Suavely Mr. Arthur manages to get the angry members to rise in honor of a great British scientist who has placed exalted responsibilities on his country. They listen to Francis' parting words: —

. . . I have called on you to build a House for Man. To-day week will disclose whether you have risen to your opportunity. The responsibility is yours.

And Evelyn Arthur says ominously, as the first-act curtain falls: —

Kindly realize that every word that young man said is — I am convinced — literally true. . . . Every word! And I solemnly say to you all, it would be better for that poor young man and for the world had he never been born.

The week has passed. The Cabinet Committee is once more set to report its decisions and its program to the young discoverer. We learn that they have passed a unanimous resolution to be submitted to him, but they are worried over what to do if he refuses to comply with its terms. The Secretary of War bluntly proposes that if he does refuse, he is to be "shut up tight and shut up for keeps," adding that if he had his way, he would simply shoot him. The majority vote to arrest him, if he cannot be persuaded. Francis is sent for and is pleased when he hears that the resolution to be read to him was proposed by Evelyn Arthur. His uncle, the Prime Minister, reads it: —

His Majesty's Cabinet-Members, in Committee assembled, most earnestly and solemnly request and entreat Francis Lightfoot to communicate his overwhelming discovery to no other human being and to destroy its secret.

Francis recoils in horror from this revelation. Unmoved by the evidence presented by Evelyn Arthur to prove that humanity is still so undeveloped that it would destroy itself with the power Francis desires to place in its hands, the young man turns on him: —

. . . You're the mummy whose hand kills . . . (*To his uncle*) I know him — history knows him . . . Anti-Christ! What can you know of Humanity, if you don't love it?

And to the Lord High Chancellor's smug and placating

Damn it, boy, the mass of mankind is still unimaginably ignorant. One must do what one can —

Francis retorts: —

Rubbish! One must do what one can't. That's why I tackled the atom.

With loathing he listens to the Secretary of War, explaining why the secret of the discovery must belong to the British alone: —

Because the battle's to the strong: an' with this weapon the Americans an' ourselves could be cock o' the walk an' teach all other peoples on the globe where they got off. . . .

Refusing to destroy the secret, Francis now opposes his power to theirs: —

. . . Yours is the Spirit of Yesterday: mine is the Spirit of To-morrow. . . . The day of the Takers is over, I tell you; the day of the Givers dawns. And I inaugurate it — with the greatest of all possible gifts: mastery over matter. At last, Man is free to enlarge the Kingdom of the Spirit; and so, whether the Sum of Things is justified or not, to justify himself. And do you think, because the Spirit of Yesterday in *you* is afraid, the Spirit of To-morrow in *me* will run away? . . . You *all* think it's a game — it's your way of evading responsibility. Very well then, if it's a game, let's play it. By God, if there's to be world drama here, I'll play Caesar. When I first took my place among you, by right, as the greatest benefactor Mankind has ever known, the first word my uncle spoke was "War." And since then: "War, Death, Despair"—to me who bring Love, Life, and Hope. Only one man among the lot of you wanted my gift—and what for? Humanity? No. To be "cock of the walk . . . the game for the game's sake." You've dragged me down—you've made me fight—very well then, by God, I'll meet you on your own atrocious level.

Still unimpressed, the ministers proceed to the next step—his arrest. Francis promptly informs them that when, a week ago, his "heart" recognized their "wickedness," he made his "preparations." As they listen to him in fascinated horror, he explains those preparations:—

Understand this: either, by *noon* tomorrow, you will be prepared to formulate, under my supervision, a constructive program satisfactory to *me,* or at *one o'clock tomorrow* England ends. (*Uproar*) Where this island was, will be a whirlpool of disintegrating atoms. . . . If, if I am interfered with in the slightest degree, or if, in the meantime (*quietly*) I should come to an unlooked-for—and convenient—end, no power at present known to man, can avert that catastrophe. (*Smiling*) That accident will guarantee the detonation.

Rejecting a final plea of Evelyn Arthur, Francis leaves. And while the Secretary of War arranges for police to follow him, adding "and, for God's sake, *tell them not to touch him,*" the second-act curtain falls.

The next day the Committee is once more awaiting the arrival of Francis. He enters, looking haggard and crushed, and tells them to what end he has finally decided to apply the power his discovery has given him. To destroy the secret would be useless, for with the many scientists in the world working on the problem, the solution is sure to be found by others. No, the Earth, apparently incapable of mastering its own destiny, must be regarded as one of "Nature's casual blunders." So it had better end, now and at once. Gravely Francis delivers his ultimatum: —

> In a brief moment, this planet and all upon it, with all its history, its hopes and its disillusions, will be wiped out. You see that clock? When the two arms of that clock coincide on noon, I will return to stand among you, a man among his fellows, and with you pass away, even as all men and this very globe itself will pass away. Our midget has spun long enough. I give it fifteen minutes more — fifteen minutes for you to come to terms with your gods.

We now live through, with the members of the Cabinet, these fifteen minutes which they believe to be their last. Gone is all need for surface-speech and for the suppression of hidden thoughts. The truth of these men's opinions of each other bursts forth with a hate that would seem to justify Francis' estimate of the children of Earth. Finally Evelyn Arthur does come to a confrontation with his gods. Turning to the others, he speaks in a low voice: —

> Prime Minister, colleagues, I must testify to the truth before I go. . . . This boy is right. Nature, not he, has put Humanity on trial; and because we have failed to evolve a faith adequate to our opportunities, she rejects us for new experiments. That is the truth and I am glad to have come to it.

But this truth the Secretary of War flouts: "To the devil with your 'Truth, Faith, Humanity!' Man can live without 'em." Convinced, like the rest, that Francis must carry the control of his world-destroying power on his person, he has come to a decision. Whipping out a revolver, he covers them: —

> Now then. You all in your hearts want him dead. Very well. Gimme a clear field o'fire. . . .

So as Francis Lightfoot crosses the threshold, the Secretary of War shoots him. His body is placed on the table. Raising himself, Francis takes a large watch out of his pocket, looks at it and sinks back dead. The watch, they now realize, must be the control, so they remove it to the mantel for safekeeping. They can scarcely believe in their salvation, and are shamed when Evelyn Arthur remarks: —

> The clock, to the great scandal of all hopeful souls, having been set back, the tortoise humanity will now cover its inch during the ensuing century.

As he finishes these words a knock is heard at the door and a letter for the Prime Minister is handed in. It is marked "Urgent. From the League of United Scientists of the World." Astounded, the Cabinet listen to the reading of it: —

> To the Prime Minister and Cabinet of Great Britain, from the League of United Scientists of the World, secretly assembled in Geneva. The League informs the Prime Minister that it is aware a scientist outside the League has proved he can control the atom. You are hereby given notice that, after years of co-ordinated labour, the League, also, has just discovered the secret of the Atom. The League has prepared its programme. And it serves notice that it requires the attendance of the Prime Minister and such of his associates as he shall select, at Geneva immediately. The League, obviously, is in a position to enforce its demands. A similar notice is being served simultaneously on the Chancellories of every civilized country in the world. Six aeroplanes are over you as you read this. They contain atomic bombs. Such bombs hang over the capitals of every civilized country.

Even while they listen the drone of airplanes is heard, growing ever louder, until they can be seen from the windows. Softly Evelyn Arthur addresses the dead Francis: —

Five minutes past twelve. The clock cannot be set back. If not you, Francis . . . another.

And as he bends down to kiss the face, the Prime Minister asks: —

Gentlemen, those wings even now sound over Europe. Are we with them or against them? What is our reply?

As they argue, Arthur, taking the fatal watch with him, to drop it "deeper than ever plummet sounded," starts for the door. And to the question: "Where are you going?" he replies with the single word: "Geneva." Hurrying to the window, they watch him go, and when the Lord High Chancellor says savagely

Idiot! Geneva. Between them the end!

the Prime Minister answers "in a ringing voice": —

No, gentlemen, between them, if Man can find faith, the Beginning!

And as "the roar of planes fills the entire theatre," the curtain falls, leaving us with the promise that the awakened forces of the world, above claims of nation and of power, will make the world safe for a free humanity.

Wings Over Europe, although acclaimed by all true lovers of the theatre, proved only a *succès d'éstime.* And its production provides yet another opportunity to judge the pernicious effect on the theatre of the absence of play-consciousness. The producers, believing that advance information would pique the curiosity of theatregoers, announced a play with a cast of twenty men and not a single woman. Irritation on the part of Theatre Guild subscribers and other theatre "lovers" began to manifest itself in such comments as: "Who wants to see a play without a woman in it?" or, "Well, that sounds as if it was going to be a fine bore." A prominent Broadway personage gave a cynical shrug as he said to me: "Well, I s'pose the subscribers will come because they've paid their money, but people don't want to see that kind of a play." Aware that he knew absolutely nothing of this play save that it had an all-male cast, I pressed him: "What kind of a play?" "Oh, *that* kind of a play," he repeated, not in the least disconcerted, "I know what it's got to be: just a regular highbrow talk-fest."

Those who demand only plays with women in them, thereby affirm, first, that the exploitation of sex is their only desideratum in the theatre, and, second, that only situations dealing with the personal relations of individuals interest them. And those who at once conclude that a play with a cast of men only must, of necessity, be a "highbrow talk-fest," thereby proclaim their rejection of the theatre as a source of ideas and inspiration. Such attitudes the profit-seeking commercial theatre fosters.

Three years later the Theatre Guild, nothing daunted, presented another original play against war: *Miracle at Verdun,* by the Austrian dramatist, Hans Chlumberg. Chlumberg, after surviving active war service, died from an accident sustained while assisting with the production of his play in Vienna, and the world was robbed of a talented playwright. Like Toller, his war experience not only filled him with revulsion, but also directed his thinking into new channels. He did not come back to Vienna a revolutionist, but he understood clearly that millions of lives had been sacrificed in vain, and that until society ceased its competition, war was inevitable. *Miracle at Verdun* does not only denounce war — that is too easy — but also a society whose peace can only breed new wars. To show, through the medium of the theatre, the millions of war dead resurrected — brought back to the realization of these truths — might, he thought, help the living to learn that they and their children will also be uselessly sacrificed, unless they hasten to build a new world.

The first scene of the play — there are eight scenes — is a military burial ground in the Argonne. Although written in 1929, the play's action is laid in 1934, twenty years after the beginning of the World War. Led by a tourist guide, a group of chattering tourists of assorted nationalities come to visit the battlefields. The Americans complain that there aren't enough dead here for the fees they are being charged. The French protest and a quarrel ensues in which the Americans tell the French they would have been lost "if we hadn't bled for you," and the French retort, "You entered the war after your ships were sunk and, of course, you didn't care about your war credits, your war profits?" It is not a pleasant scene, this, at the Verdun graves. Finally the disabled veteran, the cemetery attendant, placates them by saying that even if they have seen larger cemeteries, this one is unique because here there is a mass-grave in which French and German soldiers lie side by side. For so close were the trenches, he explains, that the wounded and the prisoners just remained in each other's trenches, for safety's sake, pressing close together for protection, binding each other's wounds, sharing each other's cigarettes, even playing cards together, "whenever there was a slight let-up." "And, in the end," asks a Frenchman, "who became the prisoners?" To which the attendant replies: —

> There were no prisoners, sir. Neither army wanted to leave the trench in possession of the enemy, so they blew it to pieces from behind the lines. (*Pause.*) And then, because they couldn't tell the French and German soldiers apart, they were all buried in this mass-grave.

None of the tourists is in the least impressed by this story of solidarity in death, except one man who has sat apart. He has heard the French attendant speak of the two survivors — a French sergeant and a German. When the tourists move on, he remains to question the attendant: "What will all the anniversary prayers in the churches tomorrow ask for the men down there in their graves?" And he mentions many of them by name. The attendant replies:

For the peace of their souls. . . . For their comfort. . . . And most of all for their glorious resurrection!

Left alone, the man whom we have guessed to be the German survivor repeats with great emotion: —

For their resurrection!

As he sits gazing off into the distance his vision unfolds for us, as the play.

It is night and a tall figure appears. He is the Messenger of the Lord and he calls upon the Dead of Verdun to arise from their graves and return home. The Lord is bringing about this miracle because He believes that the world's joy on the return of those killed in the war will be so great "that all hatred will be undermined and utterly washed away."

Presently the great cross on the mass-grave topples over, the earth begins to move, and everywhere crosses tumble. The bandaged, tattered figures of the resurrected stagger forth. Incredulously they realize that they are alive and free to go home and they decide that they will march away, two abreast, hand in hand, with a Captain and a drummer at their head. And as they start the French and the German War Ministers, arriving for the anniversary celebration, see them. Aghast, they hear the soldiers explain what has happened and the news spreads that the Day of Judgment has come — that the dead have risen!

In a moment we see the Arc de Triomphe in Paris, where the Premier is making his speech commemorating the twentieth anniversary of the beginning of the World War. Let us listen to him: —

The armistice we followed up with a victorious peace! We forced the enemy to their knees, disarmed them, diminished their territory, weakened them for generations to come, hemmed them in, fettered them on every side . . . but they have paid for it with military annihilation and economic impotence. With the power of our sword we have forced the enemy to make doubly and triply good what they laid waste in the war, and we because of them. . . . Rich and powerful as never before — we are now *invincible!* Our army is the largest, the most powerful that was ever maintained by a state in time of peace! No nation in the world is so heavily armed as we! For every poilu — a machine gun! For every squad a cannon! A tank for every file! Clouds of poison gas for every company! And so many airplanes that their brazen wings would darken the sun if any nation dared to arouse the enmity of France. Heroic dead of France! Thus are we prepared to fight and win! Heroic dead of France! Thus are we armed, that you may rest in peace, that we may prove worthy of your heroic death and do honor to your memory!

And if on this day . . . there should be a miracle: If you rose up — and walked among us . . . (Frenzied jubilation) . . . rejoicing, overcome by our ecstatic reception, and marching before us to the places that gave you birth — then I know you would say: "Sons and brothers, you have administered well our legacy! Our spirit has entered into you! Sons and brothers! We are pleased with you!"

The stage darkens for a moment and then discloses a square in Berlin where the Reich Chancellor is making his speech. And while in 1929 Chlumberg could scarcely foresee the Germany of 1934, the speech is prophetic. Voicing deepest humiliation at Germany's downfall, military impotence and economic weakness, the Chancellor vows that this will not be forever, that if Germany has "lost the power of the mailed fist . . . the next war . . . will be a war — of chemistry!" And voices shout: "Hurrah for German science! Hurrah for Germany!"

Once more the stage darkens, after which both Premier and Chancellor are seen declaiming simultaneously: —

> As we stand before this sacred monument — to you, our noble dead — we desire only that you shall be as pleased with us as we are with you. Know then, that, as you died, that your Fatherland might be great and strong — so we — swear with our lives — that you have not died in vain — at any cost — at any sacrifice . . . your Fatherland shall live and conquer. *We swear it.*

Three satiric interludes follow. That night, the news of the resurrection is received and rejected by the French Premier while in bed with another man's wife; by the Reich Chancellor in bed with the pompous partner of his domesticity; by the imperturbable British Prime Minister, sleeping alone, while his valet conducts a telephone conversation of State for him. The difference in the genius of three peoples is well burlesqued in these short scenes.

Then we return to the resurrected, homeward bound. First they reminisce happily on their lives before the war, but soon their talk drifts shudderingly back to the devastation they have since lived through. At a sign-post pointing East and West to their respective countries the German soldiers bid their French comrades farewell.

The dramatist now gives us the experiences of one French and one German soldier as typical of the reception accorded them. His purpose is to show the havoc created by the return of these men hitherto honored by lip service. They are unwelcome to their women, who have remade their lives, and to children who do not know them. Socially they are a menace, as competitors for jobs and as citizens who must be fed when there are no jobs. And so they are rejected on all sides. The French episode ends with a scene in which the villagers actually attack the returning soldiers, calling to each other: "Arm yourselves! Protect yourselves and yours against the dead!" And in the German episode the soldier, stunned by the sight of his mother in her old age scrubbing the floors of the inn, once hers, but now owned by a war profiteer, cries: "Hate — greater and stronger than before . . . Human kindness further away than ever . . . Mother! The world is just as it was. . . . Did we die in vain, Mother? In vain? In vain . . . ?"

So we come to the great scene of the play: a conference of world powers, meeting in Paris, to consider the problem of the resurrected. Statesmen and rulers are helpless in the face of a world collapsing from the terror of this miracle. Commerce and industry are at a standstill; banks have shut down. People are accumulating provisions. How is the crisis to be met? And to make the situation even more threatening, the thirteen million resurrected are demanding to know what they died for, what the living have done with the world they gave their lives to make safe and free! First of all, the high representatives of the Church, Catholic, Protestant and Jewish, agree that, according to their separate tenets, this is no miracle and no true resurrection. Then a scientific authority bores the delegates by explaining that, according to science, there can be no such thing as a miracle.

At this point sounds of alarm are heard outside and the doors are thrown open to admit a new delegation, the resurrected themselves. The others draw away from them as they sit down, on the floor, on the steps. A spokesman for the German soldiers quietly asks the Chancellor if their loved ones are being cared for, if they are hungry. The Chancellor replies: "Germany has grown poor. We are paralyzed by grim facts." At which all the resurrected cry together: "They're hungry . . . They're letting them grow hungry . . ." And when the spokesman for the French soldiers asks the Premier why, if there is peace in France, the factories are humming with the manufacture of airplane bombs and grenades, the Premier replies that "Not everybody wants to keep the peace!" At which the Italian Ambassador shouts: "You looked at me when you made that remark! Do you mean that Italy . . ." And pandemonium begins again. As the representatives reveal their suspicion and hatred of each other, the resurrected listen, shocked. Then they rise in hopelessness and proceed slowly to the door. Ashamed, the delegates begin to reassure them: "You're mentioned in the schoolbooks" — "We held divine services for you" — "Anniversary celebrations!" But the American Ambassador has come not for sentimentalities, but to give figures, and he proceeds to do so: —

The war swallowed up 170 billion dollars. And 60 billion more in property losses. Those are figures! Figures, damn it all, and not words! And the only advantage gained at such enormous cost was the extermination of the surplus human material. . . . You see, you men, it may be damned hard for you that you happened to be included in that surplus; but the economy of the world has no regard for sentiment, it recognizes only iron facts! And above all, the fundamental fact that wars are the regulating agencies that remedy the overproduction of human material. . . . To put it briefly: the stupendous costs of the first world war of the twentieth century reached a ruinous figure. If in addition to that, the discarded human material, a superfluous population of about thirteen million, now comes to life again . . .

State and Church now unite to tell the soldiers that it was not God who caused their resurrection and that it is their duty to turn back to their graves. But the soldiers do not wait for the speakers to finish. In silence and with bowed heads, they pass out, to return to their graves where alone they can hope to find peace. . . .

A closing scene brings us back to the cemetery. The German veteran awakens from his vision with a gesture of despair. The tourists come crowding back. A German boy is made to recite his lesson by a disciplinarian father: "A soldier's death is the most beautiful death of all . . . A soldier must meet death joyfully. . . ." The tourists purchase souvenirs—grenade fragments—empty machine gun cartridges—and scramble off so as to be in time for the tour of "Paris at Night." . . . The play is ended.

No doubt an overstrident production contributed to the fact that *Miracle at Verdun* did not receive in New York the response accorded it in Europe. But its success in London showed an inspiring example of play-consciousness. In the course of its run, *Miracle at Verdun* had to be moved from one theatre to another at quite a cost in rebuilding scenery. A subscription list was opened to the public in the hope that its enthusiasm would bring in the necessary funds. Promptly almost the entire amount needed was contributed in small sums by the play's admirers. This incident, described as "unique," would not be so in a play-conscious world. In any case, by the originality and truthfulness of its moving fable, *Miracle at Verdun* rates as an evocative antiwar play.

On a quite different plane is W. Somerset Maugham's play: *For Services Rendered.* It concerns an English provincial family fifteen years after the World War. Maugham shows how the entire lives of his characters have been affected by the war and how it still continues to destroy them. Moreover, he leaves no doubt that the purpose of his almost Ibsenlike play, in which we see inexorable forces closing in on the lives of these quite ordinary people, is to make us understand that they are typical of every country in the world where war has struck.

In an English village live the Ardsley family. The father, a solicitor, is the type of unthinking conservative whom neither the war nor any other experience of life could teach. The mother has a strong spirit, but is so used, since war days, to cast out all thoughts of self, that she has ignored the warnings of cancer until it is too late. Sydney, the only son, now nearly forty, has been blinded in the war; his chief occupations in life are knitting and playing chess. The eldest daughter is Eva, whose passionately loved fiancé was killed in the war; an emotionally starved spinster, she has tried to compensate for her empty life by "sacrificing" herself to her brother. The second daughter, Ethel, driven into the typical war marriage, to a farmer quite beneath her, has for years tried to hide her unhappiness, as well as the fact that her husband drinks heavily and runs after women. The youngest daughter, Lois, now twenty-six, is a handsome girl, who is prevented by her Victorian father from training for a career elsewhere and who is wondering what is to become of her in this village which does not even offer an opportunity for marriage. A friend of the family, Collie Stratton, is an ex-officer of the Royal Navy, who, having served his country for twenty years, has been thrown out into the world to earn his living. Completely untrained for business, with nothing between him and starvation but his paltry bonus, which he has invested in a garage, he has run into debt.

Let us see how logically the playwright brings this war-conditioned family to inevitable catastrophe. Lois finds herself pursued by a rich middle-aged bounder summering in the vicinity with his wife. He offers the girl Paris, luxury, escape into the world outside. She also attracts Howard, her brother-in-law, the still-handsome farmer, whose lust is so strong that the girl, to her disgust, finds herself sexually aroused by him. While trying to find a solution for her problem, she is swept to a decision by the tragedy that engulfs her eldest sister. Eva has centered her emotional need on Collie, a symbol of her lost fiancé, hoping still to experience something of a woman's fulfillment. Knowing him to be in serious financial difficulty, she offers him all the money she has in the world. When he refuses, she pitifully suggests marriage, as the condition under which he can accept her help. But Collie is too fine for this way out. The rich bounder now refuses him a loan, while Solicitor Ardsley, with cold reproach, tells him that he cannot save him from jail, since he has been giving out post-dated checks without funds. The ex-naval officer cannot face this disgrace, which would deprive him of his D.S.O., and so he kills himself.

This shock is more than Eva can endure. After accusing the others of doing nothing to help a man "who'd risked his life for you a hundred times," she collapses. In her sick mind fantasy has become reality, and she tells her family that she and the dead man had been engaged to be married. And when her fatuous father tells her how much better off she is in her "good" home, all her repression bursts through at last. Pouring out her resentment of the family which symbolizes for her all the frustration of her life, she succumbs to hysteria, beating the floor with her fists.

After this scene, which jolts them into momentary articulateness, the three men of the family — Ardsley, his son-in-law Howard and the blinded Sydney — express their attitudes toward war, which Maugham obviously wishes us to regard as typical: —

ARDSLEY: It's a terrible thing about poor Collie. No one can be more distressed than I.

SYDNEY: It seems a bit hard that after going through the war and getting a D.S.O., he should have come to this end.

ARDSLEY: He may have been a very good naval officer. He was a very poor business man. That's all there is to it.

SYDNEY: We might put that on his tombstone. It would make a damned good epitaph.

ARDSLEY: If that's a joke, Sydney, I must say I think it in very bad taste.

SYDNEY (*with bitter calm*): You see, I feel I have a certain right to speak. I know how dead keen we all were when the war started. Every sacrifice was worth it. We didn't say much about it because we were rather shy, but honour did mean something to us, and patriotism wasn't just a word. And then, when it was all over, we did think that those of us who'd died hadn't died in vain, and those of us who were broken and shattered and knew they wouldn't be any more good in the world were buoyed up by the thought that if they'd given everything they'd given it in a great cause.

ARDSLEY: And they had.

SYDNEY: Do you still think that? I don't. I know that we were the dupes of the incompetent fools who ruled the nations. I know that we were sacrificed to their vanity, their greed, and their stupidity. And the worst of it is that as far as I can tell they haven't learnt a thing. They're just as vain, they're just as greedy, they're just as stupid as they ever were. They muddle on, muddle on, and one of these days they'll muddle us all into another war. When that happens I'll tell you what I'm going to do. I'm going out into the streets and cry: Look at me; don't be a lot of damned fools; it's all bunk what they're saying to you, about honour and patriotism and glory, bunk, bunk, bunk.

HOWARD: Who cares if it is bunk? I had the time of my life in the war. No responsibility and plenty of money. More than I'd ever had before or ever since. All the girls you wanted and all the whisky. Excitement. A roughish time in the trenches, but a grand lark afterwards. I tell you it was a bitter day for me when they signed the armistice. What have I got now? Just the same old thing day after day, working my guts out to keep body and soul together. The very day war is declared I join up and the sooner the better if you ask me. That's the life for me! By God!

ARDSLEY (*to his son*): You've had a lot to put up with, Sydney. I know that. But don't think you're the only one. It's been a great blow to me that you haven't been able to follow me in my business as I followed my father. Three generations, that would have been. But it wasn't to be: No one wants another war less than I do, but if it comes I'm convinced that you'll do your duty, so far as in you lies, as you did it before. It was a great grief to me that when the call came I was too old to answer. But I did what I could. I was enrolled as a special constable. And if I'm wanted again I shall be ready again.

SYDNEY (*between his teeth*): God give me patience.

HOWARD: You have a whisky and soda, old boy, and you'll feel better.

SYDNEY: Will a whisky and soda make me forget poor Evie half crazy? Collie doing away with himself rather than go to jail, and my lost sight?

ARDSLEY: But, my dear boy, that's just our immediate circle. Of course we suffered, perhaps we've had more than our fair share, but we're not everyone.

SYDNEY: Don't you know that all over England there are families like ours, all over Germany and all over France?

For Lois the sight of her crazed sister has been a revelation. Better to run off unmarried, with an unloved man, than risk the fate of Eva. Her mother, near death, is too wise to stop her. She will tell her father, after the girl has gone. So the family, each carrying within himself his own particular hell, meet once more for the ritual of "tea." Eva, now completely mad, enters. She has put on her best frock and announces that Collie is coming to talk to her father about their engagement. Ardsley joins them, throwing Eva a cheery remark. And Maugham ends his play thus: —

ARDSLEY: Well, I must say it's very nice to have a cup of tea by one's own fireside and surrounded by one's family. If you come to think of it, we none of us have anything very much to worry about. Of course we none of us have more money than we know what to do with, but we have our health and we have our happiness. I don't think we've got very much to complain of. Things haven't been going too well lately, but I think the world is turning the corner and we can all look forward to better times in future. This old England of ours isn't done yet, and I for one believe in it and all it stands for.

(*Eva begins to sing in a thin cracked voice.*)

EVA: God save our gracious King!
Long live our noble King!
God save our King!

(*The others look at her, petrified, in horror-struck surprise. When she stops, Lois gives a little cry and hurries from the room.*)

Curtain

Treated in Maugham's characteristic vein, which never stresses the social problem manifestly inherent in his theme, *For Services Rendered* is a notable contribution to drama against war.

In *Wings Over Europe,* the question of how to end war was presented by relating it to a fabulous discovery of science. Our next play, much smaller in stature and scope, also appeals to the imagination, though the author keeps his subject within the realm of what he regards as the attainable. *If This Be Treason* was written by John Haynes Holmes with the technical aid of Reginald Lawrence. The Reverend John Haynes Holmes has for many years occupied a special position among the clergymen of New York City, because of his belief that a church must be integrated with the changing problems of life, and because of his progressive and fearless point of view on contemporary questions. A feature of his famous Community Church are its Forum meetings to which speakers of all shades of opinion are invited. I refer to this as John Haynes Holmes's play, because I read it as originally written by Holmes alone, and know that the entire content was his. His thesis is stated in the opening paragraph of the introduction to the printed play.

The subject of this play is the will of the peoples of the world to peace. Its hero is not John Gordon, President of the United States, nor Koyé, popular leader of the Japanese masses, but the common men and women whose hidden desires they express and whose latent energies they release. Its thesis is the simple proposition that if the people of any two countries involved in a war crisis were only given by their governments the same opportunity to serve the interests of peace that they are invariably given to serve the interests of war, peace and not war would come.

How peace is attained, and an imaginary war crisis between the United States and Japan averted, by arousing the people of both nations for peace instead of for war, *If This Be Treason* narrates in realistic political terms. The play opens on the day of the Inauguration of President Gordon, whom the people of the United States have elected on a peace platform. Gordon's predecessor, a militarist, has been baiting the government of Japan to an act of open hostility. With the Inaugural Ball in progress and the people rejoicing in the election of their peace candidate, news comes that Japan has taken Manila, with a loss of at least a thousand American lives. How can this slaughter be answered by anything except war? President Gordon, in the face of a Cabinet that turns against him, orders every American battleship, already strategically placed by his predecessor, to return to the home base.

During the second act we listen to the President in conflict with his Cabinet, determinedly opposing his untried philosophy of peace to their traditional advocacy of war as the only possible course. His next step is to inform Congress that, as Commander in Chief of the Army and Navy, he will not permit a soldier in the land to march nor a warship to sail. And he adds to his warning the final words of the historic challenge that gives the play its title: "Make the most of it!" At once shouts of "treason" and threats of impeachment fill the air. The ex-President asks: —

. . . Why don't you make a complete job of it, Gordon? Why not go to Japan and hand over your sword personally to the Emperor! . . . Go to Tokio and lick the dirt! . . .

To the President these taunting words come as an inspiration. While the politicians gape in dismay, Gordon orders a battleship to take him immediately to Japan. He explains: —

. . . You asked me how I would wage war if I didn't fight. Well, I've found the way . . . I shall wage war by starting at the end instead of the beginning. I'll go to Tokio for my peace conference, before, instead of after, the fighting.

To a demand for his immediate resignation, the President replies, as the second-act curtain falls: —

Refused. I shan't resign. I can't. I'm too busy. I'm going to Japan and I'm sailing tonight.

The last act takes place in Tokio. Although the great Japanese peace leader, Koyé, has been thrown into prison, his followers cheer the name of President Gordon on the streets. Since the United States had declared war on Japan, however, after the departure of Gordon, the Japanese Premier has refused to meet the visiting President. Finally he yields to the demand of the British Government, that, in the interest of mankind, the President's request for a conference be granted. The last scene of the play takes place in the conference chamber. The militarist Premier not only refuses to consider stopping the war but he also refuses to believe that the President has not come on some sinister, ulterior mission. He therefore orders his immediate arrest. Gordon's supporters try to save him by reminding the Premier that Gordon, perhaps already impeached by Congress, may now be nothing more than a private citizen. Realizing that this fact would only increase his danger, the President addresses himself to the Premier, fervidly telling him: "Wars are always lost. Victor and vanquished alike lose everything — Wealth, trade, productive enterprise, security . . . progress . . ." But he might as well try to make an impression on Mars himself.

As the Premier declares the conference at an end, news comes that the American people have ranged themselves solidly behind their President and that the Senate has been compelled to suspend the impeachment proceedings pending the outcome of his now official peace negotiations with Japan. The Japanese officials are filled with alarm at the effect of this news on their own people, for the shouts of a great crowd are heard without. Not only has the jail been stormed and Koyé freed, but the soldiers have refused to fire on the crowd that freed him. The door bursts open and part of the crowd pours into the room surrounding Koyé, who advances slowly to Gordon, welcoming him in the name of the Japanese people. Quietly Koyé explains: —

> . . . What could we do? We were not strong. We were beaten, crushed, we had failed. Then suddenly, Mr. President, as a spark from tinder, the miracle flashed across the sea. You were coming to Japan! In a day the word had gone to every corner of the land, like the wind rustling the leaves of a forest. No village so remote it did not hear — no man so humble he did not understand. *President Gordon coming to Japan to ask for peace!* At that moment, Mr. President, as though the heavens had spoken, war became impossible. Your coming was the sound of gongs before our altars. Your presence more terrible than an army with banners. We knew that America wanted peace and would bring us peace. We saw a friendly host reaching out their hands in brotherhood. We were glad, and suddenly we were brave!

And as the two men clasp hands, they are told that the Emperor requests their presence . . . It is to be peace and not the sword.

If this play seems the expression of wishful thinking rather than any coming to grips with the basic causes of war, it nevertheless makes a definite contribution to the cause of peace. For, as John Haynes Holmes says: "War some day will be abolished by the will of man," and in this sense the will-to-peace, dynamic and constructive, is a real force in the world.

Although its production antedated that of *If This Be Treason* by nearly two years, I have held to the last the discussion of *Peace on Earth,* by George Sklar and Albert Maltz, because, in its approach to its subject and in the point of view it presents, it carries furthest to the left the play against war. This play drives home to the audience the force of the playwrights' positive social philosophy and of the facts responsible for their point of view, by letting it observe the impact of these facts on the leading character of the play, who is quite unprepared for the truths they reveal. For locale, our left playwrights have taken the most seemingly peaceful place on earth: a New England college town. But when they analyze this scene, we see it in the light of the economic forces that dominate it. For the leading character of their play they have taken a young American college professor, one among thousands. When he finds behind this scene, not the peace and the freedom he believed in, but war — a war for profits manifesting itself nationally in industrial conflict, and internationally in world conflict, and when he tries to use his American birthright of freedom to tell the truth as he sees it, his martyrdom begins. The time of the play is "In a year or so," which would be *now.*

When the play opens Professor Peter Owens, living serenely with his wife and young daughter, is somewhat annoyed with himself for having agreed to participate in a meeting on behalf of one of his students who has just spent the night in jail. The youth was arrested while making an anti-war speech in connection with the strike of the town's longshoremen, who are refusing to load munitions as a protest against war. While Owens is promising his wife not to "let himself in for things," there enters unexpectedly his former classmate and closest friend, McCracken, — both are alumni of the college at which Owens now teaches, — back from a newspaper assignment in China. McCracken is a man who finds himself wherever history is in the making, especially when it involves the workers. After listening to the college group who meet in Owens' living room to plan a protest meeting against interference with free speech, Mac informs them that what they ought to do is go out and support labor's strike against war. At once Owens and the other professor present are up in arms against him, stating that it's not "the province of a university professor to get mixed up in such things." And to Mac's indignation against them — "sitting here in your ivory towers" — Owens replies: "I'm a scientist, a psychologist; I'm not a champion of causes." But they all agree to Mac's suggestion to hold their free speech protest meeting, not in a university hall, but publicly on the Green, and finally Owens, still insisting that a professor should not be actively involved, agrees to "come down and watch you."

Next we are at the street meeting. Mac, on a platform, is reading to a crowd composed mostly of students and longshoremen, those winged words from the Declaration of Independence proclaiming man's "unalienable rights." A "cop" appears, and when Mac refuses to stop, reading from the Constitution that "There shall be no law abridging the freedom of speech or of the press or the right of the people peaceably to assemble," the officer of the law pulls him down and threatens him with his club. Owens protests and insists on the legal rights of an

American citizen. The "cop" tells him to "shut up" and see how far he'll get if he tries to speak. At this Owens leaps to the platform and continues to read from America's document of freedom. The "cop's" whistle blows; Owens is pulled off the platform, more "cops" arrive, the students chant: "We demand Free Speech — We demand Free Speech," and the first "cop" announces: "You're under arrest, the whole bunch of you." So, surrounded by striking longshoremen, Professor Peter Owens steps into the reality of American life.

Back in Owens' home the next night, we learn that the student who caused all the commotion has been expelled "for conduct unbecoming a student of this University," and that the Dean is on his way to have a talk with Owens. Already his experiences have made Owens see the University and his relation to it in a new light. Especially disturbing has been his realization of the influence on the University of John Andrews, one of its trustees, who has held high national office and is a munitions manufacturer. Just how displeasing to the local magnate is this strike against shipping munitions, Owens is now beginning to understand, and when the mealy-mouthed Dean explains that "the trustees" are in a position to have the case against Owens with its "undesirable notoriety" dropped, a new Owens speaks: —

. . . I always had the notion that freedom of speech was guaranteed in the Constitution and then suddenly I discovered that when a student of mine tried to exercise that right, he was arrested. And when my friend McCracken tried to read the Declaration of Independence, he was arrested. And when I tried to say something, I was arrested too. Maybe what I did wasn't necessary. But it was certainly right. And nobody can say it wasn't. Well, I intend to find out if it's a criminal offense to read the Declaration of Independence. And John Andrews isn't going to tell me what I can or cannot do.

When the Dean adds: "All the University asks is a little more academic dignity," Owens replies: "Taking orders from Andrews isn't my idea of academic dignity . . ."

Soothing his wife, who is frankly worried over the turn things are taking, Owens can nevertheless not resist accompanying his friend Mac to the headquarters of the workers striking against war. While they are on the way, we watch the following "Interlude." We see the face of the Sheriff speaking into a telephone. He says: —

A striker was shot this afternoon, and I'm afraid the situation is getting out of hand. With the limited forces at my disposal I feel I can no longer guarantee the maintenance of law and order. I'm therefore making this formal request for assistance from the state. I urge that at least two companies of militia with full riot equipment be immediately transported into this county to be at my disposal wherever the situation warrants. I hope there'll be no occasion to use the militia and I shall try in every instance to . . .

Darkness for a second. Then another face and another voice: —

Everything's been arranged. The boat'll anchor in the harbor at about seven-fifteen. The crew'll be disembarked. A barge'll be docked and loading'll start immediately. You're to take complete charge of all operations — If the strikers should find out and try to interfere, the militia's on the way and can be relied on for co-operation. . . .

So we know that University trustee Andrews has arranged for strikebreakers to load his munitions.

At strike headquarters now, Miller, one of the strike leaders, is explaining the situation to the rest: —

That's the way things stand. They've docked a barge and they're loading munitions. They've got hold of a German boat, they're giving the sailors a bonus and they're doing it. The stuff is boxed up and marked "soap" and they've kidded them into thinking it is soap. Well, maybe we ought to go down and supervise the loading of that soap. . . .

Then Mac comes in with Owens, known to them after the "free speech" arrests of the night before. The Professor learns that a young striker was shot by a gunman that afternoon, that this will undoubtedly be used as an excuse by Andrews to have his friend the Governor declare martial law and send the militia against the strikers. As the strikers form in line to march down to the docks to "stop that scabbing," Mac says to Owens: "Want to take a look, Pete?" And Owens replies, "Yes, I think I do."

While they are on their way we watch a second "Interlude." This time we learn that martial law has been established . . . that picketing at the docks must cease . . . that "troops will be equipped with riot guns, tear gas, gas masks, machine guns and all other necessary riot equipment.". . . Workers daring to strike against war! Workers daring to prevent "scabs" from loading munitions! Let us see, with Professor Peter Owens, whose America this is. . . .

Moonlight on the dock, where a company officer is trying to hurry the German strikebreakers with their loading of cases conspicuously marked: *Soap.* The Germans are worried about the strikers, but are reassured by the information that armed deputy sheriffs as well as the militia are on the way to protect them. But the strikers are on the way, too, and arrive chanting "Stop Munition Shipments!" They tell the company officer that they are well aware that not soap, but munitions are being loaded. One German understands, and soon the rest are excited. The American strikers try to make their German brothers understand:

Nix, soap, comrade, explosif . . . nix soap, comrade, explosif, explosif, verstay?
You tell 'em, Dutch.
Don't load, comrades, strike!
Strike against war, buddies, no more war!
C'mon sailors, show your solidarity.

Finally Owens, watching in the background, is commandeered by Mac to translate. And to cheers of "Atta boy, Professor," he finds himself telling them in German that "this is a strike against war." "We," he continues in German, "must prevent the loading of munitions . . . Open the cases and see for yourselves what they contain." It is *we* now, for Professor Owens — a very big step taken here. . . . A case is opened and guncotton pulled out. Soon German sailors and American workers are on board together, throwing the cases overboard into the sea. But now police sirens are heard, and in a moment the deputies rush on, armed with guns. Exhorting the strikers not to be afraid, Mac stoops to pick up a case. A shot rings out and he falls. In the awful silence that follows, Owens steps forward and bends over the body of his friend. . . . Instinctively we know that his march to his own Golgotha has begun. . . .

It is an hour later, in a room in the University Faculty Club, where a dance is being held. We hear university shop-talk as well as war-talk. The general feeling is that "there doesn't seem much question about a war" — remember the time is *now*. The appropriate expressions of antipathy against war, and the inexcusability of again resorting to it, are exchanged. Unobserved, Owens has been standing in the doorway listening, and when Andrews, asked what he would do if the United States went to war, answers: "Well, if our Government was forced into a war, I'd support it. I'd support it a hundred percent," Owens turns to him with the one word, "Why?" The conversation that follows I shall quote, because its content is the crux of this play and makes clear why *Peace on Earth* is different from every other play against war. It is here that the playwrights present their concept of the relation of war to our social fabric, and their conviction that if we accept, without active protest, the evils inherent in our present economic system, then we, and no one else, are responsible for the continuation of war in the world. Let us listen to Peter Owens, fresh from his experience at the dock, as he takes his stand against what hitherto has been his world: —

ANDREWS: Well, if our government was forced into a war, I'd support it. I'd support it a hundred percent.

OWENS: (*Who has been standing in the doorway.*) Why?

ANDREWS: It's the only thing any patriotic American would do.

OWENS: (*Coming into the room.*) That's one reason. I have a notion you might have some others.

ANDREWS: Such as?

OWENS: You're surely in a better position to say than I am.

ANDREWS: What makes you think I have other reasons?

OWENS: Oh — offhand, I'd say you were too good a business man not to have other reasons.

ANDREWS: What do you mean by that?

OWENS: Just that.

ANDREWS: I'm afraid I don't follow.

OWENS: Nothing very mysterious. You're an industrialist, aren't you? You have, for instance, a controlling interest in a good many steel mills.

ANDREWS: That's right.

OWENS: And in other industries as well — chemicals, rubber, nitrates, textiles, rayon —

ANDREWS: Well?

OWENS: Some of these products can be converted into other products: rayon, for instance, into guncotton.

ANDREWS: Well?

OWENS: Well, that's what I mean. In supporting the government you'd naturally supply it with some of these products.

ANDREWS: Yes, I'd consider it my duty.

OWENS: I'd consider it good business.

(*There is a pause.*)

ANDREWS: I don't think I know your name.

OWENS: My name's Owens.

ANDREWS: Oh — you're the professor who's been getting publicity for himself, aren't you?

OWENS: I'm the professor who was arrested for reading the Declaration of Independence, yes.

ANDERSON: Pete, you've interrupted a rather exciting discussion.

BANKCROFT: I'd like to know what Mr. Owens would say about the war question.

OWENS: I'd say that I was opposed to war under any circumstances. I'd say that it was criminal for men like Andrews to convert textile mills into mills manufacturing munitions.

ANDERSON: Pete . . .

ANDREWS: Owens, suppose you let me talk for a moment. When rayon mills don't pay for themselves you have the choice of shutting them down, or turning out a product that does pay. That's common sense, isn't it?

OWENS: Yes.

ANDREWS: Well, I built those mills. It means a great deal to me to keep them going. I have a responsibility to the fifteen thousand workers employed in them. I have a responsibility to the twenty thousand people who hold shares in them. That's why I'm manufacturing munitions, Owens. That's why it isn't criminal.

OWENS: I can't balance the employment of fifteen thousand workers or the dividends of twenty thousand shareholders against the lives of millions of men. Maybe you can.

ANDREWS: The manufacture of munitions doesn't cause war, Owens. You ought to know that.

OWENS: If they weren't manufactured there couldn't be any war.

ANDREWS: But they are being manufactured, Owens. If I didn't make 'em, someone else would. Why shouldn't I? That's just the way things are.

OWENS: If that's the way things are — then perhaps they ought to be changed.

ANDREWS: Well, Owens, I suggest you do something about it.

OWENS: I think I will.

ANDREWS: You're pretty young, Owens.

(*There is an uncomfortable pause.*)

OWENS: You're a chemist, Kelsey. If we went to war, would you turn out poison gas?

KELSEY: I'm afraid I'd have to.

OWENS: Would you want to?

KELSEY: No.

OWENS: Then you're opposed to war?

KELSEY: Of course.

OWENS: You're a novelist, Murdock. Would you pound out rape stories for the propaganda department?

MURDOCK: No. If war comes, I'll probably head for the Canadian wilds.

OWENS: What about you, Bishop?

PARKES: No. I'm opposed to war. I'm opposed to violence in any form whatsoever.

OWENS: Bishop, when I was a senior in college, you stood up in the University chapel and called on us in the name of God to go out and fight. What'll you say in the next war, Bishop?

ANDERSON: Pete, don't you think —
BANKCROFT: Mr. Owens, I'm afraid you — } *At the same time.*

HOWARD: Bishop Parkes isn't the only man who was misled in the last war.

OWENS: No, President Howard, I know that.

PARKES: I regret deeply what I did in the last war. I regret it more than you can realize.

OWENS: I believe that. I believe that most of you are opposed to war. You've said so. I accept it. Well — there's a strike against war going on in this town; a strike against the manufacture and shipment of munitions. Support that strike, spread it, and you check the means of carrying on a war. That's what the workers in this town are doing. They've walked out on their jobs. They're being clubbed and beaten and thrown in jail — because they're against war. You say you're against war. You're people of influence — leaders of professions — some of you are receiving honorary degrees tomorrow morning. Are you willing to throw your influence into this strike? Are you willing to come out openly and support this strike against war?

(*Silence. The dance orchestra finishes a number. There is applause from the other room. Marjorie Howard, a girl of nineteen, runs into the room.*)

MARJORIE: C'mon Dad, I'm dancing the next one with you.

HOWARD: No, dear, I —

ANDERSON: I'll tell you what you do, Marjorie; take out Pete Owens here. A little dancing'll do him good.

MARJORIE: All right. Want to?

(*There is a pause.*)

OWENS: An hour ago I saw my best friend, an alumnus of this University, shot in the back. It doesn't call for dancing on my part. (*He pauses.*) Walter McCracken was interested in stopping war. He was shot and killed by a gunman hired by that man. He was killed because he was helping the strikers stop a shipment of munitions manufactured by that man. I came here to ask this University to protest against the terror and violence instigated in this town by John Andrews.

ANDERSON: Pete, for God's sake —

BANKCROFT: If you knew Mr. Andrews as well as I do, you wouldn't be saying the things you have.

ANDREWS: That's all right. Go on, Owens.

OWENS: President Howard, I ask that this University refuse to give an honorary degree to John Andrews.

ANDERSON: Pete —

OWENS: I also ask that those of you who are to receive honorary degrees refuse to accept them on the same platform as John Andrews.

PARKES: Mr. Owens — I'm in sympathy with any move against war. But I'm not in sympathy with this strike for the simple reason that it's being led by Communists. If there's been any violence I blame it on them. The Communists are trouble-makers — they always have been — and before I insult Mr. Andrews, I'd like to know who provoked this violence.

OWENS: All I know is: John Andrews called in the militia. John Andrews called in his gunmen. If they hadn't been there, there wouldn't have been any violence. If John Andrews hadn't paid his salary, that gunman wouldn't have killed McCracken. I'm no Communist and I hold no briefs for Communism. But I know this, that if you don't make trouble, you keep quiet, and if you keep quiet, you let things happen — you let war happen.

(*There is a pause.*)

HOWARD: You have no right to talk this way, Owens.

(*There is a long pause during which Owens looks around the room.*)

OWENS: All right — don't protest. Don't protest, Howard, the University needs its endowment fund. Keep your art pure, Murdock, protest is propaganda. Don't protest, Bishop, Christ needs a new cathedral — Keep quiet all of you. There are too many people in this world. Let some of them die. What do you care? Hold tight to your honorary degrees. Keep quiet. Don't protest. Let another war come. I won't keep quiet!

(*He goes out.*)

It is the eve of Commencement Day, as we have heard, and now we see four alumni returned to demonstrate what scholars and gentlemen their Alma Mater has made of them. They are in cowboy costume and drunk, and they have come to Owens' home in angry quest of him. They represent all that is most benighted in American life. Mentally atrophied, they live the life of convention, but they are the potential vigilantes of every community. . . . They have heard all about Pete Owens' arrest, his being "mixed up with strikes," his "insults" to the University's elite, and the most drunken of them keeps repeating at intervals that "Pete Owens is a dirty Red." Owens tries to get rid of them, but one insists that he will drag him on his knees to apologize to the President of the University. Finally, unable to control himself, Owens bursts out: —

Christ Almighty! You filthy, drunken swine! While you've been guzzling and reeling around the campus, one of your classmates has been lying dead.

The retort comes: —

And who the hell cares if he is? Serves him right. He's a dirty Red.

Then Owens can endure no more and orders them out. But instead they seize him, one throws a cowboy lasso over his head, they begin to cry: "Lynch him" . . . "String 'im up" . . . Owens' wife comes in. At her scream the spell is broken and, with a last warning, his fellow alumni go out. Weeping, his wife clings to him — it is for his life that she begins to fear now. But she is his *alter ego,* and when he says, holding her close, "I'm going on with this . . . The whole set-up's wrong! When things like this happen, you can't keep quiet," she understands. . . .

Next day, on the Campus, Commencement Exercises are being held. On the platform are seated those receiving honorary degrees, among them John Andrews. As the President of the University finishes his fulsome encomium — "financier, economist, pioneer in the advancement of industrial methods and techniques . . . patron of the arts, philanthropist and gentleman" — Owens, running from the rear of the audience to the front, cries: "As a member of the faculty of this University, I protest the giving of a degree to John Andrews!" The President stops speaking, and in the resulting confusion, we hear voices of the strikers in the audience: —

Down with imperialist war!
Down with the war makers!
No more profits from war!

The confusion grows, as the alumni yell: "Get the police! Throw 'em out! Throw 'em out!" Now Miller, the strike leader, leaps to the platform and cries to the audience: —

John Andrews is manufacturing ammunitions for war. He made money on munitions during the last war. Now he wants another war! The workers of this town say: Down with war!

And Owens, still in front, adds:

They say, "Stop the manufacture of munitions!" That's why they're striking. Help them! Help their strike. Help their fight against war!

This is too much for the alumni. They seize Owens and a fight ensues between them and the strikers. Amid shouts of "Give it to the dirty Reds," the police rush in. A shot is heard and one of Owens' drunken visitors of the previous night falls. At this another of them shouts: "Get that son of a bitch, Owens!" The police seize Owens and drag him off, as the second-act curtain falls.

The last act takes place ten months later. It is the night on which Peter Owens, convicted of the crime of murder, is to be executed, and we see him in his cell in the penitentiary. In another cell is the strike leader, Miller. Owens is being sent to his death, not for the crime of a murder which he never committed, but for his opinions, to which he dared give expression on the side of the workers and against war. He and Miller discuss the new war that by this time has begun in Europe, and Owens longs for a radio that he may hear the speech the President is at that moment making to Congress on the subject of America's entry into this war. For the inevitable war-provoking incident has already occurred — a United States destroyer sent "to protect American lives and property" has been blown up. The American Ambassador has called it "a shocking and inhuman butchery of innocent lives." The Government is asking for "an apology and indemnities.". . .

All this we learn in the last act, through the use of the technique of expressionism. We watch Owens live over again in his imagination all the experiences of the past ten months. We hear parts of his trial, the policeman's perjured testimony, the District Attorney distorting his opinions so as to prejudice the minds of the jury, the futile attempts of his wife and of sympathetic organizations to effect his release. Meanwhile we watch the steadily increasing momentum of pro-war propaganda; the placing of the "rescuing" destroyer directly in the War Zone; the financiers, the ministers, the blues-singers, the children, all joining the war-mad chorus. . . . The horror of this phantasmagoria is heightened by the interruption of the prison guard, who at intervals announces the passage of time toward the death hour. Owens' final vision is the trial again. The judge asks him if he has anything to say before sentence is passed upon him. And we hear him reply: —

Yes. I'm innocent. I've committed no crime. I was tried for the murder of William Morris and convicted for something else. You have no right to sentence me for murder, because I haven't been found guilty of murder. But if my crime wasn't murder, if my crime was opposition to war, if my crime was association with workers fighting against war, then I am guilty. You can sentence me for those crimes, you can hang me—but you can't stop that fight. For those crimes I'm willing to be sentenced. For those crimes I'm willing to die. . . .

Now we see the cells again, for the hour has come. The guards approach; we hear the chant of the workers' demonstration without, growing ever louder:

Fight with us, Fight against War,
Fight with us, Fight against War!

And to the sound of these words, Peter Owens, erect and unafraid, walks out of his cell to his execution, a victim of the great battle for Peace on Earth.

Peace on Earth was the first production of the Theatre Union. The response of audiences to the different elements and incidents of the play was fresh proof of what theatre can mean when it is an illuminating projection of matter vital to men's lives. A vigorous portrayal of the American scene and the American temper, in relation to the most important of world problems, *Peace on Earth* stands as another milestone in the history of American drama.

How far this final play has taken us, we can judge by a glance backward to *What Price Glory?* Extraordinarily varied in approach and treatment, this group of plays against war must arouse the admiration of every lover of vital drama.

Chapter 8 Contemporary Drama of a New Social Order: Plays of Soviet Russia

In the Introductory Chapter of this book I stated that it is the theatre of Soviet Russia which today most nearly realizes the highest function of the theatre, because its plays, with all their shortcomings, most completely integrate its audiences with the age in which they live. In the study of such drama which we have made up to this point, we have observed that its essence, from Ibsen to Odets, is its purposeful carrying on to new outposts the ways of life by which men hope to reach their goal of freedom. Therefore it is legitimate for us to wonder to what new horizons drama is pointing in the one country that has advanced to a new social order. The evils denounced by left playwrights would seem to have been abolished there. Capitalism is no more. No man can exploit the labor of another for his private profit. The vast, rich land of Russia, with all its resources and the machinery necessary to develop those resources, is the collective property of the Russian people. All matters vital to their existence as social beings are now controlled for the benefit of all by their government. Manifestly this social revolution brought to its government problems of the greatest complexity.

What import, then, could the theatre possibly have in such a situation as this? In a country requiring the dedication of all to the re-organization of the nation's economic and social life, how could the theatre be integrated with this life, with the problems that were of crucial importance to the Russian people?

At this point the leaders of this new type of government showed their understanding of the value of the theatre in its dynamic relation to life. Even before the Revolution, the Russian love of the theatre and its arts, and the high state of perfection that the theatre, the opera, the ballet, had attained there, were recognized throughout the world. What was not generally recognized, however, was the fact that only the privileged classes benefited from this rich development of the theatre arts. For the "lower" classes, not to mention the completely submerged masses, the theatre simply did not exist.

No account of the change wrought by the Russian Revolution, in the relation of the people to the theatre, could describe this as effectively as does the story of the famous Moscow Art Theatre. Buffeted by the breakers of revolution, it carried on, with unbroken continuity, a theatre so wedded to reality that it became as perfectly integrated with the new Russia as it had been with the old. And it achieved this under the guidance of the great Stanislavsky. Actor, director, teacher and founder of the Moscow Art Theatre, in 1898, Constantin Stanislavsky there developed his famous method of "psychological realism," which, not only as a method of art, but also as a philosophy, influenced the theatre of the entire world. Universally beloved, honored by the Soviet Government, Stanislavsky died at the age of seventy-five in August, 1938. He himself tells us, in his *My Life in Art,* of the transformation wrought in the theatre by the Revolution:—

The doors of our Theatre [now] opened exclusively for the poor people and closed for a time to the intelligentsia. Our performances were free to all who received their tickets from factories and institutions where we sent them, and we met face to face, right after the issuance of the decree, with spectators altogether new to us, many of whom, perhaps the majority, knew nothing not only of our Theatre but of any theatre. But yesterday our Theatre had been filled by the old public which we had educated through many decades, and today we were faced by an altogether new audience which we did not know how to approach. Neither did the audience know how to approach us and how to live with us in the theatre. We were forced to begin at the very beginning, to teach this new spectator how to sit quietly, how not to talk, how to come into the theatre at the proper time, not to smoke, not to eat nuts in public, not to bring food into the theatre and eat it there, to dress in his best so as to fit more into the atmosphere of beauty that was worshipped in the theatre. At first this was very hard to do, and two or three times after the end of an act the atmosphere of which was spoiled by the crowd of still uneducated spectators, I was forced to come before the curtain with a plea in the name of the actors who were placed in an impasse.

On one occasion I could not restrain myself, and spoke more sharply than I should have spoken. The crowd was silent and listened to me very attentively. Until the present day I cannot imagine how these two or three audiences managed to tell of what had happened to all the other visitors in our Theatre. Nothing was written about it in the papers, no new decrees were issued on the score of what had happened. Why did a complete change in the behavior of the audience take place after what had happened? They came to the theatre fifteen minutes before the curtain, they stopped smoking and cracking nuts, they brought no food with them, and when I, unoccupied in the performance, passed through the corridors of the Theatre which were filled with our new spectators, boys would rush to all the corners of the foyers, warning those present:

"He is coming."

During the war and the revolution a tremendous quantity of people passed through the doors of our Theatre—people of all descriptions, from all the provinces and of all the nationalities that compose Russia. If the Western Front gave before the enemy, Moscow would be filled with newcomers who sought to find respite in the theatre. The new audience brought its own habits, its good and bad qualities; we were forced to educate them up to the discipline of our Theatre, and we had hardly done so, when the tragic fate of

Russia dealt it a new and cruel blow, and a new stream of exiles would pour into Moscow from the north, or from the east, or from the south. They all came in through the doors of our Theatre and passed out through them perhaps forever. With the coming of the Revolution many classes of society passed through our Theatre—there was the period of soldiers, of deputies from all the ends of Russia, of children and young people, and last, of workingmen and peasants. They were spectators in the best sense of the word; they came into our Theatre not through accident but with trembling and the expectation of something important, something they had never experienced before. . . .

Thus the Moscow Art Theatre entered a new phase of its career, to find that playing to soldiers and workingmen and peasants meant playing to "spectators in the best sense of the word," who came "with the expectation of something important."

Something important! Yes, this was exactly what the Soviet Government, which of course directs the nation's collectively owned theatres, knew it must give to these millions of eager but ignorant people. It was important for these people to learn how to play their part in developing this country that had suddenly become their own, by realizing that they must develop themselves, must comprehend the purposes of their government and identify themselves with it as their instrument for bringing to fruition the ideals of their new Socialist fatherland. In other words, the State recognized in the theatre one of its most powerful agencies of education and propaganda. There, in the theatre, the people could be made to visualize the whole gamut of their new life, from the historic events of the revolution to the agricultural and industrial enterprises in which the country was now engaged. And there, too, they could learn the fundamentals of the Socialist principles that animated their government.

But it was not until the first decade after the Revolution that the new Soviet playwrights could get down to the business of writing what we may regard not only as typical Soviet plays, but also as plays sufficiently interesting in theme and treatment to offer material for the student of the drama as well as for production outside of Russia. Before we proceed to a consideration of some of these plays, it is essential to know the Soviet point of view on the relation of drama to the life of the people for whom it is being written. In the summer of 1930 there was held in Moscow, for the first time, the precursor of what two years later was to become the annual Soviet Theatre Festival. Then, however, it was given the title of the First Theatre Olympiad — and indeed one of the features of this meet, participated in by troupes from about thirty of the many nations comprising the Soviet Union, most of them speaking in a language unintelligible to the others, was a competition for prizes in the various branches of the theatre arts. But the real purpose of this first Soviet theatre congress was to give to these wholly divergent national entities, both a sense of their fundamental union, and a sense of the unity of purpose which their theatres, each expressing itself according to its own national genius, must serve. I quote from addresses made by Soviet theatre officials at this congress: —

Why is it important to speak of art today? The only significant thing in Russia today is the five-year plan involving collectivization of farms, communization of industry, and liquidation of ignorance. Art is important at present only as it serves some aspect of this plan.

The theatre is not serving industry as well as it should and the object of this meeting is to discover the cause and to suggest a remedy.

Of the several arts which make up the theatre — the arts of the dramatist, director, actor, designer, and spectator — the most important is the art of the dramatist; and in this art of dramaturgy we have at present several illnesses.

First of all, our dramatists have not succeeded in mastering the new tempo. The pace of our life today is more rapid than the pace of our plays. Our dramatists must seek to overcome this discrepancy, for drama must beat with the pulse of life. . . .

Is it not true, furthermore, that our dramatists remain too much on the outside of life as well as on the outside of the theatre? Too many are content to write as spectators of life when they should be participants. That is why they listen too much to the voice of the cities. Let them bury themselves for a space in some farm commune that they may be able to write understandingly of the land. Let them pause to hear the voice of the peasant. Silent for centuries, that voice now lifts itself throughout the steppes of Russia. To that voice we must listen.

Some dramatists, I fear, are still troubled by bourgeois conceptions of making money or of being popular. These considerations, I need scarcely say, are of the dead past. The dramatist is no longer an individual artist in the old sense. He is a worker, a builder of the foundations of a new art and of a new social organization — indeed, of a new order of mankind.

And again: —

The year 1930 has been characterized in Russia by a rate of socialist construction so gigantic that it is understandable that there should be a discrepancy between the titanic unfamiliar themes to be handled in art and the actual embodiment of these themes on the stage. Nevertheless, the theatre must accept no excuses for its shortcomings. Like every other organization in Russia it must be self-critical.

To lay hold of the philosophy of materialism is the central problem of the dramatist of today. To do this he must comprehend the ideology, now in process of being created, of the worker and the peasant. In the mind of the worker the dramatist will find material hitherto unexpressed on the stage except in terms of misery or rebellion. It is the function of the modern Soviet dramatist to show the thought-action of the worker as the moving force of life; at the same time it is his function to point out to the worker the problems with which he is faced.

The dramatist, like the worker, must study every fact from the point of view of its value, not to himself, or to abstract art, or to some mythical god, but to the collective. To regard every fact from the point of view of the mass — this alters politics, history, human relations, and — as a corollary — art.

Further than this it does not seem possible for the integration of art and life to go. But if art is to function, not for art's sake, but for life's sake, then it must have its roots in whatever is most vital either to the race as a whole, or to a particular social group. And since, under the Soviet regime, art is one of the social functions of government, it must obviously serve the great purposes of social reconstruction for which that government was founded. This theory animates the writing of Soviet drama, and it is only in its light that we can understand the new plays of Soviet Russia. I have endeavored, in selecting the plays to be considered here, to chose such as are entitled to recognition on their merits as drama, and are at the same time representative of the multifarious aspects of Soviet life. And I have also, for the sake of the interested reader, purposely included plays of which English translations are available.

After it had become firmly established in the minds of the Russian people that this new country was on its way to materialize its revolutionary ideals, the first plays to emerge were plays recreating aspects of the revolutionary experiences through which they had just lived.

One of the most famous is *Armored Train No. 14-69* by Vsevolod Ivanov, a dramatization of his novel dealing with the struggle in Siberia between the revolutionary peasants and the White Guards. Produced by the Moscow Art Theatre in 1926, its success was sensational and, as usual in the Soviet Union, other productions followed throughout the country. In America the play was produced at the Pasadena Community Playhouse.

The scene is laid near a Siberian town where the peasants are defending their farms and the lives of their families against the Whites. The leader of the Revolutionary forces, Peklevanov, knows there is a price on his head. He has been trying to enlist the active support of Vershinin, an older, influential peasant, of strong character, who refuses "to get mixed up" in the country's "troubles." But the burning by the Whites of his farm buildings and the slaughter of his two little sons, during his absence, supplies the impetus needed to bring him into the revolutionary camp. He becomes an aggressive leader, organizing the peasants for the job immediately confronting the Revolutionists, which is to prevent the Whites from getting their armored train, loaded with arms and men, into the town.

When Vershinin learns that the plan to blow up the railroad bridge has failed, he is beside himself. His cry: "Then we must block the tracks with our own bodies!" gives an idea of the temper of the time. Going about among the Russian peasants, selling sunflower seeds, is a Chinese comrade, Sing Wu, unassuming and devoted. He is with Vershinin and his men when they rush to the railway embankment, determined somehow to stop and capture the armored train. They, as well as the audience, can already hear the whistle in the distance. Reminded that under the old railway regulations, every train must come to a stop if there is an impeding body on the tracks, Vershinin asks for volunteers to perform this heroic deed for the Cause. And when the peasants murmur "It's suicide," and one says bluntly: "Lie down yourself," Vershinin is quite ready to do so. But the others will not hear of the sacrifice of so valuable a leader and while they argue, the tension is increased by the rumble of the approaching train. After agreeing to sacrifice himself, one peasant, mad with terror, finds that he cannot go through with it. Then Sing Wu quietly clambers up to the tracks. What, after all, can he do better with his body than to give it now, when the Revolution needs it? The student Mitia says to him gently: "Lie down, brother. Lie down, dear brother." Sing Wu places himself on the track, the headlight of the onrushing locomotive sweeps across the stage, while the curtain quickly falls. . . . Battle for the armored train follows, at the end of which, while the peasants sing, the victorious revolutionists drive the train into the town.

But Vershinin's joy at bringing the news to their leader turns to grief when he is confronted with the body of Peklevanov, that day assassinated by a Japanese spy posing as a flower-vendor. While the rest rush off to see the armored train, Vershinin pauses in grief beside his dead comrade. Then he orders the armored train to move on to the general uprising for which Peklevanov had been about to give the signal. And as his wife sobs over the body, covered by an improvised red flag, the sound of the train, symbol of the victorious Revolution, is heard moving as the final curtain falls.

It is not difficult to understand how this simple tale, stirring a thousand memories of suffering and hardship, should have gone straight to the hearts of the audience, — an inspiration to the new generation whose fighting lay on other fronts. Even the inept English translation cannot dim its vivid picture of the time, its humor, its excitement, its "feel" of great things happening. If there can be such things as Soviet classics, *Armored Train No. 14–69* would take first place in that category.

Another famous play dealing with this period of civil war, but on a quite different plane, is the fascinating *Days of the Turbins* by Michael Bulgakov. Produced by the Moscow Art Theatre in 1926, its appearance created such a storm of protest that it was withdrawn early in 1928 and banned from the stage for a period of four years. The reason for this was that while the dramatist undoubtedly did depict the end of a class hostile to the new Government — the notorious Czarist military caste which had made up the White Guards — he did not portray the Turbins and their officer friends as monsters, but as very human creatures cornered in a new world that was utterly alien to them. When Chekhov painted the useless and idle landowning class, in just the same way, exposing them as doomed human creatures to be pitied and not hated, he was judged "revolutionary." But, since Chekhov's day, the Czarist White Guards had proved the people's bitterest enemies and those who survived in the new social order were suspect. Therefore the play was condemned as dangerous to the new order. But as each year brought the Government greater security, the fear aroused by the Bulgakov play diminished and it became one of the most admired of the new Soviet plays.

An intelligent performance of *Days of the Turbins* by the Yale University Dramatic Association in 1934, while it did not succeed in creating the Russian atmosphere so essential for this play, gave an excellent idea of its values and afforded its American audience an opportunity to judge for itself the quality of an outstanding Soviet drama.

The "Days of the Turbins" are those of the winter of 1918 in Kiev, the capital of the Ukraine. Fighting was still going on between the Ukrainians and the Bolsheviks, and the situation was further complicated by a division among the Ukrainians themselves. For Germany was protecting the Ukraine against Bolshevism with its own troops, headed by a native general to whom had been given the old title of Hetman. The only native troops permitted him, however, were a few White Guard regiments, made up of former Czarist officers and cadets. To these belonged the Turbin brothers and their officer friends.

The peasants at that time were both against the Bolsheviks and against the German-controlled Hetman, of whose patriotic integrity they were suspicious. A widespread popular uprising followed under the leadership of Petliura, whom the Hetman's White Guards had to defeat first, in order to establish a united Ukrainian front against the Bolsheviks. This is the situation in Bulgakov's play, which presents not the usual pattern of Whites fighting Reds, but one of Whites fighting other Whites, while the shadow of the advancing Reds looms over all.

The important element of *Days of the Turbins* lies not in its historic matter, however, but in its colorful portrayal of what life had been like in this officer class, at the time of the play still ready to die for the old regime. In their tasteful living room we meet the Turbin family: Alexei, about thirty, a Colonel of Artillery, earnest and high-minded; his brother Nikolka, eighteen, a gay military cadet; and Elena, their handsome sister, married to Talberg, a careerist Colonel of the General Staff. Here too we meet Alexei's three fellow-officers, daily visitors at the Turbin home, one of whom, the handsome Shervinsky, a talented singer determined to achieve an operatic career, revolution or no revolution, is in love with Elena. When the play opens Nikolka, strumming a guitar, is singing a ribald anti-Petliura popular song which soon gives way to a White Guard drinking song:—

> Brimless hats askew
> Boots all shiny new
> We Cadets are marching and here's our
> White Guard line.

So we watch them during an evening singing, drinking, eating, jesting, going off to take baths, warmly welcoming a young country cousin who unexpectedly arrives to live with them, while studying at the University in Kiev, damning the peasants, damning the Hetman and his guzzling Germans who are taking things easy, wondering when Petliura or the Bolsheviks will descend upon them. Much delayed, Talberg finally arrives and tells Elena in private that the town is surrounded by Petliura troops, that the German staff is planning to leave secretly for Berlin at once and that there is just one place for him. Elena begins to understand what manner of man her husband is, and even the brothers, to whom she imparts nothing save that Talberg is off to Berlin on a "mission," remark shrewdly: "He resembles a rat . . . and our house resembles a ship." . . . Then the gaiety continues just as if the old life were flowing on uninterrupted and there were no such thing as Revolution stalking outside. Shervinsky plays the piano and makes loves to Elena, they sit down to dinner and they drink, until all, including Elena, are merrily tipsy. Then Nikolka gets his guitar and they all sing, first gypsy songs, later a Czarist military march with the line: —

> We have conquered and the enemy has fled, has
> fled, has fled —

at which the drunken country cousin blurts out the forbidden toast: "To the Czar!" Alarmed, they drown out these dangerous words with louder Tra-la-las. Mishlayevsky, another officer, draws his revolver and drunkenly shouts that he is going out to shoot commissars. They take his revolver away from him. Then Shervinsky tells the current legend that the Czar is still alive and ready to lead them back to Moscow. To the horror of Alexei and Elena, the rest begin to sing the Czarist national hymn, "God Save the Czar." But soon they are beyond singing. Mishlayevsky has to be carried out. And after Elena lets Shervinsky make love to her, a clock strikes. It is three o'clock in the morning. . . . No treatise could give a more complete picture of a social class whose life the Russian Revolution was extinguishing than this brilliant act of Bulgakov's play.

After a scene showing the desertion of the Hetman with the

German generals, and another showing one of the disreputable ruffian bands that swelled the number of Petliura's followers, we come to the scene in which Alexei, bitterly realizing the hopelessness of the White cause, refuses to sacrifice his few troops and declares the campaign against Petliura ended. His words, as the audience knows, mark the end of the White cause everywhere in Russia:—

. . . Listen, my friends! To me, as a fighting officer, has been entrusted the task of throwing you into battle. If only there were something to fight for . . . but there isn't. I declare before the world that I will neither lead you nor let you be led . . . I tell you that the White cause in the Ukraine has collapsed. It has fallen to pieces. Dead . . . buried!

So he sends them home from the headquarters as Petliura's machine guns are heard outside. Nikolka refuses to leave his brother, there is a clatter of cavalry, a shot bursts through the window and Alexei falls, but Nikolka evades Petliura's drunken band and escapes.

The last act, two months later, is again in the Turbin home. It is Christmas Eve, a tree is being decorated, and in spite of their grief for the death of Alexei, there is gaiety. Even though the Reds, victorious over Petliura, are expected in Kiev within half an hour, the White Guard Christmas celebration must go on. Elena promises to divorce her husband and marry Shervinsky—so there is another reason for celebration. Only Captain Mishlayevsky has a new point of view. He is a realist and he understands, however dimly, that there is no use fighting against the Bolsheviks because, as he puts it, "the day of the simple people has come." And when the irreconcilable Captain Studzinsky says sadly: "Once there was Russia, a great Empire," Mishlayevsky replies:—

And it will be again, it will be . . . Not the kind there was in the past, but a new kind. Tell me this. When you will be beaten on the

Don — and beaten you will be, I prophesy — and when your Denikin will sneak off abroad — and that I prophesy also — where will you go then?

And to Studzinsky's terse: "Abroad also," Mishlayevsky retorts: "I'll remain here in Russia. Come what may . . ."

As they sing the same songs we heard in the first act, the cannon-shots of approaching Bolsheviki are heard. And the play ends thus: —

(*All except Studzinsky rush to the window; the sound of the "Internationale" draws ever nearer.*)

NIKOLKA: Gentlemen, do you know this evening is a great prologue to a great historical play?

STUDZINSKY (*glumly*): For some a prologue — for me, an epilogue.

For some a prologue — for others an epilogue. These words of the playwright Bulgakov have become a classic phrase in Soviet Russia. *Days of the Turbins,* one of the least patterned and most literary of the Soviet plays, is entitled to be regarded as dramatic literature. In that theatre-of-the-armchair, its perusal will prove an interesting experience.

Let no one conclude, however, that because plays dealing with the revolutionary struggle appeared earliest, that the interest of Russian audiences in this theme has abated. Quite the contrary.

In the first place, the early plays are kept in the theatres' repertories — in Soviet Russia, every theatre is a repertory theatre — so that they may keep green the picture of those heroic days for new groups of theatregoers. For example a play written in this same year, 1926, *Lyubov Yarovaya,* by Konstantin Trenev, tells the story of a woman teacher, active in the revolutionary movement, who, believing her husband dead, discovers that he is an *agent provocateur* for the Whites.

A complicated story of the Civil War is woven about Yarovaya's struggle between her love for this husband and her loyalty to the Cause. His capture is regarded by the Reds as of the utmost importance, and when Yarovaya discovers that he is escaping in disguise, in spite of the fact that he is her husband and that she still loves him, she causes his arrest. It is the finale, as always, that underscores the play's propaganda note, for Lyubov Yarovaya's anguish at the fate of her husband and her part in it is mitigated by the realization that it is only now that she herself has really become a loyal Bolshevik. This play I saw in Moscow in the fall of 1937, playing before a packed house, eleven years after its first showing.

In the second place, new plays on the revolutionary period are constantly being written. One of the most exciting and popular of these is *Intervention* by Leo Slavin, produced in 1933. The scene is Odessa, the time early in 1919, when the city was occupied by the allied interventionary armies. This was a critical period for the harassed Soviet power and the play gives vivid pictures of speculators, gangsters, White Guard officers and other friends of the interventionists. Also we watch Bolshevik workers, procuring and hiding arms, trying to enlist the interest of the foreign soldiers in the revolutionary cause and cautiously spreading plans for an armed uprising against the invaders. After every phase of the complex situation has been cleverly exploited by the playwright, the day arrives for the Allies to evacuate Odessa. Russian émigrés, too, hurry aboard the ship. And we have a typical Soviet finale. One of the most interesting characters in the play is Célestin, a French soldier. Hitherto indifferent and foot-loose, he becomes more and more impressed with the ideals of this country he has been sent to "save." So, when the troops are embarking, Célestin announces that he and another French soldier have decided to remain. He exhorts the returning soldiers to tell about the failure of intervention in Odessa and how the workers and soldiers there put human brotherhood above all difference in language, race and creed. Just as the steamer pulls off, a huge Cingalese soldier, also won by the Bolsheviks, leaps to the wharf and joins the other two. The scene changes to the historic Potemkin Steps, up which we see these three musketeers of the Revolution marching to their new life.

Thus the plays of the type I have just discussed are, to the people of Soviet Russia, not only symbols of past achievements, but also a constant stimulus to the vast accomplishment they know is still ahead.

Among the many important post-revolutionary tasks was that of making clear to the people the difference between revolutionary internationalism and capitalist imperialism. No better material could be found to interpret this difference than imperialist methods as they were in China. China's economic and political status in relation to the Far Eastern situation as well as its growing revolutionary movement were necessarily of deep concern to the Soviet Union. In 1926, a play was produced in Moscow, with the title of *Roar China.* Its author was Sergei M. Tretyakov, a famous writer, whose knowledge of the Far East had been obtained at first hand. As a professor in the University at Peking he had the opportunity of studying Chinese conditions and of observing the shameless exploitation of China by foreign powers. *Roar China* was produced by Meyerhold, its impression enhanced by popular knowledge that the incident reported by Tretyakov in his play was true in every shocking detail, having occurred while he was in China in 1924.

The action of the play takes place on the wharf of the town of Wan-Hsien, on the Yangtze River and on board the British gunboat and covers a period of twenty-four hours. When the plays opens, it is morning and Tretyakov thus describes the scene:—

Out in the middle of the River Yangtze lies the Imperialist gunboat, Cockchafer.

On the wharf there is the usual harbour chaos of cranes, ropes, overturned boats, packing cases, barrels and stacks of bales . . . Occasionally the head and shoulders of a boatman appear, carrying a huge bale of skins, which he tips over on to the bank, before going down to his boat for more. Coolies are engaged in removing these . . . They are shabby — most of them wear dirty cotton trousers, a handkerchief round their heads, and coarse bast sandals. Some are naked to the waist, others wear sleeveless cotton jackets. While they are working they hang their huge flat hats on their chests, and some wear a ripped sack over their heads and shoulders, like a coalheaver. The older ones still wear their pigtails, though when carrying a load they twine them round their heads, but the younger ones are completely shaven. While they are working, they chant rhythmically to their stride — "hai-ho, hai-he." The Compradore leads the chant every now and again, but otherwise sits and drinks tea, fanning himself all the time. He is wearing a light blue gown and a European straw hat. His hair is parted in the middle and soused with pomade. On the wharf there is a hawker selling tea. He carries a complete kitchen, with stove and kettle and little bowls, hanging from a wooden yoke across his shoulders.

When the scene begins, the work is going slowly, the chanting is monotonous. One by one as they come back empty-handed, the coolies stop and sit down in any scrap of shade they can find. They put on their wide hats, and begin to smoke long straight pipes — too hot and weary to talk.

In the Theatre Guild production this scene was unforgettable. No curtain was used, and before the play actually began a crowd of coolies, boatmen, beggars, hawkers, women, sat about or passed along the wharf, talking, laughing, arguing, gesticulating. The audience, on arriving in the theatre, immediately began to absorb the atmosphere of this teeming life. They also realized that the people on the wharf were not American actors "made up," but actually Chinese men and women. The Theatre Guild demonstrated its flair for creating theatre at its highest level by securing out of New York's Chinatown the Chinese needed for the play. Journalists, a poet, an engineer, a medical student, as well as regular Chinese actors made a living China for this drama. In connection with the casting there occurred a significant incident. Two young Chinese, before consenting to be interviewed, sought information as to the subject matter of the play. "Does this play," they asked, "do honor to our country?" When the story of *Roar China* was told them, they were wholly enthusiastic. . . .

As the eyes of the audience passed beyond the wharf, they beheld water, real water, on which rested sampans with their graceful, rust-colored sails. Later, after the play had begun, these boats moved apart, to reveal the British gunboat, its guns trained on the shore and on the audience. The entire scene was a symbol, pictorial and psychological, of predatory imperialism ready to attack its prey.

The play opens with the arrival on the wharf of a rich merchant to buy skins from the American, Ashlay. But he merely instructs the compradore and departs on hearing Ashlay's approach, as he has no desire for personal contact with him. For to this insolent American, as to the Europeans we shall meet, the Chinese are not human beings like themselves, but inferior creatures to be "kept in their places," used and despised. And here, as in all genuinely social plays, the characters, individualized for the purposes of drama, are only symbols — symbols of the class, the economic viewpoint, the civilization and the social outlook they represent. How this American trader regards the Chinese coolies we learn from his anger at their slowness: "Jesus Christ, what scum. Ten of these yellow dagoes couldn't take on one American."

From a smart, young "kept" journalist, Ashlay learns, to his fury, that he has been overpaying the coolies by giving them ten cents, while the Chinese exporters themselves have cut that amount in half—to ten coppers. Ashlay orders the compradore to inform the coolies that he is paying them the lower rate, but they refuse to accept it. So he throws some coins into the crowd and watches with amused contempt while they fight among themselves for the precious coppers. A boatman, Chee, rushes up to Ashlay, showing his empty hands and demanding his ten cents. A policeman strikes him and gradually the cheated coolies run away, dispersed by the blows of the police.

Now we see signs of activity on board the gunboat. A French merchant, with his wife and daughter, is on deck to meet Ashlay. Business over, the Cabin Boy beckons a boatman to come and take Ashlay ashore. The boatman is Chee, who shouts back something in Chinese which the Boy interprets as a refusal to come because the American does not pay enough. At this unheard-of insult, a young Lieutenant points his revolver at Chee with a peremptory order to come. Terrified, the Boy seizes the officer's hand and is thrust into the river. When no effort is made to save him, Chee hurries over, rescues him, and is compelled to take Ashlay. We see the boat coming back through the water. Presently Chee ceases rowing and asks Ashlay for his ten cents. Ashlay informs him that he'll get what he deserves when they're ashore. Chee rests on his oars and Ashlay, in fury, throws five coppers at him. When Chee throws them back, he advances on Chee and strikes him. And as Chee leans over to ward off a second blow, the boat tilts, Ashlay is thrown overboard, and Chee rows off alone to shore. But the American fails to come up and when some sailors from the gunboat bring him ashore, he is dead. Even without the excitement that now prevails on the wharf, we know that here is an "incident" that supplies the foreign invader with full opportunity to demonstrate his power.

Among those who, from the shore, watch Chee's quarrel

and its consequences, is one man who attracts our attention. He is dressed as a stoker, and unostentatiously mingles among the crowd. We soon gather, from the comments he lets fall, first to one worker and then to another, enlightening their ignorance, rejecting their superstitions, that he is circulating among them for a special purpose. This is a character we meet again and again in Soviet plays: the awakened worker who has espoused the cause of Communism. He is a new version of the *raisonneur* in plays of an earlier age, not only interpreting events in the light of his social philosophy, but also actively propagandizing. In *Roar China* it is the Stoker who tells the coolies there is a country, near by, where workers are not afraid of the "white" man. It is the Stoker who holds the boatmen back when some of them are ready to respond to Ashlay's call for a new boatman. It is the Stoker who compels Chee to run, to hide himself, and "never answer if anyone calls you, not even if it is your own son's voice."

On board the gunboat excitement runs high. Tourists and missionaries begin to arrive for "protection." Rumor has already turned Ashlay's death into "murders" and the French merchant talks of the insult to the "prestige of the Great Powers"—of "Washington," "compensation" and what not. The Daieen, the elderly, dignified Mayor of Wan-Hsien, with his student interpreter, comes on board to express to the Captain his deep regret at the accident. He is amazed to learn what the British Captain demands as "amends" for the "murder": the execution of the "murderer" next morning at nine o'clock, or, if he cannot be found, the execution of two other men of the Boatmen's Union—a refusal to comply to be answered by the general bombardment of the town. And the Captain's first act on hearing the Student's departing words—"This very day the whole civilized world shall know of your monstrous cruelty"—is to issue an order to occupy the telegraph office and the radio station.

Scenes among the boatmen follow. They learn through the Chairman of their Union that two of their number must die unless Chee is found. One of them cries: "Let them kill Chee, he is the guilty one!" The Stoker replies: "He is not guilty" — and proceeds to tell them how the "coolies" of another country drove out the masters, "even the English," and that they are now fighting, not for themselves alone, but for coolies everywhere. From the gunboat across the water comes the sound of dance music. The terrified boatmen beg the Student to tell "them" on the boat that they will ferry them and take no money at all, that they have sons. . . . "Kiss their feet. Implore them for mercy!" "Why — why should we die?" Looking hard at this boatman, the Stoker says to the Student: "You tell them that a coolie will always die for a coolie."

On the gunboat, where the white colony in evening dress has been enjoying a banquet, speeches are in progress on what the "civilized" countries have done for these "pagans," these "vermin-infested savages." The Captain is informed that the Daieen has come once more. Prostrating themselves, the Chinese kneel before the Captain, imploring him not to have the two boatmen executed. So the Captain generously changes his order from beheading to — strangulation. The Cabin Boy has been listening. As soon as the deck is deserted, we see him approach the door of the Captain's cabin, tie a rope to the rail above the door and make a loop at the other end. For an instant the ship's moving searchlight illuminates the boy. Then we hear a groan and in the dim light we see his body hanging in front of the Captain's door — his people's age-old gesture of "revenge" against the oppressor. . . .

Morning. The people of the town are weary from a sleepless night. The women moan as the Chairman of the Union announces that the two boatmen who must die will be chosen by lot. One chopstick has been broken in two — the rest are long.

A very old boatman, who has already volunteered to be one of the doomed, draws the first short stick. But the second boatman is young, the father of a little son, and his anguish is pitiful. Watching him, one of the boatmen turns in rage to the Stoker, to whom the balloting has been entrusted, and asks him "When — when will they come?"

STOKER: Who?

1ST BOATMAN: They over there who drove out their masters.

STOKER: They are here.

1ST BOATMAN: Show me one of them.

STOKER (*pointing to the boatmen*): He is one — and he is another and you are one. We don't need to wait for others. We must fight ourselves, gun in hand. We must raise all the towns together. Do you know Sun Wen? Do you know Canton? Do you know what is written on the chests of the Canton workmen? — "Die for the people."

After the acrid scene of Ashlay's funeral ceremony, in which the Daieen and other prominent Chinese join, the Captain orders the Europeans back to the boat and tells the hangmen they have three minutes left in which to do their job. We watch first the garroting of the old boatman, then that of the young one. But when the journalist tries to get a "scoop" by photographing the gruesome sight, the crowd forms a solid wall between him and their dead comrades. The Captain, determined to know if his show of power was effective, offers the boatmen one dollar to take him to his ship. As one man, they raise their oars for an instant, then lower them sharply to the ground. The Captain draws his revolver, but before a fresh issue can arise, a telegram is handed to him. There is trouble in Shanghai and his gunboat is needed there at once. Covering the crowd with rifles, the sailors, with their Captain, retreat. The Stoker, who has shed his disguise, stands revealed in his uniform of the revolutionary Canton Workers' Militia.

He picks up the crumpled telegram which the Captain has dropped, reads it with the Student, and shouts to the crowd: —

They have got to go. Their guns are wanted down the river. The aliens are collecting all their strength at Shanghai. In Shanghai there is revolution. Look! They're running. (*He snatches a gun from a policeman, jumps on to the wharf edge and shouts after them.*) Run.

THE CROWD: Run! Run!

STOKER (*brandishing the gun*): I swear, by this gun — you shall not come back! Count your hours. Your end is near. China is roaring. Oh, you can see me at last. Shoot! I may fall, but ten will rise in my place. . . .

STUDENT (*shouting*): Roar over the whole earth! Roar China in the ears of all the world! Roar China the story of this crime! Out of our China . . .

THE CROWD: Out! Out! Out!

Curtain.

How prophetic was this Soviet play, in 1926, of the awakened China of today, rising to protect itself, not only against the exploitation of the West, but against the even more shameless imperialism of the East!

The end of the Civil War period brought Soviet Russia face to face with a staggering economic crisis and the need for drastic reconstruction. To meet this emergency Lenin developed his New Economic Policy, the famous NEP. While it lasted, NEP not only afforded an opportunity to amass private wealth, but also caused a temporary wave of disillusionment to spread through the less firmly rooted revolutionary elements. At the same time the people of the country were going through a period of the most violent adjustments in their personal relations, hence in their emotional life. Extreme laws had been passed affecting marriage and divorce, which led to excesses and to the shirking of personal responsibility. Thus in the early twenties the plunge into a new sex orientation, the pressing economic problems, and the presence of the Nepmen, as the private traders under the NEP were called, all contributed to make Soviet life a tempestuous, but also an exhilarating, experience.

One of the early plays to depict the reaction of youth to this difficult time is *Rust,* the work of Vladimir Kirchon and André Uspenski, produced in Moscow in 1926. The Theatre Guild, using the title *Red Rust,* also presented this play, in a much too free adaptation. Humanly and with humor, the playwrights show us a group of young men and girls, as different in aims, tastes and behavior, as a similar group anywhere. But all of them, even the most ill-informed and misguided, know that they must justify their conduct by the standards of Communism.

Crowded into the cramped quarters of a Students' House, struggling against discomfort to prepare themselves for their future tasks, the students discuss everything from the wheat situation and bureaucratic red tape to the unescapable sex problem. A young peasant, to whom the mental effort of learning comes very hard, says to them:—

> Comrades . . . I came here to study and I don't want to be bothered with your sex problems. . . . All your chatter is the result of laziness. . . . Your so-called sex-problem is all your lazy minds can warm to. . . . I am a peasant. In the country we work at the plow, planting and reaping. And when we go home at night we sleep so soundly that we wouldn't care a damn if the rats came along and ate up your sex problem. Work, study, Comrades!

Although it is the sex problem which the English version makes the major theme of the play, yet we see that some of these students are much less disturbed by sex than by the discrepancy between their revolutionary ideal and the inequality they behold around them. The young poet of 1926 drinks vodka to forget "a revolution that has become a matter of kopecks," and one of the most intense of the students is ready to kill himself because there are profiteers again. "The rust has eaten into them," he proclaims tragically, "and it will eat into all of us. This is not my Russia, not the Proletariat for which thousands of our comrades lie dead. . . ." The protest of youth expressed in this play, against the corrosion wrought by the Nepmen, created a profound impression. And it also furnishes one of many examples of Soviet plays outspoken in their criticism of administrative policies and abuses.

In the main story of *Red Rust,* we find the divergent attitudes toward the new sex freedom typified in the characters of Terekhin and of Nina. Terekhin, who has been in the revolutionary movement since boyhood, is a domineering brute. He made a hero of himself during the revolution and is now pushing himself forward politically. The new sex liberty means to him old-fashioned license and promiscuity. After indulging in a passing physical attraction to Nina, he marries her, solely in order to get the advantages of a separate room away from the common sleeping quarters of the other students. Nina, on the other hand, has the highest ideals of love and marriage. In the conflict between them, each has supporters among the students. Lisa, for example, who sleeps with a different student every night, including Terekhin, dubs Nina "hopelessly middle-class" and no true Communist, while Fedor, in every way Terekhin's antithesis, and deeply in love with Nina, agrees with her that "true Communists" see in sex freedom the way to a higher love-relation, and not a "reversion to the animal." After having bullied Nina into having an abortion, Terekhin is so irked by her unhappiness that he treats her, publicly as well as privately, with the utmost cruelty. When, at the close of a scene between them, during a students' party, Nina runs out of the room, Terekhin follows her. A shot is heard and students rush in crying that Nina has killed herself.

We now come to the most interesting part of the play: the action taken by the students' "cell" to consider a complaint made by some of its members against Terekhin as the cause of Nina's suicide. At their meeting the conflicting points of view are presented: —

"We shall not allow one of our comrades to be tortured into committing suicide!"

"No real Communist has a right to kill himself."

"She clung to him like a fluttering bourgeois!"

"We stood by and watched a valuable Communist life destroyed by a bully."

While Terekhin insists that the cell has no right to judge his private life, Fedor solemnly asks that the cell vote for his expulsion from the Party: —

Among us are certain individuals who are more dangerous than our millions of enemies outside the frontiers of Russia . . . Because we respect the memory of their physical deeds during the revolution, we allow them to express theories which are like abscesses in a healthy body, and some debauched members of the Party accept these theories with delighted enthusiasm, because it enables them to indulge their lazy libertinism, and from *these* Communists the entire world judges us. . . . Terekhin's unworthiness is only the first, and I propose that he be expelled from the party. And in addition, that in his records be written that he is a disgrace and a pollution to the Communist Cause.

To which another male student retorts:

Now listen to me, Comrades, you are none of you going the right way. If we continue, we shall soon have another revolution. We are not at a district political meeting now. I don't see any kid-gloved ladies present. What's it all about? A comrade has killed herself. What makes you think that Terekhin was to blame? She killed herself, therefore she was a bad Communist. Why should a good Communist, who was at the front during all the glorious years, be blamed for her death? They quarrelled. And you? Is there no one else here who quarrels with his woman? If a man of the party is to be expelled every time some kid kills herself—then the devil help us! We shall soon have no party to expel him from!

The scene is a long and animated one, and it is not difficult to understand that for Soviet audiences this was not theatre, but a page out of their own lives. . . . Finally the students' cell votes for expulsion. Within the hour, however, the Party Commission of Control reviews the case and we hear the opinions of older Party members. The majority decide that expulsion is too severe, that a warning and a severe reprimand are sufficient and the decision of the cell is annulled.

But the students refuse to let the matter end there, especially those who suspect that it was not Nina who fired the fatal shot. Terekhin is trapped by a girl student who has purposely gone to live with him, into believing that in his sleep he has repeatedly confessed to the murder of Nina. Beside himself, he does confess, imploring her not to expose him, telling her that he and she have great things to do together for the Cause. The girl calls "Fedor!" and he and other students, who have been planted where they could hear, rush in, seize Terekhin and drag him off as the curtain falls. . . .

A quite different type of play, reflecting in a humorous vein, the confusion of youth during this NEP period, is *Squaring the Circle* by Valentin Katajev, one of the best known of the new Russian playwrights. Produced by the Moscow Art Theatre in 1928, it became one of the most popular plays in the Soviet Union, running for years in professional and nonprofessional theatres throughout the country. Other countries, including the United States, have also seen it. The purpose of the play was to burlesque the misconception on the part of earnest Soviet youth that love could be regulated according to social theories. Realize the fact that these boys and girls had to solve the problems of their love-life under the most trying of housing conditions, and you have the setting for Katajev's "jest in three acts," as he himself calls his play. Let us follow his own description of the physical scene:—

A typical room in an overcrowded, noisy, municipalized tenement in Moscow, barnlike, dusty and neglected. A battered door on the right, rear.

In one corner lies a dilapidated striped spring mattress propped on four bricks, which is a bed at night and a sofa during the day. On it lies a grimy pillow in a mildewed ticking and without a pillow-case. Beside the improvised couch stands a decrepit stool. A pair of old trousers against one wall and a crude home-made radio are the only embellishments of this corner, which is Vasya's.

Abram's corner on the other side of the room contains only a pile of books, papers and booklets, and a few nails in the walls for clothes.

In the foreground on one side is an untidy iron sink. From the middle of the ceiling hangs a lone, unshaded electric bulb, which glares at the room and brings out sharply its chaotic poverty.

Directly under the lamp stands a heavy wooden park bench which must have been dragged here by heroic efforts; initials and a large pierced heart betray its earlier career. On the bench lies a preposterously thick volume of Lenin, useful to bewilder poor Abram's head in daytime and to support it as a pillow at night.

The one window in the room, with a broken window-pane, stuffed with a rag and decorated with the pendent remnant of a thick sausage, is in the foreground, left, facing the audience.

Into this room, Vasya and Abram, having secretly married on the same day, bring their brides, to the consternation of all four. Vasya, a very earnest and simple young worker, has fallen for the charms of Ludmila, *toute femme,* as the French say, who purrs and talks baby-talk. Abram, who is also sincere, but far less serious, has won Tonya, an intensely serious-minded Young Communist worker, sternly dedicated to the Cause and to the rejection of everything that threatens her shibboleth of complete sex equality. All, except the unregenerate Ludmila, are active "Komsomols," members of the League of Communist Youth. How Ludmila has a partition built down the middle of the room, in order to divide it into two separate halves, how she prettifies her and Vasya's half into a good old-fashioned home, while Tonya leaves her half in a mess and reads economic treatises aloud to Abram, must be read to be appreciated. The dialogue is rich with satire of all the ill-digested theory and fantastic living characteristic of those early Soviet years.

But sexual attraction has its own laws, even in a Revolutionary State, and Vasya, bored to despair by Ludmila's baby-talk, realizes that he has fallen genuinely in love with Tonya, while, on the other side of the partition, Abram, in revolt against the Communist discipline maritally imposed upon him, knows that married happiness for him lies in the arms of Ludmila. The two girls respond fervently to the call of love, but complications follow because each married partner does not dare confess to the other, for fear that he or she would succumb from grief. Finally the tangle is straightened out with the aid of an older Communist, who says to them:

> You got married, all of you, as if you had been running away from a fire, without thinking of consequences, and then turn your room into an art theatre, and in the meanwhile you put me to all the trouble of divorcing and marrying you properly. I must remind you, comrades, that I have other business to attend to . . .

The essence of this play, however, lies not in its absurd story, but in the humorous way in which the efforts of Soviet youth to be one hundred per cent. Marxists are satirized. Abram is always in a dither as to whether he is behaving according to Communist "ethics," Tonya is always warning against "bourgeois tricks," and a favorite phrase, influencing a decision on almost anything, is that it "can't hurt the Revolution." Thus has the use of satiric farce for social criticism, that delighted Russian audiences in the pre-revolutionary plays of Gogol, been retained in Soviet plays as an instrument for education.

The new sex orientation brought into the foreground another problem with which Soviet playwrights felt themselves called upon to deal. This problem grew out of the new status of women, whose equality under the law found immediate practical realization because of the urgent need for workers in every field of activity. The competent women soon rose to positions of responsibility, causing jealousy and resentment on the part of those males whose masculine superiority complex not even the Revolution had as yet been able to eliminate. There were also women incapable of shedding the skin of their old sex subservience, as well as those who shed it very slowly, after a process painful not only to themselves, but also to others connected with them. There are many Soviet plays dealing with the various aspects of this problem, some very crude, showing how the fine work of women in the industrial drive — the First Five Year Plan had by now begun — was being impaired by male sabotage in a factory, or on a collective farm, where, in one play, I remember a male character shouting that no "woman agronomist" could tell him what to do.

One of the very best of the Soviet plays dealing with this problem I first read in the German translation used by Piscator, when he produced it at his theatre in the pre-Hitler Berlin that was then the most important theatre centre of the world. There it was given the title *Woman at the Front,* which conveys the essence of the play, as the Russian title, *Inga,* does not. For its author, Anatol Glebov, does not, in the play, make Inga's problem any more important than he does the problems of the other women characters, or, for that matter, those of the men. The play was produced in Moscow in 1929, one year after the inauguration of the First Five Year Plan.

The scene is a large clothing factory of which the handsome, thirty-year-old Inga is the manager. The superior of every man there, placing her work for the Socialist State above all other considerations, she is nevertheless enough of a woman to respond to the passionate love of Dmitri, Chairman of the Factory Committee. Their relation is complicated, however, by the fact that Dmitri has been married for eleven years to Glafira, who loves him deeply, and that he is devoted to his child. We have by this time realized how preposterous is the popular idea of a Soviet play as a dull monstrosity with a tractor for a hero and a locomotive for a heroine. *Inga* is an especially interesting example of the interweaving, in Soviet plays, of incalculable human factors with the social factors that call for an impersonal dedication to the ideal. A delightful moment of the play illustrates this. Resentful of Inga is Ryzhov, the assistant manager, because he has been repeatedly and publicly criticized by her for his incompetence. He loses no opportunity to humiliate her by allusions to her love affair with Dmitri. The following dialogue takes place between Ryzhov and Nemtsevitch, a rather cynical, university-bred engineer: —

RYZHOV: I am not even allowed to drink! But the woman manager and the chairman of the Factory Committee may make love in broad daylight! I suppose you think that's fair?

NEMTSEVITCH: Well, what can you do about it? The implacable laws of physiology. You Marxists do not appreciate Freud. Strictly speaking, if you look at it objectively, is it your Marx that rules the world?

RYZHOV: What do you mean?

NEMTSEVITCH: Freud, friend, Freud! Not *class,* but *sex!*

RYZHOV: You can go to the Devil with your bourgeois deviation! They've put a woman over us — that's why it's Freud!

While, on the one hand, we watch Inga's superb control of her work, speeding up the output, insisting on the importance of the æsthetic in the garments produced, hurrying on the construction of the factory's new buildings, — all of which gives us a picture of Soviet factory management, — on the other hand, we watch the increasing complication of her personal life. Urged by Dmitri, she finally agrees to his leaving Glafira and living with her, although she knows the whole factory is buzzing with the affair. For Glafira makes no secret of her despair at losing Dmitri. She actually attempts suicide, which leads to one of the finest themes in the play, the efforts of Somov, a highly intelligent old party worker, to lead Glafira to a new life by winning her to active interest in the Cause. When she is recovering from the effects of the poison, Somov says with all his heart: —

. . . Strength will come. You won't notice it, but it will come. Have more faith in yourself, Glafirushka. Move everything inside of yourself, rebuild it. We live in such a stirring day. Everything old goes into the meltingpot. They're even accusing *me* now . . . they say that I'm lagging behind. Never mind. Even *I* can still put up a good fight. And you're young! You have only to live and breathe deeply! You *are* silly — shedding tears! Work! Study! Start a new life! What is there to cry about? Before you had only Mitya to love you and defend you, but now the whole world is yours! And the whole collective is for you! . . . Do you think you're all alone? We'll all back you up so that your life will get on the right track. Do you hear? And what's more: I'll take you under my personal wing! . . . I must. I must, Glafirushka! Every life matters now. All of you here are my army. I am responsible to the Party for you, for the whole factory. The fight is raging. Every factory is a trench in the Five-Year Plan. A trench of the new life. If something is wrong in the army, something threatening the life within — *who* is responsible? . . .

So we see Glafira, throwing off her sexual bondage, looking younger, wearing her red kerchief at a rakish angle on her newly-bobbed hair, enjoying the communal life of which she now forms a part. There are still unpleasant scenes between her and Inga, and between both women and Dmitri, when they meet in connection with their factory work. But Glafira has become a human being, a social being, in her place at the front, though she still loves Dmitri and her child is her greatest joy.

The playwright goes on to show how the relation between Inga and Dmitri comes to its inevitable end. For Inga resents his constant intrusion of their personal relation into what she regards as a strictly impersonal relation — their work in the factory. She knows that their discord is undermining her efficiency, her prestige, and is, besides, a bad influence on the workers. Somov — another version of the recurrent *raisonneur* character in Soviet plays — even expresses doubt as to Inga's present value to the factory, and to Dmitri's angry: ". . . But this is a personal matter" — he replies:

There are no personal matters! Everything has a social significance to us. We are constantly watched by the masses. We set the example for them. Thousands of eyes are watching us. What do you mean by personal?

Inga knows that she must choose, and she chooses what to the Soviet "woman at the front" is greater than any personal happiness: service to the Cause. Apparently after all, it is Marx and not Freud who "rules" in the new Russia.

From this same period come two plays illustrating the use of the theatre as a vehicle for special propaganda. While these plays, written by outstanding Soviet playwrights, were enormously popular with Soviet audiences, readers must decide for themselves if they are sufficiently interested in the specific Soviet problems presented to read them. These two plays are *Tempo* by Nikolai Pogodin, produced in Moscow at the famous Vakhtangov Theatre in 1930, and *Bread* by Vladimir Kirchon, produced in the same year at the Moscow Art Theatre. *Tempo* brought home to Soviet audiences the necessity for a superhuman effort of speed, if the tremendous construction projects of the Five Year Plan were to be realized. *Bread* showed the government campaign against the "Kulaks" and other peasants who were hoarding and trafficking in grain, thus keeping bread from the hungry cities.

While the theatre was thus helping to bring Soviet industrial and agrarian undertakings to successful fruition, there were problems on other "fronts," which it was also the theatre's job to handle. It is always necessary to remember that the theatre in the Soviet Union is a function of government and *not* a commercial enterprise conducted by individuals for private profit. Therefore the same play may be—and if important and popular it always is—produced simultaneously in many parts of the country, often in different theatres in the same city, distinguished by varying styles of production. Thousands of Soviet citizens, from Leningrad to Tiflis, are constantly seeing the same play on the same night, and we may judge from this fact how enormous is the influence of a theatre thus integrated with the life of the people. The only approach to this we have ever beheld in the United States were the twenty-three simultaneous productions in American cities by the Federal Theatre in October, 1936, of Sinclair Lewis's anti-Fascist play: *It Can't Happen Here.* But we can readily imagine the educational and propaganda value of simultaneous productions all over this country of the Federal Theatre's brilliant *Living Newspaper.* Imagine how Americans from coast to coast would profit from the instruction provided for them by this form of dramatized journalism. The truths about Power and the Consumer, about Labor and Injunctions, about Slums and Housing, could thus be made clear and alive through the medium of the theatre. That is the Soviet way, and that is why we can follow in its plays the history of the country's struggles and problems.

One of these problems was that created by the "bourgeois intellectual" who was saturated with the philosophy of life held by the pre-revolutionary Russia intelligentsia. Could persons of this type and background become true Communists, not merely external, lip-serving supporters of the new order? Trained specialists in every field were sorely needed, but if inwardly they were antagonistic to their new world or desired its termination, then these intellectuals were not merely valueless, they were actual enemies, who had to be watched and unmasked. The most interesting play of the period to present the story of such an intellectual is *The Man with the Portfolio* by Alexis Faiko, produced in Moscow in 1928.

Granatov is a young scientist, son of a Czarist general, now deceased. After the Revolution his wife fled to Paris with their little son, but Granatov remained in Russia to engage in counter-revolutionary activity. When his secret organization was discovered, a number of his fellow-plotters were executed, but Granatov's connection with the group never came to light. Thoroughly frightened, however, Granatov decides to identify himself actively with the new government. His ability soon brings him to the top and after a few years of prominence in the academic circles of Leningrad, he is appointed to the faculty of the Moscow Institute of Revolutionary Culture and Science. We first meet him in his compartment on the train as he is leaving for Moscow. This opening scene is lively, for a group of young Communists, his admiring students, have come to see him off and to bring him, as a parting gift, a fine leather portfolio. To Granatov this gift seems a symbol of the new life of achievement and fame which will forever obliterate his past.

But the first person he meets on the train is a former member of his counter-revolutionary society. Granatov tries to get rid of him. In the dining car, he learns that the man has in his possession a document which will hopelessly incriminate Granatov. To make matters worse, Granatov sees here also another link with his past, his dead father's valet, who approaches him and asks for money. Beside himself with fear, Granatov refuses and resumes his excited conversation with his former associate who now threatens blackmail. As the desperate Granatov and his companion reach a platform on their way back through the cars, Granatov fells the man and throws him off the speeding train. He does not know that the curious valet has watched the crime from the rear.

Positive that he has now quite buried his past, Granatov soon wins great popularity in Moscow, especially delighting his old professor, Andrasov, now a sincerely convinced Communist. He decides to strengthen his position by marrying Zina, the sister of the Director of the Institute. But hardly has he proposed to Zina when another ghost out of his past appears: his wife with their son. Furious as well as frightened, he tells her that it is dangerous for them to be seen together and, giving her money, informs her that he can have nothing further to do with her.

A new Director of the Institute is to be elected and it is a foregone conclusion that the choice will be Granatov's old teacher, Andrasov. As he enters the cloakroom on the day of the election, Granatov is shocked to find his wife waiting for him. Having been refused admission to his apartment, she has come there to implore him to return to her and to their child. But he refuses and hurries her away. Then there steps out of the shadow the valet, who this time fortifies his request for money by reminding Granatov of what he saw happen on the train platform. Granatov promises the valet to see him at his home and hastens to the election. The happy old professor hears speech after speech commending him in the most glowing terms. But Granatov has determined to leave no shadow of doubt as to his hundred per cent. Communism. When his turn to speak comes he urges the faculty not to place this great scientific institute in the hands of a man who is not above suspicion as an enemy of the new order. To prove this serious charge he reads aloud a poem written by Andrasov a number of years previously, satirizing the future of Russia under Communism. This calumny uttered by his beloved pupil is more than the old professor can endure. As he rises to reply, he clutches his heart and drops to the floor, dead.

Still his colleagues cannot believe that Granatov's conduct was motivated by anything other than excessive devotion to the Communist cause, and some of them even want to prove their faith in him by electing him Director of the Institute. But that past, of which he is still a part, now closes in on him. The sums demanded by the blackmailing valet grow exorbitant. His unhappy wife commits suicide and sends his young son to apprise his father of the tragedy. Meeting the boy on the threshold, Zina decides to slip into another room and wait. There she is witness to a terrible scene. For, driven beyond control by the abomination of his life, Granatov seizes the terrified boy and savagely shakes him, asking the child if he knows what kind of damnable society he is going to have to live in. When Zina emerges and faces him, he knows that the end has come. Nevertheless he goes to the Institute, to deliver a lecture on "The Intelligentsia and the Revolution." Very effective is the last scene of the play. Granatov's lecture platform is the stage and his audience is the theatre audience, in which the members of the faculty are seated. But instead of delivering his lecture, Granatov tells the story of his own life, declaring himself a threefold murderer — of his former associate, of Andrasov, and of his wife. And he ends by saying to his dumbfounded audience: —

> Why did I do all this? Because inwardly I hated the new era and could not free myself from the heritage and traditions of the past. That is why the more I tried to escape the net of the past the more deeply I became entangled in it. This is my confession — the confession of a member of your intelligentsia . . .

Concluding, Granatov quietly leaves the platform and, before the audience can recover, they hear a shot. The Man with the Portfolio has left a world to which he could not adjust.

In this conflict of the intellectual with the demands of a new social order antipodal to all the tenets he has cherished in the past, lies a problem not confined to the boundaries of Soviet Russia alone.

But the Russian intellectuals had to adjust. They had to discover their true relation to the new ideological basis on which their Government functioned, or find themselves not only useless for the great work in which it was engaged, but also condemned as social enemies. The scientists especially had to learn that there was no such thing as a "scientific" detachment from belief or non-belief in Communist theory, that the work of scientific discovery had to be approached from the point of view of its service to the Revolutionary cause. The most widely produced and acclaimed Soviet play to show the scientist — as a symbol of the intellectual — undergoing this transformation of mental adjustment is *Fear,* by Alexander Afinogenyev. One of the interesting features of *Fear* is that it does not confine its criticism to the behavior of anti-Soviet elements, but frankly criticizes some of the stupid methods used by the Government in dealing with them. Clearly, the time had come when the Soviet Government felt itself sufficiently strong to invite that "self-criticism," which had, by now, begun to express itself more and more freely in Soviet plays. Such criticism could never be of the social and economic principles animating the Government, but it could point out what the Russians knew from one of their famous pre-revolutionary plays, that there is "enough stupidity in every wise man" to make him do exceedingly foolish and ill-advised things.

Fear was produced by the Moscow Art Theatre in 1932. The chief character is Professor Borodin, aged sixty, renowned Director of the Institute of Physiological Stimuli in Moscow. He is the typical, pre-revolutionary intellectual. He will have nothing to do with the new "politics" and hates the proletarians — "ignorant upstarts" he calls them — who are put in positions of authority. To him it is unthinkable that Elena, daughter of a metal worker, who, figuratively, drops her aitches and never heard that *Faust* is something to read as well as hear the music of, should be appointed research assistant and be given the preference in his scientific institute over Kastalsky, the cultured son of a former Senator.

But the playwright makes it very clear that if Kastalsky is bitterly anti-Soviet and a potential plotter, it is because his "wrong social origin" makes him suspect and precludes him from ever attaining a position commensurate with his ability. Indeed all the characters are selected so as to stress the various elements involved in an ideational conflict. One of the important departmental heads of the Institute is Professor Bobrov, married to Borodin's young daughter, Valya. He is finding it increasingly difficult to maintain his loyalty both to the Soviet system, in which he thoroughly believes, and to his obstreperous father-in-law and volatile wife. Valya is a sculptress, so befuddled by all the new theories, which she does not understand, that when she tries to create "proletarian" art, the result is, of course, execrable. The ambitious, proletarian Elena is married to Tsekhovoi, a graduate student at the Institute. Tsekhovoi is a neurotic, due to his inner insecurity and the terror of discovery that on his application for Party membership he lied about his "wrong social origin." Knowing that he might as well commit suicide as admit that his grandfather was a Czarist Admiral and his father a Military Prosecutor, he stated that his father was a petty postal clerk and his mother dead. But his mother, a silly woman, turns up and Kastalsky, learning the truth, exposes Tsekhovoi, knowing that the crime of hiding one's social origin is expulsion from the Party. Expelled also from the Institute, Tsekhovoi naturally goes to pieces and is destroyed. His five years of Communist activity, his scientific studies, count for nothing.

Thus the question the playwright dares to ask is: What is more important, a man's ancestry, or what he is now ready and eager to make of himself in his new world? And finally there is Clara Spasova, whose prototype is the German Social-Revolutionary Clara Zetkin, later an active Communist in Russia. The character, made up to look like the famous Zetkin, is that of a splendid old-time Bolshevik of sixty, now a prominent Party leader, wise, reasoned, unfanatical. It is Clara who saves the sculptress Valya from the idiocy of trying to make a factory worker of herself; it is "Auntie Clara" who knows that little Natasha, an ardent, intelligent example of Communist youth, is not conditioned by the fact that her grandfather was a Military Prosecutor, and it is Clara who knows that wrongheaded old Professor Borodin is no menace to the Soviet State but a tremendous asset, and that he must be made to understand the error of his thinking.

How this purpose is accomplished, the play tells. Outraged at everything that is happening under the new Government, Professor Borodin organizes a laboratory for the study of human behavior in Soviet Russia. "We shall test thousands of individuals — strictly scientifically, without any bias," he cries. "The laboratory will prove that our life is going to the dogs — that we are headed straight for the abyss." The Communists in the Institute are eager too for the experiment, for as Elena says: "We shall prove that the old stimuli of envy, jealousy, fear are disappearing and that the stimuli of collectivity and the joy of life are beginning to grow!" But a snag is struck. To Borodin, the "pure" scientist, the investigation of every human type is of value, but to Elena, only such types matter as are of importance to the new Soviet state. Thus she protests:

ELENA: Our Laboratory of Human Behavior is investigating milk-women, expelled bookkeepers, and even paupers. I don't see why we should study the behavior of such social categories.

BORODIN: I study people, not social categories.

ELENA: There are many more people in the factories.

BORODIN: From the point of view of science, a milk-woman is just as interesting as a factory mechanic.

ELENA: For our purposes, the factory mechanic is more interesting.

BORODIN: I don't know anything about your purposes. You young people have a distaste for facts. You're concerned only with bare purpose. And science doesn't like these "bare purposes."

ELENA: It's necessary to know *why* to collect facts. Now we are working with our eyes shut — blindly.

BORODIN: All of us are more or less blind.

ELENA: I don't approve of this method.

BORODIN: In that case, give up your place to Kastalsky. To him, *I* am the method.

KIMBAYEV: And what about self-criticism, Comrade Borodin?

BORODIN: Indulge in your self-criticism as much as you like, but don't touch me . . .

This fundamental difference of approach between the "pure" scientist and the scientist with a social philosophy, who wants scientific data collected for a definite social purpose, takes the form of a battle at the meeting of the faculty to discuss the conflict. The Communists protest against supplying Borodin with data which he alone compiles and interprets. His son-in-law, Professor Bobrov, says unhappily:

. . . I have kept my peace too long . . . It is not easy for me to raise my hand against Professor Borodin . . . But he is committing a grave scientific error. He is intent on explaining the behavior of people by the simplest animal stimuli. This error is the result of his political views. It is against this that I must take my stand.

And Elena continues:—

. . . We protest against Borodin's attitude. You are concerned with the behavior of man in general, irrespective of his class connections. You are interested only in classless eternal stimuli. From that point of view the Revolution may appear to be the result of rage, Socialist competition may be explained by sexual activity, and shock-brigading as the result of hunger. But this is to us a theory utterly foreign and politically harmful.

BORODIN: You cannot possibly know what conclusions will be reached—because I don't know them yet myself . . .

BOBROV: The conclusions have been suggested by Kastalsky. He wants to discredit the present system of governing people.

But the anti-Soviet forces win a temporary victory. Elena, for her lack of faith in Borodin, is demoted and the plotter, Kastalsky, is promoted. But Bobrov carries the issue into the newspapers and the Borodin case is soon a *cause célèbre*. Meanwhile Borodin is determined to give his lecture on the findings of his investigation as scheduled, and once more we see the stage as the platform of a lecture hall with the faculty facing the theatre audience, which Borodin addresses as follows:

I'm coming now to the end of my lecture. You have seen in the case of the rabbits that at the basis of their behavior are the stimuli that rouse them. . . . Analogously, we are able to discover the ruling stimulus of a social environment and thus forecast the path of development of social behavior. The time is coming when this science will take the place of politics. We have decided to bring as much good as we can to our country and to analyze what stimuli lie at the base of the behavior of contemporary man. Together with comrades who are members of the Communist Party . . . we have managed to make a survey—an objective survey—of several hundred individuals of various social strata. . . . Those who are interested may study the material at their leisure. I should like to point out, however, that the common stimulus of the behavior of eighty per cent of all those investigated was—fear.

VOICE IN AUDIENCE: What?

BORODIN: Fear! . . . Eighty per cent of those who have been studied live under the constant fear . . . of losing social security. The milk-woman is afraid that her cow will be confiscated; the peasant is afraid of compulsory collectivization; the Soviet worker is afraid of the endless purgings; the Party worker is afraid that he will be accused of deviations; the scientific worker is afraid that he will be accused of idealism; the technical worker is afraid that he will be accused of sabotage. We live in an epoch of great fear. Fear compels talented intellectuals to renounce their mothers, to fake their social origin, to wangle their way into high positions. Yes, yes. In high places the fear of exposure is not so great. But fear stalks everyone. Man becomes suspicious—shut in—dishonest—

careless — and unprincipled. Fear gives rise to absences from work, to the lateness of trains, to breakdowns in industry, to general poverty and hunger. No one attempts anything without an outcry, without having his name inscribed on a blackboard, without the threat of arrest or exile. The rabbit who has seen a boa constrictor is unable to move from the spot. His muscles petrify. He waits, submissively, until the rings of the boa constrictor squeeze him and crush him. All of us are rabbits . . . In view of this, can we work creatively? Of course not! . . . Destroy fear — destroy everything that occasions fear — and you will see with what a rich creative life our country will blossom forth! With your permission, I shall stop here.

The floor is given to Clara Spasova, who in the dignity of her years and standing speaks movingly: —

CLARA: We live in the epoch of great fear. You and I, Professor, are old enough to know that fear has lived on earth for many hundreds and thousands of years. Ever since the earth has known a world of slavery and oppression, fear has existed as a mighty weapon for the suppression of man by man. . . . The priests threatened us with heavenly punishment for resisting the Tsarist Government; the professors told us from their rostrums that man conditioned to physical labor had no talent for science and for government. They tried to frighten us. But the oppressed are not rabbits, Professor Borodin. They fought in the detachment of Spartacus; they shouted about freedom from the pyres of the Inquisition. They spat in the faces of their executioners. They called to the good fight from the platform of the scaffold. . . . It was thus that fear gave birth to fearlessness! The fearlessness of the oppressed who have nothing to lose, the fearlessness of proletarians — of revolutionists. . . . Today a man is great; tomorrow he is nothing — nobody — if he betrays the trust of the working class which has advanced him to the high place. You, too, are a great man, Professor, and you, too, will be exposed pitilessly, because you are defending—not the Soviet worker, but the bureaucrat; not the Party member, but the fellow who has wormed his way into the Party; not the technical worker, but the sabotager; not the peasant, but the kulak. This fear stalks behind the man—yes, it stalks behind those who deceive us, who wait for the return of the old order. . . . Know then, Professor, be guided by it in the future: we are fearless in the class struggle—and merciless with the class enemy. . . . When we break the resistance of the last oppressor on earth, then our children will look for the explanation of the word "fear" in a dictionary. But until then, temper yourself in the fearlessness of the class struggle! Prepare yourself for the new advances of the enemy, and strike with all the might of which the strong arms of the working class are capable! . . .

Borodin is arrested and hears his frightened colleagues, including the counter-revolutionary, Kastalsky, calumniate him as having attempted to incite the Institute against the State. And all that Borodin can say is: "Monstrous! monstrous!" But the Soviet authorities know too that the charge is monstrous, and in the last scene we see the Professor, aged by his experience, but free. Elena has been appointed the Director of the Institute, but when Borodin hands her the keys to his study, she says warmly: "You'll open it yourself and you will take charge of the new graduate students." At this Borodin shakes his head and says: "I am no longer of any use to science or to you. I have been too seriously mistaken in people and in my conclusions. I cannot step across those mistakes." But when "Auntie Clara" places her hands on his shoulders and says to him with a twinkle: "You can trust me. I am an old woman, but I am sure that you and I can still be useful. It's too soon to throw us away on the ash-heap. Of course, they might retire us on a pension. . . ." Borodin cries:

No, no! Why pension me off? I want to work . . . I will tell how I joyously greeted every manifestation of fear and how I failed to notice fearlessness. . . . I did not understand real life. And life penalizes those who shun it . . . with loneliness. . . . That is a really frightful vengeance! I think I'm weeping, but I'm not ashamed . . . because now I will go to those who masterfully demand the keys to all the studies and I will give them all of my keys. I accept your conditions, my new director. (*Then to Clara*) You and I can still be useful. . . .

Fear shows that the time had come for a change of attitude toward the pre-revolutionary intellectual as well as towards the innocent sufferers from a "wrong social origin." No longer should these elements have to die like the Man with the Portfolio. Once they understand the application of revolutionary principles to their field of work, they become one with the proletariat.

A year or two earlier "self-criticism" in a lighter vein found expression in a satiric farce, *The Bedbug*, by the famous Soviet poet, Vladimir Mayakovski. Produced in 1930 at the Meyerhold Theatre, *The Bedbug* not only satirizes undesirable elements of the time, but presents an imaginary picture of the Soviet Union in the year 1980, when everything will have become completely mechanized and sanitized. The hero of the play is Prissypkin, a proletarian, so impressed with the fact that he is marrying into a "bourgeois" family that he calls himself "Pierre Skripkin." Yet he insists on a "thoroughly red" wedding, and his blunders in the arrangements for it are a burlesque on that attempt at conformance with the new order which does not come from any real knowledge or understanding. To offset this we are shown a group of his young coworkers in a House of Communist Youth, disgusted at Prissypkin's behavior. During the wedding festivities, everybody gets tipsy and under cover of this the playwright allows his characters the widest latitude in spoofing the Revolution, the

Bolsheviks, Party shibboleths, and so on. Jokes and puns fly, the wedding party gets completely drunk, and finally the house is set on fire. The firemen come too late, and nothing is saved except the cellar, which has, however, been flooded into a solid mass of ice.

Fifty years elapse and when the curtain rises, it discloses a meeting hall in the year 1980. This is a large amphitheatre supplied with the most elaborate mechanical equipment, including radios, each with a mechanical arm attached at the side. Some workers enter and while tinkering discuss how funny it must have been in the old days when real people attended meetings. A uniformed person appears and, talking into a microphone, tells of the discovery in Moscow of a man frozen into solid ice. It has been established that he is still alive and that he dates from the year 1930. But in view of the diseased condition of men's bodies and their filthy habits at that time, all Russia must now vote on the question whether or not he is to be brought back to life. At once the mechanical arms begin to go up and you hear from the radios: "Siberia, Yes" . . . "Ukraine, No," until all parts of the Union have been heard from. The ayes have it and reporters are admitted, who, upon being given the news, dash to microphones into which they shout: "Wave length 792, Chicago Herald Tribune — Resurrection!" . . . "Wave length 537, Paris Soir — Resurrection!" . . . It is an amusing picture of a completely mechanized world.

Quite overpowering is the sight of the laboratory in which Prissypkin is now to be thawed back to life. Snow-white from ceiling to floor, with the most fantastic equipment for asepsis, prophylaxis, etc., the professors and attendants, swathed in white protective accoutrements, expose not so much as an inch of human anatomy. As the Soviet citizen of 1930 emerges from the ice-block and the scientists of 1980 contemplate him with intense interest, a small, dark object is seen moving on his collar. It is a bedbug, that long extinct species, which no living scientist of 1980 has ever seen! What a find! What a moment for science! But before anyone can catch the precious specimen, it has disappeared. What a catastrophe! The entire resources of the city must be utilized to find and catch the bedbug. . . .

In the meantime however we are shown the havoc wrought in the perfectly ordered Russian community of 1980 by Prissypkin himself. His pernicious influence is seen, for example, in the corruption of the dogs of the city, whom he has taught to hop about on their hind legs, begging for food. But, far worse, Prissypkin's guitar was thawed out with him, and on it he plays those antisocial rhythms called jazz, which spread among the young like wildfire.

Comes the moment when the bedbug is discovered crawling up the wall of a building. This is the signal for the appearance of the Director of the Zoological Garden with a glass box in his hand, followed by attendants, ladders from the fire-department, photographers with all kinds of apparatus, people with telescopes, and so on. Day and night the creature has been sought and now the equipment and excitement involved in the great bedbug-catching scene are sufficient to trap a gorilla. At last a voice cries: "I have it!" And a moment later the Director steps forward to make a speech to the crowd, bidding them rejoice with him in the name of Science, but requesting them to be patient until "the animal shall have been rested and refreshed."

The remaining scenes depict the hopeless unregenerateness of Prissypkin and the loathing he inspires in the ultra-mechanized Russians of 1980. Finally they decide that since he is, after all, just as much of an extinct animal as his bedbug, the only thing to do is to put him into a cage and exhibit him. In the last scene we see him publicly exhibited in his cage, which bears a sign labeled: "Bourgeoisius vulgaris." The people are prevented from getting close because the creature spits and swears. And when the man of 1930 howls with shame and loneliness, the children are hurriedly marched away, the cage is covered and removed and the place where it stood fumigated.

A farce like *The Bedbug* would delight any audience; no wonder that for Soviet audiences it was a veritable riot. But it was more than that. For its lampooning of much that had been regarded as sacrosanct furnished Soviet citizens with a psychological release that was invaluable.

With the beginning of the Second Five Year Plan in 1933, the tensions under which the country had been living noticeably decreased. Their ideals no longer seemed far away and almost unattainable. In industrial development they were making extraordinary progress — there was no longer any need for plays like *Tempo.* Everywhere food supplies and the comforts of life were increasing — there was no longer any need for plays like *Bread.* A new generation of Soviet-trained scientists and intellectual workers was beginning to carry on — the Men with Portfolios were, for the most part, either extinct or usefully assimilated, like Professor Borodin. Everywhere rose the feeling that there was no such word as impossible in the vocabulary of the new world. This buoyant faith in themselves and in the future, which is the strongest impression one carries away from Soviet Russia, naturally furnishes the dominant note for the plays of recent years. Achievements of the Revolution and the Civil War period are by no means forgotten, but alongside of these run the plays telling, not with urgency, what *must* be done, but with pride, what *is* being done.

No recent Soviet play seems to me to record so inspiringly this sense of accomplishment as Pogodin's *Aristocrats,* produced in Moscow in 1935, in two totally contrasted styles of production, one at the Vakhtangov Theatre, the other at the Realistic Theatre, both of which I attended in the autumn of

1937. The subject of *Aristocrats* is the rehabilitation of criminals by awakening in them a sense of achievement and self-respect derived from performing socially useful work. Proceeding on the Socialist principle that the vast majority of crimes spring from economic causes and that most criminals are victims of social maladjustment, the Soviet Government had been doing experimental work in the "re-education" of criminals with great success. *Aristocrats* tells the story of how the White Sea Canal, linking the White and Baltic Seas, was built by convicts, who, through the experience of creative achievement, were themselves re-created into useful Soviet citizens.

The scene is the White Sea Prison Camp at which a new batch of prisoners has just arrived, men and women. They include every variety of criminal, from murderer, burglar, pickpocket and incendiary, to bourgeois anti-Soviet engineers, convicted of sabotage and counterrevolutionary activities. While waiting to be registered, Sonya, a young woman who has sunk to the lowest depths, and Kostya, known as the Captain, who has lost every shred of human decency, recognize each other with pleasure. They at once agree that the prison camp will never get any work out of them and Kostya practices his skill at thievery by relieving Engineer Sadovsky of his gold cigarette case.

Both the Chief of the project and the Director of the prison camp, Gromov, are beautifully drawn characters whose psychological insight into the human creatures with whom they have to deal, and patience in dealing with them, are their assets in the uphill job of rehabilitation. We see their methods, when Gromov informs the "wrecker," Sadovsky, that he has been appointed chief construction engineer of the camp. Sadovsky only smiles, and Gromov knows that he has an anti-Soviet "sabotager" with him still. The other engineer, Botkin, a former aristocrat and inventor, behaves in exactly the same way and the rest of the engineers follow their lead.

In the meantime the Chief is carefully trying to elicit some response from Sonya, whose wild behavior and vodka drinking are demoralizing the women prisoners. Sullenly Sonya snaps back replies to the Chief's friendly questions; but when he learns that her father was a railroad worker, killed in a disaster, and says to her: "Ah, I see . . . My father was a worker too. Died of consumption. It's all easy enough to understand now . . ." — this real understanding stirs something in Sonya. At her third interview with the Chief, who to her astonishment orders tea "for two," she still refuses to do any work in the camp, but promises that she will not drink any more vodka. And after she has left him, the Chief says aloud: "Well, we haven't done much this evening, comrade, but still it seems as if we've broken the ice."

Tougher still is Kostya, the Captain. Immediately asserting his leadership over his gang of "hoodlums," as he calls them, he keeps them in rebellion with his scorn against "slaving like a hod-carrier for the Soviet Government." For are they not now, as one of the pickpockets puts it, the only "real aristocrats"? Finally Kostya can no longer endure the "clawing at his soul," as he calls the persistent efforts being made to change him, and in an hysterical outburst slashes himself with a knife, shouting: "I'm not going to work . . . I won't work . . . I'll see myself damned first . . . I'll kill everyone of you . . . and myself too . . . I won't work!" But to Sonya, who by this time, to her own amazement, is leading a women's wheelbarrow "brigade," and who, having rushed in to quiet him, tells him he's making a fool of himself, Kostya says in astonishment: —

> Really? . . . I can't understand what they want of me? Why did they think up this canal? Why should they want crooks to work?

And after Sonya and the Doctor have left him, he lies quite still and repeats to himself: "Why should they want crooks to work?"

Elsewhere the engineers are experiencing their own inner conflicts. Botkin, in spite of the fact that he and Sadovsky have made a pact never to succumb to Soviet "re-forging," cannot endure mental inaction. He spends his evenings making a model, working out his own able plans for the building of the canal. But as a creative mind he cannot let them remain sterile, he must see them carried out. "We're letting ourselves be carried into sheer barbarity and sectarian fanaticism!" he cries to Sadovsky. "I'm tired of believing in a future I can't see. I can't live any longer in this vacuum." So Botkin submits his plans, they are accepted, and his part in the work of construction and reconstruction has begun. . . . And it is Kostya who is put in charge of the thieves and worse to be sent with Botkin on the first rock-blasting expedition. For Gromov knows well that the psychological moment for Kostya has come. He summons him to his office and in the presence of the astonished Botkin, the following dialogue takes place: —

GROMOV: So it's you who play cards for girls?

THE CAPTAIN: No familiarity, please. Prisoners are supposed to be treated with courtesy.

GROMOV: I wanted to have an unofficial talk with you.

THE CAPTAIN: Well, you're the big shot here.

GROMOV: I'm about the same age as you. What year were you born?

THE CAPTAIN: 1898.

GROMOV: And I was born in 1899.

THE CAPTAIN: Ain't it funny, the kind of mugs who get to be Red generals?

GROMOV: You gamble for girls, you get locked up . . . and for what? For petty hooliganism. You're a clever chap and yet how you've let yourself slip down in the world. Just look at yourself. A plain tramp—a caricature of a man . . . I'm ashamed of you before this engineer sitting here.

THE CAPTAIN: Then shoot me! Lead me out, stand me up against a wall, and get this over with!

GROMOV: So that's all life is for, you think—just to get a bullet in you? Taking cheap risks—"Let's stake our youth on a flip of the cards," er—that sort of thing? Bah! You talk like a cheap novel: "Nothing left in life, no joy, no honour, no friends, no family . . . nothing but filth, vodka, whores." Rot! You're a strong man full of energy. You have a good mind, talent, organizing ability. How are you any worse than me?

THE CAPTAIN: Cut it out, Chief, and start your quiz.

GROMOV: Sit down. (*The Captain sits down ready for cross-questioning.*) You're appointed commander of the rock-blasting expedition. (*To Botkin.*) Show him why we need this blasting work done.

BOTKIN (*to the Captain*): Look here, please. (*Points to the model.*) Do you know anything about hydraulic engineering? (*Silence.*) You see, these are the sluices. . . .

THE CAPTAIN: Very interesting. I wonder if I could tell a cow from an airplane. . . .

How Kostya takes charge of this strange expedition with zeal and humor; how he teaches the elegant Botkin the "proper approach to people who have never worked before," how he gets the blasting done well ahead of schedule, and, as a reward, his sentence reduced by one year; how Sadovsky can no longer hold out in the face of all this activity and at last steps into a responsible job, makes more than lively reading. And the brisk dialogue brings completely to life the characters, the scene, and the great issues involved, human as well as social.

But before the play is over Kostya gives everybody great concern by his unexpected backsliding. In this connection it is again interesting to note how, as in *Inga,* the personal, emotional factor is shown as inextricably bound up with the impersonal social problem. For poor Kostya has lost his heart to one of the prisoners, a pretty girl assigned to clerical work, who has believed his preposterous yarn that he is a great aviator. When, undeceived, she hurls the epithet of "thief" at him and leaves him for another, the bubble of his inflation is pricked. He steals the office typewriter and, with one of his "hoodlums," makes his escape. And here again we have an interesting bit: the showing up of an important Soviet official as unworthy of his post. For the Educational Director of the Prison Camp, incapable of understanding the agitation of Gromov over Kostya's defection, finally remarks: "He's not worth bothering with any longer. We've got thousands of them." Gromov replies: —

> Thousands. . . . They're just figures for you — zeros, are they? — these human lives the Party's entrusted to us. . . .

But Kostya turns back and appears in Gromov's office, tattered and dripping. And when he asks: ". . . Tell me, am I done for? Am I never to be anything but a criminal — a thief?" — Gromov replies gruffly: "Cut out your whining! This isn't a young ladies' boarding school." . . . But he gives the order that no punishment is to be administered to Kostya.

Typical, once more, of the Soviet play, which ends always on the positive note of progress and achievement, is the final scene of celebration held upon the completion of the canal. Botkin and Sadovsky, decorated by the government, are to be released, speeches are made — a few halting words by Sonya, a fluent and characteristic speech by the irrepressible Kostya, and a final speech by Gromov drawing together all who once were outcasts under the banner of their common Cause. And as Kostya asks them to "listen to the water singing in the locks," the curtain falls.

If the Soviet theatre, however, offered its audiences nothing but the kind of plays we have been considering, it would represent a special theatre, extremely limited in scope. Such is not the case. What makes the Russian theatre the most outstanding in the world today is that, in addition to this integrated drama, it also supplies the other elements necessary for an inclusive and balanced theatrical fare. If we stretch this term "theatre" to include opera, ballet and the dance, add the classics and foreign plays, including Shakespeare, Molière, Schiller, Shaw and O'Neill, children's theatres, "national" theatres such as the Gypsy, the Jewish, the Ukrainian, the Uzbek, and invest this with the most original and even lavish staging to be seen anywhere, we can get a faint idea of the scope and content of the Soviet theatre today.

And while Moscow is the theatre centre of the Soviet Union, theatre thrives everywhere in this vast land from the new, ultra-modern theatre building at Rostov-on-the-Don, with its great concert halls on the top floor, its four floors of spacious lounges and buffets, its plaza approach and high location affording a view for miles across the Steppes, down to the little stages in the Recreation Halls of Collective Farms, proudly exhibited to the visitor as "our theatre." And let no one think that these farmworkers' amateur groups are not ambitious. Shakespeare's *Romeo and Juliet,* Molière's *The Knaveries of Scapin,* and Schiller's *Intrigue and Love* do not frighten these "stage collectives."

Furthermore, in the summer the Russian theatre goes on tour. You may not find a Moscow theatre open in Moscow, but you are likely to find one of its most famous companies performing in Odessa or in Tiflis. While staying in Yalta, the Crimean summer resort on the Black Sea, I saw at an open air theatre in its park, a performance by a visiting Ukrainian company; and a little back from the quay, under a large tent, I watched workers and peasants, many brought from outlying districts in great lorries, howl with delight at a visiting *Zirk*—circus—from Moscow. In Kharkov, I had to choose between a Trade Union group performing a play I expected to see later in Moscow and a visiting provincial theatre doing *Uriel Acosta.* Unhappily I chose the latter. The provincial company's brave struggle with this classic did not conclude until well after midnight. Soviet Russia fairly seethes with theatre, from the village where children give a playlet, fairy tale or propaganda, and the town school whose pupils perform an opera, the music for which was written by their music teacher, all the way to the great theatres of Moscow.

Now let me describe briefly what theatrical fare was available in Moscow early in the autumn of 1937.

Out of the wide array of classics from all countries which Moscow has been providing for its audiences, there were three of which I could avail myself during my stay. The first was a production of Shakespeare's *Much Ado About Nothing* at the Vakhtangov Theatre, beyond compare the wittiest and most original production of a Shakespeare comedy I have ever seen. And it was straight Shakespeare, for happily the early Soviet practice of giving the classics a Marxian slant has been abandoned. I saw this performance well in advance of the Theatre Festival period and, so far as I could judge, there were less than a half-dozen foreigners in a house filled to capacity. To see an audience composed preponderantly of Russian workers ecstatic at a Shakespeare performance was an unforgettable experience to carry back to America. The second classic was the Maly Theatre's production of Ostrovski's *Enough Stupidity in Every Wise Man,* played with that ebullient use of social caricature of which the Russians have always been masters. The third, offered as the *pièce de résistance,* was the Moscow Art Theatre's much-heralded production of a dramatization of Tolstoi's *Anna Karenina.* To me the attempt to transmute the content of a great novel into the special form required by the theatre is rarely, if ever, justified, and the dramatization of *Anna Karenina* proved no exception. But the Moscow Art

Theatre's pictorial and psychological re-creation of a social epoch, of a code of morals and manners that have passed from the world forever, was worked out to the last meticulous detail. And if the play dragged for me, it did not for the Russian audience. A young Russian woman sitting beside me said, out of a full heart, as she wiped her eyes: "Wasn't it terrible to be alive then!"

Next, one could attend the lavish production of Glinka's opera, "Russlan and Ludmila," based on the tale by Pushkin, the centenary of whose death was then being commemorated in Moscow by a superb exhibition depicting his life and work in relation to the social conditions of his time — an exhibition such as only the Russians seem to know how to assemble. Or one could attend the equally lavish production of the Tchaikovsky ballet, "The Sleeping Beauty." At the delightful little Gypsy Theatre off on a cobblestoned side-street, *The Wedding in the Camp* was played. This State Gypsy Theatre, the only Gypsy theatre in the world, was organized in 1931. Since the Revolution, the gypsies have been transformed from illiterate, nomadic tribes into a national entity with their own teachers, poets, playwrights, and a national theatre through which they preserve and present their primitive native art. Very popular is the State Jewish Theatre, — anti-Semitism does not exist in the Soviet Union, — which has a varied repertory. On this occasion it was offering a "musical saga," called *Sulamith,* utilizing a Biblical theme and Jewish national melodies. An earlier production was Shakespeare's *King Lear,* said to be an extraordinary achievement.

The two official theatres for children, — and this means theatres whose personnel, including actors, is entirely adult, conducted for youthful audiences, — The Central Children's Theatre and the Central Theatre of Youthful Spectators, were offering respectively *The Golden Key,* by Alexei Tolstoi, and an adaptation of Calderón's *His Own Jailor*. It is the policy of the latter theatre to present classical and historical plays of interest to Soviet youth, as well as new plays dealing with aspects of their own life. The former theatre addresses itself to younger children. *The Golden Key* is a gorgeous fairy tale, with a wicked magician, animals that speak and puppets that come to life. But to the good old moral that money is the source of all evil and virtue its own reward is added a new lesson: that the most wonderful thing in the Land of Happy Childhood is free, creative work.

We come finally to the meat of this varied and vital Soviet theatre—the new plays in the fabric of which their own lives and destinies are interwoven. The old favorite, *Lyubov Yarovaya,* the lively *Intervention,* the inspiring *Aristocrats*—all furnishing one with a living experience of the events they portray—I have already described. Others on the list were two very new plays by young writers: another effective intervention play, *The Year '19,* by Josef Prut, and *Glory* by Victor Gusev, a study in free verse of two contrasted types of young Soviet aviators.

The last play I saw in Moscow in 1937 stands in an entirely different class of creative achievement. This was Gorky's picture of pre-revolutionary Russia: *Egor Bulychev,* given a superb production at the Vakhtangov Theatre. This play was the first of a planned trilogy, of which only it and the second, *Dostigayev,* were completed before Gorky's death in 1936.

Egor Bulychev portrays the cultural level and social outlook of the rich merchant class during the period of the World War. Representative of this class is Bulychev, dying of cancer, symbol of a social order itself incurably diseased. Bulychev has lusted for money and has ridden roughshod over others to get it; has lusted for women and taken them. Even now he is sleeping with the servant, Glafira, who adores him. His ménage consists of a stupid wife, a scheming daughter and son-in-law and his illegitimate daughter, Shura, who loves him and who is the only human being he loves. With clairvoyance born of his realization that the end is approaching, he sees his world bare of illusion. In his cynical disbelief in the Czar, the Church and the creed by which he has lived, he reflects the general skepticism of his class.

His provincial household presents for the most part a pandemonium, in which an unctuous priest, Bulychev's wealthy, hypocritical sister-in-law, an Abbess, his money-minded business associates and others come in and out, expressing their alarm at the "great commotion" in the land. We hear reports of happenings in the Duma, of the death of Rasputin, of the abdication of the Czar and other rumors of revolutionary activity. In the meantime we get a picture of the ignorance and superstition then to be found even in this abode of wealth. A fraudulent "healer," a "witch-woman" and a halfwit, are brought in to essay their curative powers on the rapidly failing Bulychev — a scene of mediæval credulity. Yet to the very end Bulychev remains himself, domineering, sensual, yet ingratiatingly human, as Gorky always depicted human creatures who had caught even a glimmer of the divine spark of understanding.

Bulychev hears the Abbess, fled from her convent, tell that the peasant women screamed in her face: "Our husbands, the soldiers, are the nation!" And he lives to hear a revolutionary demonstration pass his own window, singing as they go. But in a world to which this new era has come, an Egor Bulychev is finished.

Tremendous in its symbolism was the closing scene in the Vakhtangov production. Bulychev lies dead in his closed bedroom at the right of the stage. Shura, grief-stricken at the loss of her father, is with him. Presently singing is heard without, the sound of a new demonstration. Opening the door of the bedroom, Shura emerges into the living-room, listening. Then, as if self-reproachful, she turns back again to the dead.

But as the singing grows louder and nearer, she cannot resist its call. With one last look backward, she leaps up a short flight of stairs at the head of which a window looks out on the street. The revolutionists pass the house, their voices loud and clear, and as Shura waves to them, the curtain falls.

Bulychev is dead, but his daughter will help to build the new world.

In this new world the Russians have not only continued the glorious traditions of their theatre, but they have added to it the indispensable element which, before the Revolution, it lacked: plays of vital meaning for the Russian people.

Chapter 9 ❧ Conclusions in a Changing World

❧ Following the forward road with plays as our sign-posts, we find we have traveled far. We have come from Ibsen's Nora, breaking through her sex-chrysalis and emerging as a human being, to Soviet Inga, enjoying complete sexual, political and economic equality, but placing the social responsibility thus imposed on her beyond mere egotistical claims for self-realization. We have come from the groping of Wedekind's sex-obsessed characters to the psychological clarification with which O'Neill illuminates the sexual complications troubling men and women today. We have come from Hauptmann's weavers, rebelling against their exploitation, to the workers and peasants of Soviet Russia, hopefully building their own nation, in which profit-making and exploitation have been abolished. The plays considered in this book have taken us marching through a changing world. And no one who has marched along with these plays can fail to be inspired by their pioneering efforts, by the way in which they have interpreted those new vistas of life which the playwrights' fellow-travelers, advancing so much more slowly, cannot or will not yet see. To the examples selected here many others could be added, that show the same high purpose, the same conviction that vital drama must be integrated with its age.

But the record of the theatre and of audiences is neither praise-worthy nor admirable. Their combined rejection of the play of genuine importance is responsible for its unequal struggle and for its frequent failure. And since the American theatre and American audiences are, after all, closest to our hearts, the problem is how to win a permanent place in our theatre for plays of significance to Americans living today, how to make such plays an organic part of our theatre and hence of our national cultural and social development.

Let us turn first to the subject of the theatre. On the American commercial theatre I shall waste few words. Under the present economic set-up, the production of a play must be considered in terms of real estate, of rentals, of people with money to invest who find "show business" more glamorous than merchandising or Wall Street, and, finally, of careerists on and off the stage. To this theatre the play does not matter and the audience exists only to be mulcted as thoroughly as possible. If occasionally the commercial theatre does produce a superior play, we may rest assured that it has been selected not because of its inherent values, but because some producer, with a canny business sense, was convinced that it possessed "audience-appeal." "Show business" is first, last and always the cynical exploiter of audiences and the most sinister obstacle in the way of vital theatre.

When we turn away from the commercial theatre, we find, as the plays considered in these pages have demonstrated, that the vital contributions to the American theatre have been made by essentially noncommercial producing organizations. We have seen how the Provincetown Players and the Theatre Guild carried the American theatre forward from infantilism into robust and intransigent youth, while outside of New York, the Pasadena Community Playhouse and a few other theatres of this type produced plays on the assumption that audiences not only possess the capacity to think, but would also enjoy the experience of being stimulated to think in the theatre. On the other hand, the "little theatres" of the country, with few exceptions, have been timid and vacuous, passionately dedicated to stage-carpentry as a noble end in itself and to the presentation of worthless Broadway "successes." Finally, impelled by a change in American social and economic conditions, stimulated by original workers' theatre groups in pre-Hitler Germany and by the new theatre in Soviet Russia, American workers' play-producing groups also developed, leading to the formation of the Theatre Union. The Group Theatre, operating virtually on a commercial basis, endeavors also to maintain its ideal of a "collective" organization and of presenting to the audiences of today plays of significance and moment. But the Group Theatre is treading a thorny path, the Theatre Union was unable to survive, and the Theatre Guild can no longer be distinguished from a commercial theatre. How then are the American people to obtain a vital theatre? How are they to be made familiar with the type of play which will help interpret their lives to them in this changing world and give them the vision of that new and better life, which, despite the threat of war clouds, is unmistakably discernible on the horizon?

The most hopeful present answer to this question lies in the Federal Theatre, which in a few short years has already made itself the theatre of the American people and which, when its function as a relief measure is ended, must be continued by the Government as one of its permanent cultural and educational functions. The achievements of the Federal Theatre throughout the country — the high average of the type of plays selected for production; the variety of fare, from pageants and the dance to that brilliant contribution, the *Living Newspaper;* the providing of production opportunities for racial, sectional and foreign groups; the inspiration and new outlook it has given to millions of citizens, most of them underprivileged and new to the theatre — all this cannot be recounted here.

Nor, when I say that in the Federal Theatre lies the chief hope of the American people to see important plays, am I unmindful of the fact that Government censorship is an imminent danger. We have already had evidences of such Federal Theatre censorship, locally as well as nationally. It is quite unrealistic to fancy, in so critical a juncture in the world's history, that those who have the power will not use it to suppress anything they regard as threatening to the *status quo*. And by the same sign those under whose direction the Federal Theatre has been placed will naturally observe caution when selecting new plays to be produced. Such an impasse seems today unavoidable and the only way to meet Federal Theatre censorship, whenever it comes into the open, is for the vigilant minority to bring the issue before the American people to whom this theatre belongs. It is rather ironic that certain political and economic questions should be regarded as taboo in connection with a project which owes its very existence to economic collapse.

However, when we see the kind of plays that have been produced everywhere by the Federal Theatre, there seems more immediate cause for rejoicing than for alarm. I am especially happy to record here productions of Ibsen's *Ghosts, An Enemy of the People* and *The Wild Duck;* Hauptmann's *The Weavers;* Shaw's *On the Rocks;* Chiarelli's *The Mask and the Face;* Lawson's *Processional;* Paul Green's *In Abraham's Bosom* and *Hymn to the Rising Sun;* a large number of O'Neill's plays; Anderson's *Gods of the Lightning;* Howard's *The Silver Cord;* Chlumberg's *Miracle at Verdun;* Peters' and Sklar's *Stevedore;* Bein's *Let Freedom Ring;* Odets' *Awake and Sing;* Katajev's *Squaring the Circle.* To this list should be added a few of the new plays produced by the Federal Theatre, such as Clarke's and Nurnberg's *Chalk Dust,* dealing with problems affecting the freedom of American schoolteachers; Lashin's and Hastings' *Class of '29,* showing the effect of unemployment on our college graduates; Saul's and Lantz's *The Revolt of the Beavers,* an allegory introducing to children the evils of industrial exploitation and the need for union and solidarity among the workers; and, finally, of course, Sinclair Lewis' anti-Fascist warning, *It Can't Happen Here.*

The production of vital *new* plays is one of the Federal Theatre's important functions. Therefore playwrights who present contemporary social or individual problems must be able to look upon it as *their* theatre. Such playwrights know that Broadway will have none of them. And their dilemma often drives them completely out of the playwriting field or turns them into cynical purveyors of pabulum for the commercial theatre.

By far the most novel and noteworthy contribution made by the Federal Theatre is the *Living Newspaper.* Presenting educational propaganda by the terse method of the newspaper, it utilizes the screen, charts, the living actor, the loud speaker, lighting, whatever medium its producers deem effective for their purpose of arousing the American people to an active interest in matters vital to their very existence. The too few productions of the *Living Newspaper* are *Triple-A Plowed Under,* dealing with the agricultural problem and the critical economic situation of the farmers; *Injunction Granted,* a history of the unfair treatment of labor by the courts; *Power,* educating the consumer of electricity in the audience by identifying him with the baffled consumer on the stage, struggling to understand the meaning of a "Kilowatt hour" and why he pays what he does for the amount of electricity that represents; and *One Third of a Nation,* a highly informative and moving portrayal of the housing conditions under which one third of the people of America are compelled to live, because of the uncontrolled manipulation of "real estate." In addition to these there were presented in Chicago, *Spirochete,* part of the nationwide campaign of education on the subject of syphilis; in Oregon, a *Living Newspaper* on *Flax,* and in New Orleans, one on *Flood Control.* The audience response to this feature of the

Federal Theatre's program, which should be made available to the entire country, again demonstrates the importance of a theatre truly integrated with the lives of the people.

Let us turn now from our analysis of the attitude of the American theatre toward the vital play to that of our audiences. Subjected to a barrage of the most tawdry ballyhoo, termed "publicity," by those who have theatre to sell, audiences in America are kept in a dither of excitement by the exploitation of the personal, the cheaply titillating and the sensational. The result is that going to the theatre is not a simple, natural enhancement of people's lives, like attending a symphony concert or an art exhibition or even the cinema, but an artificially stimulated excursion self-consciously undertaken as an experience quite extraneous to the theatregoer's ordinary life.

To realize what a healthy attitude toward the theatre is like, and what a contrast to that of New York theatre audiences, one must see audiences in Moscow. To Moscow theatregoers the theatre is as natural a part of their regular existence as eating or conversing. Their work day and their theatre evening flow into each other, one is merely the continuation of the other. We are beginning to observe something of this in our Federal Theatre audiences, who are quite different in their attitude toward the theatre and the play from other American audiences.

But so whipped-up are the typical American audiences by the high pressure technique of the commercial theatre, that the compulsion to attend a theatrical offering reputed to be "a hit" attains the proportions of hysteria. And those who can afford to buy the choicest seats exhibit this compulsion no more extravagantly than those who often make sacrifices to secure even the topmost places. This is theatre-consciousness in its most virulent form!

In this spurious concept of the theatre, American audiences are aided and abetted by American newspaper theatre-reviewing, misnamed "drama criticism." Conventional and superficial, devoid of any fundamental philosophy of life to serve as a basic standard of criticism, subscribing to the Broadway concept of the theatre as a source of diversion and amusement, American newspaper theatre-reviewing supinely maintains the attitude imposed on it by the commercial theatre.

Thus American audiences have been so conditioned that they are almost mentally atrophied as to any understanding of the real values of the theatre. Not only is independent judgment on the part of the theatregoer in relation to plays almost non-existent, but the average theatregoer is also in complete ignorance of plays that are not being trumpeted. The vicious circle is complete: the audience is psychologized into the reactions of an excited herd, and the play of significance, if produced at all, has little or no chance to survive — the fate, as we have seen, of many of the finest plays discussed in this book.

The basic reasons, however, for the rejection by audiences of serious plays dealing with the problems of their time are those inherent in the social and economic conditions under which we live. Since the World War these conditions have grown more menacing to people on all rungs of the social ladder. Life all along the line is a worrisome and frightening affair, and frightened people consciously or unconsciously seek escape from the reality which oppresses them.

Therefore, while the people of a nation are divided on real issues, — social, economic, political, — they also have one common desire: to lose themselves as often as possible in a make-believe world which represents life as they would like it to be. This explains the commercial theatre's pet phrase of the "audience-appeal" of a play; herein lies that common denominator which solaces the businessman and his lady in the second row as well as the clerk and his girl in the second balcony. Why do the superficial plays of Rachel Crothers, for example, fill the theatre with audiences really divided by their economic status? Because to those on the uppermost rungs of the economic ladder, the sight and sound of well-groomed, comfortable men and women, ordering servants about in charming homes, seem reassuring proof that their world is not on the rocks but eternally secure. And to those on the lower rungs this care-free world of material ease and physical loveliness represents all that in their frustration and ignorance they fancy they would ask of life. In this sense, then, of the common need of today to seek the illusion of security, the Colonel's lady and Judy O'Grady may be said to be sisters under the skin.

But let the theatre house a play like *Peace on Earth* and all the false lull of security is gone. Those at both ends of the social scale who, for a variety of reasons, cling to the economic *status quo,* shrink from being drawn into the real world of profit-makers and war, of industrial conflict and sudden death, of endowment-controlled universities and truthtellers legally murdered. The vast majority of Americans prefer to crawl into the silken cocoons Broadway spins for them. This explains why, although the cocoon was hardly as silken as that of a Crothers' play, security-seeking audiences flocked with shuddering ecstasy to *Of Mice and Men.* They understood perfectly that this sensational piece about brutal, subhuman underdogs was nothing to get alarmed about; that this yarn, with its spurious daring and its spurious "social note," was mere theatrical excitement without any significance whatsoever for anybody. It is the really daring play of import that falls between two stools and is shunned by that compact majority, in all social classes, whom Ibsen long ago designated as the real enemy of the people.

In a world that must inevitably come, however, people will have unified social and economic interests and audiences will no longer be conditioned either by a commercial theatre or by the fear of economic disaster. That such unified interests bring with them no danger of uniformity in intellectual content or in taste, the theatre of Soviet Russia amply demonstrates. Every year workers in the theatre — playwrights, producers, actors, scenic designers, critics — come from all over the world to attend the Annual Soviet Theatre Festival in Moscow, to learn and to be freshly inspired by the achievements of the Soviet theatre.

Nor was it an accident that the pinnacle of achievement in the theatre of Germany was reached in those postwar years when the people of the quasi-Socialist Republic had at least quasi-unified social interests. At that time Reinhardt created many of his inimitable productions; outstanding foreign plays were produced, such as *Strange Interlude;* Piscator produced plays as bold in content as they were in style and method of presentation, while workers' theatre groups flourished. It was then, too, that Bert Brecht made his socially implemented German adaptation of John Gay's *The Beggars' Opera,* under the title of *The Three Penny Opera,* for which Kurt Weill wrote his satiric score. This period was one of richness and significance, producing a world-renowned theatre which Nazism destroyed and in the place of which it has created nothing. Indeed there can be no more revealing commentary on Fascism than its utter barrenness in the field of the drama. Germany, Austria, Hungary, Italy, are today destitute of plays of any value; their drama is as sterile and empty as their destructive political philosophy.

So it would seem, as we look back over the way we have come, that the plays and theatre most profoundly integrated with life are those dedicated to the realization of man's age-long dream of freedom, individual and social; of justice, which implies every form of equality; and of human brotherhood, which means peace. It is a thrilling story, this, of the play's part in progress, born of the vision and the courage of pioneer playwrights and of such producers as share with them their concept of the highest purpose of the theatre. If audiences have failed to rise to these plays, it is because men's lives are still so motivated by greed and fear, because their ignorance is still so deep and so widespread. But vital plays and the theatre that produced them have been man's companions through the centuries of his upward struggle, voicing for him, often inarticulate in his emergence, his search for individual and social fulfillment. During the portentous conflict in which men of this age are aligned, the vital play and the theatre will continue, as they have always done, to point the way in a changing world. They, too, will march on.

Appendix

I. *A LIST OF PUBLISHED PLAYS REFERRED TO IN THIS BOOK*

Afinogenyev, Alexander: *Fear*. In *Six Soviet Plays*. Houghton, Mifflin Company, Boston.

Amiel, Denys: *Mr. and Mrs. So And So*. (*Monsieur et Madame un Tel*. Untranslated. A. Fayard et Cie., Paris.)

Anderson, Maxwell, and Stallings, Laurence: *What Price Glory?* In *A Treasury of the Theatre*. Simon and Schuster, New York.

Anderson, Maxwell, and Hickerson, Harold: *Gods of the Lightning*. Longmans, Green & Co., New York.

Anderson, Maxwell: *Elizabeth the Queen; Mary of Scotland; Both Your Houses*. Samuel French, New York. *Winterset; The Wingless Victory; High Tor; The Masque of Kings*. Dramatists Play Service, New York (paper). Anderson House, Washington, D.C. (bound).

Anet, Claude: *The Lost Girl*. (*La fille perdue*. Untranslated. Bernard Grasset, Paris.)

Ansky, S.: *The Dybbuk*. Liveright Publishing Corporation, New York.

Aristophanes: *Lysistrata*. In *A Treasury of the Theatre*. Simon and Schuster, New York. *The Peace; The Birds; The Acharnians*. In one volume of *Everyman's Library*. E. P. Dutton and Company, New York.

Baum, Vicki: *Grand Hotel*. Doubleday, Doran and Company, New York.

Bein, Albert: *Let Freedom Ring*. Samuel French, New York.

Bourdet, Édouard: *The Captive*. Brentano's, New York. (*La Prisonnière*. Librairie Théatrale, Paris.)

Brieux, Eugène: *Damaged Goods; The Three Daughters of M. Dupont; Maternity*. In a volume entitled *Three Plays by Brieux*. Brentano's, New York. *The Red Robe* in *Chief Contemporary Dramatists, First Series*. Houghton, Mifflin Company, Boston. *Les Hannetons* and all works in French. P. V. Stock, Paris.

Browne, *see* Nichols.

Bruckner, Ferdinand: *Sickness of Youth; Criminals*. (*Krankheit der Jugend; Die Verbrecher*. Untranslated. Europa Verlag, Zurich.) *Races*. Alfred A. Knopf, New York.

Bulgakov, Michael: *Days of the Turbins*. In *Six Soviet Plays*. Houghton, Mifflin Company, Boston.

Chekhov, Anton: *The Cherry Orchard; The Three Sisters; Uncle Vanya*. In *The Plays of Tchekov*. The Modern Library, Random House, New York.

Chiarelli, Luigi: *The Mask and the Face*. Based on the original, by C. B. Fernald. Samuel French, New York. (*La maschera e il volto*. A. Mondadori, Milan.)

Chlumberg, Hans: *Miracle at Verdun*. In *Twentieth Century Plays — Continental*. Thomas Nelson and Sons, New York.

Clarke, Harold A., and Nurnberg, Maxwell: *Chalk Dust*. Samuel French, New York.

D'Annunzio, Gabriele: *The Dead City*. (*La citta morte*.) Translated by Arthur Symons. Brentano's, New York.

Euripides: *Electra; The Trojan Women*. Oxford University Press, New York.

Ford, John: *'Tis Pity She's a Whore*. In *Eight Famous Elizabethan Plays*. The Modern Library, Random House, New York.

Galsworthy, John: Collected Works. Charles Scribner's Sons, New York.

Gay, John: *The Beggars' Opera*. In *Eighteenth Century Plays*. *Everyman's Library*, E. P. Dutton and Company, New York.

Geddes, Virgil: *The Earth Between*. Samuel French, New York.

Glebov, Anton: *Inga*. In *Six Soviet Plays*. Houghton, Mifflin Company, Boston.

Goethe, Johann Wolfgang von: *Faust.* Translated by Bayard Taylor. The Modern Library, Random House, New York.

Gorky, Maxim: *The Lower Depths.* (*Night's Lodging.*) In *Dramas of Modernism and their Forerunners.* Little, Brown and Company, Boston. *Egor Bulychev.* In *Four Soviet Plays.* International Publishers, New York.

Green, Paul: *In Abraham's Bosom.* Robert McBride and Company, New York. *Hymn to the Rising Sun.* Samuel French, New York.

Hart, Moss, and Kaufman, George S.: *You Can't Take It With You.* Farrar and Rinehart, New York.

Hastings, *see* Lashin.

Hauptmann, Gerhart: *The Weavers.* In *Dramatic Works, Vol. I; The Assumption of Hannele, Vol. IV; Before Dawn, Vol. I. The Weavers* also in *Chief Contemporary Dramatists, First Series,* Houghton, Mifflin Company, Boston.

Hellman, Lillian: *The Children's Hour.* Alfred A. Knopf, New York.

Hickerson, *see* Anderson.

Holmes, John Haynes, and Lawrence, Reginald: *If This Be Treason.* The Macmillan Company, New York.

Houghton, Stanley: *Hindle Wakes.* Samuel French, New York. Also in *Contemporary Plays: English and American.* Houghton, Mifflin Company, Boston.

Howard, Sidney: *The Silver Cord.* Samuel French, New York. Also in *Dramas of Modernism and their Forerunners,* Little, Brown and Company, Boston.

Ibsen, Henrik: Collected Works edited by William Archer. Charles Scribner's Sons, New York.

Ivanov, Vsevolod: *Armored Train No. 14–69.* International Publishers, New York.

Johnston, Denis: *The Moon in the Yellow River.* Samuel French, New York.

Katajev, Valentin: *Squaring the Circle.* In *Six Soviet Plays.* Houghton, Mifflin Company, Boston.

Kaufman, *see* Hart.

Kingsley, Sidney: *Dead End.* Random House, New York.

Kirchon, Vladimir: *Bread.* In *Six Soviet Plays.* Houghton, Mifflin Company, Boston.

Kirchon, Vladimir, and Uspenski, André: *Red Rust.* Brentano's, New York.

Kirkland, Jack: *Tobacco Road.* The Viking Press, New York.

Lantz, *see* Saul.

Lashin, Orrie, and Hastings, Milo: *Class of '29.* Dramatists Play Service, New York.

Lawrence, *see* Holmes.

Lawson, John Howard: *Processional.* In *Contemporary Drama, American Plays, I.* Charles Scribner's Sons, New York.

Lewis, Sinclair: *It Can't Happen Here.* Dramatists Play Service, New York.

Living Newspaper: *Triple-A Plowed Under; Power; Spirochete; One Third of a Nation.* In *Federal Theatre Plays.* Random House, New York.

Maltz, *see* Sklar.

Maugham, W. Somerset: *The Constant Wife.* Samuel French, New York. *The Breadwinner; For Services Rendered.* Doubleday, Doran and Company, New York.

Moody, William Vaughn: *The Great Divide.* Samuel French, New York.

Nichols, Robert, and Browne, Maurice: *Wings Over Europe.* Samuel French, New York. Also in *Dramas of Modernism and their Forerunners.* Little, Brown and Company, Boston.

Nurnberg, *see* Clarke.

Odets, Clifford: *Waiting for Lefty; Awake and Sing,* in one volume. *Paradise Lost; Golden Boy,* in single volumes. Random House, New York.

O'Neill, Eugene: Collected Works. Random House, New York.

Ostrovsky, Alexander: *Enough Stupidity in Every Wise Man.* In *Moscow Art Theatre Plays, 2nd Series.* Brentano's, New York.

Peters, Paul, and Sklar, George: *Stevedore.* Covici, Friede Inc. New York.

Pogodin, Nikolai: *Tempo.* In *Six Soviet Plays.* Houghton, Mifflin Company, Boston.

Raphaelson, Samson: *Young Love.* Brentano's, New York.

Reed, Mark: *Yes, My Darling Daughter.* Samuel French, New York.

Rice, Elmer: *The Adding Machine.* Samuel French, New York.

Romains, Jules: *The Dictator* (*Le Dictateur*); *Donogoo; Boën; Musse.* (Untranslated. Librairie Gallimard, Paris.) *Le Dictateur* also in *La Petite Illustration,* October 23, 1926. *Dr. Knock.* (*Knock.*) Samuel French, New York.

Saul, Oscar, and Lantz, Lou: *The Revolt of the Beavers.* Dramatists Play Service, New York.

Schnitzler, Arthur: *The Lonely Way.* In *Representative Continental Dramas—Revolutionary and Transitional.* Little, Brown and Company, Boston. *Light o' Love.* (*Playing With Love.*) In *Continental Plays, Vol. I.* Houghton, Mifflin Company, Boston. *Living Hours.* In *Chief Contemporary Dramatists, Second Series.* Houghton, Mifflin Company, Boston. *Professor Bernhardi.* Victor Gollancz, London. *Hands Around.* (*Reigen.*) The Modern Library, Random House, New York. *The Vast Domain.* (*Das weite Land.*) Poet Lore, Boston.

Shairp, Mordaunt: *The Green Bay Tree.* The Baker International Play Bureau, Boston.

Shaw, George Bernard: Collected Works. Dodd, Mead and Company, New York.

Shelley, Percy Bysshe: *The Cenci* in *Shelley's Poetical Works,* variously published.

Sherriff, R. C.: *Journey's End.* Coward-McCann, Inc., New York.

Sklar, George, and Maltz, Albert: *Peace on Earth.* Samuel French, New York.

Sklar, *see also* Peters

Sophocles: *Œdipus, King of Thebes.* Oxford University Press, New York.

Stallings, *see* Anderson.

Steinbeck, John: *Of Mice and Men.* The Viking Press, New York.

Toller, Ernst: *The Transformation; Masses and Man; The Machine Wreckers; Hinkemann.* In *Seven Plays.* Liveright Publishing Corporation, New York.

Tretyakov, Sergei M.: *Roar China.* International Publishers, New York.

Uspenski, *see* Kirchon.

Walter, Eugene: *The Easiest Way* in *Chief Contemporary Dramatists, Second Series.* Houghton, Mifflin Company, Boston.

Wedekind, Frank: *The Awakening of Spring; Earth-Spirit; The Box of Pandora.* In *Tragedies of Sex.* Boni & Liveright, New York. *Earth Spirit* in *Continental Plays, Vol. II.* Houghton, Mifflin Company, Boston. *Marquis von Keith.* (Untranslated. Europa Verlag, Zurich.)

Werfel, Franz: *Mirror-Man.* (*Spiegelmensch.*) Untranslated. Europa Verlag, Zurich. *Goat Song.* In *The Theatre Guild Anthology.* Random House, New York.

Wexley, John: *They Shall Not Die.* Alfred A. Knopf, New York.

Wolf, Friedrich: *The Sailors of Cattaro.* Samuel French, New York.

II. *NOTES ON PLAYS AND PRODUCTIONS*

Chapter 1

Grand Hotel. Produced in New York, 1930.

The Moon in the Yellow River. Produced by the New York Theatre Guild, 1932.

Dead End. Produced in New York, 1935.

The Silver Cord. Produced by the New York Theatre Guild, 1926.

You Can't Take It With You. Produced in New York, 1937.

CHAPTER 2

Alla Nazimova production of *Ghosts*. Reached New York in December, 1935, after an extensive tour.

Thornton Wilder version of *A Doll's House*. Produced in New York, 1937.

William Archer: London press comments on a private performance of *Ghosts* in "Ghosts and Gibberings," *Pall Mall Gazette,* April 8, 1891.

Shaw's *The Quintessence of Ibsenism* (1913) is still a stimulating discussion on Ibsen's work, even though its special slant on so-called "idealism" lacks validity for the reader today.

The Weavers. Produced in English in New York by Emanuel Reicher, 1915. *Hannele*. (*The Assumption of Hannele*.) Produced in English in New York by Eva Le Gallienne, 1924.

Tobacco Road is based on the novel *Poor Whites* by Erskine Caldwell. Produced in New York, 1933.

The Awakening of Spring. Produced in English in New York, for one performance, 1917.

Mrs. Warren's Profession and censorship. The People of the State of New York *v.* Arnold Daly and Samuel W. Gumpertz, *New York Law Journal,* July 9, 1906.

On the Rocks. Produced in New York by the Federal Theatre, 1938.

The Federal Theatre. In 1935 the United States Government, endeavoring to meet the country's staggering unemployment crisis, created a Works Progress Administration, one of the projects of which was to be known as the Federal Theatre.

Justice. Produced in New York, 1916, with John Barrymore. *The Fugitive*. Produced in New York, 1917. *The Mob*. Produced in New York at the Neighborhood Playhouse, 1920.

The Three Daughters of M. Dupont. Produced in English in New York, 1910. *The Red Robe*. Produced in English in New York, 1920, under the title of *The Letter of the Law*. *Les Hannetons*. Produced in

English in New York under the title of *The Incubus,* 1909; under the title of *The Affinity,* 1910, and under the original French title, 1922.

Hands Around (*Reigen*) and censorship. The People of the State of New York *v.* Philip Pesky, Vol. 230, *New York Appellate Division Reports,* page 200.

The Three Sisters and *The Cherry Orchard.* Produced in English by Eva Le Gallienne at the Civic Repertory Theatre, New York, in 1926 and 1928 respectively. *Uncle Vanya.* Produced in New York, 1930.

Chapter 3

Hindle Wakes. Produced in New York under the title of *Fanny Hawthorn,* 1922.

Readers interested in the economic basis of monogamy are referred to *The Origin of the Family* by Friedrich Engels.

The Constant Wife. Produced in New York, 1926, with Ethel Barrymore.

Mr. and Mrs. So And So. (*Monsieur et Madame Un Tel . . .*) Produced in Paris, 1925.

The Mask and the Face. First produced in New York, 1924. In 1933 produced by the Theatre Guild, when the faithful and excellent translation of W. Somerset Maugham was used. It is regrettable that this has never been printed because the available Fernald version, "based on" the original, mutilates the play's fine values.

Sickness of Youth. (*Krankheit der Jugend.*) Played in various European cities and produced in New York, in the obscure little Cherry Lane Theatre, 1933. The English adaptation was made by the American playwright, the late Patrick Kearney.

The Captive. Faithfully and beautifully translated by Arthur Hornblow, Jr. and perfectly produced by Gilbert Miller in New York, 1926.

The Captive and censorship: Liveright *v.* Waldorf Theatres Corporation, Vol. 220, *New York Appellate Division Reports,* page 182.

Readers interested in the subject of *The Captive* are referred to Havelock Ellis' *Studies in the Psychology of Sex,* Vol. VI: *Sex in Relation to Society;* and Vol. II: *Sexual Inversion.* Also to *The Basic Writings of Sigmund Freud* in the Modern Library.

The Green Bay Tree. Produced in New York, 1933.

The Children's Hour. Produced in New York by Herman Shumlin, 1934.

The Dead City. (*La citta morte.*) Produced in New York, 1923, with Eleonora Duse.

The Lost Girl. (*La fille perdue.*) The French title has a double significance, since *fille* means both "girl" and "daughter" and the daughter has also been "lost" to her father since early childhood.

The Earth Between. Produced in New York by the Experimental Theatre at the Provincetown Playhouse, 1929.

Chapter 4

The Dybbuk. Produced in New York at the Neighborhood Playhouse, 1925.

The Emperor Jones. Produced in New York by the Provincetown Players, 1920. *The Hairy Ape.* Produced in New York by the Provincetown Players, 1922. The "I.W.W." (Industrial Workers of the World), the first revolutionary organization of industrial as opposed to craft unions, founded in Chicago, 1905. *All God's Chillun Got Wings.* Produced in New York by the Provincetown Playhouse, Inc., 1924. *Desire Under the Elms.* Produced in New York by the Provincetown Playhouse, Inc., at the Greenwich Village Theatre, 1924. *Marco Millions.* Produced by the New York Theatre Guild, 1928. *Lazarus Laughed.* Produced in Pasadena, California, by the Pasadena Community Playhouse, 1928. *Diff'rent.* Produced in New

York by the Provincetown Players, 1920. *The Great God Brown.* Produced in New York by Kenneth Macgowan, Robert Edmond Jones and Eugene O'Neill, 1926. O'Neill's letter explaining this play appeared in various New York newspapers, February 14, 1926. *Strange Interlude.* Produced by the New York Theatre Guild, 1928. *Mourning Becomes Electra.* Produced by the New York Theatre Guild, 1931. My authority for the statement that Electra or A-lektra may be interpreted as signifying the Un-mated is Professor Gilbert Murray in his Introduction to his translation of the Electra of Euripides. . . . The unexpected success of *Mourning Becomes Electra* in London, where it was not produced until 1937, is another tribute to O'Neill's genius. For the notoriously late and leisurely diners of London, who regard their playgoing as after-dinner entertainment, to be willing to reach a theatre before seven and remain, with two short intervals, until after eleven, in order to live through an unrelieved tragedy, was indeed an unheard-of event in the London theatre. *Dynamo; Ah, Wilderness!; Days Without End.* Produced by the New York Theatre Guild, 1929, 1933, 1934, respectively.

Eugene O'Neill was awarded the Nobel Prize for Literature, 1936, the Swedish scientist having stipulated in his bequest that the annual Nobel prizes were to be awarded to those who, in their given fields, had contributed most to the benefit of mankind.

Chapter 5

Masses and Man. Produced in English under the title of *Man and the Masses* by the New York Theatre Guild, 1924. *The Machine-Wreckers.* Produced in English by the Boston Repertory Theatre, 1927. *Hinkemann.* Produced in English in New York by Maurice Schwartz, under the title of *Bloody Laughter,* 1931.

The Sailors of Cattaro. Produced in New York by the Theatre Union, 1934.

The Dictator. (*Le Dictateur.*) Produced in Paris at the Comédie des Champs-Élysées, 1926. *Donogoo* at the Pigalle; *Knock or the Triumph of Medicine* at the Comédie des Champs-Élysées; *Boën, or the Possession of Wealth* at the Odéon; *Musse, or the School of Hypocrisy* at the L'Atelier, 1934–1935. *Knock* was produced in New York by the American Laboratory Theatre, under the English title of *Dr. Knock,* 1928.

The Adding Machine. Produced by the New York Theatre Guild, 1923, during its finest experimental period. Beginning its official career as the Theatre Guild at the Garrick Theatre, New York, 1919, this organization was the outgrowth of the Washington Square Players, founded in New York in 1915 by a group of young writers, artists, actors and others to help create a theatre of ideas and of new art forms in America.

Processional. Produced by the New York Theatre Guild, 1925. Excellently revived in New York by the Federal Theatre, 1937. The two bitter industrial conflicts referred to in the text in connection with this play involved the textile workers in Lawrence, Massachusetts, 1919, and the coal miners in Herrin, Illinois, 1922, resulting in the so-called "Herrin Massacres." *The Ku Klux Klan.* "King Kleagle" and "Goblins" are actual examples of the nomenclature assumed by Klan.

Gods of the Lightning. Produced in New York by Hamilton MacFadden and Kellogg Gary, 1928. Readers interested in the Sacco-Vanzetti case are referred to: *The Case of Sacco and Vanzetti,* by Felix Frankfurter; *Facing the Chair,* a pamphlet, by John Dos Passos; *The Sacco-Vanzetti Case,* by Osmond K. Fraenkel; and *The Letters of Sacco and Vanzetti.*

Elizabeth the Queen. Produced by the New York Theatre Guild, 1930; also *Both Your Houses* and *Mary of Scotland,* 1933. *Winterset.* Produced in New York by Guthrie McClintic, 1935. *The Wingless Victory.* Produced in New York by Katharine Cornell, 1936. *High Tor.* Produced in New York by Guthrie McClintic, 1937. *The Masque of Kings.* Produced by the New York Theatre Guild, 1937.

Goat Song. Produced by the New York Theatre Guild, 1926.

Chapter 6

They Shall Not Die. Produced by the New York Theatre Guild, 1934. Readers may be interested to know that after the first trial of the Scottsboro case, Ruby Bates, the *real* Lucy Wells, came to New York to help raise funds for the appeal of the case. Shy and retiring, pale and wearing glasses, she looked like a country school-mar'm. She had never seen a play before and described *They Shall Not Die* as giving "a very good picture of what happened to me and what the trial was like and how things are in the South."

Waiting for Lefty. First presented in New York under the auspices of *New Theatre Magazine* in January, 1935, by a Group Theatre cast including its author. In March, 1935, presented at the Longacre Theatre, New York, by the Group Theatre. Readers interested in the censorship experiences of this play are referred to a pamphlet entitled *Censored!* published by the National Committee Against Censorship of the Theatre Arts, which also contains information on the censorship of *They Shall Not Die, Stevedore,* and other plays of social protest.

Awake and Sing was produced by the Group Theatre in New York, in February, 1935; *Paradise Lost* in December, 1935; *Golden Boy* in 1937.

Chapter 7

Aristophanes' three so-called antiwar plays are *The Acharnians, The Peace* and *Lysistrata.* The last, which is also the best and best-known, is a feminist protest against war, as a nuisance which keeps lovers and husbands away from panting bosoms and waiting arms. A lively and ribald satire, its underlying serious note is all but lost sight of in the hilarity the play arouses.

Journey's End. Given a London Stage Society production on a Sunday evening in December, 1928, the play opened to the London public in January, 1929, and in New York in March, 1929.

What Price Glory? Produced by Arthur Hopkins, New York, 1924.

Wings Over Europe. Given its first production anywhere by the New York Theatre Guild, 1928. It is important to note that in the original last act (also printed), Lightfoot meets his death by being run over just as he is about to return at the fatal noon hour. The Theatre Guild wisely requested the authors to change this accidental death to the deliberate murder by the Secretary of War, thus greatly strengthening the power and significance of the play. . . . In connection with the action taken by a fictitious "League of United Scientists" in the play, it is interesting to note that in 1937, nine years after the production of *Wings Over Europe,* the American Association for the Advancement of Science, at its annual congress, decided to further the initial step already taken in England and elsewhere to unite the scientists of the world into a body which would seek to apply the findings of science to a solution of the social and political problems disrupting the world.

Miracle at Verdun. Produced by the New York Theatre Guild in 1931. The original play is divided into thirteen scenes. The English version effectively transposes two of the early scenes and reduces the number to eight.

For Services Rendered. Produced in New York, 1933.

If This Be Treason. Produced by the New York Theatre Guild, 1935. The character of Koyé is based on that of the well-known Tolstoian Japanese pacificist leader, Kagawa.

Chapter 8

The quotations from speeches of Soviet theatre officials at the First Theatre Olympiad are taken from an article by Hallie Flanagan in the *Theatre Guild Magazine,* September, 1930.

The Armored Train was also produced in New York in Yiddish.

Roar China. Produced in an adapted version by the New York Theatre Guild, 1930. The only available English translation follows the original play. A "compradore" is the chief native employee in a European house of business in China.

Red Rust. Produced by the New York Theatre Guild, 1929.

Squaring the Circle. Produced at the Lyceum Theatre, New York, 1935, where 108 performances were given.

The Man With the Portfolio. Produced by Maurice Schwartz at the Yiddish Art Theatre, New York, 1931.

Schiller's *Intrigue and Love* (*Kabale und Liebe*), like *Anna Karenina,* is produced in the Soviet Union because of the revealing picture it presents of another social epoch.

Egor Bulychev. Produced in New York, in Yiddish, by the Artef Players.

Chapter 9

The Federal Theatre. In connection with the establishment of a Federal Theatre in America it is important to note that State or National Theatres have existed in European countries for many years, but they have been art theatres, without social significance. Readers interested in an account of the accomplishments of the Federal Theatre are referred to the book *Bread and Circuses* by Willson Whitman. Oxford University Press, New York.

The Three-Penny Opera. The Brecht-Weill version of *The Beggars' Opera* produced in Berlin in 1928 enjoyed a sensational run. Produced in English, in New York, in 1933, it failed chiefly because its current social implications had not been translated into an idiom readily intelligible to American audiences.

Index

Index